AUSTRALIAN PUBLIC POLICY

Progressive ideas in
the neoliberal ascendency

Edited by Chris Miller and Lionel Orchard

P P

First published in Great Britain in 2016 by

Policy Press
University of Bristol
1-9 Old Park Hill
Bristol
BS2 8BB
UK
t: +44 (0)117 954 5940
pp-info@bristol.ac.uk
www.policypress.co.uk

North America office:
Policy Press
c/o The University of Chicago Press
1427 East 60th Street
Chicago, IL 60637, USA
t: +1 773 702 7700
f: +1 773 702 9756
sales@press.uchicago.edu
www.press.uchicago.edu

British Library Cataloguing in Publication Data
A catalogue record for this book is available from the British Library.

Library of Congress Cataloging-in-Publication Data
A catalog record for this book has been requested.

ISBN 978-1-4473-1268-0 paperback

ISBN 978-1-4473-2110-1 ePub

ISBN 978-1-4473-2111-8 Mobi

Cover design by Robin Hawes
Front cover: image kindly supplied by www.istock.com

Contents

List of figures and tables

Figures

Tables

Contributor biographies

Jon Altman is a research professor at the Centre for Aboriginal Economic Policy Research (CAEPR) at the Australian National University. He has a disciplinary background in economics and anthropology. In 1990, he was appointed the foundation director of CAEPR – a position he held until 2010. Since migrating to Australia in 1976, Professor Altman has focused on Indigenous economic development, mainly in remote Australia, and on Indigenous public policy nationally. He has been an outspoken critic of the paternalism of recent Indigenous policy in Australia, especially the 2007–12 Northern Territory National Emergency Intervention. Professor Altman maintains a close relationship with Kuninjku people in western Arnhem Land where he undertook his doctoral research. In 2003 Professor Altman was elected a fellow of the Academy of the Social Sciences in Australia and in 2012 an honorary fellow of the Royal Society of New Zealand.

Fran Baum is Matthew Flinders Distinguished Professor and an Australia Research Council Federation Fellow at Flinders University, Adelaide. She is also Foundation Director of the Southgate Institute for Health, Society and Equity and conducted a range of research on aspects of the social determinants of health and health equity and comprehensive primary health care. She is a member of the Global Steering Council of the People's Health Movement. She also served as a Commissioner on the World Health Organization's Commission on the Social Determinants of Health from 2005 to 2008. She is a Fellow of the Academy of the Social Sciences in Australia and of the Australian Health Promotion Association. She is a past National President and Life Member of the Public Health Association of Australia.

Deborah Brennan is Professor in the Social Policy Research Centre (SPRC) at the University of New South Wales and adjunct Professor in the Centre for Children and Young People (CCYP), Southern Cross University. She is the University of New South Wales lead of a Collaborative Research Network that links the SPRC and the CCYP to build research capacity in relation to children, families and young people. Deborah is one of Australia's leading researchers in comparative welfare, family policy and gender and politics. She is the author of *The Politics of Australian Child Care* (1998, Cambridge University Press) and co-editor with Louise Chappell of *'No Fit Place for Women', Women* *in New South Wales Politics, 1856–2006* (2006, UNSW Press), as well as numerous scholarly articles on gender, politics and family policy.

John Buchanan is Professor and Director of the Workplace Research Centre, University of Sydney Business School. Until recently his major research interest has been the demise of the classical wage earner model of employment and the role of the state in nurturing new forms of multi-employer coordination in the labour market. Building on this he is now devoting special attention to the evolution of the labour contract, the dynamics of workforce development and the relationship between work and health. His most recently co-authored book is *Safety in Numbers: Nurse–patient ratios and the future of health care* (with S. Gordon, J. Buchanan and T. Bretherton; 2008, Cornell University Press).

Paul Burton is Professor of Urban Management and Planning and Acting Director of the Urban Research Program at Griffith University. He was previously Head of the School for Policy Studies at the University of Bristol. Paul is a founding member of Regional Development Australia, Gold Coast and directs the Griffith University/City of Gold Coast Growth Management Partnership. His research interests include the relationship between research and policy; the theory and practice of public participation and community engagement; and the everyday professional lives of urban planners. He recently completed an analysis of the role of urban agriculture in building urban resilience and is currently developing a major programme of work to measure the legacy associated with the Commonwealth Games, to be held in the City of Gold Coast in 2018.

Janine Chapman is a research fellow at the Centre for Work + Life, Hawke Research Institute, University of South Australia. Her background is in psychology with expertise in both psychological and sociological perspectives of behaviour and behavioural change. She has a keen interest in a range of worker safety, health and wellbeing issues, in addition to workplace policy. She is currently project manager for a large multimethod project investigating the intersection of work and sustainable living in Australia.

Dr Daniel Connell works in the Crawford School of Public Policy at the Australian National University, Canberra, where he teaches courses dealing with environmental policy and communications, and transboundary rivers. His research focuses on issues related to the institutional design and governance arrangements applying to rivers in federal or multilayered political systems such as Australia, South Africa, the United States, Mexico, the European Union (Spain), India, China and Brazil. His publications include *Water Politics in the Murray-Darling Basin* (2007, Federation Press) and *Basin Futures: Water Reform in the Murray-Darling Basin* (co-edited with Quentin Grafton; 2011, Australian National University E-Press). He is also a co-editor of *Federal Rivers* (with Dustin Garrick, George R.M. Anderson and Jamie Pittock; Edward Elgar, 2014).

George Crowder is Professor of Politics in the School of Social and Policy Studies, Flinders University, Adelaide. His research interests concern contemporary political theory, in particular the political implications of the idea of value pluralism associated with Isaiah Berlin. He is the author of *Liberalism and Value Pluralism* (2002, Continuum), *Isaiah Berlin: Liberty and Pluralism* (2004, Polity), and most recently, *Theories of Multiculturalism: An Introduction* (2013, Polity), and the co-editor of *The One and the Many: Reading Isaiah Berlin* (with Henry Hardy; 2007, Prometheus).

Mark Davis teaches in the School of Culture and Communication at the University of Melbourne. He is the author of *The Land of Plenty: Australia in the 2000s* (2008, MUP), which examines the impact of the new conservatism on Australian public culture, and *Gangland: Cultural Elites and the New Generationalism* (1997, 1999, Allen & Unwin), which analyses the ongoing tenure of Australia's 1970s and 1980s cultural establishment in the context of the culture wars and media disparagement of young people.

Jago Dodson is Professor of Urban Policy in the School of Global Urban and Social Studies, Royal Melbourne Institute of Technology (RMIT) University, Melbourne, Australia. After completing his PhD on housing policy at the University of Melbourne he undertook a post-doctoral fellowship at RMIT University before taking up a research fellowship within the Urban Research Program at Griffith University and subsequently served as Director of that Centre. His research has covered an array of urban planning and policy topics, addressing problems of transport policy, public transport and disadvantage, oil vulnerability, urban form and structure, urban governance, infrastructure policy, housing policy and climate change adaptation. Much of his work addresses the links between economic, social, technical, governance and policy processes in cities. Jago's teaching has included the first-year subject 'Understanding the Australian city' at Griffith and he has also been a regular commentator on urban issues in the media and public sphere.

Judith Dwyer is Director of Research in the Department of Health Care Management at the Flinders University School of Medicine. Professor Dwyer is a former CEO of Monash Health in Melbourne, and of Flinders Medical Centre in Adelaide. Professor Dwyer was the inaugural President of Women's Hospitals Australasia, is an experienced board director, and was listed as one of 'Australia's Smart 100' by *The Bulletin* in 2003. She is a Research Program Leader for the Lowitja Institute, Australia's national Aboriginal health research institute, and teaches in the Flinders Master of Health Administration programme. Her research is focused on Aboriginal health services and policy and the governance of the Australian health care system. She is the lead author of the popular text *Project Management in Health and Community Services: Getting good ideas to work* (with Z. Liang, V. Thiesen and A. Martini; 2013, Allen & Unwin) now in its 2nd edition.

Colin Fudge is President of RMIT Europe and Vice President of RMIT University. Professor Fudge has worked in universities and in government in the UK, Sweden, Australia, and the European Commission. Previously he was Chair, European Union Expert Group on the Urban Environment; Founding Director of the World Health Organisation (WHO) Collaborative Research Centre on Healthy Cities and Urban Policy; Chair European Sustainable Cities and Towns Campaign; Visiting Professor, European University Institute, Italy, Tokyo University, Chalmers University and Royal Institute of Technology, Sweden, Member of the English Commission for Architecture and the Built Environment (CABE) and Patron of the UK Urban Design Group. He has contributed through interdisciplinary and transdisciplinary research on public policy formulation and implementation; cities, sustainable development and adaptation to climate change; public health; demographic change and urban design. He was awarded Royal Professorship of Environmental Science by the Swedish Academy of Sciences and an Honorary Fellowship of the Royal Institute of British Architects.

Dr Zareh Ghazarian is a Lecturer in Politics in the School of Political and Social Inquiry at Monash University. He holds a BSc and BA from Deakin University and a BA (Hons) and PhD in Political Science from Monash University. He is a leading commentator on politics and appears regularly on national and international television and radio. Dr Ghazarian's teaching and research interests include elections, institutions of governance, political leadership and comparative politics. He has published widely in academic journals and co-authored *Australian Politics for Dummies* (with Nick Economou; 2010, Wiley). Dr Ghazarian is currently completing a book on the party system in the Australian Senate since the end of the Second World War.

Robyn Hollander is an Associate Professor and a member of the School of Government and International Relations at Griffith University. She leads the Federalism, Regionalism and Devolution in the Centre for Governance and Public Policy. She has a long-standing interest in federalism and public policy, particularly in relation to economic reform and the environment. Her current work focuses on federalism, political culture and moral values. In 2013, she was part of a team that won a large Australian Research Council grant to study federal culture in Australia and abroad.

Ralph Horne is Director, Research and Innovation for the College of Design and Social Context at RMIT University. He is interested in urban social and policy change for environmentally sustainable design and development. He has extensive experience of environmental techniques and sustainability appraisal and has a specific research interest in relations between housing and households in the context of climate change and resource scarcity. He combines research leadership and participation in research projects concerning the environmental, social and policy context of production and consumption in the urban environment.

Dr Charlotte Liu is an Assistant Professor in teacher education at the University of Canberra, lecturing in education foundations and educational research methods. Her research interests include comparative education policy, early childhood teaching and teacher effectiveness, with a focus on mathematics education.

Ian Lowe is Emeritus Professor of Science, Technology and Society at Griffith University in Brisbane as well as an adjunct professor at Flinders University and the University of the Sunshine Coast. He is a Fellow of the Australian Academy of Technological Sciences and Engineering. He has published 12 books, including, *Bigger or Better? Australia's Population Debate* (2012, University of Queensland Press), as well as more than 50 chapters and over 50 journal articles. He has been involved in a wide range of government advisory bodies and was made an Officer of the Order of Australia in 2001 for services to science and technology. He received in 2000 the Prime Minister's Environmental Award for Outstanding Individual Achievement and the Queensland Premier's Millennium Award for Excellence in Science. He was also awarded the 2002 Eureka Prize for Promotion of Science. In 2009 the International Academy of Sciences, Health and Ecology awarded him the Konrad Lorenz Gold Medal.

Chris Miller was Professor in Social Work and Social Planning, School of Social and Policy Studies at Flinders University, South Australia, from 2008–12. Prior to that he was Professor in Applied Social Studies at the University of the West of England, UK. He has a disciplinary background in sociology and politics, and completed his doctorate in UK local government decentralisation and public service trade union responses. Whilst at Flinders he was Interim Dean, School of Social and Policy Studies. He worked closely with the Wentworth Group of Concerned Scientists on water policy in the Murray-Darling Basin, and made numerous public commentaries focused on achieving sustainable communities. From 2002–08 he was Editor of the international *Community Development Journal*. Previous books include *The Dilemmas of Development Work: Ethical Challenges in Regeneration* (with Paul Hoggett and Marjorie Mayo; 2008, Policy Press); *Producing Welfare: A Modern Agenda* (2004, Palgrave Macmillan); and *Public Service Trade Unionism and Radical Politics* (1996, Dartmouth Publishing Group).

Damian Oliver is Leading Research Analyst at the Workplace Research Centre, University of Sydney Business School. He has a decade's experience in applied research examining the links between work, training and education. His particular areas of expertise are the intersection of industrial relations issues and workforce development strategies, the youth labour market, the apprenticeship and traineeship models of skills development, and the transition from education to employment. His research career includes time spent at Griffith University (Brisbane), the University of Duisburg-Essen (Germany), and three years at the National Centre for Vocational Education Research (Adelaide). He has an honours degree and PhD in industrial relations from Griffith University as well as qualifications in business (from the Queensland University of Technology) and economics (from the University of Adelaide).

Lionel Orchard is Associate Professor in the School of Social and Policy Studies at Flinders University, where he teaches public policy. He has published on Australian urban and housing policy, Australian public policy and its reform, and the debates about new social democratic ideas and policies. He is the co-author of *Public Goods, Public Enterprise, Public Choice: Theoretical Foundations of the Contemporary Attack on Government* (with Hugh Stretton; 1994, Macmillan) and co-editor of *Markets, Morals and Public Policy* (with Robert Dare; 1989, Federation Press).

Barbara Pocock is Inaugural Director of the Centre for Work + Life, at the University of South Australia. Professor Pocock, who was initially trained as an economist and completed her doctorate in gender studies, has been researching work, employment and industrial relations and the complex intersections with households, families and social life in Australia for over 25 years. She is actively involved in policy development and public commentary. Professor Pocock has published widely and given visiting lectures in the US, Canada, the UK, New Zealand, Switzerland, and China. Recent books include *The Work/Life Collision* (2003, Federation Press), *The Labour Market Ate My Babies: Work, Children and a Sustainable Future* (2006, Federation Press), *Living Low Paid: the Dark Side of Prosperous Australia* (with Helen Masterman Smith; 2008, Allen & Unwin), *Kids count: Better early childhood education and care in Australia* (co-edited with Alison Elliot and Elizabeth Hill; 2007, Sydney University Press), *Time bomb: work, rest and play in Australia today* (with Natalie Skinner and Philippa Williams; 2012, University of New South Wales Press).

John Quiggin is an Australian Laureate Fellow in Economics at the University of Queensland. He is prominent both as a research economist and as a commentator on Australian economic policy. He is a Fellow of the Econometric Society, the Academy of the Social Sciences in Australia and many other learned societies and institutions. He has produced over 1,200 publications, including six books and over 200 refereed journal articles, in fields including decision theory, environmental economics, production economics, and the theory of economic growth. He has also written on policy topics including climate change, microeconomic reform, privatisation, employment policy and the management of the Murray-Darling river system. His latest book, *Zombie Economics: How Dead Ideas Still Walk Among Us*, was released in 2010 by Princeton University Press, and has been translated into eight languages.

Natalie Skinner is a Senior Research Fellow at the Centre for Work + Life in the Hawke Research Institute for Sustainable Societies at the University of South Australia. Her research addresses the impact of psychosocial factors in the workplace on work–life interaction and wellbeing. She has a particular interest in the intersection between time, flexibility and work intensity. She manages the Centre's Australian Work + Life Index (AWALI) survey. Recent books include *Time bomb: work, rest and play in Australia today* (with Barbara Pocock and Philippa Williams; 2012, University of New South Wales Press).

Ben Spies-Butcher is a Senior Lecturer and Director of the Masters of Policy and Applied Social Research in the Sociology Department at Macquarie University. He has a PhD in Economics from the University of Sydney and his work focuses on the political economy of social policy. Ben is a Fellow of the Centre for Policy Development and a Research Associate at the Retirement Policy and Research Centre at the University of Auckland. His most recent co-authored book is *Market Society* (with D. Cahill and J. Paton; 2012, Cambridge University Press). Ben has been an active member of a number of human rights and social justice organisations and was co-convener of the Australian Greens during the 2013 federal election.

James Walter is Professor of Politics at Monash University, and Professor Emeritus (Australian Studies) at Griffith University. He has published widely on Australian politics, leadership, ideas, institutions, political history and policy making. His recent books include *What were they thinking? The politics of ideas in Australia* (2010, University of New South Wales Press), winner of the Henry Mayer prize for Australian politics, 2011 and *Understanding Prime-Ministerial Performance* (2013, Oxford University Press), with Paul Strangio and Paul 't Hart. He is currently completing a history of the Australian prime ministership, and commencing a comparative history of policy determination in the post-war period.

Louise Watson is a Director of the Education Institute at the University of Canberra. Professor Watson engages in policy research relevant to all sectors of education and training, including early childhood education and care. She has published extensively on education policy in Australia and has served on many advisory committees. She was a member of the expert panel appointed by the Australian government to review Base Funding for higher education, which reported in October 2011.

Acknowledgements

This book began to take shape through a number of informal discussions and reflections about future directions and debates in Australian politics and public policy and the available literature in this field. From a base in the new School of Social and Policy Studies at Flinders University, Lionel willingly shared his deep knowledge of public policy while Chris attempted to interrogate Australian issues and history from a European perspective. From different starting points both brought a shared experience of the corrosive impact of neo-liberalism on public value and collective well-being.

We would like to thank colleagues from the School who supported this venture and, in particular facilitated the financial support for the workshop that brought contributors together in April 2013. We thank all contributors for their commitment and tolerance, for making the book's preparation the smooth process it was and engaging with the collaborative spirit of the workshop. We thank Bernie Fraser for his foreword. Those who reviewed the book proposal and draft chapters provided feedback helpful in reshaping the organisation and presentation of the book.

At Policy Press, we thank Emily Watt and her team for the support, encouragement and responsiveness throughout the process. As ever it is always a pleasure to work with Policy Press.

Lionel thanks his colleagues at Flinders, especially George Crowder and Rob Manwaring for their support. Closer to home, he thanks Sue for her ongoing support and many helpful suggestions, and Olivia, Michael and Sophie for their interest and engagement. Chris would like to thank his former Flinders colleagues, especially Fiona Verity and Mick Piotto for their insights on Australian social policy. In particular, he thanks all those at the Wentworth Group of Concerned Scientists for the opportunity to work with them on water reform in the Murray-Darling Basin, especially Tim Stubbs and Caroline McFarlane. He is as ever indebted to Mavis for her continuing support, encouragement and much more besides. Finally, thanks go to Megan and Laurie for their support for our 'Antipodean' adventure and their willingness to endure regular summer vacations in that sun-kissed continent.

Foreword

Bernie Fraser

If (like me) you have been waiting patiently for Australia to show the world how a progressive country can meld a competent and competitive economy with a fair and compassionate society, prepare yourself for further disappointment!

It's not that this goal is utopian: it is no more than what the major political parties have promised us in every election campaign for decades.

This excellent collection of essays on policy making in Australia is rich in insights into why governments invariably deliver much less than they promise. In many areas the high failure rates owe a lot to a pervasive 'market liberalist' (or 'neoliberalist') framework of thinking about policy choices – in short, to an ideology built upon faith in markets and distrust of governments.

A feature of the collection is the prominence it gives to all manner of social policies, and to longer-term 'sustainability' policies (notably population and climate change), as well as traditional economic policies. This mix is appropriate: as important as growing employment and containing inflation are, the ultimate test of government policies – by government's own benchmarks – is whether or not they help to build a prosperous, fair and caring society.

Markets do certain things well – like allocating resources efficiently – where self-interest is an obvious (and legitimate) driver. But it is not in their make-up to afford ordinary people access to quality health and education services (for example), to clean environments, or to reasonable safety nets if they happen to fall through the cracks. These and other community interests have to be driven largely through progressive government policies.

The essays provide informed analysis and commentary on the evolution of more than a dozen different policies in Australia over recent decades. They highlight shortcomings in several social policies that the authors believe are largely attributable to overzealous efforts to apply market liberalism (and to eschew government involvement) in the areas concerned.

These lessons should be heeded. They come at the very time the present government is gearing up for what is foreshadowed to be a particularly strident application of market liberalism. Public spending is set to be cut sharply and widely in the quest for budget surpluses and, down the track, to open the door for tax 'reform' – very much code these days for further reductions in personal income tax. The overweighting of self-interest against community interest inherent in this approach does not auger well for any moves soon towards a fairer, more just society.

The puzzle is that this free market ideology should continue to have the hold it does over policy makers, given its demonstrable failures. The policies followed in the United States and Europe that ushered in the global financial crisis and prolonged its miseries are but the most recent demonstration. They are also the most grotesque, with the 'trickle down' of unemployment and bankruptcy to tens of millions of ordinary people accompanied by a spurt up of bonuses and bailouts to many of the culprits.

Australia avoided the ravages of the Global Financial Crisis (GFC), assisted by a more hands-on approach to financial regulation and the adoption of countercyclical economic policies in place of recession intensifying austerity measures. Despite this, and more than 20 years of sustained economic growth, Australia is still a long way from establishing a prosperous and fair society. As the authors of these essays remind us, income inequalities have risen, education and other standards have fallen, big gaps remain in our infrastructures and Indigenous and other vulnerable groups continue to find life a struggle.

Some answers to the puzzle emerge in several essays that focus on developments in the processes of policy making, as distinct from its subjects. It is clear that institutional support for market liberalism from big business groups, lobbyists and like-minded think tanks has been unscathed by GFC and other setbacks; rather, it has been emboldened by recent changes in Canberra.

Conversely, the credibility of institutions naturally disposed towards the alternative approach of a pragmatic mix of market and government actions – with an explicit bent towards community interests – has taken some hits in recent times. The previous government could have been expected to defend the case for the responsible use of fiscal policy in support of pressing social change but instead pursued a fetish for budget surpluses. And some dubious spending decisions helped to discredit the whole notion of governments having a vital and positive role to play in the nation's advancement. Meanwhile, the trade union movement – another natural source of support for the alternative approach – has seen its influence diminished by declining membership, the spread of enterprise agreements and multiple scandals.

The road to a stronger, fairer and more just Australia is clearly long and rough. Disenchantment will lead some to disengage. These essays provide valuable insights into both the challenges and possible ways forward in many policy areas: the collection is a real marshalling point for everyone committed to continuing the journey.

Bernie Fraser was Secretary of the Australian Treasury (1984–89) and Governor of the Reserve Bank of Australia (1989–96). More recently, he was Chairman of the Australian Government's Climate Change Authority (2012–14).

Part One

SETTING THE SCENE

ONE

Towards a new progressive policy agenda

Chris Miller and Lionel Orchard

Introduction

Australian politics and public policy are at an impasse and face many challenges given economic, political and social turbulence in both the domestic and global spheres. The overwhelming defeat of the Rudd Labor Government in the 2013 federal election and the decisive election of a Liberal–National Party Coalition Government led by Tony Abbott as Australia's 28th Prime Minister make the likelihood of progressive public policy a more distant prospect. Yet Labor's defeat is also an opportunity for progressives to think again about public policies addressing the key issues of today. This book brings together leading authors strongly engaged in public debate to examine trends, generate insights about current policy directions, and articulate ideas for a new progressive policy agenda. While mindful of the complexity and dilemmas entailed in such a project, and the deep-rooted dominance of neoliberal thinking over many years, pursued to varying degrees by both Labor and Liberal Coalition Governments, our aim is to help build analysis of the ways in which such an agenda can be pursued. With some exceptions (for example, McClelland and Smyth, 2010), recent discussions of Australian public and social policy have been mainly built around, on the one hand, change and improvement in public policy processes, and on the other hand, contributions from journalists and politicians reflecting on contemporary political and policy directions and dilemmas (for example Kelly, 1994, 2009; Tanner, 2011; Gallop, 2012; Megalogenis, 2012). There are also various contributions to the policy debates about economic rationalism and centrist and centre-left alternatives, material to be discussed in more detail later. We hope this book contributes critical insights building on these perspectives. This chapter, along with Mark Davis's contribution (Chapter 2), sets the scene, providing some context about contemporary Australian public policy.

The history, socioeconomic and political context of nation states leads each to respond to what may appear as common dilemmas in slightly different ways. Our focus is on Australia but without losing sight of debates and policies elsewhere. We believe that after 30 years of neoliberal ideas and policies holding sway, it is important that in seeking a progressive public policy future, we return to the universalist foundational values of social democracy on which post-war policy was largely framed but modified and extended to give prominence to sustainability, equity, gender and caring principles. In these ways, we hope that the book contributes to the re-imagination of social democratic values and public policies for the changed circumstances of the 21st century. It is also important to consider what kind of institutional frameworks and public institutions are required to deliver new progressive policies. How do social democratic values shape different policy domains, how far have these values been undermined and with what effect, for example in relation to the downgrading of mainstream provision and the elevation of more marginal concerns? How important is the 'high wage/low tax' formulation that has shaped so much recent policy in Australia and beyond to thinking about progressive policy in the future? Any progressive programme will also need to address the obsession with unsustainable consumption and economic growth that so far have been marginal in the development of public policy. Our premise is that if Australia can address such challenges it will be able to continue its rich tradition as a social laboratory and retain its distinctiveness.

The actions and inactions of the Rudd and Gillard Governments, and the response of the Coalition parties then in opposition, raised serious questions about policy process, direction and implementation. In what feels like a period of permanent global uncertainty focused on global financial and environmental instability, and both forced and voluntary migration, many of the values, principles and policy tools dependent upon full employment, social solidarity, and a young and growing population have come to be questioned. Given that public policy seems to have lost the surefootedness it once may have had and with few signs that neoliberal thinking has run its course, we set out to address three interrelated questions: how can we better understand what has been happening across important policy domains; to what extent are current policies fit for purpose in such uncertain times; and how might progressive policies be defined and defended in such circumstances? In what follows, responses to these questions in the contributions to the book are woven through a more detailed account of the history, current directions and possible futures in Australian public policy.

In addition to the 'Setting the Scene' chapters (Part One) and the final chapter, the book has four main parts.

In Part Two, 'Economics, Welfare and Work', John Quiggin considers the continuing capacity of neoliberal economics to prosper despite its numerous failures, while Barbara Pocock, Janine Chapman and Natalie Skinner revisit the relationship between work and unpaid care. Ben Spies-Butcher examines the impact of neoliberalism on welfare policy and attitudes towards those not in paid employment, while John Buchanan and Damian Oliver argue that industrial relations policy, a critical feature of the Australian Settlement, has been deeply damaged by neoliberal policies.

Part Three, 'Culture and Society', has contributions from Jon Altman on the ways in which neoliberalism has underpinned contemporary Indigenous policy, and George Crowder, who considers the potential impact of greater social and cultural diversity on public policy and Australian identity. Deborah Brennan examines the marketisation of childcare, while Louise Watson and Charlotte Liu demonstrate how neoliberalism has shaped education policy. Fran Baum and Judith Dwyer explore how health policy has steered a pragmatic course through competing ideological approaches and Lionel Orchard reviews the tensions in housing policy, where private ownership and housing as an individual capital asset dominate thinking to the exclusion of many from decent accommodation.

Part Four, 'Environment, Population and the Cities' addresses some key challenges for a sustainable Australia. Ian Lowe considers the debate on population growth, a debate concerned not solely with optimum numbers for economic and environmental sustainability but also with social diversity, asylum seekers and identity. As cities take on a growing significance globally, sometimes appearing to compete with the nation state as centres of power and significance, Paul Burton and Jago Dodson consider Australia's approach to urban development and the potential impact of an emergent national urban policy. Using water reform in the Murray-Darling Basin as an exemplar, Daniel Connell considers Australia's inability to grapple with the shifts required in natural resource management as a consequence of previous over-exploitation and future climate change. Ralph Horne and Colin Fudge provide important international perspectives and comparisons for the development of more sustainable environmental and urban policy in Australia.

Part Five, 'Politics and Government', centres on the challenges facing public policy given existing institutional arrangements and political relationships. James Walter and Zareh Ghazarian identify the decline in trust between governments and citizens as a critical concern, and in particular challenge the dominant models of leadership characteristic of contemporary neoliberalism. Robyn Hollander argues that given growing centralism there is a need to revisit the strengths of federalism and the capacity of state governments to act creatively and with local knowledge. Chris Miller argues that the restoration of trust and better policy making is possible if governments at all levels engage more fully with citizens to address current and future dilemmas.

Finally, our concluding chapter distils common themes reinforcing the key arguments and their significance for the future of public policy while acknowledging that not all aspects of Australian public policy have been examined in the book.

Australian policy accommodations

The Australian outlook is often portrayed as pragmatic and adaptable. This is certainly true in the history of Australian politics and public policy. While metropolitan ideas and ideologies, often transposed from other countries, have inevitably shaped Australian political and policy practice, as indeed Australian policy and practices have been influential elsewhere and especially in the UK, there has always been some scepticism about their relevance and their more or less careful adaptation to the Australian setting. The 'Australian Settlement', or more accurately the 'Australian white British/European Settlement' to the extent that it rested on the continuing negation of Indigenous Australians and, for many years, a strictly enforced monocultural ethnic immigration policy, reflects this 'pragmatism'. As with all things political, the 'Settlement' reflects important values and principles resulting from social and political struggle. For those who qualified for membership, the Settlement was grounded in notions of social and economic protection, faith in government, but ambiguity and caution about an expanded and interventionist state, commitment to the egalitarian 'fair go', within the context of relatively low levels of 'unearned' inequality, and a strong system of industrial arbitration – coming together in what some have called the Australian 'wage-earners welfare state' (Castles, 1985, 1988; Kelly, 1994; Buchanan and Oliver, this collection)

These ingredients acted as a starting point for future change and was to some extent only possible in a settler society that, while adopting some features from its colonial inheritance, was relatively 'legacy free', especially in respect of the lived and assumed practices of class. Australia's size and geographical diversity and the consequent challenges for governance, reinforced by different settlement histories of convict and free migration, isolation and distance from its colonial master and ongoing dependence on labour and new migrants to reproduce and build the colony, made for some unique foundations for a nation state. They were all contributory factors to the 'antipodean' experiment, as was the need to impose social and political order (see Fenna, 2012, for reflections on the distinctiveness and similarities of the Australian 'Settlement' in these respects by comparison with experiences in other settler societies).

Pragmatism can be viewed as sound judgment in relation to seemingly opposed political ideologies applied appropriately to the specificity of the Australian situation, or the outcome of reasoned reflection on the effectiveness and appropriateness of various political practices and institutions found elsewhere. It can also be read as whatever is politically feasible at a given moment, the outcome of political conflict and opportunity. More recently, rather than take political decisions based on assessment of what is required long-term to address actual or potential major policy issues and dilemmas, pressing ahead sometimes against powerful interests, the pragmatic outlook might be seen as more closely allied to preferences for short-term fixes echoing opinion polls, focus groups and views in the popular media so as to avoid the risks of electoral displeasure.

Whether the pragmatism and adaptability has been principled and sound or more thinly based and rushed, the Australian political and public policy experience in the late 20th and early 21st centuries has taken place against a quite different ideological backdrop. Since the late 1970s, public policy has been powerfully influenced by the dominant ideology of the times – the neoliberal defence of negative freedom, markets, deregulation, privatisation and small government – and what Jon Altman (Chapter 7) refers to as the 'Canberra consensus', that might appear as a smaller and less polished mirror of its Washington counterpart. At its heart is a set of economic ideas of which the free market and small government are the linchpins. John Quiggin (Chapter 3) succinctly sets out the macroeconomic principles of neoliberalism, or what he calls 'market liberalism', and the persuasive hold they now have internationally despite their failure over time and in multiple places, with the Global Financial Crisis (GFC) the latest and most extreme manifestation of that failure.

In practice, neoliberalism is a dynamic, complex, multifaceted, even contradictory set of ideas, variously applied as a distinctive political project across different countries. Its proponents have had to work hard to secure the positions of power and influence necessary both to put policies in place and to win the ideological arguments, something that has never been entirely achieved. Mark Davis (Chapter 2) shows in some detail the arguments and interests shaping the neoliberal political project, not a 'natural' phenomenon but something carefully constructed, and the way neoliberal ideas and assumptions have found their way into everyday language and expectations. Similarly, Jon Altman (Chapter 7) illustrates this process in respect of Indigenous policy while Louise Watson and Charlotte Liu, Fran Baum and Judith Dwyer, and Daniel Connell (Chapters 10, 11 and 15) show how policy language and directions in education, health care and water management have acquired neoliberal inflections.

While neoliberalism has shaped much change in recent Australian public policy, the pragmatic accommodation of competing principles and values continues to be evident. With the exception perhaps of the Howard Government, the policies and directions of the Hawke, Keating, Rudd and Gillard Governments – Labor or minority Labor Governments – have navigated the increasingly relentless demands of the global turn to neoliberalism without entirely abandoning the legacy of social democracy. What the Liberal Coalition Government, elected in 2013, will do remains unclear, although a number of the leading spokespeople, but not always Prime Minister Tony Abbott, defend neoliberal standpoints unequivocally.

The Hawke and Keating Governments (1983–1996) attempted to balance a neoliberal emphasis with social democratic commitments. The then relatively protected and thus vulnerable and rigid Australian economy experienced major deregulation and exposure to global markets, while key public institutions were privatised. This was combined with the 'trilogy' commitment to reduce the size of the government deficit and expenditure and limit levels of taxation. It was pursued alongside a tripartite corporatism – the 'Accord' – that sought to balance business and labour interests and pursue creative and progressive social policies in welfare, health and education. The Hawke/Keating policy mix was an early expression of 'third way' or 'new social democratic' thinking that became so influential in the UK, Europe and later, albeit briefly during Clinton's presidency, the USA.

The policies of the liberal–conservative Howard Government (1996–2007) were more explicitly neoliberal in many respects, as reflected in the pursuit of fiscal discipline and budget surpluses, labour market deregulation, and welfare and public sector reform. Nevertheless, the Howard Government encountered numerous limitations when it came to policies as opposed to rhetoric and struggled in particular with the attempt to further reform labour relations beyond the Keating changes (see John Buchanan and Damian Oliver, Chapter 6). Howard remained conservative or populist in other areas – particularly on the issues of immigration and refugees, although it is common practice for neoliberal governments, for example in the USA and the UK, as well as other political entities such as the European Union, to impose strict regulations on who can participate in the free movement of labour, a policy often seen as being at the core of neoliberalism. As Mark Davis argues, it is more accurate to speak of neoliberal conservatism than the more restricted economic formulations of neoliberalism. Likewise, Howard was not averse to state intervention, as illustrated by his Indigenous policies. Running against the grain of his espoused neoliberalism, Howard's 'Northern Territory Intervention' was justified as a response to a 'crisis' of child abuse and community disintegration, despite the lack of effort to connect the policy with the stated problem. However, as Jon Altman argues, the intervention was not without a neoliberal infusion.

The election of the Rudd Labor Government in 2007 saw some winding back of neoliberal policies in industrial relations and wage setting, a strong Keynesian fiscal response countering the impacts of the GFC on the Australian economy, and more equity and inclusion in welfare and social policy. But the broad policy parameters – positive about markets, sceptical about government intervention – set in the Hawke, Keating and Howard eras proved difficult to shift in fundamental ways. The spectre of climate change rose to prominence during the first decade of the century and was declared by Rudd to be the "greatest moral challenge of our times". Yet both sides of Australian politics have had difficulty traversing these issues, as evidenced by both the opposition to the Gillard Government's carbon price legislation and Rudd's announcement on his brief and ultimately unsuccessful return as Prime Minister in 2013 that he would effectively abandon the policy.

Similarly, Rudd's proposed mining tax on excessive profits was much watered down by the Gillard Government and there is little sign of government wanting to regulate coal seam gas explorations. Similarly, water reform in the Murray-Darling Basin (see Chapters 15 and 19 by Daniel Connell and Chris Miller), that began with all-party support, underpinned by the Water Act 2007, to return the valuable iconic Basin to a healthy river system, ended in a thoroughly botched pragmatism that failed to tackle the long-standing problem of over-use of water for irrigation. Instead, a powerful farming lobby implacably opposed to reform was appeased. The irony is that these interests will themselves lose out if the basin environment continues to decline. Larger environmental questions about over-consumption and the related obsession with continued economic growth have yet to figure on the agenda of any political party, beyond the Greens. As Ian Lowe (Chapter 13) argues, the political and policy tension between those who argue for further encouragement of economic and population growth and careful management of fragile environmental resources in Australia remains.

Policy inertia and complacency

On the face of it, the Australian public policy orthodoxy through the period since the early 1980s has been broadly successful, particularly in the economic arena. Judged by the latest Organisation for Economic Cooperation and Development's (OECD) assessment of the best country in which to live, Donald Horne's 'Lucky Country' metaphor continues to resonate in attitudes of the Australian public and elites, even if some commentators argue that the exploitation of mineral resources as the main basis for Australia's recent luck has been handled very poorly (Cleary, 2011). A rough bipartisan consensus about the virtues of continuing market-oriented reform is reinforced within mainstream media and intellectual debate. This consensus continues to shape Australian politics and public policy. Government 'efficiency', 'competence' and 'trust' dominate the debate and rarely are current relationships between state, market and civil society or market rationale questioned. Similarly, as Ralph Horne and Colin Fudge demonstrate (Chapter 16), Australia has yet to properly grapple with the critical issues of climate change and environmental sustainability. In this it seriously lags behind initiatives and awareness in both the global north and south with potentially major implications for future policy directions.

The public policy changes unleashed in the 1980s and 1990s have been the subject of much debate. This has centred on the impacts of 'economic rationalism' on national politics and policy, the early Australian expression of concern about neoliberalism (Pusey, 1991; Carroll and Manne, 1992; Emy, 1993; King and Lloyd, 1993; Rees et al, 1993); the influence of 'public choice' theory in shifting understandings of the role of government in neoliberal directions (Self, 1993, 2000; Stretton and Orchard, 1994); the influence of neoliberal assumptions in the policy reforms of the period (Argy, 1998, 2003; Woodward, 2005); and reflections on the impact of the reforms on the idea of the Australian policy settlement or the 'Australian Way' (Smyth and Cass, 1998). Equally, there was some concern about the dominance and influence of neoliberal assumptions in Australian public policy and the economic and social policies associated with it during the Howard era. There was hope that the 2007 election of Kevin Rudd's Labor Government would see greater attention to the wide range of social, environmental, international and cultural issues facing Australia (Manne, 2008). For some, glimmers of a progressive future moving beyond neoliberalism were evident in Rudd's conventional Keynesian responses to the 2008 GFC that prevailed despite the subsequent issues faced by this initiative in the wake of substantial problems over implementation (Manne and McKnight, 2008).

Also indicative of a shifting balance in mainstream discussion in political and policy debates in recent years has been the publication of centrist and centre-left policy manifestos for Australia's future, each setting out to varying degrees comprehensive agendas for economic, social, environmental and political reform (Stilwell, 2000; Duncan et al, 2004; Stretton, 2005; Davis and Lyons, 2010). The question of how best to respond to increased risk in the social, work and environmental spheres, in the context of deregulated global markets and the impact of neoliberal policies on patterns of inequality, continues to attract attention (Western et al, 2007; Marston et al, 2010). The growing presence of centre-left think tanks, such as the Centre for Policy Development and Per Capita, and new public policy research centres, such as the Grattan Institute, pursue research and advocacy across a wide range of policy areas – economic, social, health, and environmental. Nevertheless, the impact of ideas and argument from these sources has with some exceptions been marginal. For long periods during the Gillard Government, the Liberal Coalition led consistently in the opinion polls and, apart from a brief period upon the return of Rudd as Prime Minister in June 2013, were set to win comfortably, as they ultimately did in the 2013 federal election, having already taken Victoria, New South Wales and Queensland from Labor in the 2011/12 state elections.

Thus, the traction of new ideas amidst what then seemed like the declining influence of neoliberalism proved somewhat patchy and difficult, given the ongoing dominance of centre-right views and, perhaps, the lack of clarity about how to respond to seemingly intractable policy problems or map a broader social democratic vision: a problem reflected here too with most contributors struggling with the latter. Most of our contributors highlight the dilemmas confronting policy while presenting ideas and arguments edging away from neoliberal thinking and reconnecting with social democratic ideas but in somewhat muted ways.

There is a continuing inertia and complacency in Australian politics and policy making, although this might alter with the Abbott Government. To date this has been expressed in a number of ways, for example the erosion of the idea that government can be a positive source for wellbeing, the diminished role or value attached to professional expertise, the undue influence of a media fixated on sound bites and immediacy, an inability amongst politicians to communicate complex policy issues in accessible ways and with due regard to those who might be required to make major adjustments, and significant problems with policy implementation and poor political leadership (Manne, 2011; Tanner, 2011; Garnaut, 2013).

There is also the issue of just how influential neoliberal ideology and ideas have been in shaping politics and public policy. It can be argued that the impact has been very uneven across different societies and that the Australian experience reflects the continuing role of established political institutions and policy ideas coming from other quarters (Cahill et al, 2012). What neoliberalism did well was to exploit major fault lines in the previous regime that had previously been exposed by left-leaning critics from both mainstream social democracy and social movement radicals. In particular these focused on the position of women, young people, Aborigines and minorities, as well as other shortcomings of earlier social reforms, especially the poor quality and bureaucratic management of many public services. With the weakening of grand narratives, the growing fragmentation of class, the loss of confidence in the capacity of the state and the emergence of counter-cultures, neoliberalism was able to advance ideas of individual choice and freedom from the state, while also, and somewhat contradictorily, remobilising conservative values to fend off calls from young people for greater freedoms and slow down, if not halt, demands for equity across all spheres by those so-called minorities. At another level it brought forward a greater emphasis on evidence and accountability and the questioning of expertise. Its solutions were always absolutist in terms of the pre-eminence of markets. Nevertheless, it has demonstrated a capacity to adapt, and thereby opened a gap between rhetoric and neoliberalism as practised.

The emergence of policy process and the role of political institutions as a key concern

One of the most important other influences on Australian public policy is the continuing emphasis on managerialism and 'process' thinking, which, while not intrinsically associated with neoliberalism, have taken on a neoliberal hue, with its emphasis on efficiency, regulation and control within reduced budgets. It has also demanded that senior public servants look to the private sector for managerial role models and techniques, leading to a growing emphasis on heroic leaders exercising absolute managerial control and in general the uncritical adoption of new management speak within the public sector. Thus the study and teaching of public policy in Australian universities has been overtaken by a vision primarily focused on the clarity and logic of the procedures associated with it. This is reflected in the dominance of *The Australian Policy Handbook*, first published in 1998 and now in its 5th edition (Althaus, Bridgman and Davis, 2013). Much advocacy of change and innovation in public policy practice, especially that associated with the Australian and New Zealand School of Government (ANZSOG) stresses the latest process vogues – in recent times, the need for more innovative coordination across government agencies and levels of government, as in 'joined-up' and 'whole of government' approaches, improved collaboration across sectors through partnerships, greater levels of community engagement in the development of policy, and the more sophisticated marshalling of evidence to support policy change (O'Flynn and Wanna, 2008; Argyrous, 2009; Scott and Baehler, 2010; Lindquist et al, 2011).

Such initiatives have in part reflected new thinking and transformations with regard to the important public service values of efficiency, inclusiveness, service accessibility, professional and service cooperation in adopting a holistic service user focused approach, service quality and accountability and effectiveness by using the best available data and greater transparency in decision making. We do not underestimate the importance of policy process, political institutions, the role of key actors or the importance of engaging with what will be more assertive and articulate as well as diverse sets of publics. Indeed, for some, the perceived problems with key policies and programmes of the Rudd and Gillard Governments can essentially be attributed to process failures – 'top-down' decision making, insufficient time to carefully consider options, and lack of care in developing a 'business case' for these policies (Howard et al, 2012).

James Walter and Zareh Ghazarian, Robyn Hollander, Chris Miller, and Daniel Connell (Chapters 17, 18, 19 and 15) address key aspects of the policy process – leadership, institutional frameworks and citizen engagement. Hollander points to the important role federalism has and can play in allowing for experimentation and local specificity with sometimes quite different approaches to policy problems and ensuring that a 'one size fits all' approach has not been enforced on what is a highly diverse country, despite an ongoing trend towards centralism. An implication of Chris Miller's contribution on the need to address the growing problem of a depoliticised citizenry is that federalism will only continue to work in progressive ways if politics is once again felt to be meaningful at the everyday local level beyond federalism, and if socially aware and informed citizens are able to hold politicians to account in more participatory ways than is allowed for in representative government.

James Walter and Zareh Ghazarian highlight the limitations of contemporary approaches to political leadership, as displayed across the political spectrum, and argue for a leadership style more suited to complexity and uncertainty. Daniel Connell argues that getting institutional arrangements right is critical even when substantive policies are agreed. He argues that arrangements for the management of the Murray-Darling Basin have changed in neoliberal directions with both positive and negative consequences.

Other chapters highlight institutional and political problems. For example, Ian Lowe, and Paul Burton and Jago Dodson (Chapters 13 and 14) illustrate some of the inherent tensions in the current federal–state relationships, especially those related to the respective capacities for policy making, income generation and spending responsibilities. Louise Watson and Charlotte Liu (Chapter 10), however, provide examples of Labor's efforts in education policy, especially under Gillard, to build more of a long-term partnership between federal and state governments and thereby bring about less autonomy for both.

Mainstream public policy: social, economic, urban and housing policies

Social policy continues to be riven by tensions between generosity and toughness, fairness and responsibility, and the question of just how far social provision should be integrated into economic and employment policy. Australians have not entirely lost sight of their welfare heritage of a 'wage earners' welfare state', underpinned by wages at least sufficient to support a family with three dependent children and a single breadwinner, in which everyone who could work would want to work for the rewards offered, the self-respect that accompanies work and the subsequent ability to be an active and contributing member of society. Consequently, and acknowledging the still to be achieved goal that women too must be included as an equal part of the paid workforce, those unfortunate enough to be outside the workforce are still treated with respect, and offered support to re-enter the labour market, or can live with security and dignity if they are either unable or not required to do so. However, there are growing signs of impatience with, and even the demonisation of, those out of paid work, and continuing emphasis given to 'hard-working' and 'responsible' families.

Like most northern countries, Australia remains at best ambiguous in how it values and rewards those engaged in unpaid caring work, an increasingly important issue, as highlighted by Barbara Pocock, Janine Chapman and Natalie Skinner (Chapter 4). As Ben Spies-Butcher (Chapter 5) argues, attitudes and policy on social welfare are changing, albeit not as dramatically as some writers have argued, and the collective or shared sense of belonging to a common project of 'the making of Australia', built on fairness and free of social distinctions, is continually challenged by the market-driven emphasis of neoliberalism. A philosophy of 'each against all', accompanied by the view that expressions of 'collectivism' or 'common purpose' only undermine individual freedom and expression, with no benefits beyond those of law and order, shape policy directions in many areas. Deborah Brennan, Louise Watson and Charlotte Liu, Fran Baum and Judith Dwyer, and Lionel Orchard (Chapters 9, 10, 11 and 12) explore the tensions between individualism and collective responsibilities in relation to family, education, health and housing policy, respectively.

Economic policy and priority setting in resource allocation in Australia's mixed economy continues to be hampered by assumptions about the virtues of private choice and competition through markets and the vices of public and government involvement (John Quiggin, Chapter 3). Nevertheless, major economic and regional imbalances – the 'two-speed' economy – have threatened the sense of integration in Australian society and express the continuing failure to address urban and regional development questions. The recent debate on water reform in the Murray-Darling Basin highlighted the absence of any long-term approach to regional development as well as how to ensure a sustainable farming industry under changed environmental circumstances. Daniel Connell (Chapter 15) highlights the shortcomings in the policy process that would enable the engagement and building of an institutional framework needed to address such complex issues. The problems of Australia's cities – infrastructure backlogs and bottlenecks, car dependence and poor public transport, housing supply and price issues – continue to grow without much conscious policy attention while investment in an ageing public infrastructure – schools, hospitals, community facilities – continues to be patchy. Paul Burton and Jago Dodson (Chapter 14) examine recent developments and the significance of a national framework for urban policy and related infrastructure issues, and consider its potential impact under a Coalition Government. Lionel Orchard (Chapter 12) examines the current problems in building an effective housing policy, addressing investment, taxation, supply and regulation issues across the different housing tenures.

Developing responses to these economic and social questions takes place against the backdrop of what some claim is Australia's uniqueness as a high wage/low tax society. While there is some question about whether the Australian economy really is high wage, other issues lurk behind this understanding. How are patterns of income and tax burdens distributed? Is the tax system sufficiently progressive and to what extent are progressive taxes critical to the future of Australian society? Are private incomes sufficient to ensure appropriate health care, decent and secure housing, a decent life in old age, good education for all children, provision for the needs of children in large families, and the capacity to save to cover periods of unemployment, illness or disability? Does a low tax economy ensure the provision of enough public facilities – hospitals, schools, public transport, roads, parks and recreation facilities, environmental protection, and so on – and at a quality sufficient to attract all sections of the community? Do indirect subsidy flows in the tax system distort policy development and directions in key areas like housing and health? To what extent does a 'high wage/low tax' arrangement include all sections of the Australian community and who, if anyone, is excluded?

The real debate is not the extent to which the Australian income and tax system has worked so far, although that is important, but rather whether it can deliver satisfactory solutions to these issues in the future. A high wage/low tax economy could be justified in an economy guaranteed to deliver secure, well-paid employment for all those able to work. A global, dynamic and fiercely competitive economy, currently transforming relationships between the global north and south, offers no such guarantees. In circumstances of increasing uncertainty, what role should the state play in ensuring security for all? The 'five giant evils' of unemployment, poverty, ill health, insufficient education, and inadequate housing, identified by the influential British Liberal, William Beveridge in 1942, whose ideas helped frame post-war settlements between the state, capital and labour, could be added to and further refined for life in the 21st century but they are never far from the door. While the evidence might indicate that more Australians are levering themselves out of universal services and into private market options it is not clear whether this shows a strong commitment to markets or is mainly in response to fear and anxiety over the consequences of not doing so. Although market-driven neoliberalism presents itself as the only option for our times it is not at all certain that the public has lost faith in state-based solutions, although impatience with 'under-performing' governments reflects neoliberal values. A number of our contributors address these questions. For example, John Quiggin addresses the problem of rebuilding macroeconomic policy and public finance to deal with future infrastructure and human service demands. Fran Baum and Judith Dwyer, Louise Watson and Charlotte Liu, and Lionel Orchard all raise similar concerns of how to maintain equity of access in the policy areas they examine – health care, education and housing. Ben Spies-Butcher points to changes in welfare policy that may make public/private balances in the system more difficult in the future.

The fragility of Australian identity: irrationality in public policy

Australian public policy development has been much less focused recently on the wider examination and contest of other public values, especially equality, fairness, sustainability, cultural diversity, identity and recognition, and the ways in which those values could be given substantive and institutional expression (Stewart, 2009). Public policy academics have been criticised for retreating from public debate and abandoning consideration of wider questions and responses in favour of more narrow instrumental objectives and falling in with government attempts to introduce research output measurements (Shergold, 2011).

There have been numerous examples of public policy drift and a lack of leadership energised by a vision of a distinctive Australia capable of addressing the challenges and uncertainties of the times. In Indigenous policy, fear about what is revealed of the Australian identity and its capacity to tolerate the unacceptable limits the ability to address major issues of life chances, opportunities, cultural differences and the consequences of failed policies over many years. The seemingly intractable nature and continuing deterioration in the condition and wellbeing of especially rural and remote Indigenous peoples, underscored by anxiety about the 'other', continues to undermine a well-intentioned policy to 'close the gap', although Fran Baum and Judith Dwyer highlight some areas of progress in health (Chapter 11). Meanwhile, debate about whether Australian Aborigines should be formally acknowledged in the Constitution evokes memories of 'white Australia', 'terra nullius' and even reverting to whether Indigenous peoples could or should ever be considered to be part of a country called 'Australia' and, if so, at what price to them (Jon Altman, Chapter 7).

In the area of refugees and asylum seeker policy, especially in relation to those arriving by boat, who tend to be escaping from the more troubled countries in the region, such as Afghanistan, Pakistan, Sri Lanka and Iraq, both Labor and the Coalition have striven to demonstrate that they have the toughest approach and are most determined to stop the growing number of boats, often fragile and ill-equipped to deal with the perilous crossing from Indonesia, bringing asylum seekers to Australian shores. People travelling in this way have quite erroneously been perceived as illegitimate claimants to refugee status and as 'queue jumpers'. Rudd added to the tough stance in the mid-2013 announcement that no unprocessed asylum seeker attempting to land by boat would ever be allowed to gain refugee status in Australia but would instead be landed on Manus Island in Papua New Guinea and 'resettled' there even if subsequently granted asylum. This decision only further raised the stakes, in particular on the question of whether it breached Australia's commitment to international treaties.

While the debate has reflected differences over how best to process applicants while acknowledging the trauma suffered, especially for unaccompanied minors, complying with obligations under the Human Rights Convention and avoiding placing asylum seekers at personal risk of death by drowning, other fears lie not too far below the surface. Australia has a long history of fearing an invasion from the north of 'alien' others who would swamp the 'newly' settled country. It also has a history of trying to closely manage the influx of new migrants, in relation to numbers and skills but especially ethnicity and skin colour, and only recently did it abandon the 'white Australia' policy. Pre-election 2013 Abbott went further, following his emphatic and oft repeated 'stop the boats' slogan with the appointment of a three-star general to oversee his 'Sovereign Borders' strategy, a symbolically war-like footing. Once in office, Abbott's determination to bury this issue allowed the Australian navy to board boats and tow them back into Indonesian waters, raising accusations of mistreatment and illegality.

With an estimated population in 2014 of still only 23.5 million there remains an overriding anxiety that population growth, a desired or even necessary policy objective, provided it is not too great, will be driven by those who are in some way 'unsuitable' (Ian Lowe, Chapter 13). The fact that refugees make claims based on their human right to asylum undermines Australia's capacity to control immigration using the traditional markers of education, sought-after skills, age, family circumstances and country of origin, a case of where a rational approach to policy making is overturned by world events beyond the control of nation states. More fundamentally, current asylum seekers bring cultural challenges of integration, heightening fears fuelled in part by the so-called 'war on terror' and a sense that the much heralded success of multiculturalism, which in reality is relatively small-scale in what remains a predominantly 'white' country, will be put at risk in the same way that it is claimed has happened in the UK and elsewhere in Europe.

There can be few other contemporary examples of public policy being as driven by irrational fear and anxiety and in defiance of all the evidence as Australia's current approach to asylum seekers, although the 'Northern Territory Intervention' had many similarities. Instead, sufficient real and news-grabbing events, such as sunken boats, unaccompanied children kept in detention, hunger strikes, suicides and rooftop protests continue to hold political and policy attention. The current drama that has been played out against asylum seekers has all major parties seeking the leading role in pursuing the harshest policies in this area. This stands in contrast to the bipartisan and inclusive leadership of earlier times, particularly led by conservatives like Malcolm Fraser, in confronting the rising reactions of the Right during the period of high Asian immigration in the 1970s and 1980s following the Vietnam War. George Crowder (Chapter 8) explores some of the tensions surrounding multiculturalism, arguing that overall Australia remains tolerant and that multiculturalism has so far not generated the same degree of negativity as found elsewhere.

Social cohesion, the sustainability of welfare and the value of public goods

Beneath specific political, institutional, social, economic and resourcing questions lie more fundamental concerns about Australia's identity. Australia continues to be successfully held together by the opportunity to participate in a still relatively successful economy, a stable political system and, for most, an agreeable climate in an outstanding environment. Nevertheless, there is growing unease about what provides the glue binding societies together, and what provides political legitimacy and a sense of belonging if competitive markets underpinned by individual consumption drive everything. Moreover, these are global markets in which capital moves effortlessly to those regions able to supply the cheapest labour, thereby injecting a heightened sense of job insecurity, while the increasing global movement of people presents nation states with new problems of diversity and inclusion. Consequently, there has been much discussion about the need to create 'active citizens', shifting the balance between rights and responsibilities away from the former and towards the latter. These concerns are also evident in the widespread introduction of often vaguely formulated policies aimed at increasing 'social inclusion', building 'social capital' or the 'big society', looking to the third sector to play a greater role in service delivery and community building, and in efforts to promote new forms of governance through intersectoral partnerships.

Australia is not alone, however, in facing such uncertainties about the future of progressive public policy in the neoliberal era, as the international perspectives and context provided by Mark Davis, John Quiggin, and Ralph Horne and Colin Fudge (Chapters 2, 3 and 16) indicate. In most OECD countries, questions have been raised about the state's capacity to provide public decommodified goods and services. Doubts are often raised about whether the state can 'afford' such provision in the context of a changing demographic profile, higher standards and broadening expectations. Closely aligned are those who question the justice and fairness of universal provision in contexts where increasing numbers are deemed sufficiently well off to purchase services. Removing so-called middle-class welfare beneficiaries, it is argued, would thereby leave greater access to those who cannot afford private provision and remove from the poor the burden of subsidising the rich. These doubts are evident too in more specific areas of policy, such as those efforts to extend the working life by raising the age at which pensions can be accessed, investments in skill training rather than education, and increasing the eligibility criteria for social security benefits with a view to making the unemployed more 'job ready' and 'flexible', often with lowered benefit levels, and away from what are perceived as dysfunctional lives.

Such 'economic' considerations continue to ignore the social function and indeed benefits of universal public provision, especially in respect of non-monetary provision such as health care or education rather than child benefits. Not only do such services generate a sense of social inclusion but they are also more likely to ensure the quality of provision as well-educated, articulate and rights-aware users of such services expect and demand equity, efficiency, effectiveness and ongoing improvement in them.

Doubts about the costs of welfare exist alongside the argument that the state should not make such provision regardless of cost. Entitlements to public services, usually financial benefits, are said to breed dependency, diminish a recipient's sense of self-respect and undermine their ability to take responsibility to problem solve and provide for themselves and their families. However, welfare payments were never designed to replace work but to provide support over a limited period of time, and related to family circumstances when someone was unable to work through no fault of their own, with the expectation that they would return to paid employment as quickly as possible. During a period of full employment and with relatively high wages there was little argument with the rationale for such provision. Circumstances changed with an increasingly insecure labour market that has become a more permanent feature, and consequent rising unemployment and lower government tax revenues. Those in work, often struggling to remain employed, living with relatively lower incomes and family commitments requiring two wage earners or multiple jobs, can now more easily look differently upon those out of work and in receipt of welfare benefits, especially when this seems to be ongoing rather than the result of illness, disability, retirement or temporary lay-off. Anti-welfare arguments have been so well orchestrated as to have a profound impact to the point that it has become almost unacceptable to speak positively of those in receipt of benefits, let alone argue for increased benefits. Across the political spectrum the goal, at least at the level of rhetoric, is to radically reduce the number of benefit recipients, not because of changes in the labour market or how we think about unpaid care, but because it is argued that recipients do not have any entitlement to benefits and are a drain on otherwise 'hard-working families'.

The stigmatisation and punishment of those who have become 'dependent' upon welfare have little merit and are unlikely to produce new 'responsible' citizens of those so chastened. After all, life for those on welfare means accepting fewer, more restricted and less rewarding opportunities and a much lower standard of living, or having to create an alternative high-risk household 'economy' by supplementing welfare benefits with either undeclared work or illegal activities. If the goal is to ensure that the vast majority of those eligible are in gainful employment then the first requirement is to ensure the ready availability of such work. Beyond the availability objective are the more important ones of ensuring that the conditions of work create opportunities for individual creativity, fulfillment and development, while these are in harmony with an equally valued personal, family and social life. Indeed, in a less consumer-oriented world the time spent by all in paid employment may be much reduced. Only in this way will those in work find satisfaction and a sense of wellbeing with what they are doing, with those outside the labour market having a positive incentive to actively seek to be part of it.

We are now more than ever aware of the non-material benefits of paid work for men and women as well as the need to fulfil ourselves in other ways too as parents, carers, citizens, community members and in our own personal goals. Add to this that on average we are living longer than our forebears, with the expectation of a fulfilling life, and a 'third age', in retirement, and we can see that all modern societies require major investment in education and health care, not simply for purely economic reasons. We are also aware of the diminishing returns and ultimate futility of ever increasing consumption, in terms of personal satisfaction, happiness and economic and environmental sustainability. The challenge for social democracy, after a long period in which neoliberalism has been dominant and persistent, is to create a cohesive vision embracing new social, economic and political arrangements and relationships built upon knowledge and insights about the fundamentally new challenges and changes taking place.

Australians continue to demonstrate resilience in the face of adversity and a seemingly boundless capacity to 'bounce back' from disasters, both natural and caused by humans, as seen recently in response to extensive flooding in Queensland (2011), the Victorian bush fires (2009) and throughout the ten-year Millennium drought. However, this capacity does not necessarily equip people to plan for a more uncertain future, one requiring major policy and behavioural adaptations of a long-term nature. Rather, resilience born out of adversity reaffirms a belief in the ability of Australians to carry on as before after such setbacks have been addressed. The paradigm that economic growth, social and political progress are assured and guaranteed by a uniquely 'Australian way' remains dominant. This was further reinforced, both by the relatively light economic impact of the 2008 GFC, although current (early 2014) projections are less optimistic, and the belief that Australia succeeded where others have failed in developing a respectful multicultural society. In response to this 'pragmatic complacency', we hope that the arguments of this book help in building new understandings of both the strengths and the limits of where we are now and more expansive views about where we might go.

References

Althaus, C., Bridgman, P. & Davis, G. (2013), *The Australian Policy Handbook,* 5th edn, Allen & Unwin, Sydney

Argy, F. (1998), *Australia at the Crossroads: Radical free market or a progressive liberalism?* Allen & Unwin, Sydney

Argy, F. (2003), *Where to From Here? Australian egalitarianism under threat,* Allen & Unwin, Sydney

Argyrous, G. (ed), (2009), *Evidence for Policy and Decision-Making: A Practical Guide,* UNSW Press, Sydney

Cahill, D., Stilwell, F. & Edwards, L. (eds), (2012), *Neoliberalism: Beyond the Free Market,* Edward Elgar, London

Carroll, J. & Manne, R. (eds), (1992), *Shutdown: The Failure of Economic Rationalism and How to Rescue Australia,* Text Publishing, Melbourne

Castles, F.G. (1985), *The Working Class and Welfare: Reflections on the Political Development of the Welfare State in Australia and New Zealand, 1890–1980,* Allen & Unwin, Wellington

Castles, F.G. (1988), *Australian Public Policy and Economic Vulnerability: A Comparative and Historical Perspective,* Allen & Unwin, Sydney

Cleary, P. (2011), *Too Much Luck: The Mining Boom and Australia's Future,* Black Inc., Melbourne

Davis, M. & Lyons, M. (eds), (2010), *More than Luck: Ideas Australia Needs Now,* Centre for Policy Development, Sydney

Duncan, M., Leigh, A., Madden, D. & Tynan, P. (2004), *Imagining Australia: Ideas for our Future,* Allen & Unwin, Sydney

Emy, H.V. (1993), *Remaking Australia: The state, the market and Australia's future,* Allen & Unwin, Sydney

Fenna, A. (2012), 'Putting the 'Australian Settlement' in Perspective', *Labour History,* No. 102, pp. 99-118.

Gallop, G. (2012), *Politics, Society, Self: Occasional Writings,* UWA Publishing, Crawley, Western Australia.

Garnaut, R. (2013), 'Ending the great Australian complacency of the early twenty first century', Victoria University 2013 Vice-Chancellor's Lecture, Melbourne, 28 May: http://research.vu.edu.au/wp/2013/06/ending-the-great-australian-complacency/

Howard, J.H. with Allan, P., Katsigiannis, T., MacDonald, M., Stewart-Weeks, M., Sturgess, G., Suggett, D. & White, P. (2012), *Public Policy Drift: Why governments must replace 'policy on the run' and 'policy by fiat' with a 'business case' approach to regain public confidence,* Institute of Public Administration Australia (IPAA) Public Policy Discussion Paper, Canberra

Kelly, P. (1994), *The End of Certainty: Power, Politics & Business in Australia,* 2nd ed., Allen & Unwin, Sydney

Kelly, P. (2009), *The March of Patriots: The Struggle for Modern Australia,* Melbourne University Press

King, S. & Lloyd, P. (eds), (1993), *Economic Rationalism: Dead End or Way Forward?,* Allen & Unwin, Sydney

Lindquist, E.A., Vincent, S. & Wanna, J. (eds), (2011), *Delivering Policy Reform: Anchoring Significant Reforms in Turbulent Times,* ANU E Press, Canberra

Manne, R. (ed), (2008), *Dear Mr Rudd: Ideas for a Better Australia,* Black Inc., Melbourne

Manne, R. (2011), *Making Trouble: Essays against the New Australian Complacency,* Black Inc., Melbourne

Manne, R. & McKnight, D. (eds), (2008), *Goodbye to All That? On the Failure of Neo-Liberalism & The Urgency of Change,* Black Inc., Melbourne

Marston, G., Moss, J. & Quiggin, J. (eds), (2010), *Risk, Welfare and Work,* Melbourne University Press

McClelland, A. & Smyth, P. (eds), (2010), *Social Policy in Australia: Understanding for Action,* 2nd edn, Oxford University Press

Megalogenis, G., (2012), *The Australian Moment: How we were made for these times,* Penguin, Melbourne

O'Flynn, J. & Wanna, J. (eds), (2008), *Collaborative Governance: A new era of public policy in Australia?,* ANU E Press, Canberra

Pusey, M. (1991), *Economic Rationalism in Canberra: A Nation Building State Changes its Mind,* Cambridge University Press

Rees, S., Rodley, G. & Stilwell, F. (eds), (1993), *Beyond the Market: Alternatives to Economic Rationalism,* Pluto Press, Sydney

Scott, C. & Baehler, K. (2010), *Adding Value to Policy Analysis and Advice,* UNSW Press, Sydney

Self, P. (1993), *Government by the Market? The Politics of Public Choice,* Macmillan, London

Self, P. (2000), *Rolling Back the Market: Economic Dogma & Political Choice,* Macmillan, London

Shergold, P. (2011), 'Seen but not heard', *Australian Literary Review,* 4 May, pp. 3-4

Smyth, P. & Cass, B. (eds), (1998), *Contesting the Australian Way: States, Markets and Civil Society,* Cambridge University Press

Stewart, J. (2009), *Public Policy Values,* Palgrave Macmillan, Basingstoke

Stilwell, F. (2000), *Changing Track: A new political economic direction for Australia,* Pluto Press, Sydney

Stretton, H. (2005), *Australia Fair,* UNSW Press, Sydney

Stretton, H. & Orchard, L. (1994), *Public Goods, Public Enterprise, Public Choice: Theoretical Foundations of the Contemporary Attack on Government,* Macmillan, London

Tanner, L. (2011), *Sideshow: Dumbing Down Democracy,* Scribe Publications, Melbourne

Western, M., Baxter, J., Pakulski, J., Tranter, B., Western, J., van Egmond, M., Chesters, J., Hosking, A., O'Flaherty, M. & van Gellecum, Y. (2007), 'Neoliberalism, Inequality and Politics: The Changing Face of Australia', *Australian Journal of Social Issues,* 42, 3, pp. 401–18

Woodward, D. (2005), *Australia Unsettled: The Legacy of 'Neo-liberalism',* Pearson Education Australia, Sydney

TWO

Neoliberalism, the culture wars and public policy

Mark Davis

Introduction

The roles available in the highly scripted, highly charged repertoire that passes for much public debate on politics and public policy are by now so well known as to have become generic. First there is a beleaguered, 'silenced' 'mainstream' of 'battlers' who inhabit the 'real Australia' of the suburbs and the bush, and whose fears and concerns are systematically ignored. Second are those who would silence them – the 'latte sipping', 'politically correct', inner city dwelling, 'new class', 'cultural elites' of an all-pervasive Left, who peddle their 'bleeding heart' causes out of self-interest and against the popular interest, supported by 'nanny state' government regulators and credulous, left-leaning accomplices in the publicly owned media. Finally there is a third group of self-styled defenders of the 'battlers', who are the arbiters of this stand-off and who set the rules of the game: a retinue of permanently outraged commercial radio talkback hosts, chronically incredulous conservative newspaper columnists, high profile conservative politicians, and even billionaire magnates, who nevertheless portray themselves as anti-elite friends of the 'little people' on whose behalf they speak. Their role is to endlessly promote the above divide and its sustaining narrative that society's so-called ills, from cruelty to asylum seekers, to sexism and the inequality of women, to racism and multiculturalism, to global warming, are little more than the pure-spun product of the fevered imaginations of a 'politically correct' Left.

This, then, is the terrain of the culture wars, so-called because they are fought out not across the traditional class and religious–sectarian divides that once defined Australian politics, but across the supposed stark and intractable cultural differences between Left and Right, between 'mainstream' and 'cultural elites', between the inner city and the 'real Australia' of the suburbs and the bush, between the (white) national interest and a threatening, benighted global cosmopolitanism. But if this culture-based politics might seem like something ephemeral, a sideshow to distract from 'real politics' that underestimates a deeper historical shift in the way politics is enacted. Many high profile policy debates, over such things as gay marriage, global warming, Aboriginal rights, and asylum seekers, are now transmuted through the lens of the culture wars, configured primarily as 'left-versus-right' issues rather than being understood primarily in policy terms. Traditionally 'serious' policy areas such as employment rights, health, education, national security, and foreign policy, too, are increasingly understood in normative and polarising cultural terms. They are to be understood as the irrational attachment of recalcitrant groups to outmoded social practices and forms of social organisation, whether it be work rights defended by unions, ongoing public support for government-owned health and education services, or the threat of terrorism posed by radical Islam and the 'clash of civilisations'.

Culture as politics

The recent cultural turn in political debate goes beyond the descriptive senses in which politics has always been cultural and tribal. Culture, now, is a political means and end. In the post-World War Two era, as Raymond Williams has said (1987, 12–13, 87–93), 'culture' began to gain new meanings such that it no longer referred mainly to arts-focused creative practices and upper class leisure pursuits, and instead came to refer in a more anthropological sense to 'whole ways of life'. In contemporary political parlance 'culture' prescribes and proscribes certain ways of life on the assumption that these are times of necessary social and economic transformation. As Rupert Murdoch famously said in 1990 when asked what it might take to fix the economic malaise of the time: 'Oh, you know: change the culture' (Frow and Morris, 1993, vii). 'Culture', now, designates a particular set of ideals to do with work and its organisation, entrepreneurship, welfare, class, national belonging, militarism and national security, crime and punishment, sexuality and gender roles, race, and human rights, that have come to the fore with the emergence of new forms of conservatism in the west since the 1970s.

Since then terms such as 'new right', 'neo-conservatism', and 'neoliberalism' have often been used interchangeably and with little historical precision to describe the political forces behind the broad-scale economic and political transformations that subsequently took place in many western nations. Yet in order to understand the role of culture in today's politics some conceptual and historical precision is necessary. Briefly, 'new right' refers to different nationally based groups that emerged in the 1960s and 1970s in the UK, the US, across Europe, and in Australia. Despite similarities in their deregulatory free market agendas such groups have had differently inflected responses to issues such as race, religion, and nationalism. 'Neo-conservatism' refers to a specific group of post-1960s US intellectuals, many of them former leftists such as Daniel Patrick Moynihan, Daniel Bell, Irving Kristol, Norman Podhoretz, and Midge Decter and their successors. Kristol famously described them as having been 'mugged by reality' (Nash, 2006, 556), and who (at least in the early stages), retained faith in governments and worried about the social instability engendered by markets.

Of the above formations neoliberalism is deserving of the closest attention in the present context since it combines specific economic and cultural projects, and because it involves a transnational project oriented around changing the basic relationship between the state, the citizen, and capital in as many national settings as possible. The close links between the neoliberal economic and cultural projects can be traced to its roots in the 1930s and the work of Austrian School economists Ludwig von Mises and Friedrich Hayek. The term 'neoliberalism' was coined by participants including Mises and Hayek at a 1938 colloquium and sought to describe their desire to reformulate classical laissez-faire liberalism (Stedman Jones, 2012, 6). Concerned by the rise of fascism and totalitarianism in Germany, Italy and Soviet Russia they saw parallels between autocratic state central planning and a trend towards socialism in Britain and the US. Inspired by the free market ideas of 19th century neoclassical economists and putting faith in Adam Smith's 'hidden hand of the market', their achievement was to weld anti-Keynesian free market economics to a broader conservative political project, and to work as activists to integrate their ideas into emerging conservative movements in the UK and the US. The key economic idea is that the price signal operates far more efficiently to distribute resources than government planning. In turn, this is then wedded to the political idea that central planning leads to totalitarianism. The central message of Hayek's *The Road to Serfdom* (1994) flatly stated that 'planning leads to dictatorship' (1994, 78). This was music to the ears of a US conservatism dismayed by a post-war world that everywhere seemed to be heading towards a leftist collectivism. Politics, Hayek argued, was a 'battle of ideas' to be fought over the long term. His Mont Pelerin Society, founded in 1947, kept the flame of free market thinking alive during a post-war period in which Keynesianism dominated policy making, and steadily gained the support of powerful US corporate leaders opposed to state interventionism and determined to undo the legacy of New Deal. Hayek's early visits to the US helped galvanise a broader conservative movement that leading conservative Frank Meyer, among others, would later coalesce in the 1950s. This brought together disparate conservative strands that included the Burkean conservatism of figures such as Russell Kirk, economic libertarianism, and the fervent anti-communism represented by cold warriors such as Meyer and James Burnham, as part of a broad 'fusion' of conservative movements, paving the way for the conservative resurgence of the 1970s (Nash 2006, 235–86).

By the 1970s Hayekian neoliberalism had made its influence felt across a broad US conservative movement. It included disparate groups such as cold war Hawks, business groups, Chicago School economists, Virginia Public Choice theorists, anti-civil rights activists, and the evangelical New Right, that came together under the banner of anti-communism, opposition to 'big government', 'individual freedom', and distaste for the verities of post-1960s 'permissive society' (Jones, 2012, 137–47). In the UK think-tanks such as the Institute for Economic Affairs and the Centre for Policy Studies, which counted Sir Keith Joseph and Margaret Thatcher as patrons, were, as Daniel Stedman Jones has written, 'crucial in bringing the thought of Hayek and Friedman to wider public attention in Britain' (2012, 161), and helped drive Thatcher's revamping of Conservative Party policy. As she famously said in a 1975 meeting, having pulled a copy of Hayek's *Constitution of Liberty* (2006) from her briefcase and before slamming the book down on the table: "This is what we believe".

On both sides of the Atlantic this neoliberal–conservative ascendency was occasioned by bitter culture wars. Groups were singled out on the basis of race, gender and sexuality to illustrate the indulgences of 'politically correct' attachments to non-market forms of group rights and the debased nature of government support for special privileges for disadvantaged people. In the UK, for example, Thatcher's programme unfolded amid talk of 'madhouse' 'politically correct' local councils (Gabriel, 1998, 82–6), and coded attacks on racial minorities (Gilroy, 1993; Gabriel, 1998). These, as Anna Marie Smith has argued, explicitly placed Britain's decline in a post-colonial context requiring economic recovery (1994, 4). In the US, as Dan Carter has written, summarising work by Thomas and Mary Edsall, Conservatives gained electoral ascendency through the 1980s and 1990s in so far as they were able to portray their Democrat opponents as 'the party of blacks, of homosexuals, of the undeserving poor, of big-spending bureaucratic defenders of the welfare state, and of those unwilling to defend American interests abroad' (1999, 80).

From the outset neoliberalism has been both institutional and prosaic, and has sought to make itself part of everyday life by writing into daily cultural practices particular ideas about liberty, personal responsibility, opportunity, entrepreneurship, equality, and the role of the state. 'Economics are the method', as Margaret Thatcher said, 'but the object is to change the soul' (Harvey, 2007, 23). Neoliberalism, as such, is hegemonic. That is, it seeks to integrate itself into everyday life as a normative form of 'common sense'. It works through a process whereby, in Terry Eagleton's pithy definition, ideology 'is subtly, pervasively diffused throughout habitual daily practices, intimately interwoven with "culture" itself, inscribed in the very texture of existence from nursery school to funeral parlour' (1991, 114). Potently, neoliberalism's advocates sought to emphasise ways in which ideas similar to their own were already part of everyday life. In particular, neoliberals sought to dovetail their ideas with traditional working class ideas around work and self-reliance, the prizing of merit over managed forms of equality, deservedness, and aspirations to such things as home and business ownership. The achievement of leaders such as Thatcher, Reagan, and later in Australia, John Howard, is that they were able to synthesise neoliberal free market discourse into an authentic morality that spoke to such traditions, and yet smooth over the contradictions between free markets, finance and transnational corporatism, and the threats they posed to the work security and rights of their constituencies.

Neoliberalism, in short, was never merely an economic philosophy. It also has a moral and ethical dimension that makes it a distinctive and potent cultural force. As Wendy Brown has explained, the political convergence of neoliberalism and conservatism was never unproblematic. The contradictions between them manifest as a tension between 'a market-political rationality and a moral-political rationality, with a business model of the state in one case and a theological model of the state in the other' (2006, 698). Neoliberalism and neo-conservatism are nevertheless convergent since neoliberal depoliticisation has prepared the ground for a neo-conservative movement whose 'incompatibility with even formal democratic institutions does not spur a legitimation crisis because of the neoliberal devaluation of these practices and institutions that neoconservatism then consecrates' (2006, 702). In what follows I suggest further points of convergence. To capture these I speak of neoliberal-conservatism rather than simply neoliberalism, to reflect the conservatism-friendly ethical and moral dimensions of neoliberalism, and the epistemic closeness of neoliberalism to the cultural politics of a broader conservative movement generally opposed to such things as planned forms of wealth redistribution, social collectivism and 'communism', 'special rights' for minorities and women, 'elites', and 'big government'. In using this portmanteau term I do not seek to suggest there has been any simple homogenisation under the banner of neoliberalism of the diverse strands of thought and complex local histories that make up contemporary conservatism. Nor do I seek to discount the tensions Brown points out. Rather, while keeping such complexities in mind, I seek to capture the ways in which neoliberal thought has nevertheless been integrated with and is often consistent with the cultural as well as the economic politics of mainstream forms of conservatism, at least in the Australian context.

None of this is to suggest that the neoliberal–conservative transformation has been total and conclusive. At every step it has been contested and resisted. We live among traces of social democracy interleaved with ascendant forms of free market thinking, where discourses of social democracy, social liberalism, and economic liberalism clash in debates over everything from road funding to childcare. This is especially the case in Australia, where strong ('egalitarian') expectations around equality have never been fully overturned. There can be little doubt that the adoption of neoliberal ideas has shifted the political spectrum rightwards and along the way changed the structure, cultures and practices of most public institutions, and with it their relationship to citizens ('clients'), as well as the nature and culture of citizenship itself. Yet, neoliberalism, for all its manifest successes, is a protean, complex cocktail of contradictory ideas, spread unevenly from an array of institutional powerbases that deserve to be understood in their cultural and local specificity, rather than as a totalising or universalising force.

Australia's culture wars

Neoliberal–conservative cultural imperatives nevertheless track back into Australian debates with considerable consistency. Australia's culture wars date back to the vicious public campaign led by mining magnate Hugh Morgan in the 1980s against Aboriginal land rights, and the parallel campaign against Asian immigration led by historian Geoffrey Blainey. These campaigns were a proving ground for early forms of rhetoric against so-called leftist 'elites', who were accused of purveying the 'black armband' view of history and labelled the 'guilt industry' (Markus, 2001, 66, 77). They also helped cohere a nascent Australian conservative movement around a strategy that combined Hayek-inspired approaches to economic 'reform' with attacks on minority rights. This found voice among economic 'dries' in the Liberal Party and at think-tanks such as The Centre for Independent Studies and the Institute of Public Affairs. Such was the spread of the movement that since 1979 more than 60 privately funded conservative think tanks have been founded in Australia (Boucher and Sharpe, 2008, 49). Opposition leader John Hewson's refusal in 1993 to negotiate to support the Mabo Native Title Bill, on the back of private party polling that showed that older white men made redundant by the recession of the early 1990s thought Aborigines were getting benefits denied to them (Megalogenis, 2012, 254), demonstrated the neoliberal–conservative integration of culture and politics. While Hewson has since emerged as a compassionate social liberal, his line of argument, as well as being politically opportunist, was consistent with neoliberal–conservative economic thinking that no group, even one suffering systemic injustice, should have 'special privileges' accorded to it by the state since this is 'rent-seeking' and reeks of 'planning' and impedes the otherwise efficient operations of the open market.

The supposed division between the interests of 'elites' and those of 'ordinary people' set up by such debates is summed up by the shorthand term 'politically correct', which was imported to Australian debate from the US in the early 1990s (Bennett, 1993). Despite referring to a largely manufactured phenomenon the term has since done much cultural work to marginalise the Left. The power of this expression is that it compactly illustrates the key neoliberal–conservative division between 'them' and 'us', which is also a division between those who would prescribe state interventionism and those willing to work hard and take a risk in an open market. Economics here, in two short words, is rendered into culture. Media debates about 'victim feminism' in the mid-1990s, following the publication of Helen Garner's *The First Stone* (1995), signalled the introduction of a similar, neoliberal–conservative logic into public discussion of feminism. The terms of such debates, which were imported from the US, signalled a shift in rights debates away from the positive notions of freedom ('freedom to do') that had underpinned post-war consensus politics, with the government expanding freedom as helpmate and enabler to marginalised and disadvantaged people via welfare. Now emerged a more clearly neoliberal–conservative notion of negative freedom ('freedom from'), where freedom is defined in individualist terms by an absence of government intervention, and where feminism is a matter of individual responsibility rather than group rights (Davis, 1999, 75–98). This is at the same time a shift from the collective to the individual, where group rights are transmuted into 'personal responsibility' for one's ethical choices.

John Howard's 1998 *Future Directions* manifesto, as Geoff Boucher and Matthew Sharpe have shown, combined dry economics with culture wars attacks on 'guilt purveying' reassessments of Australian history and traditionalist support for family and religion. The publication would confirm Howard as potential party leader of choice for a new group, the Lyons Forum, founded in 1992 to promote Christian conservatism within the Liberal Party (2008, 67). The Forum, which drew inspiration from the influence of conservative Evangelicals in US cultural debates, would have an important impact in debates on such things as euthanasia, censorship, in-vitro-fertilisation (IVF) access for gays and lesbian couples, and gay marriage (Maddox, 2005: Boucher and Sharpe, 2008, 67–9). The subsequent Howard Government built disparagement of elites into a 'civic religion' that was developed around militarised ideas of national belonging and identity and national sporting success and that was designed to 'inspire and unite contemporary Australians in a time of rapid change and cultural disorientation' (Boucher and Sharpe, 2008, 79). The foregrounding of national security and border protection issues after 2001 was part of this project. As such the culture wars seek to address an integration crisis and the social fragmentation caused by free market approaches to such things as employment rights. The 'history wars' of the early 2000s made the terms of such debate explicit. Were we to celebrate (white settler) Australian history and identity writ large in heroic national mythology about such things as 'Simpson and his donkey', or adopt what Geoffrey Blainey dubbed the 'black armband' view of a history focused obsessively on the tragedy of Aboriginal dispossession? The 'Intervention' of 2007 exemplified the terms on which the new neoliberal–conservative social contract with Indigenous Australians was offered. What had been a matter of public ethics was reframed as a crisis of the private morality of Aboriginals and Torres Strait Islanders, which was deemed to literally require military supervision.

The public–private logic of rights versus 'individual responsibility' animates most neoliberal–conservative responses to public issues. For example, in relation to attitudes to asylum seekers, rights become privileges that rely on the testing of individual worth. In marriage heterosexual unions can be publicly consecrated but homosexual unions are private matters. In multiculturalism, any non-white racialised tradition is seen as a private matter. The neoliberal–conservative campaign against climate science, too, has made headway in so far as those who would deny the reality of global warming have been able to reframe the debate in cultural terms. As with other culture wars issues, the spectacle offered, and promoted in conservative sections of the media and by think-tanks such as the Institute of Public Affairs (IPA), is of a struggle between a righteous, overtaxed mainstream versus a self-interested lobby of left-leaning 'rent-seekers'. In this case the targets are scientists reliant on government grants and operating in league with an irrational 'greenie' left, and who are prepared to misrepresent the facts accordingly. The underlying economic argument is of course that miners and polluters represent a more noble private sphere, and should be allowed access to the environmental commons without limit, not least since in Hayekian terms the environmental commons are *literally* without limit and should be beyond the reach of inefficient and burdensome state 'planning' or taxation.

Perhaps the most important neoliberal–conservative cultural battlefield has been work rights. As John Frow and Meaghan Morris have written, Murdoch's 1990 remark about 'changing the culture' was 'quoting a formula of the neoliberal rhetoric now broadly shared in Australia (as elsewhere), by bureaucrats, politicians, economists journalists, and financiers as well as union and corporate leaders, namely: economic problems need cultural solutions' (1993, vii). 'Changing the culture', as such, involved 'challenging the conduct of other people's everyday working lives … fewer workers must produce more for less' (1993, vii–viii). The result has been, since the 1980s, a slowdown of wages growth against increasing demands for productivity, attacks on such things as penalty rates and other entitlements, and the growth of private contracts and casualised, short-term labour.

The hollowed out public sphere

Changing the expectations of government is central to these culture wars. Run-down public education institutions and long public hospital queues all create incentives to abandon public systems. Punitive approaches to such things as unemployment benefits make clear that the state provides only minimal welfare services and 'safety nets' for disadvantaged people, in a climate where there is relentless pressure to reduce taxation, especially on the wealthy. Again, the central idea has been to foster an ongoing shift from public to private, a struggle that is fought out at every level of government and policy making. If good policy making is traditionally impartial, rational and evidence-based so as to best serve the public interest, then the challenge facing policy makers today is that market logic and ideologically driven debates about culture have become integrated into the very substance of politics, including policy making itself.

Neoliberal-conservatism has transformed governance processes such that policy makers work in an environment where populist–cultural politics often trumps sound policy. Asylum seeker policy and global warming are two obvious examples. They also work in an environment where government has been 're-engineered' as part of a neoliberal project to make a primary role of the state the facilitation of markets (Wacquant, 2012). Wacquant's insight is important since it acknowledges that, rather than understanding the state in agonistic tension with markets, the state has become a principal agent of neoliberal hegemony. This re-engineering has affected every stage of the policy making process, from the identification and solution of problems to delivery and evaluation. Many steps in the policy process have themselves been privatised, such as the outsourcing of policy development to think-tanks and their delivery via private contractors operating in quasi-markets created by government, for example unemployment agencies. Every stage of the process, too, is increasingly subject to a surveillance and evaluation culture of performance audits and benchmarking, with built-in carrots and sticks designed to measure and change behaviours.

This re-engineering of the state has involved considerable effort to 'change the culture' of administration processes. The introduction of New Public Management approaches to policy making in the Australian Public Service in the 1980s was itself a response to government downsizing. This was founded in neoliberal public choice theory and ideological assumptions about the rational economic behaviour of the public, the self-interested behaviour of public servants, and their potential responsiveness to competitive market pressures (Hughes, 2003). Such assumptions neatly bring together the belief that public servants tend to favour only more public spending, with populist political narratives about public waste versus private 'efficiency', 'small government', and low taxation regimes. While empire-building and low performance cultures undoubtedly provided an opening for such initiatives in many cases, and while accountability should be central to all policy making and implementation, results have been mixed (Hughes 2003, 11).

One symptom of this transformed political culture is weakening democratic cultures and a citizenry disengaged from and cynical about political processes. As Brown says, 'the hollowing out of democratic culture' has resulted in

... the production of the undemocratic citizen. This is the
citizen who loves and wants neither freedom nor equality,
even of a liberal sort; the citizen who expects neither truth
nor accountability in governance and state actions; the
citizen who is distressed not by exorbitant concentrations
of political and economic power, routine abrogations of
the rule of law, or distinctly undemocratic formulations of
national purpose at home or abroad. (2006, 692)

What, then, are the prospects for progressive policy makers, and indeed,
for progressives more generally, in this transformed environment? A
central issue is whether public policy can be implemented in genuinely
new and humanely enabling ways in a new information-saturated
environment, or whether, as seen in 'third way' and 'big society'
projects, governments will continue with technocratic projects founded
in neoliberal–conservative assumptions about minimal government,
private sector 'efficiency', cultures of dependence, and the idea that
state interventionism corrupts the moral worth of individuals and
perpetuates societies that are 'broken'.

The search for an alternative model

The pessimistic possibility haunting all these obstacles to genuinely
progressive policy making is that just as the post-war consensus era
was often understood as an era of 'embedded liberalism', this is an era
of embedded neoliberalism where neoliberal–conservative ideas have
become immovable 'common sense'. The privileging of market-based
solutions to the fundamentally biochemical problem of global warming
is a case in point. Yet the reality that equally haunts the present era
is that neoliberal–conservative approaches to public policy across the
broad spectrum of areas such as global warming, health, education,
housing, water, asylum, and indigenous issues, have enjoyed limited
success. Even the question of whether deregulated free markets can
produce stable, sustainable economic progress is vexed in the wake
of the economic crises that have spread across the globe since 2008.

As such the task facing progressive policy makers and progressives
more generally, requires a thoroughgoing assessment of deeper issues
holding the present consensus in place, and formulating alternative
responses. Contra to prevailing mythologies, the neoliberal–
conservative free market ascendency of the 1970s did not simply
happen as if by some natural evolutionary step in human progress.
Neoliberal-conservatism was successful because it offered an organised

response to the economic and social crises of the times, including the outset of a broader crisis in post-war Western liberal modernity. These crises encompassed firstly a crisis in Fordist industrialism and profitability with the failure of Keynesian economics in a climate of economic stagnation and yet rising inflation ('stagflation'). Secondly, there was an associated crisis of US monetary hegemony with the US currency crisis of the early 1970s and subsequent collapse of the Bretton Woods agreement. Thirdly there was a broader crisis of identity in the West amid the sense that (white) Judeo–Christian Western culture had lost its way and the West was losing its global hegemony. These possibilities were underlined by the emergence of 1960s counterculture, an emerging post-colonial crisis of mobility and immigration from the late 1960s on, the growing economic power of the Organization of the Petroleum Exporting Countries (OPEC) nations and Japan, the successes of independence movements in former colonies and client nations in the 'third world', and the loss of the Vietnam war.

In most cases, the 'solutions' offered to these and more recent 'globalisation crises' such as untamed refugee mobility, terrorism, and global warming, have been simplistic and retrograde. They have involved laying new planks for economic domination, sponsoring crude nationalism and re-establishing immigration borders amid coded white cultural supremacist rhetoric, re-establishing gendered social roles and family structures, turning away from human rights, undermining good governance, and pretending that environmental catastrophes are leftist ideological imaginings and that the commons has no limits. Yet the inevitable failures of such responses, which mostly comprise an attempt to 'turn back the clock', have not addressed the fundamental and ongoing economic, cultural, humanitarian, and ecological crises of modernity.

As such the task facing progressives, including progressive policy makers, is to address these failures in a more enlightened, progressive way so as to imagine and articulate new post-neoliberal–conservative possibilities and narratives for modernity and democracy. It is easy to agree at the outset that such a future must be sustainable, accepting of difference and supportive of human rights. But behind these more or less obvious nostrums lie more difficult questions of how to manage real and intractable cultural differences across the globe, how best to manage scarcity, how best to create wealth, how to manage inequality and ensure reasonable standards of fairness and how to manage looming environmental crises equitably. Perhaps most of all, it requires us to ask who are the 'we' of a reimagined modernity, since it seems improbable that such a project should be run exclusively from traditional global centres of power and privilege. Other pressing questions loom. What will be the role of the state and the role of markets, and the relationship between them? How will the forces of global finance be managed? What does 'development' look like in different places and who will pay? What will citizenship and public culture look like in an increasingly connected world? According to what principles will a de-centred, de-westernised global governance be organised?

We can tentatively point to some possibilities. It seems obvious that the way forward will involve some form of (re)managed capitalism and with it the rethinking and renovation of older forms of secular liberalism. If this might seem to cut across the traditional progressive–leftist wariness of liberalism then, as Wendy Brown suggests:

> If ... the institutions as well as the political culture comprising liberal democracy are passing into history, the left is faced both with the project of mourning what it never wholly loved and with the task of dramatically resetting its critique and vision in terms of the historical supersession of liberal democracy, and not only of failed socialist experiments (2006, 691).

The paradox of such mourning is that it raises on the one hand the prospect of formulating a new post-liberal politics and on the other the possibility that for all its (white patrician) weaknesses liberal democracy and its close cousin modernity are not as easy to 'forget' or to 'step outside' as is sometimes imagined. What remains is to fashion a durable reconfigured liberal democratic politics that might lend real weight to such liberal virtues as secularism, pluralism, inclusion, due process, and enlightened social progress, in a framework that takes difference seriously. A similar process of reimagining generic political antagonisms might be applied to economics. There is no necessary contradiction, for example, between support for government and support for markets. Thinking about new ways to work with and through capital seems necessary, given that the possibility of socialist revolution has receded to pinpoint size in the planetary rear-view mirror, and given the urgency, as Tim Jackson has argued, of inaugurating a viable post-consumption economics in the face of finite planetary resources (Jackson, 2009). To argue alongside neo-Marxists such as Slavoj Žižek that socialism remains possible is to indulge a fantasy, useful and invigorating though his Lacanian–Marxist critique remains. Nostalgia for the prospect of staging such a revolution is no doubt one of the things that have been holding many progressives back from starting work on new solutions. What shape can capitalist modernity take in an age where injustice is legion, where resource scarcity and planetary limits are definitive? What will be its institutions and cultures? This is our new question.

What we are talking about, then, is building a movement, since practical opportunities for change, whether at the level of policy development or at the level of broader social change, will not otherwise occur in any widespread way. Signs of hope can be found in the emergence of the Occupy movements that, while short-lived, put in place an effective shorthand narrative about global inequality and the oligarchic 'one percent'. The Arab spring, for all its undemocratic as well as democratic twists and turns, showcased the potential of social media as an organising tool. As this chapter is being written, momentum is building across southern Europe, amid massive youth unemployment, against neoliberal 'austerity' prescriptions whereby seemingly limitless funds are available to bail out mismanaged banks and other finance organisations but none to assist distressed peoples through economic stimulus. People are becoming alert to the politics whereby, in Kenneth Galbraith's classic formulation, profits are privatised and losses are socialised, and are demanding an ethic of care from governments that cuts across neoliberal prescriptions.

There is a lesson, too, in Obama's 2012 US election victory. Armed with sophisticated analytics to capture emergent groups and appeal to their important issues, and to buy media appropriately, the campaign marked the emergence of new ways of understanding the voting public that outflanked neoliberal–conservative politics based on race- and immigration-based division and the demographic typecasting of an under-educated, middle-aged white constituency who have themselves been major victims of economic reform and deindustrialisation. As a campaign official interviewed about the campaign's use of data responded, the era of 'guys sitting in a back room smoking cigars, saying, "We always buy 60 Minutes"' is over (Scherer, 2013).

A crucial task facing policy makers and progressive change makers alike is to thus imagine publics in new and sophisticated ways, and to work to renew public cultures. Any such process will no doubt require progressives to reset a key aspect of their critique. Thus far progressives have proceeded against neoliberal-conservatism by attacking it directly, pointing out its manifest failures such as sluggish and inconsistent global economic growth, growing underclasses, extensive global inequality, deregulatory scandals, human rights scandals, and environmental crises. The progressive approach to global warming, for example, has been to warn of its dire consequences, and to parade scary facts that might hopefully galvanise people and governments into action. Obviously such facts are needed along with robust critique. But in its narrowness this strategy speaks to an old leftist morality and self-righteousness, and to a touching faith in old-fashioned notions of 'public education' that little understand our transformed public cultures. As should be clear after decades of demystification around neoliberalism, including a decade of increasingly fervent educative approaches to getting action on climate change, this approach has failed. Academics, in particular, risk being stuck, wheels spinning in the rhetorical dead-end of endless critique. What is needed is not just scary facts that will hopefully galvanise people into action, but a positive guiding narrative for the future, replete with heroes, stories, literatures, music, films, and tales of hope, opportunity and moral courage. The focus should not only be on the price of inaction, but on the rewards of action. Those of us who believe urgent change is required need to speak of possible futures, and also of new ways of being and indeed, ways of life. For if there is one thing to be learned from neoliberal–conservative ascendency, a lesson that the Left seemingly forgot after the 1960s, it is the importance of connecting social change to culture.

References

Bennett, D. (1993) '"PC" Panic, the Press and the Academy', *Meanjin*, vol 52, no 3, pp 435–46

Boucher, G. and Sharpe, M. (2008) *The Times will Suit them: Postmodern Conservatism in Australia*, Sydney: Allen & Unwin

Brown, W. (2006) 'American nightmare: Neoliberalism, neoconservatism and de-democratization', *Political Theory*, vol 34, no 6, pp 690–714

Carter, D. (1999) *From George Wallace to Newt Gingrich: Race in the conservative counterrevolution, 1963–1994*, Baton Rouge: Louisiana State University Press

Davis, M. (1999) *Gangland: Cultural Elites and the New Generationalism* (2nd edn), Sydney: Allen & Unwin

Eagleton, T. (1991) *Ideology: An Introduction*, London: Verso

Frow, J. and Morris, M. (1993) *Australian Cultural Studies: A Reader*, Sydney: Allen & Unwin

Gabriel, J. (1998) *Whitewash: Racialized Politics and the Media*, London and New York: Routledge

Garner, H. (1995) *The First Stone: Some Questions About Sex and Power*, Sydney: Picador

Gilroy, P. (1993) *Small Acts: The Politics of Black Cultures*, London: Serpent's Tail

Harvey, D. (2007) *A Brief History of Neoliberalism*, Oxford: Oxford University Press

Hayek, F.A. (1994) *The Road to Serfdom* (50th anniversary edn), Chicago: University of Chicago Press

Hayek, F.A. (2006 [1960]) *The Constitution of Liberty*, London and New York: Routledge.

Hughes, O.P. (2003) *Public Management and Administration: An Introduction* (3rd edn), Basingstoke: Palgrave Macmillan

Jackson, T. (2009) *Prosperity without Growth: Economics for a Finite Planet.* London and Washington DC: Earthscan

Maddox, M. (2005) *God under Howard: The Rise of the Religious Right in Australian politics*, Sydney: Allen & Unwin

Markus, A. (2001) *Race: John Howard and the Making of Australia*, Sydney: Allen & Unwin

Megalogenis, G. (2012) *The Australian Moment: How We were Made for these Times*, Melbourne: Viking

Nash, G.H. (2006 [1976]) *The Conservative Intellectual Movement in America since 1945* (30th anniversary edn), Wilmington: ISI Books

Scherer, M. (2013) 'Inside the Secret World of the Data Crunchers Who Helped Obama Win', *Time.com*. Available at: http://swampland.time.com/2012/11/07/inside-the-secret-world-of-quants-and-data-crunchers-who-helped-obama-win/

Smith, A.M. (1994) *New Right Discourse on Race and Sexuality: Britain, 1968–1990*, Cambridge: Cambridge University Press

Stedman Jones, D. (2012) *Masters of the Universe: Hayek, Friedman, and the Birth of Neoliberal Politics*, Princeton and Oxford, Princeton University Press

Wacquant, L. (2012) 'Three Steps to a Historical Anthropology of Actually Existing Neoliberalism', *Social Anthropology* 20: 166–79

Williams, R. (1987) *Keywords: A Vocabulary of Culture and Society* (2nd edn), London: Flamingo

Part Two

ECONOMICS, WELFARE AND WORK

THREE

Macroeconomic policy after the Global Financial Crisis

John Quiggin

Introduction

Since the mid-1970s, Australian economic policy has been driven by a set of ideas based on the claim that a market economy, with minimal government regulation, will outperform any alternative. The central goal of policy has been to reduce the scope and extent of government activity, with the aim of promoting productivity growth. The dominance of these ideas may be seen in the very names of government departments like the Department of Finance and Deregulation and institutions such as the Productivity Commission.

The same set of ideas, with variations, has been dominant throughout the world, beginning in the economic turmoil of the 1970s and reaching its peak of confidence in the 1990s. The ideology that unifies them has been given various names: 'Thatcherism' in the United Kingdom, 'Reaganism' in the United States, 'economic rationalism' in Australia, the 'Washington Consensus' in the developing world, and 'neoliberalism' in academic discussions. Most of these terms are pejorative, reflecting the fact that it is mostly critics of an ideological framework who feel the need to define it and analyse it. Politically dominant elites do not see themselves as acting ideologically and react with hostility when ideological labels are pinned on them. From the inside, ideology usually looks like common sense. The most neutral term that could be found for the set of ideas described by these pejoratives is market liberalism, and this is the term that will be used in this chapter.

Market liberalism created the preconditions for the Global Financial Crisis (GFC) and, repackaged as 'austerity', ensured that the crisis became a sustained depression engulfing most of the developed world. The failure of austerity is now widely recognised within the economics profession, even by bodies like the International Monetary Fund, which has traditionally had the role of enforcing painful adjustments on indebted governments.

Australia avoided recession during the GFC, in large measure because of policies of fiscal stimulus adopted both there and in China, Australia's most important export market. However, the Labor Government failed to defend the stimulus policy against conservative attacks, instead focusing its efforts on defusing the issue through a rapid return to budget surplus. At the same time, and despite some promising initial responses, the crisis provoked no rethinking of the dogmatic commitment to small government, adopted in response to the perceived need to be seen as 'economically conservative'. However, the failure of the microeconomic part of the market liberal agenda produced pressing needs for more government expenditure on health, education, environmental and infrastructure services. The resulting contradictions have produced an atmosphere of crisis, despite the strong performance of the economy as a whole.

This chapter describes the ideology of market liberalism, the macroeconomic policies and institutions it produced, and the failure of those policies and institutions that produced the GFC and the subsequent deep recession in most developed countries. Although it is impossible to prescribe a fully developed alternative policy framework at this point, new directions in macroeconomic policy are sketched out, including countercyclical fiscal policy, the need for an increase in public sector revenue and expenditure, and new approaches to monetary policy and financial regulation.

Market liberalism

In *Zombie Economics: How Dead Ideas Walk Among Us* (Quiggin, 2012)[1] the resurgence of market liberalism in the 1970s, and the displacement of the post-war economic consensus built on Keynesian macroeconomic policy, the social democratic welfare state and the mixed economy are described. The central ideas of market liberalism as it developed in the years leading up to the GFC are:

- The Great Moderation: the idea that the period beginning in 1985 was one of unparalleled macroeconomic stability.
- The Efficient Markets Hypothesis: the idea that the prices generated by financial markets represent the best possible estimate of the value of any investment.
- Dynamic Stochastic General Equilibrium: the idea that macroeconomic analysis should not concern itself with economic

aggregates like trade balances or debt levels, but should be rigorously derived from microeconomic models of individual behaviour.
- Trickledown economics: the idea that policies that benefit the well-off will ultimately help everybody.
- Privatisation: the idea that any function now undertaken by government could be done better by private firms.
- Austerity: the belief that the best response to a crisis like that of the present is for governments to balance their own books, and wait for the private sector to recover.

Taken together, these ideas supported the vision of an 'ownership society' in which individuals and families managed their assets to achieve the best possible outcomes for themselves. The ideal type of ownership was the ownership of equity capital, traded in sophisticated financial markets. More mundane assets, such as houses, and the associated mortgages, should ideally be securitised, through devices such as home equity loans and associated derivatives, to unlock the capital value they represented. The most important of assets for most people, the 'human capital' embodied in their labour power, was to be commodified in the same way, and marketed, in Tom Peters's phrase, as 'The Brand Called You'(Peters, 1997).

The role of government, in the market liberal view, should be limited to a few basic tasks: providing a legal framework, along with the police and defence forces necessary to maintain that framework, correcting a limited range of 'market failures' and providing a basic 'safety net' for those unable, through bad luck or disability, to provide for themselves. The associated programme of microeconomic reform was one reducing the role of direct intervention by governments and increasing the role of markets and market based policy instruments. In macroeconomic policy, the defining feature of market liberalism is a rejection of Keynesian economic theory and the associated policy of macroeconomic stabilisation through policies of fiscal stimulus during recessions and depressions. The macroeconomic policy prescribed by market liberalism is one that relies exclusively on monetary policy, and in which a low and stable rate of inflation is the primary target. Fiscal policy is aimed at maintaining balance between revenue and expenditure, and at constraining the total share of resources allocated to public expenditure.

In Australia, market liberalism is most commonly called 'economic rationalism'. The most distinctive feature of Australian economic rationalism, compared to the versions of market liberalism found in other countries, is its relentless focus on 'productivity', sought largely through labour market 'reforms' such as those embodied in the Howard Government's Work Choices package. The 'recession we had to have' in 1989–91, deeper and more sustained than contemporaneous slowdowns in the United States and elsewhere, did much to discredit the macroeconomic ideas associated with economic rationalism. Only after the adoption of the Keynesian *Working Nation* package in 1994 (Commonwealth of Australia, 1994) did the labour market begin to recover from the recession. Arguably, this experience contributed to the greater willingness of Australian policy makers to embrace Keynesian stimulus as an immediate reaction to the GFC.

Macroeconomic policy under market liberalism

During the 1990s, the experiments of the 1980s coalesced into a more or less standard approach to macroeconomic policy, followed with minor variations in most developed countries. The central element was the primacy of monetary policy, based on the use of interest rates as the sole policy instrument and inflation rates as the primary target. The use of fiscal policy for macroeconomic stabilisation, the hallmark of the Keynesian era, was abandoned or discouraged. Instead the primary goal of fiscal policy was to maintain the government budget balance at levels consistent with stable ratios of debt to national income. Prudential policy, that is the management of risk in the financial sector, was separated from monetary policy and treated as a regulatory function, to be undertaken in as 'light-handed' a manner as possible.

There were some variations in the approach. For example, the US Federal Reserve did not adopt a formal target range for inflation until 2012, although it was generally known that policy was based on a 'comfort zone' of 1–2% for the Fed's preferred inflation measure. In the Eurozone, the separation between monetary policy, operated by the European Central Bank and targeted solely at inflation, and fiscal policy, operated by national governments, was sharper than elsewhere, with the result that the austerity policies adopted after the GFC have been harsher and more damaging.

Even under a system of inflation targeting, central banks did not ignore the real economy entirely. Booming conditions in the real economy were seen as raising the danger of high inflation in the future, while depressed conditions implied that this risk was low. Hence, an inflation target could be implemented using what is known as a 'Taylor rule', in which the central bank sought to keep both the current inflation rate and the rate of growth of output (seen as an indicator of future inflation) near their long-run target levels. The result was that both the inflation rate and the rate of growth of real output could be stabilised.

This worked well as long as economic fluctuations were modest, so that, in the event of a recession or slowdown, a cut in interest rates was usually sufficient to restore growth. However, the sustained slump that has followed the GFC in North America and Europe has shown up the inadequacy of this policy. Although most Organisation for Economic Co-operation and Development (OECD) economies have high levels of unemployment and underemployment, inflation has remained at or close to its target level. This outcome led the former chair of the European Central Bank, Jean-Claude Trichet, to describe his own performance as 'impeccable' (Trichet, 2011), at a time when most of the economies in Europe were severely depressed, and when the complete collapse of the euro as a common currency appeared likely.

The GFC and Australia's escape

The apparent triumph of market liberalism collapsed with surprising rapidity during the GFC. Nevertheless, although the ideas supporting market liberalism have been refuted by experience, they continue to dominate the thinking of policy makers and opinion leaders, particularly as regards macroeconomic policy, and have ensured that there has been no effective macroeconomic response to the crisis. The financial phase of the crisis was surprisingly short-lived. The major banks were bailed out on generous terms. They rapidly returned to profitability, and resumed their old practices of market manipulation, insider trading and massive bonus payments. Recent scandals include major tax frauds, rigging of commodity markets and of the London Interbank Offered Rate, known as LIBOR, which forms the basis of global bond markets (House of Commons Treasury Select Committee, 2012), and multimillion dollar payments to bankers whose incompetence is obvious to all. By contrast, the real economy in the US and Europe has yet to recover the ground lost in 2008 and 2009. The problems of the Eurozone are even worse than in the US because the institutional structure, combined with the rigid ideological positions taken by key officials, has prevented any effective response to a depression that is now more than three years old, and shows no sign of ending.

The crisis has invalidated most of the popular explanations for the Great Moderation. The idea that improvements in monetary policy, administered by central bankers such as Alan Greenspan, have been a force for economic stabilisation looks rather silly now. A crisis generated within the financial system has brought about a crisis against which the standard tools of monetary policy, based on adjustments to interest rates, have proved ineffective. If the pretensions of central banks have been shaken, those of financial markets have been utterly discredited. There is now no reason to accept the claim that financial markets provide individuals and households with effective tools for risk management. Rather, the unrestrained growth of financial markets has proved, as on many past occasions, to be a source of instability. The collapse of the Great Moderation has destroyed the pragmatic justification that, whatever the inequities and inefficiencies involved in the process, the shift to market liberalism since the 1970s delivered sustained prosperity. If anything can be salvaged from the current mess, it will be in spite of the policies of recent decades, and not because of them.

Australia's escape

Australia stands almost alone in the developed world, both in the vigour with which Keynesian policies of fiscal stimulus were used during the GFC and in the success of our macroeconomic outcomes. As the crisis emerged in the US, the first Rudd Government undertook a highly effective fiscal stimulus, coordinated its fiscal policy with the monetary policy of the Reserve Bank and fixed major vulnerabilities in the system of prudential regulation, most notably the absence of a deposit guarantee.

The results speak for themselves. Almost alone in the OECD, Australia escaped recession, whether this is judged on the 'two quarters of negative growth' rule of thumb or a more general assessment of economic performance. Inflation has remained quiescent, sitting right in the middle of the Reserve Bank's target range. Unemployment remains near its 30-year low. Despite unfavourable demographic trends associated with the ageing of the baby boomers, the employment-population ratio is near an all-time high. At the same time, and despite the global crisis, some of the chronic imbalances that threatened the Australian economy when Labor came to office have abated. The bubble in house prices that emerged in the early 2000s has deflated gradually, in marked contrast with the disastrous bursting of such bubbles in many other countries. Household savings rates, negative in the last years of the Howard Government, have recovered strongly to levels not seen since the 1980s. The ratio of foreign debt to national income has declined, and debt has been redirected from financing consumption (including consumption of housing services) to financing investment, primarily in the mining sector. It is also possible that a coalition government, faced with strong advice from Treasury in favour of fiscal stimulus, would have abandoned the focus on headline measures of budget balance that characterised the Howard–Costello era. Under the actual circumstances of the crisis, however, the opposition, then led by Malcolm Turnbull and Julie Bishop, with Joe Hockey as Shadow Treasurer, opposed the stimulus and proposed instead to pursue permanent tax cuts.

It is, of course, possible to argue about the appropriate division of credit between the Rudd/Gillard Governments, their predecessors, the success of monetary policy under the Reserve Bank, and the favourable external circumstances of the mining boom. But on the most important question of how we managed to avoid the effects of the GFC, there can be little doubt that it was government policy that was responsible. The close coordination between fiscal and monetary policy means that there is no sense in separating the credit due to the Reserve Bank from that due to the government. In retrospect it has been claimed that demand from China, and the mining boom more generally, meant that stimulus was unnecessary. This claim is nonsense for at least three reasons. First, minerals prices fell sharply in the immediate aftermath of the crisis, making Australia more, rather than less, vulnerable. Second, the rapid Chinese recovery was due to the policies of fiscal stimulus very similar to those adopted in Australia. Finally, the failure of economic recovery in other countries that turned rapidly to austerity once the immediate crisis was past is a further demonstration of the validity of the Keynesian analysis.

Despite this relative success, Australia's current policy debate, focused almost entirely on the idea of budget surplus and on public debt, reflects neither the success of Keynesian policies in Australia nor the global failure of the austerity policies that drive the politic rhetoric of the conservative parties. Much of the blame for this fiasco must go to former Treasurer Wayne Swan. Whatever the substantive merits of the policies he oversaw, Swan failed to show any conviction in defending them. The huge success of Keynesian stimulus should have resulted in a fundamental reconsideration of the 'fiscal conservatism' inherited from Howard and Costello. Instead of pursuing a target of balance or small surplus every year, Keynesian theory prescribes a countercyclical policy of deficits in recession and surpluses in booms. While occasionally paying lip service to this idea, Swan's public rhetoric mostly treated the GFC as an embarrassing departure from reality and the return to budget surplus as a holy grail. His oft-repeated promise to return the budget to surplus by 2012–13 was, of course, a disastrous failure in practice. Even worse was the rhetorical gift to the spurious economic analysis propounded by then Opposition Leader Tony Abbott, in which budget surplus is the sole goal of fiscal policy.

The current situation

The failure of the Great Moderation calls for a rethinking of the macroeconomic experience of the 20th century, and in particular, the crisis of the 1970s. Considered as a whole, the performance of developed economies in the era of market liberalism looks considerably less impressive than that of the post-war period of Keynesian social democracy. Yet the Keynesian era ended in the chaos and failure of the 1970s. Until the current crisis, that failure was taken as conclusive. Whatever its merits, Keynesian economic management had proved unsustainable in the end, while the methods of market liberalism seemed to promise the continuing stability of the Great Moderation.

Economies can collapse to a point where only large-scale monetary expansion and fiscal stimulus can revive them. But having revived the economy, can Keynesian policies restore and sustain full employment in a system that is inherently prone to crisis? An answer to this question will require radical new directions in macroeconomics. Economists are only beginning to understand the lessons of the GFC and its implications for economic theory and policy. The failure of market liberalism, the Great Moderation, and of supporting economic theories like the Efficient Markets Hypothesis has forced (at least some) policy makers to relearn the basic lessons of Keynesian economics. The GFC has shown, once again, the effectiveness of Keynesian macroeconomic policy, and the failure of fiscal austerity, as responses to recession. In the long term, the GFC must lead to a radical remodelling of economic theory that will entail the development of new policy instruments for macroeconomic management. In the short term, however, it is necessary to take the institutions and policy instruments of market liberalism as a starting point, and to consider how they can be modified to allow more control over the economy.

Countercyclical fiscal policy

The most important lesson from the crisis is that, when macroeconomic policy really matters, both monetary and fiscal policy are necessary, and they must be used together. The two crucial requirements for Keynesian fiscal policy are that:

- the government budget balance should be countercyclical, with deficits during slumps and surpluses during booms;
- it should be sustainable over the course of the economic cycle.

A countercyclical budget balance tends to stabilise the economy. When private economic activity is weak, the government can stimulate demand directly, by increasing its purchases of goods and services, or indirectly, by reducing taxes and increasing transfer payments such as pensions and benefits. To some extent the second of these processes happens automatically. When the economy is in recession, tax revenue declines and unemployment increases, leading to higher expenditure on benefits. Conversely, during booms, the budget automatically returns to surplus.

However, the effectiveness of these 'automatic stabilisers' may be undermined if governments are excessively concerned with annual measures of budget balances. Instead of using budget surpluses to build up assets, governments may run the surplus down through tax cuts or popular, but economically dubious, expenditure programmes, leaving less room for stimulus when the economy inevitably declines. A far more serious problem, evident in European and US responses to the GFC, is the adoption of 'austerity' policies aimed at restoring budget balance during a sustained recession. Such policies played a major role in exacerbating the Great Depression of the 1930s, and contributed to the rise of Hitler in Germany and the military takeover of politics in Japan (Quiggin, 2011; Blyth, 2012). Reliance on automatic stabilisers is a sensible fiscal policy during periods when economic fluctuations are modest, as they were for the decade leading up to the GFC. However, more severe shocks such as those of the GFC, or the 1989–91 Australian recession, require a more active policy response.

The second requirement of fiscal policy is sustainability, which may broadly be stated as the requirement that the ratio of public sector net worth (the difference between assets and debt) to national income should remain stable over the long term. A policy that allows debt to grow without limit cannot be sustained indefinitely, though there is no clear point at which the debt position becomes untenable. Broadly speaking, debt will increase when the government budget is in deficit and decrease when it is in surplus. So, if stability is to be sustained, deficits and surpluses, appropriately defined, must balance over time.

There are two main measures of the government's net financial position. First, and most important, is the net worth of the public sector, that is, the difference between the value of publicly owned assets and the debt incurred to finance those assets. Historically, these two values have been about equal, so the net worth of the Australian Government has been around zero, ranging from 6% of Gross Domestic Product (GDP) just before the crisis to negative net worth of minus 6% in 2011–12. Net worth is the most relevant measure of a government's financial position in the long run. The second measure is net financial worth, which excludes nonfinancial assets such as schools, hospitals, roads and so on, but includes the value of public enterprises such as Australia Post. Investments in nonfinancial assets generate a flow of services, but no monetary return. Hence, they must be financed over time by tax revenue. In Australia, state governments own most of these types of assets, so the impact on the Commonwealth is modest.

By looking at the results of privatisation and other asset sales one can see clearly the importance of using correct measures. Asset sales improve the government's cash balance in the year they take place, and they reduce 'gross' measures of public debt, which do not take assets into account. Selling income-generating assets will make no difference to the government's financial position, unless the asset is sold for more than its value in continued public ownership. In other words, only if the interest that can be saved, by using the sale proceeds to repay debt, exceeds the value of the flow of dividends and retained earnings from the continued public ownership of the asset, will there be a net benefit.

Turning from measures of the government's financial position at a point in time to measures of annual flows, the most useful concept of budget balance, sometimes called primary budget balance, is simply the difference between government revenue and operating expenditure. This measure does not include interest on government debt or income flows from financial assets. Assuming the rate of interest on government debt is equal to the rate of growth of national income, the addition of interest to the existing debt will leave unchanged the ratio of debt to national income. This point may best be illustrated by an example. Suppose public debt is equal to 30% of national income, which is initially one trillion dollars a year, so that debt is $300 billion. Suppose too that the rate of interest on public debt and the rate of growth of national income are both 5%. With a primary balance of zero, public debt will grow by the amount of interest paid, which is $15 billion (5% of $300 billion). But national income will also grow by 5%, to $1.05 trillion. It is easy to check that the ratio of debt to income remains unchanged at 30%, and that this result does not depend on the specific values in the example.

It is, not, however, generally desirable to pursue the goal of primary balance every year. Countercyclical fiscal policy requires governments to run deficits during recessions and surpluses during booms. Sustainability requires that, over the course of the economic cycle, deficits and surpluses must balance out. Although the precise measurement of budget balances and public balance sheets is complex, the central issue is the very simple one raised at the beginning of this section. In the language of economists, fiscal policy satisfies the long-term intertemporal budget constraint if, and only if, it is consistent with a stable long-term ratio of public debt to national income.

Taxation and expenditure

In macroeconomic analysis of fiscal policy, the primary emphasis is on measures of budget balance, and on the economic impact of deficits and surpluses. In the longer term, however, balance must be maintained one way or the other. The crucial questions are how much of national income should be allocated to the public sector as government revenue, and which services should be provided or funded with that revenue. For most of the 20th century, both the size of the public sector, relative to the economy as a whole, and the scope of public sector activity, expanded.

The resurgence of market liberalism from the late 1970s onwards was centred on the belief that most productive functions performed by the public sector could be better handled by the private sector. This belief was supported by the development of theories of property rights and public choice in which government intervention in the economy was viewed as inefficient and as motivated primarily by a desire to redistribute income. However, the crucial theoretical underpinning of this belief was the idea, inherent in the Efficient Markets Hypothesis, that private capital markets do a better job of allocating investment than can ever be achieved by governments.

Market liberals sought to roll back the growth of the state through privatisation, deregulation, contracting out of public services and scaling back efforts to redistribute income. These efforts achieved substantial success both in cutting back the scope of the public sector and in reversing the egalitarian shift in income distribution that had taken place in the era of Keynesian democracy. By the time of the GFC, the role of the public sector in the provision of infrastructure had been greatly reduced, and substantial shifts towards for-profit provision had taken place in health, education and other services traditionally provided by governments. These efforts stopped the growth in the government share of national income. In Australia, the Commonwealth Government's share of national income has remained broadly constant between 20% and 25% since the 1984 'Trilogy' commitment of the

Hawke Labor Government. This promise, initially made for a single Parliamentary term, required the government to allow no further growth in the revenue and expenditure shares of national income and to reduce the size of the deficit. With the exception of the periods of fiscal stimulus in 1990 and 2009, these commitments have hardened into dogma.

To the disappointment of market liberals, however, all their efforts have been insufficient to reverse the 20th-century growth in the government share of national income. There are two main reasons for this. The first is that the sectors of the economy in which government has historically played a crucial role, most notably health and education, are growing in their relative economic importance, while the sectors where market provision works best, most importantly manufacturing, wholesale and retail trade and primary production, are generally declining. The second, more significant factor has been the failure of attempts to introduce for-profit provision of infrastructure and key services in place of public (or publicly supported nonprofit) provision. Examples include:

- Telecommunications: the failure of Telstra (the privatised replacement of the former Telecom Australia) to provide modern broadband services has forced governments to re-enter this field with the creation of the National Broadband Network.
- Roads: the attempt to finance road infrastructure through privately built and financed toll roads on the Public–Private Partnership (PPP) model has almost invariably ended in failure. Either the public has paid far more than the true cost of the infrastructure (the most common outcome in the 1990s) or the private investors have lost their money (most common since 2000). Now that neither party is willing to accept substantial losses, it has proved virtually impossible to induce private investors to tender for road projects on the traditional PPP model.
- Electricity: the introduction of market competition was expected to produce large reductions in prices but has distorted investment decisions and led to massive increases in costs.
- Education: for-profit providers of vocational education and training have repeatedly exploited weaknesses in the pricing system to generate large profits, while providing training of little value. Internationally, for-profit education has been a comprehensive failure in the United States at both the school level (Edison Schools) and in the tertiary sector (University of Phoenix).

The catastrophic failure of financial markets in the current crisis represents an even more fundamental failure for the market liberal project. In some circumstances, private operators may do a more efficient job of delivering some kinds of services than their public counterparts, using existing infrastructure. It is now apparent, however, that leaving the provision of new infrastructure to the judgements of financial markets has been a disastrous mistake. This means that, in future partnerships between public and private sectors, the balance in the existing PPP model must be reversed.

The financial crisis also undermines a crucial argument for lower rates of taxation, particularly on high income earners. Market liberals claimed that the incentive effects of lower tax rates would lead those at the top of the income distribution to devote more effort to productivity activity and less to tax minimisation. In reality, both unproductive financial speculation and aggressive attempts to undermine the tax system have expanded massively during the era of market liberalism. There is no evidence that an increase in the tax burden on high income earners would have any adverse effects on the performance of the economy as a whole.

The need for an expanded public sector role in infrastructure, health and education services implies that the share of national income allocated to the public sector as government revenue must increase. The Rudd and Gillard Labor Governments made some initial steps in this direction, with the increase in the Medicare levy to partially fund DisabilityCare Australia (the national disability insurance scheme) and a scaling back of tax expenditures such as the Fringe Benefits Tax Exemption for motor vehicles. But these measures are not nearly sufficient to fund the necessary expansion of public provision. The expansion of health, education and infrastructure services will require an additional 3–5% of national income over the coming decade or so. To fund that it will be necessary either to raise the rate of Goods and Services Tax (GST) substantially, to 12.5% or 15%, or to raise income tax rates, particularly for high income earners, as well as extending the kinds of measures that have already been taken. Such measures have been seen as politically impossible until recently. However, the increase in the Medicare levy to fund DisabilityCare Australia went through smoothly, and the Rudd Government's changes seem to have been received without too much concern raising the possibility that the levy could be increased further in the future.

Monetary policy

Despite its comprehensive failure to prevent the GFC, and the failure of monetary policy to generate a recovery, inflation targeting remains the preferred approach of central banks around the world. The United States Federal Reserve, which previously operated an informal policy of targeting an inflation 'comfort zone', announced an official inflation target of 2.0% in 2012. In many countries, however, the issue is somewhat academic, since interest rates are at or close to zero, so that the conventional version of inflation targeting, based on small adjustments to interest rates, is not applicable. Yet, in countries such as Australia, with low but positive interest rates, inflation targeting remains dominant.

The most modest change that could be made is to increase the inflation target, say to a range of 3–4%. Changing the inflation target would simply be an adjustment of the parameters of the policy regime that has prevailed since the early 1990s. The International Monetary Fund (IMF) suggested this idea in the early stages of the crisis. More recently, and starting from a situation of price deflation, the Japanese Government has sought to increase the rate of inflation. A more fundamental shift in policy, advocated by economists including Christina Romer and Paul Krugman, would be to target the nominal (current dollar) value of GDP rather than the rate of inflation, a policy called nominal GDP targeting. The key merit of this approach is that it takes account of economic activity as well as inflation, and includes an automatic trade-off between the two.

In periods of strong growth in real activity, policy leans towards controlling inflation, so that the rate of growth in nominal GDP is kept close to the target. By contrast, in recession periods, the nominal value of GDP declines, implying the need for monetary stimulus. The other critical feature of nominal GDP targeting is that, unlike inflation targeting, it does not ignore the past. If the economy is in recession, the aim of nominal GDP targeting is not merely to achieve a return to growth from a low basis, but to return to the pre-recession trend of economic activity.

As with fiscal policy, a shift to nominal GDP targeting would not have much effect during periods where economic fluctuations are modest. By contrast, in the severe and sustained recession observed in most developed countries since the GFC, both real and nominal GDP have fallen far below the levels implied by pre-crisis trends, even as inflation has remained close to its target values. In this context, a nominal GDP target implies a far more expansionary monetary policy than an inflation target. More importantly, a nominal GDP target implies a commitment to sustain monetary expansion until growth is restored.

Financial regulation

The most distinctive feature of Australia's policy approach in the years leading up to the GFC was a more cautious and restrictive approach to prudential regulation. In large measure, this reflected the near-collapse of the banking system that occurred in during the 1990 recession, following the deregulation of the 1980s. In addition, the political unpopularity of the major banks meant that restrictions on mergers (the 'Four Pillars' policy) were retained, and financial innovations were viewed less favourably than elsewhere.

Australia's approach to monetary policy and financial regulation differed only in minor and subtle details from that adopted in other developed countries. The fact that Australia escaped serious problems during the GFC might, perhaps, be due to such subtle details in policy frameworks, but if so, no one has identified yet the crucial differences between Australia's approach and those that failed so badly elsewhere. Alternatively, it might be that those managing Australia's system did a better job than their counterparts elsewhere. That might be a cause for satisfaction, but there is no guarantee that similar skill will be shown the next time the system runs into crisis. Finally, it was largely a matter of luck that Australia escaped the initial impact of the crisis and therefore had time to implement an effective programme of fiscal stimulus, expansionary monetary policy and guarantees to financial institutions.

Moreover, the system came closer to collapse than is commonly realised. Both Westpac and National Australia Bank (NAB) secretly borrowed billions from the US Federal Reserve in 2008. If the Fed had not been willing to act as a lender of last resort in this instance, the job would have fallen to the Reserve Bank of Australia that had quietly bailed out Westpac in 1991. The GFC exposed a major regulatory weakness in the absence of a guarantee on bank deposits. Such a guarantee had been resisted by the major banks, which correctly foresaw that they would be made to pay for an explicit guarantee, whereas, in the absence of such a guarantee, they could rely on being bailed out, overtly or covertly. After briefly flirting with the disastrous idea of a guarantee limited to $20,000 per account, which would surely have caused a bank run, the government introduced an unlimited guarantee of deposits in September 2009. This was originally intended to be temporary, but was made permanent in 2011, with a limit of $250,000 per account.

More generally, the crisis exposed fundamental flaws in the reasoning underlying the light-handed regulation introduced in the 1980s, and extended by the Wallis Review in 1996. Examination of the outcomes in Europe and the US suggests that the policy framework adopted in the 1990s played a major role in generating the crisis and requires radical modification.

Beyond financial capitalism

The policy proposals described earlier represent a feasible medium-term response to the failure of market liberalism in the GFC, aimed at achieving sustainable full employment. In the longer term, however, a reform programme of this kind would imply radical changes to the economy and society. In part, these changes would be a reversal of the programme of deregulation and privatisation that began in the 1970s. It is obviously impossible, however, to turn the clock back to the 'social democratic moment' of the late 1970s. Social and family structures, life expectations and technology have all changed radically since then.

What, then, would be likely to emerge in the place of the failed structures of financial capitalism? In macroeconomic terms, the most important changes would involve what Keynes (1936) called 'a somewhat comprehensive socialisation of investment'. In part, this would involve governments returning to their traditional role of undertaking large-scale investment in infrastructure, particularly at times when private investment is weak.

In a more globalised world, it is important to manage international flows of investment. Measures such as a tax on high volume financial transactions (Tobin tax) would help to reduce the volume and volatility of short-term capital flows. Similarly, experience has shown that controls on capital flows, anathema under market liberalism, can be a useful tool. Nevertheless, it is impossible to restore the level of control over global capital flows that facilitated the Keynesian boom of the post-war era. It is, therefore, necessary to undertake financial regulation at a global level, and to construct what has been called a 'new global financial architecture'. Attempts to do this so far, through the 'Basel process', have only served to facilitate destabilising financial speculation. A new approach, in which the primary objective is to tame and constrain the financial system, rather than to set it free, is needed.

Macroeconomic management must also take account of requirements for sustainability, particularly in relation to climate change. For example, periods of slow economic growth should be taken as an opportunity to accelerate investments in renewable energy, and close down old fossil fuel power plants. The primary requirement in all of this is the need for governments to take the ultimate responsibility for stabilising the macroeconomy. During the years of the Great Moderation, this task was left to financial markets and to central banks, which have proved unequal to the task. Both the traditional instruments of fiscal policy and new policy instruments suited to a globalised world need to be deployed.

Concluding comments

Australia's escape from the GFC owes much to the willingness of policy makers to break with the dogmas of market liberalism and intervene decisively to prevent financial collapse and offset the shocks to the real economy arising from the global recession. Unfortunately, they have, for the most part, regarded the GFC as a one-off shock, never to be repeated. Australia's success in managing the crisis has been seen as proof that its macroeconomic policies and institutions are in no need of change, while the catastrophic failures of similar policies and institutions in other developed countries have been largely ignored. An adequate response to the GFC will require fundamental changes in macroeconomic policy and in the economic theory that guides policy.

Note
[1] This is the Australian edition, in which the chapter on austerity is replaced with a discussion of economic rationalism (that is, market liberalism) in Australia.

References
Blyth, M. (2012) *Austerity: The History of a Dangerous Idea*, Oxford University Press

Commonwealth of Australia (1994) *Working Nation: Policies and Programs*, Australian Government Publishing Service, Canberra

House of Commons Treasury Select Committee (2012) *Fixing LIBOR: Some Preliminary Findings*. Available at: www.publications.parliament.uk/pa/cm201213/cmselect/cmtreasy/481/48102.htm

Keynes, J.M. (1936) *The General Theory of Employment, Interest and Money*, Macmillan, London, Chapter 24

Peters, T. (1997) 'The Brand Called You', Fast Company. Available at: www.fastcompany.com/28905/brand-called-you

Quiggin, J. (2011) *Zombie Economics: How Dead Ideas Walk Among Us*, Princeton University Press (US paperback edition)

Quiggin, J. (2012) *Zombie Economics: How Dead Ideas Walk Among Us*, Black Inc, Melbourne (Australian paperback edition)

Trichet, J-C. (2011) 'Transcript of the questions asked and the answers given by Jean-Claude Trichet, President of the ECB and Vítor Constâncio, Vice-President of the ECB, 8 September'. Available at: www.ecb.int/press/pressconf/2011/html/is110908.en.html

FOUR

Putting together work and care in Australia: time for a new settlement?

Barbara Pocock, Janine Chapman and Natalie Skinner

The regulation of work, and the social and political institutions that underpin it, have been a prominent issue in public policy in Australia for over a century. This chapter falls into three sections. In the first, we discuss the nature of successive work/care regimes distinguishing breadwinner man/caring woman from more recent forms of social reproduction where women do both paid work and household care. In the second, we outline recent data about the effects of the current work/care arrangements on women and men using evidence from the Australian Work and Life Index (AWALI) survey. In the third, we turn to the future and policy changes that would help relieve the work/care strains that negatively affect many workers.

Work and its settings have been sites of some of Australia's most bitter public policy fights and deep social division. The fierce strikes of the 1890s − that saw shearers and maritime workers fighting for their right to bargain collectively rather than individually − heavily influenced the shape of the federation settlement and the industrial and conciliation institutions that persisted for most of the 20th century (Turner, 1978). In the early decades of union organising such struggles were often bitter, prolonged and bloody. These disputes continued into the late 20th century, such as the 1998 maritime dispute and later still the 2007 campaign against the decollectivising 'Work Choices' proposals of the Howard Government (Muir, 2008).

Elsewhere in this volume, Buchanan and Oliver point to some key categories that are essential for understanding the heat in this area of public policy. Beyond these categories are other important concepts and issues that arise out of the social location of work and the fact that no production or formal employment can occur without the social production of workers and society. Beneath the world of production and paid work lies the essential domain of social reproduction and unpaid work. These domains exist in a tight embrace. However, the nature of this relationship varies under different public policy and gender regimes. Understanding the mechanisms and means of social reproduction is essential to understanding the world of work, and the public policy debates that flow around it. The shift in the nature of the gendered regime of social reproduction makes analysis of the categories of gender and social reproduction particularly salient and helps explain why recent policy issues have included working time, flexibility, leave and the security of employment contracts.

From breadwinner man to dual earner households

The work and care patterns of Australians unfold within a complex social, cultural and institutional 'work/care regime' (Pocock, 2005). Several factors construct such regimes, including the dominant gender regime that shapes particular institutions, cultures and action that are time and place specific (Pocock, Skinner and Williams, 2012). The balance of class forces between employers and employees and the role and nature of the state also affect the prevailing work/care regime. Such regimes are historically specific and individuals' experiences vary by socioeconomic status, ethnicity and location. Delineating particular work/care regimes is an exercise in generalisation that does violence to many particular experiences that run counter to a dominant pattern. Nonetheless, it is useful to consider some common characteristics to highlight change and draw out the context of public policies and debates as they emerge.

When Australia's federation settlement was shaped, the dominant work/care regime placed men as breadwinners in the public sphere of paid work, and women as carers in the private sphere of the home. While there were many women – widows, daughters and mothers – who did both, the wage system was built on the assumption that men's earnings supported a family while women worked for pin money or did not work at all. A cornerstone of this regime was the male breadwinner wage. In 1907 Justice Higgins brought down the famous Harvester decision that required the H.V. McKay Company to pay a living wage to its male employees in exchange for tariff protection by the state from international competition. This living wage was defined by Higgins as that which met a worker's normal needs living in a 'civilized' community, defined to include the sustenance of a worker and his family – assumed to include a dependent wife and three children – in 'frugal' comfort. In 1912, Higgins cemented the inbuilt disadvantage for women by setting the female rate at 55% of men's – and this discriminatory approach prevailed until the early 1970s, until a series of equal pay decisions implemented a limited form of equal pay for equal work (Thomson and Pocock, 1997).

In short, production and employment were assumed to be largely the business and responsibility of men, while women were assumed to be dependent upon men in terms of an income, and took their place in the domestic sphere, looking after their men, children and home. In terms of public policy, this model of work and social reproduction was accompanied by a particular set of working conditions that enshrined and protected the 'proper worker', or what Joan Williams (2010) has termed the 'ideal worker': that is, a worker who is full-time, available for overtime when required, and who is expected to work steadily over decades. This 'ideal worker' casts a long shadow over the terms and conditions available to those who do not meet the standard trajectory. Those with caring responsibilities cannot meet the demands of full-time work, and deviating from the standard can carry penalties in terms of lifetime earnings, accumulation of leave, and access to careers, training, promotion, retirement funds, and a host of other formal and informal working conditions and amenities.

There were always women (and men) for whom this model did not hold. From federation and before, many women found themselves with children and, in the absence of social security support, were forced to both earn and care, while many men earned a breadwinner wage despite having no caring responsibilities. However, the model prevailed as the dominant archetype as long as men made up most of the workforce. From the 1970s, however, it began to unravel.

Figure 4.1 shows the proportion of men and women participating in the labour market in 1966 (top figure), and in 2011 (bottom figure). Over this 45-year period men's participation (the top line in both figures) declines a little across the age spectrum, from nearly 100% from the late teens through into the fifties in the 1960s, to just over 90% from the mid-twenties through to the fifties in 2011. The picture is very different for women. Women's participation (the bottom line in both figures) rises dramatically across the age spectrum between 1966 and 2011. Indeed, over this period the 1966 participation dip associated with the arrival of children and early mothering in the twenties and thirties almost disappears. By 2011 almost 70% of women were in the paid labour market from their twenties through to their fifties. This increase represents a sea change in women's patterns of social reproduction. They have come to look like men in labour market participation over their life course, taking on a paid job alongside men – albeit much of their employment is part-time. However, men's

Figure 4.1: Changes in the proportion of people participating in the labour market, 1966–2011

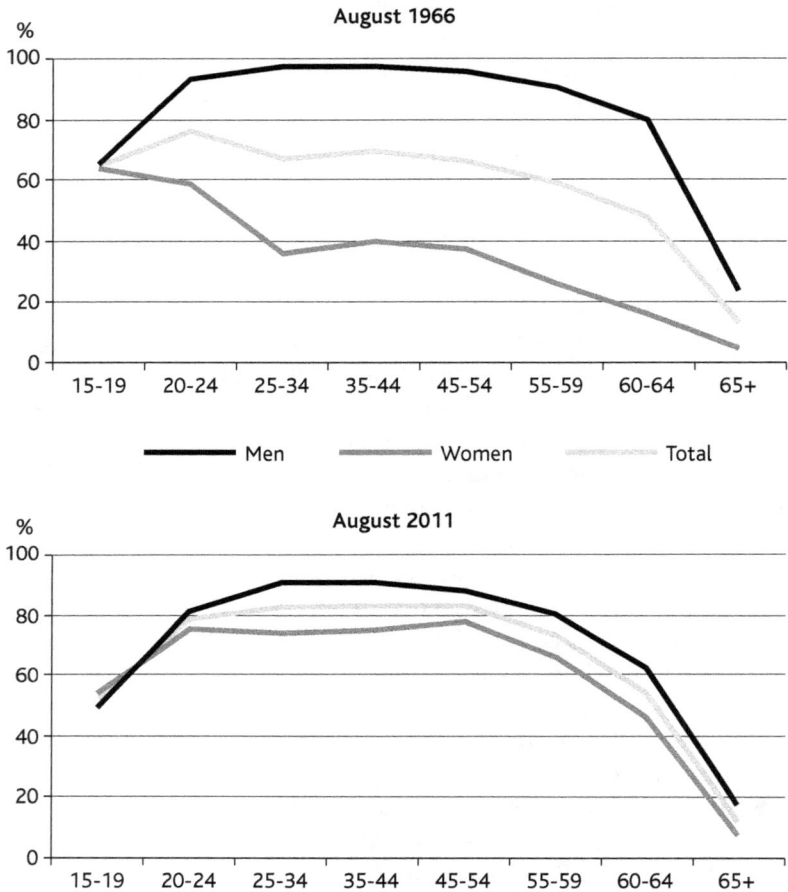

August 1966

%
- 100
- 80
- 60
- 40
- 20
- 0

15-19   20-24   25-34   35-44   45-54   55-59   60-64   65+

──── Men   ──── Women   ──── Total

August 2011

%
- 100
- 80
- 60
- 40
- 20
- 0

15-19   20-24   25-34   35-44   45-54   55-59   60-64   65+

Source: Labour Force, Australia (cat. no. 6202.0); Labour Force Historical Time Series, Australia (cat. no. 6204.0.55.001)

slightly lower rate of employment is not associated with a significant redistribution of unpaid work.

The shift of many thousands of women into the paid labour market transforms the capacity of women to maintain social reproduction: to look after their partners, children, parents and friends; to cook and clean; to read in schools and support sport and extracurricula activities of school children; to care for the older and infirm people; to be present in streets and homes in ways that create community linkages and fabric. When a large portion of women's hours are removed to the labour market and to commuting to and from work, then an equivalent portion of their time is not available for the social reproduction of home and community. Many of these latter activities are then given up or squeezed in alongside a job, producing the 21st century 'time bomb' in which many working women live (Pocock, Skinner and Williams, 2012).

'Breadwinner man/caring woman' has been replaced by 'male earner/female earner + carer', and the burden of adding paid work on top of unpaid work and care is reflected in the policy discourse of 'work–life conflict'. Men are not immune from its effects, with many working long hours and new fathers increasing their hours of work to compensate for the loss of their partners' income when a baby arrives (Pocock, Skinner and Williams, 2012). However, the biggest impact is upon women with caring responsibilities.

For much of the 20th century the public policy preoccupations in the sphere of work focused upon issues affecting full-time workers. More recently, while wage levels remain a consistent preoccupation, security of employment, the conditions of part-time work, leave to accommodate family responsibilities including paid parental leave, the provision of social supports like childcare, the undervaluation of paid care work and gender pay equity, have been significant preoccupations. Before turning to consideration of these, however, it is useful to consider the dimensions of the 'work/life collision' (Pocock, 2003) that have contributed to this debate.

The current work/life experiences of Australian working men and women

The cost of work–life conflict on individuals, families and societies as a whole is high. There is strong evidence of a link between work–life strains and a range of serious health outcomes such as burnout/exhaustion, stress, psychosomatic symptoms and physical health problems (Allen, Herst, Bruck and Sutton, 2000; Hammig, Gutzwiller and Bauer, 2009; Amstad, Meier, Fasel, Elfering and Semmer, 2011). From an economic perspective, high levels of work–life conflict have been linked with higher turnover, lower organisational commitment, and reduced levels of individual performance and productivity (Amstad, Meier, Fasel, Elfering and Semmer, 2011). Numerous studies have attested to the increasing number of Australian workers struggling to reconcile their working lives with commitments outside the home. In 2005, for example, the Australian Survey of Social Attitudes found that over 70% of respondents aged 18 to 65 would like to spend more time with their family and have more leisure time, and nearly 40% of workers would prefer to spend less time at work.

Here we explore the dynamics of men's and women's experiences of work–life conflict using data from the Australian Work + Life Index (AWALI), one of the largest and most comprehensive national surveys measuring how work intersects with other life activities. AWALI is a cross-sectional survey representative of Australian workers, first collected in 2007 and subsequently in 2008, 2009, 2010 and 2012. Over this five-year period, AWALI has surveyed 12,691 workers in total, benchmarking levels of work–life conflict. AWALI includes information about the work–life relationships experienced by men and women across a number of professions and industries, as well as detail about actual and preferred hours of work, employment type and sociodemographic data.

One of the main findings is that experience of work–life conflict has remained steady since 2007, with a consistent and sizeable group of workers affected by negative work–life interference. Men, particularly fathers and the self-employed, work the longest hours and would prefer to reduce their working hours, indicating a poor fit between work and other life commitments. With regard to occupation and industry, managers and professionals, and workers in the mining, information and professional industries, stand out as reporting the longest working hours and the poorest fit with the hours they would prefer to work (Skinner, Hutchinson and Pocock, 2012).

One of the most consistent patterns, however, relates to differences in work–life relationships for men and women, and – more specifically – for mothers and fathers. In general, women's work–life outcomes are consistently worse than men's when differences in work hours are accounted for. In addition, mothers' work–life outcomes are worse than fathers', whether single or partnered (Skinner, Hutchinson and Pocock, 2012; Chapman, Skinner and Pocock, forthcoming). Table 4.1 shows the work–life outcomes of employed men and women surveyed between 2007 and 2012 – with and without parenting responsibilities – who work part time (34 hours or less per week), full time (35–44 hours per week) and long full time (45 or more hours). There are strong gender patterns associated with working hours. Most part-timers are women (70.7% overall). A substantial proportion of part-timers are mothers (39.7%) or men without children (20.5%). Only 8.8% of part-timers are fathers. Men comprise the largest group within the full-time workforce; just over half working 35–44 hours are men (57.6%) of which 24.8% are fathers, and a similar proportion are women without children (27%). Only 15.4% of those working

Table 4.1: Employees' work–life interaction and fit with preference, by gender, parenting responsibilities and hours of work

	Men		Women		
	No children	Children	No children	Children	All
Work often/always interferes with activities outside work (%)					
Part time (≤34 hours)	13.4	17.2	12.4	17.3	14.9
Full time (35-44 hours)	15.2	19.7	15.4	26.9	18.1
Long full time (≥45 hours)	34.8	37.1	38.8	50.0	37.8
Work often/always interferes with time with family or friends (%)					
Part time (≤34 hours)	13.8	20.9	14.0	17.3	15.9
Full time (35-44 hours)	18.1	23.3	17.7	34.6	21.9
Long full time (≥45 hours)	35.7	44.4	39.2	59.3	41.7
Work often/always interferes with community connections (%)					
Part time (≤34 hours)	8.8	13.9	9.5	11.2	10.5
Full time (35-44 hours)	13.5	15.8	15.0	20.2	15.5
Long full time (≥45 hours)	26.3	31.4	30.9	40.1	30.3
I often/always feel rushed or pressed for time (%)					
Part time (≤34 hours)	25.5	42.9	42.4	65.7	48.3
Full time (35-44 hours)	39.1	49.7	52.0	71.2	50.1
Long full time (≥45 hours)	54.5	66.2	70.6	90.5	65.1
I am not satisfied with work–life balance (%)					
Part time (≤34 hours)	13.6	10.5	12.5	12.4	12.4
Full time (35-44 hours)	15.3	12.4	16.5	24.1	16.3
Long full time (≥45 hours)	24.8	25.2	32.0	47.0	28.2
Fit with preference*					
Part time (≤34 hours)	+7.0	+5.8	+3.0	+2.1	+3.7
Full time (35-44 hours)	−2.0	−1.0	−4.1	−5.6	−2.9
Long full time (≥45 hours)	−9.6	−9.7	−11.9	−13.3	−10.4

*Difference in hours between actual and preferred working time. Minus sign (–) denotes a preference for fewer hours, plus sign (+) denotes a preference for more hours.

long hours are mothers. Men predominate in long (45+) hours work (72.8%), fairly equally divided between men with and without children (37.6 and 35.2% respectively). Women without children comprise 18.3% of long-hours workers, whereas less than 10% of those working long (45+) hours are mothers (8.9 per cent).

As reported in Table 4.1, AWALI respondents were asked to report on the extent to which work interfered with (1) activities outside work, (2) time spent with family and friends, and (3) community connections; (4) how often they experienced chronic time pressure; (5) general satisfaction with work–life balance, and (6) how their actual hours compared with preferred hours.

From Table 4.1, we can see a clear relationship between the length of the working week and higher work–life conflict, and generally this holds for all employees. Overall, working long hours is associated with the worst work–life outcomes in all groups, and both men and women have poorer work–life outcomes when they have children. However, women's interference is more sensitive to increases in working hours, and this is especially the case for mothers. There is little difference between men and women without children for interference with activities outside work, time spent with family and friends, or community conflict. Similarly, there is little difference in the responses of fathers and mothers who work part-time hours.

Those working full-time and long full-time hours show a different pattern. Approximately one third of mothers working full time report that work always or often interferes with outside activities (26.9%) and time with family or friends (34.5%), and this rises to over half of mothers who work long full-time hours (50% and 59.3%, respectively). In comparison, interference with outside activities applies to 37.1% of fathers working long full-time hours.

A much larger proportion of employees report often or always feeling pressed for time, and unsurprisingly this increases for those who have children. The extent to which people feel rushed and pressed for time is a simple and direct indicator of the 'busyness' of working lives. On this item, gender differences are also apparent for those without children – a significantly higher percentage of women often or always experience chronic time pressure than men in all groups, particularly when working 45 hours or more (70.6% of women without children in comparison to 54.5% of men). In relation to parenting, over two thirds (65.7%) of mothers working part time and 71.2% of full-time mothers are time poor in comparison to under half of working fathers. Furthermore, 90.5% of mothers working long hours report always or often feeling rushed and pressed for time, in comparison to 66.2% of fathers working equivalent hours. This pattern is mirrored in responses to satisfaction with overall work–life balance, with almost half (47%) of long-hours mothers reporting dissatisfaction in comparison to a quarter of men (25.2%). Parenting responsibilities made no difference to men's work–life satisfaction, regardless of hours worked.

The extent to which work hours fit with working time preferences is also a major factor affecting work–life relationships (Baxter, Gray, Alexander, Strazdins and Bittman, 2007; Losoncz, 2011). Employees working part time reported that on average they would prefer longer hours, with men reporting that they would like to work almost a full day longer. This is particularly the case when we consider men working short part-time (1–15) hours; fathers in these jobs would prefer to work at least one day more a week (7.5 hours), whereas men without children would prefer to work 11 more hours. Women, whether mothers or not, would prefer an additional 5.5 hours per week. For those working longer part-time (16–34) hours, a preference for longer hours is evident for most groups. However, for women these longer part-time hours are a much better fit with preferences. Women without children would prefer to work only 1.8 hours a week, whereas mothers report a very good fit with preferences (+0.3).

In contrast, full-time women report a substantially wider discrepancy between actual and preferred hours. Full-time women with and without children reported a preference for working over half a day less. On average, employees working 45 hours or more were working substantially more than they would like (10.4 hours), however the discrepancy was greatest for mothers (13.3 hours). Previous research has shown that women's actual and preferred work hours show greater variation across the life course compared to their male counterparts, strongly linked to childcare needs (Drago, Wooden and Black, 2006; van Wanrooy and Wilson, 2006).

Working full-time and long full-time hours is where the greatest contrasts in work–life outcomes occur, and when combined with parenting is a major source of time pressure and work–life strain, with working mothers bearing the heaviest burden. Almost all – 90.5% – of mothers working 45+ hours per week report often or always feeling rushed or pressed for time, and half are not satisfied with their overall work–life balance. In contrast, working hours have no effect on men's reports of work–life balance, and in some cases satisfaction is higher for fathers than non-fathers, despite longer working hours. Combining parenting with full-time work has also been shown to compromise women's health, a link not observed for women working part time or men working full time (Hewitt, Baxter and Western, 2006). Men, however – especially fathers – are working considerably longer than they would like, even when taking into account the effect on their earnings.

These gendered patterns of engagement in paid work and unpaid care/domestic work are by international standards relatively entrenched. Australia is one of the most unequal countries with respect to men's and women's sharing of domestic and care work, with the gender contrast being strongest for parents (Sayer, England, Bittman and Bianchi, 2009; Craig, Mullan and Blaxland, 2010).

The policy consequences of a changing work/care regime

Concern over work/life pressures has been such that they have reached across the parliamentary spectrum. All parties have been drawn into debate about the appropriate terms and conditions underpinning workplaces and care. While positions have differed, on some issues – like paid parental leave – conventional political lines have become blurred. Work, care and family issues were key areas of public policy and electoral interest in the previous four national elections and continue to be significant.

On the conservative side, in 2001 Prime Minister John Howard (leader of the Coalition Government 1996–2007) acknowledged that the pressures faced by modern working families amounted to a national 'barbeque stopper'. His response was the Baby Bonus that gave parents a sizeable cash bonus on the birth of a child (available to all, regardless of their labour market participation). Since 2007 and the election of a Labor Government there have been some important policy reforms, including the introduction of Australia's first national paid parental leave scheme, childcare reform, and the introduction of a right to request flexibility in the National Employment Standards. In recent elections a group of 31 Australian academics from 19 universities have offered a set of evidence-based 'Benchmarks' against which various party 'work and family' proposals can be assessed in an election context (see www.workandfamilypolicyroundtable.org/). The Work and Family Benchmarks released in April 2013 highlight eight issues as priorities in need of public policy action: childcare, paid parental leave, job security, flexibility and working time, pay equity, the tax/transfer system, superannuation and the care issues arising from an aging Australia (Work and Family Policy Roundtable Benchmarks, 2013).

Parental leave

The paid parental leave debate reveals much about Australian political processes and actors. Both major parties have come late to paid parental leave, given the International Labor Organisation's almost century-long support for paid leave for working mothers on the arrival of a new baby. Among developed countries, only Australia and the US lacked a system of paid parental leave in 2009. On the Labor side, many male-dominated unions historically prioritised other forms of paid leave and some harboured a strong attachment to the idea of mothers staying at home to care for children. The Gillard Government introduced a national Parental Leave Payment (PLP) from 2011, providing 18 weeks paid leave at minimum wage on the birth of a child. Unlike the Baby Bonus this acknowledges the contribution of working mothers to the workforce. The scheme provides financial support to primary carers of newborn and newly adopted children, allowing them to take time off work to care for their child, enhancing the health and development of mothers and children. It also encourages women to continue in the workforce and promotes gender equality. Eligibility rests upon Australian residency, income ($150,000 or less), and an employment/ work test. Emphasising the work-related rather than welfare-related nature of the payment, PPL is usually made through employers to eligible long-term employees while others receive their payment via the Family Assistance Office. Recent figures show that half of the 150,000 PLP applications are mothers who earn less than $43,000 per year, suggesting that the scheme is providing support for those least likely to have access to employer-paid parental leave (Baird and Whitehouse, 2012).

On the conservative side Tony Abbott has become converted to paid parental leave, turning away from his earlier staunch opposition: in July 2002 he said that compulsory paid maternity leave would occur only over the Howard Government's 'dead body' (ACTU, 2010). The power of personal experience in shaping public policy is revealed in Abbott's self-styled 'slow and late' conversion, which he explained by reference to his daughters' reduced life options (Abbott, 2012). Unfortunately, reliance on personal experience alone as the basis for policy reform is likely to mean a very long wait on many issues and might help explain why paid parental leave took so long, given that most parliamentary policy makers and political leaders have been men. Abbott's scheme is a generous one, offering 26 weeks paid leave at full income replacement (capped at $150,000), financed by a 1.5% levy on companies with taxable income greater than $5 million per annum. While his recommendation is likely to face firm anti-levy opposition from business and his own party, the design ensures full income replacement. It would be particularly advantageous for higher-paid women, but may provide no benefit for those women who work part time, where a payment at minimum wage would be higher than their normal weekly wage.

Many employees would value full income replacement while on paid parental leave, and many employers recognise this by providing some employer-funded paid leave at full wage. Employers should certainly be encouraged to extend the period of paid leave, given that many Australian mothers and parents would like to take up to a year's leave with a new baby. Further, there is a good case for ensuring that new parents continue to accumulate superannuation when they take parental leave, so that they are not penalised in retirement. However, there are other pressing work/family priorities and much debate over how expenditure should be prioritised (Summers, 2013).

Other work–family policy reforms

Paid parental leave and arrangements on the birth of a new child are a small part of the work–family challenge that Australians face. Finding appropriate, affordable, accessible quality childcare is a major challenge for many who return to work after parental leave, as is finding an employer who will meet parents' need for flexibility and part-time work. Beyond care of children, an increasing number of workers are also likely to face significant care responsibilities for someone with a disability or an older parent, partner or friend. These more diverse and often more demanding types of care require a wide range of policy responses.

Provision of unpaid care is essential to the wellbeing of Australia's society and economy. Children, frail older people, disabled and sick people, all require care. In 2009, 12% of the population (2.6 million people) had caring responsibilities for people other than children (ABS, 2012). The provision of unpaid care has a significant impact on workforce participation throughout the life course, especially for women. Recent disability and health care reforms are built around an increased reliance on unpaid carers (FaHCSIA, 2012). At the same time, the national productivity and participation agenda calls for (and in the case of income support policy, mandates) increased labour force participation among women, older people and those with disabilities (Australian Government, 2010; Daley, McGannon and Ginnivan, 2012). This makes the duality of carers' jobs of increasing importance (Work and Family Policy Roundtable Benchmarks, 2013, p 13).

Australian women often undertake part-time or casual work as a strategy to reconcile work and care, but such jobs often lack the security and predictability of full-time employment. Many workers seek changed hours of work and the Labor Government's 2010 introduction of a formal 'right to request' (RTR) flexible working arrangements in the National Employment Standards was a response to this need. This allows those with children under school age to request changes to their working arrangements. However, RTR lacks an effective appeal mechanism to contest an employer's unreasonable refusal. Further, eligibility is limited to workers with 12 months service with their employer. Research shows that most workers do not know about the RTR, that men are less likely than women to make a request, and are more likely to be refused (Skinner, Hutchinson and Pocock, 2012).

Systemic and structural reforms

We began by reflecting on major changes that have occurred over a short time span with regard to gender and engagement in paid employment that has resulted in a shift away from the 'male breadwinner' towards dual earner households. This radical social change has not been accompanied by a matching level of policy reform, although there have been some important and substantive changes. So far we have focused on what we consider essential and achievable reforms to existing policy that are urgently required to enable men and women to participate fully and equitably in paid work and also perform essential and valuable care for family and community. Bolder and deeper change is needed at a systemic and structural level to achieve real gender equality in work and care, and a decent quality of life for all citizens. Here we canvass two such reforms – universal income security and reduced working hours. The Australian Council of Trade Unions (ACTU's) 2012 Independent Inquiry into Insecure Work (Independent Inquiry Into Insecure Work in Australia, 2012) recommended a number of reforms, including strengthening workers' rights to decent working time by introducing a right to refuse overtime, and a base for minimum hours of paid work for part-time and casual workers, along with a range of reforms to provide greater employment security and access to entitlements such as paid leave for casual workers.

Theorists such as Guy Standing have advocated for a universal basic income, arguing that economic security would enable access to both decent quality work and the opportunity to engage in activities not currently valued, such as care work and participation in community (Standing, 2011). There is also convergence among researchers from diverse disciplines that a shorter working week is not only preferable but quite possibly necessary to address the social and ecological challenges (Rosnick and Weisbrot, 2006; Abrahamse and Steg, 2009; Hayden and Shandra, 2009; Schor, 2010; Strazdins, Broom, Banwell, McDonald and Skeat, 2011). They argue that reducing work hours can increase the quality of life, in terms of time for family, community, leisure and health. They challenge the assumption that a 'standard' job involves full-time hours, and instead call for better quality part-time jobs, that provide security, stability of work hours and scheduling, and a sufficient income to support a decent quality of life (Lyonette, Baldauf and Behle, 2010). Broad uptake of a reduced working week would also require substantial change to cultural norms and assumptions around the meaning and implications of reduced hours of work, the entrenched cultures of long hours and 'face-time'. Such norms define many occupations, and explicitly preference workers willing and able to prioritise paid work, with the consequence of disadvantaging workers managing both paid work and care for others from access to decent quality jobs and career pathways.

Conclusion

Despite recent advances, many public policy challenges remain in the domain of work and family policy as we respond to changing workforce and population demographics. The slow adoption of basic measures and employer resistance to improvements in job security or more worker say over the times and place of work, have restrained change. While some have readily recognised the need to provide new leave, flexibility and supervisory practices in their organisations to accommodate changes in family and working life, others have not adapted, and workers and their dependants bear the cost. Long hours are a widespread problem and measures like reducing the length of the average working week, or regulating against long working hours, are desirable, but seem far from the current political agenda.

More change is needed to ensure a good society that enables workforce participation while supporting social and family relations, where work and care can easily be combined. This is particularly critical to gender equality and the quality of life for working women. In the long run, productivity is dependent upon social reproduction before all else, making the successful combination of work, care and family an ongoing economic, as well as social, goal.

References

Abbott T. (2012) 'Why I changed my mind on paid parental leave', *Mamamia website*, www.mamamia.com.au/news/tony-abbott-writes-for-mamamia-about-paid-parental-leave/

Abrahamse, W. and Steg, L. (2009) 'How do socio-demographic and psychological factors relate to households' direct and indirect energy use and savings?', *Journal of Economic Psychology*, vol 30, no 5, pp 711-720

ACTU (2010) 'Paid parental leave "over my dead body", says Abbott', 9 February, Media Release available at: www.actu.org.au/Media/ Mediareleases/PaidparentalleaveovermydeadbodysaysAbbott.aspx

Allen, T.D., Herst, D.E.L., Bruck, C.S. and Sutton, M. (2000) 'Consequences associated with work-to-family conflict: A review and agenda for future research', *Journal of Occupational Health Psychology*, vol 5, no 2, pp 278-308

Amstad, F.T., Meier, L.L., Fasel, U., Elfering, A. and Semmer, N.K. (2011) 'A meta-analysis of work-family conflict and various outcomes with a special emphasis on cross-domain versus matching-domain relations', *Journal of Occupational Health Psychology*, vol 16, no 2, pp 151-69

Australian Bureau of Statistics (2012) 'Caring in the Community Australia', Cat. No. 4436.0, Canberra: ABS

Australian Government (2010) 'Australia to 2050: Future Challenges, Intergenerational Report 2010', Canberra: Commonwealth of Australia

Baird, M. and Whitehouse, G. (2012) 'Paid parental leave: a first birthday policy review', *Australian Bulletin of Labour*, vol 38, no 3, pp 184-98

Baxter, J., Gray, M., Alexander, M., Strazdins, L. and Bittman, M. (2007) 'Mothers and fathers with young children: Paid employment, caring and wellbeing', Commissioned report by the Australian Institute of Family Studies for the Department of Families, Community Services and Indigenous Affairs, Canberra: FaHCSIA

Chapman, J., Skinner, N. and Pocock, B. (forthcoming) 'Work-life conflict in the 21st century Australian workforce: 5 years of the Australian Work + Life Index (AWALI)'

Craig, L. and Mullan, K. (2010) 'Parenthood, gender and work-family time in the United States, Australia, Italy, France, and Denmark', *Journal of Marriage and Family*, vol 72, no 5, pp 1344-61

Craig, L., Mullan, K., and Blaxland, M. (2010) 'Parenthood, policy and work-family time in Australia 1992–2006', *Work, Employment & Society*, vol 24, no 1, pp 27-45

Daley, J., McGannon, C. and Ginnivan, L. (2012) *Game Changers: Economic Reform Priorities for Australia*, Melbourne, Grattan Institute

Drago, R., Wooden, M. and Black, D. (2006) 'Who wants flexibility? Changing work hours preferences and life events', Institute for the Study of Labour (IZA) Discussion Paper No. 2404, Bonn: Institute for the Study of Labour (IZA)

FaHCSIA (2012) *National Carer Strategy*, Canberra: Department of Families, Housing, Community Services and Indigenous Affairs

Hammig, O., Gutzwiller, F. and Bauer, G. (2009) 'Work-life conflict and associations with work- and nonwork-related factors and with physical and mental health outcomes: a nationally representative cross-sectional study in Switzerland', *BMC Public Health*, vol 9, no 1, p 435

Hayden, A. and Shandra, J.M. (2009) 'Hours of work and the ecological footprint of nations: an exploratory analysis', *Local Environment*, vol 14, no 6, pp 575-600

Hewitt, B., Baxter, J. and Western, M. (2006) 'Family, work and health. The impact of marriage, parenthood and employment on self-reported health of Australian men and women', *Journal of Sociology*, vol 42, no 1, pp 61-78

Independent Inquiry Into Insecure Work in Australia (2012) *Lives on Hold: Unlocking the Potential of Australia's Workforce*, Melbourne: Australian Council of Trade Unions

Losoncz, I. (2011) 'Persistent work-family strain among Australian mothers', *Family Matters*, no 86, pp 79-88

Lyonette, C., Baldauf, B. and Behle, H. (2010) '"Quality" part-time work: A review of the evidence', Warwick, UK: Institute for Employment Research, University of Warwick

Muir, K. (2008) *Worth Fighting For: Inside the Your Rights at Work Campaign*, Sydney: University of NSW Press

Pocock, B. (2003) *The Work/Life Collision*, Sydney: Federation Press

Pocock, B. (2005) 'Work/care regimes: Institutions, culture and behaviour and the Australian case', *Gender, Work & Organization*, vol 12, no 1, pp 32-49

Pocock, B., Skinner, N. and Williams, P. (2012), *Time Bomb. Work Rest and Play in Australia Today*, Sydney: NewSouth Publishing

Rosnick, D. and Weisbrot, M. (2006) 'Are shorter work hours good for the environment? – A comparison of U.S. and European energy consumption', Washington DC: Center for Economic and Policy Research

Sayer, L.C., England, P., Bittman, M. and Bianchi, S.M. (2009) 'How long is the second (plus first) shift? Gender differences in paid, unpaid, and total work time in Australia and the United States', *Journal of Comparative Family Studies*, vol 40, no 4, pp 523-545

Schor, J. (2010) 'Sustainable work schedules for all', in L. Starke and L. Mastny (eds), *2010 State of the World. Transforming Cultures. From Consumerism to Sustainability*, New York: W.W. Norton and Company, pp 91-95

Skinner, N, Hutchinson, C. and Pocock, B. (2012) 'The big squeeze: work, home and care in 2012, The Australian Work + Life Index', Adelaide, SA: Centre for Work + Life University of South Australia

Standing, G. (2011,) *The Precariat. The New Dangerous Class*, London: Bloomsbury Academic

Strazdins, L., Broom, D.H., Banwell, C., McDonald, T. and Skeat, H. (2011) 'Time limits? Reflecting and responding to time barriers for healthy, active living in Australia', *Health Promotion International*, vol. 26, no 1, pp 46-54

Summers, A. (2013) 'There is a better way to help mothers return to paid work'. The Saturday Age. May 18 2013, p 16

Thomson, C. and Pocock, B. (1997) 'Moving on from masculinity? Australian unions' industrial agenda', In B. Pocock (ed) *Strife: Sex and Politics in Labour Unions*, St Leonards NSW: Allen & Unwin, pp 67-92

Turner, I. (1978) *In Union Is Strength: A History of Trade Unions in Australia, 1788–1978*, (2nd edn), West Melbourne, VIC: Thomas Nelson (Australia)

van Wanrooy, B. and Wilson, S. (2006) 'Convincing the toilers? Dilemmas of long working hours in Australia', *Work Employment and Society*, vol 20, no 2, pp 349-368

Williams, J.C. (2010) *Reshaping the Work–Family Debate: Why Men and Class Matter*, Cambridge, MA: Harvard University Press

Work and Family Policy Roundtable Benchmarks (2013), www. workandfamilypolicyroundtable.org/wp-content/uploads/2013/04/ Benchmarks-2013-for-website.pdf.

FIVE

Welfare reform

Ben Spies-Butcher

Recent discussions of welfare reform have been unusually divided. Many see the Australian welfare state transformed by neoliberal economic restructuring, which has increased inequality and left many vulnerable (Bryson and Verity, 2009; Jamrozik, 2009). Others have argued that alongside market restructuring Australian governments have also renovated past social protections, expanding social spending and addressing new forms of social insecurity (Castles, 1994; Mendes, 2009). The diversity is partly explained by the focus of enquiry. Looking specifically at aggregate social spending, and on the distribution of social spending, confirms a substantial renovation (Fenna and Tapper, 2012). However, a number of associated changes potentially contradict this. Economic and social reforms have undermined the basis of older forms of social protection, increasing reliance on social spending (Smyth, 2006). Policy change has also concealed some of the largest increases in public assistance, via the tax system, which exaggerate, rather than mitigate, market inequalities (Stebbing and Spies-Butcher, 2010). Finally, the nature of spending has changed, increasing conditionality for many (Mendes, 2009).

This chapter starts from the premise that understanding changes in Australian social policy requires an historical analysis of the Australian Settlement and its transformation. Much of the increased social spending has been a direct response to the new challenges facing workers and their families as the Settlement has been unwound. Some of the most fundamental challenges that remain emerge because policy has not always been sensitive to the potential inequalities generated by market reforms, or political strategies have failed to maintain a sense of solidarity with those marginalised from paid work. The chapter begins with an overview of the original wage earner settlement and its demise. It then discusses how social policy reform has responded by modestly renovating welfare institutions. An account of the shortcomings of this renovation follows, exploring both how this has happened and the potential implications of these trends. It suggests that Australia's welfare state has certainly felt the impact of neoliberalism, but this has not been a simple process of 'shrinking the state', rather it suggests a 'hollowing out' of social protection (Wilson et al, 2013).

Vale full employment

Australia has been described as a 'wage earner's welfare state' (Castles, 1985). Australia has had lower taxes and social spending than many European countries, leading it to be classified along with the United States as a liberal, market-orientated welfare state (Esping-Andersen, 1990). However, inequality in Australia has also been much lower than in other liberal welfare states. Castles (1985) explained this anomaly, claiming other policy instruments, especially labour market policies, performed the function of European social spending. Australia introduced centralised wage fixation and incorporated social needs into wages, so that workers would be guaranteed enough to raise a family. From 1945 it also committed to promoting full employment, with unemployment remaining below 2% for most of the 1950s and 1960s (Smyth, 1994).

The limited social spending that did exist – such as pensions for older people and unemployment benefits – complemented these labour market policies. Means tests were relatively generous, ensuring most workers could access some payment and only the relatively well off were excluded, thus reducing stigma. Unlike European social insurance models, where those on higher incomes usually received higher payments, Australia's system of low, flat-rate benefits were better suited to low wage workers than to the middle class (Castles and Shirley, 1996). The old age pension and unemployment benefit offered manual workers a much higher proportion of their usual working income than was the case for higher paid professionals. Social spending has been more efficient at reducing inequality, allowing Australia to maintain relatively egalitarian outcomes with lower taxes. Hence, the title of a 'wage earner's' welfare state (Castles, 1985).

This system of social protection, however, rested on policy settings beyond traditional social policy, generally called the Australian Settlement (Beilharz, 2008). Workers were able to maintain a strong bargaining position through restrictions on immigration and through tariff barriers that protected domestic industries. The demands on social policy were also reduced by social norms around the nuclear family. Male wages were significantly higher than female wages, reflecting an assumption that men were the breadwinners in the household, and so needed higher incomes to provide for a family (Ryan, 1984). The nuclear family allowed a trade-off between paid and unpaid work, where the male breadwinner earned enough to support a family, and in turn was supported by the unpaid work of a housewife, who would care for the breadwinner and their children. The system was effective at reducing inequality, although it clearly also limited the horizons of many, and marginalised those outside this norm, such as single parents, as well as many immigrants and Indigenous people who were excluded from these protections.

Both the broader economic policy settings, and the social norms around the family, began to break down from the 1970s. An economic crisis saw the simultaneous rise of inflation and unemployment, undermining the credibility of Keynesian macroeconomic policies supporting full employment. Australia followed an international trend towards neoliberal policy settings (Bryson and Verity, 2009). Economic policy refocused on reducing inflation. Governments deregulated financial markets, reduced industry protections, privatised government assets, and introduced competition policy in other areas. Industrial relations were also partly deregulated, with wages set at the enterprise, rather than industry level, and by a substantial increase in casualisation (Borland et al, 2001). This weakened the bargaining position of disorganised and less skilled workers, increasing wage inequalities (Harding, 1997). Technological change and pressures from the international economy also saw a decline in manufacturing, leaving many traditional breadwinners out of work. The result has been growing inequalities in labour and capital incomes (Productivity Commission, 2013). This is combined with a substantial increase in very high incomes (Atkinson and Leigh, 2007), especially among corporate managers, and a shift in national income from wages to profits, that coincide with the deregulation of the economy (Stilwell and Jordan, 2007).

Widening market inequalities were reinforced by changes to the internal redistribution undertaken within the family. As family and gender norms have changed, so the distribution of paid and unpaid work has also changed. Relationships have broken down, and women have entered the paid workforce. On the one hand this has meant a growing number of households without market income and reliant on government payments (Saunders, 2007). Single parents struggled to balance paid work and care responsibilities and are dramatically overrepresented among poor households (Productivity Commission, 2013). On the other hand, more families now have multiple market incomes. This brings with it new pressures to balance work and 'life'. As Pocock and her colleagues point out elsewhere in this volume, the impacts of these pressures are diverse. But women face particular challenges, as they have increased their participation in paid work while often retaining primary responsibility for providing unpaid care. This is only reinforced by the prevalence of insecure work (Pocock et al, Chapter 4, this volume).

Renovating the welfare state

Neoliberalism has played out differently in different locations. Unlike in the United States and the United Kingdom, a left of centre government undertook Australia's reforms. This long period of Labor rule from 1983 to 1996 is unparalleled in the English-speaking world. Labor did not oppose the trend towards integration with global markets. It did, however, combine deregulation with new social commitments, an approach that later became known as the Third Way (Frankel, 1997). Most significantly, Labor entered an Accord with the trade union movement, committing to increase the 'social wage' through social policy in return for union restraint in wage negotiations (Stilwell, 1986). Feminist activists, known, sometimes disparagingly, as femocrats, also worked closely with the government to promote new social policy and labour market measures to help women gain greater financial independence (Eisenstein, 1995; Brennan, 1998 [1994]; Sawer, 2003). While the social wage elements of this reform process often fell short of initial expectations, and market liberalisation went much further than many unions or feminists supported, the extension of social policy during this period can be seen as 'refurbishing' the wage earner model for new circumstances (Castles, 1994).

This compact saw the extension of social policy in the traditional areas of health and pensions. Following the abolition of short-lived universal health insurance by the Fraser Coalition Government, Medicare was reintroduced in 1984 as part of the Accord (Gray, 1991). Later, superannuation was also added to the Accord (Quiggin, 2010), granting new contributions to worker pensions in return for lower wage demands. Consistent with the 'wage earner' model, employers are responsible for workers' benefits, giving the appearance of a small state. Both initiatives were contested. Indeed, Medicare was overturned in its original form. However, the longevity of the Labor Government ensured both were entrenched.

These measures addressed long-established social needs related to the risk of losing income in illness or old age. However, new claims, many related to the distribution of care work, became more pressing with the renegotiation of gender roles (Esping-Andersen, 1999; O'Connor et al, 1999). Here too, Australia renovated social protection, including social wage increases under the Accord (Brennan, 1998, 165–8). This reflected both social goals of poverty alleviation – especially for children – and economic motivations to increase female labour force participation.

While significant, the changes have also been uneven. Family benefits have increased to be among the highest in the Organisation for Economic Cooperation and Development (OECD) (Stebbing and Spies-Butcher, 2010). Funding for childcare also increased rapidly, although still not keeping pace with growing demand (Brennan, 2007). However, Australia was one of the last rich countries to introduce publicly funded parental leave. In general, this spending follows similar patterns to earlier programmes. Family payments are targeted, with the highest payments going to those on the lowest incomes, but with most families receiving some benefit. Paid parental leave is set at the minimum wage, rather than being linked to the parent's income. Childcare benefits are largely means-tested. The combined effect is that while deregulation has increased inequality from market income, social policy changes have tended to reduce inequality, slowing the overall trend. This continued after 1996, with the Coalition increasing family assistance. The Coalition did more to support breadwinner families than to encourage women into work (Brennan, 2007) and supports income-related parental leave payments; however, increased spending has helped contain broader trends towards inequality.

A neoliberal welfare state

Describing Australian social policy reform as a modest 'refurbishing' or 'renovation' of a longstanding egalitarian tradition is controversial. While it is true that the expansion of health and family payments have mitigated the inequitable effects of broader economic and social trends, inequality has increased (Productivity Commission, 2013). Many of these reforms were directly linked to trade-offs, such as reducing wage increases and deregulating the labour market. It is therefore contentious to focus simply on the benefits, without also acknowledging the impact of falling wages and insecure work that were a necessary corollary. Market reforms have also extended beyond 'economic' areas such as industry and employment policies. Competition policy has been introduced within social services that were previously publicly run, and public funding has been extended to private providers, potentially stratifying access. In addition, policies aimed at protecting those outside paid work have become more paternalistic and punitive. As a result, the overall impact of policy may be much less egalitarian than initially suggested.

This has rarely been achieved through overt retrenchment of the welfare state. Despite the anti-welfare state rhetoric of politicians such as Margaret Thatcher and Ronald Reagan, social policy research suggests there are few instances in which existing social programmes are successfully abolished. As social policies develop, Paul Pierson (1995) argues, so do constituencies in favour of retaining them, making them more difficult to remove. This is also the case in Australia, where there have been few instances of payments or services being abolished, the original Medibank excepted. Policies have however been reshaped.

A more recent literature on neoliberalism has highlighted a disconnect between the free market rhetoric of neoliberal think-tanks and the often interventionist nature of neoliberal reforms in practice (Levi-Faur and Jordana, 2005; Braithwaite, 2008). 'Actually existing neoliberalism' (Brenner and Theodore, 2002; Cahill, 2010) identifies a political project to weaken social control of the economy, rather than a set of economic ideas (Mirowski, 2009). In Australia, the expansion of the market has gone hand in hand with expansions in state capacities. For example, deregulation has frequently involved the creation of new regulatory agencies and a significant expansion in scope and even physical size of legislation (Cahill, 2010). Thus, financial market deregulation saw the creation of the Australian Prudential and Regulatory Authority, while labour market deregulation involved establishing a new Building and Construction Commission with extensive powers.

Within the welfare state, the literature on actually existing neoliberalism has focused on the expansion of marketisation and punitive surveillance (Wacquant, 2012). Neither trend necessarily suggests a contraction of the state, but rather a reshaping of state programmes. Social programmes that were once designed to shield citizens from the risk of losing market income can instead expose citizens to the risks of market fluctuations and discipline workers back into the labour market. The most obvious form of this is mutual obligation (McClure, 2000). This refers to a set of reforms that seek to redefine the obligations of those receiving government payments. In practice, this has extended what international scholars have referred to as 'workfare', labour market programmes that increase the requirements of, and surveillance placed upon, recipients of government payments (Peck, 2000). In Australia this includes programmes like 'work for the dole', which require some benefit recipients to undertake unpaid work to remain eligible for payments. It also includes more onerous monitoring and reporting regimes. Those found to have broken these rules are then 'breached' and their payments are withheld, often for extended periods (Grahame and Marston, 2012).

The development of mutual obligation is highly paternalistic, reflecting neoconservative theories that poverty is the result of perverse cultural norms (Mead, 1997) and are usually focused on stigmatised and marginalised groups. Initially work for the dole applied only to young unemployed people but was later expanded to include other groups (Wilson et al, 2012). Some see a similar logic in recent reforms to Indigenous social policy associated with the Northern Territory Emergency Intervention, which introduced compulsory income quarantining. This means that recipients can only spend their payments on items and at outlets approved by the state. This scheme is expanding to other groups, such as long-term unemployed people, through trial sites in areas with high unemployment (Billings, 2011; Mendes, 2012). Critics argue that the logic of these schemes is not to protect citizens, but to enforce social norms about participation in the market – they are paternalistic rather than decommodifying (Peck, 2000). This is particularly the case given little evidence that the programmes assist participants to find paid work (Borland and Tseng, 2011).

While retrenching existing entitlements is politically difficult, entitlements can be redefined and eroded over time. The ability of different recipients to defend the adequacy of their entitlements has increasingly reflected their relative marginalisation. Older pensioners have been the most successful in gaining greater support. Indexation arrangements have been updated, so that the old age pension is now linked to average wage rises, rather than inflation, and the Rudd Government introduced a separate one-off increase following the Harmer Review. In contrast, unemployment benefits remain linked to inflation and have not received any additional increase, producing a growing gap between these different forms of social support. In between are disability and parenting payments, which have been linked to wages, but were excluded from the discretionary increase (Whiteford, 2012).

More explicit adverse changes have been justified as a means to encourage work. Reforms under the Howard Coalition Government narrowed the definitions of disability and single parenthood. This created new employment obligations for those affected, subjecting them to mutual obligation requirements. Because the unemployment benefit has lagged behind other social support, it also reduced their payments (Grahame and Marston, 2012; Lantz and Marston, 2012). The Gillard Labor Government extended these reforms (Miletic and

Harrison, 2012), and the Abbott Government has signalled further changes.

Alongside growing paternalism, critics of neoliberalism also argue social policy has been transformed by marketisation. This involves the extension of competition in areas where other norms have traditionally determined the allocation of resources. For example, Australia has led the world in introducing competitive tendering to provide job training and placement for unemployed people – a system known as the Job Network (Ramia and Carney, 2001). This replaced a public system, with services now offered by non-government and for-profit providers who compete for contracts and are paid per outcome achieved. In education, funding to non-government schools has outstripped public school funding and fees for technical and higher education have increased (see Watson and Liu, Chapter 10, this volume). In childcare direct funding for non-profit and local government service providers has shifted towards subsidies for consumers that can be spent at for-profit facilities (Brennan, 2007). The new National Disability Insurance Scheme, DisabilityCare, follows a similar model of consumer based funding to be spent in a competitive market (Foster et al, 2012).

Marketisation can change the nature of social provision. By creating a market, the state constructs citizens as 'consumers' exercising individual choices. This reinforces a broader social process of individualisation (Clarke et al, 2007). It also shifts responsibility for managing risk from governments and corporations onto individuals and households. This is most obvious in the United States, in what Jacob Hacker calls 'the great risk shift' (2006). Reforms to strengthen the role of the market in employment have facilitated a growth of casual employment. Casualisation means labour incomes are less reliable, as the risk of market fluctuations is passed from the employer onto the employee. In the US, less secure employment also has implications for health care and pension rights, which have traditionally been provided by employers. Thus, a growing proportion of the workforce are obliged to purchase their own private health insurance and pension scheme. Access to health insurance is risk rated, so the sick pay more, and pension schemes no longer guarantee benefits, instead workers invest in market based schemes and get a return based on the market performance of their fund. This leaves them vulnerable to market fluctuations like the Global Financial Crisis.

The Australian experience is less dramatic, but is broadly consistent with Hacker's analysis (Marston et al, 2010). Here labour market changes have protected minimum wages, but facilitated casualisation and greater wage differentials (Wilson et al, 2013), meaning wages increasingly change with market conditions rather than social need. The introduction of compulsory superannuation also changed the nature of this form of savings. Where most schemes were 'defined benefits', meaning workers would be guaranteed a pension based on their final salary, the new schemes are 'defined contribution', meaning the contributions into the scheme are set, but the end payment is dependent on the performance of the fund, making workers more dependent on market conditions (Quiggin, 2010). More broadly, marketisation facilitates a change in the way services are purchased and provided. It allows for the entry of private competitors to public schemes, and can facilitate user payments.

Marketisation reflects not only neoliberal support for the market, but also financial constraints on the state. Pierson has argued that as the population ages and economic growth slows in developed economies, so an increasing proportion of government spending must be dedicated to existing social programmes, restricting funds for new forms of social support (2001). Marketisation is a response to the fiscal pressures this creates. By encouraging private forms of social provision governments can shift part of the cost onto the individual through 'user pays' schemes. However, unlike privatisation, the state remains a central player in these newly formed 'markets'. States set the rules, determine who can compete and provide most of the funding – these are 'quasi' or 'managed' markets (Le Grand and Bartlett, 1993; Davidson, 2009). Indeed, the state often creates new forms of financial support to encourage private provision. Private health insurance is supported by rebates and superannuation by generous tax concessions. Thus social spending can actually increase with marketisation.

Much of the additional financial support for private forms of welfare spending is poorly captured in traditional budgeting processes. Superannuation and private housing purchase, for example, are supported by generous tax concessions. Tax concessions are reductions in tax rates that apply to certain forms of spending, for example if your employer pays money into your superannuation account this is taxed at a lower rate than if they paid you directly. Because tax concessions reduce revenue, rather than increasing spending, they are not captured in the budget. But they have the same effect on the budget bottom line, and on individual behaviour, because you only get the concession if you undertake the action. Thus, more economists now acknowledge tax concessions are equivalent to spending (Surrey and McDaniel, 1985).

Tax concessions and rebates for private welfare spending have grown considerably since the 1980s, along with marketisation of welfare

(Stebbing and Spies-Butcher, 2010). However, this support is radically less egalitarian than traditional social spending. Because these benefits support private spending (you receive a rebate or concession based on how much you contribute) support is higher for those that can afford to spend more. If the support is given as a tax concession, then the rate of support also increases with income. The cost of tax concessions for superannuation now rival total spending on the old age pension, yet the bulk of these benefits go to those on the highest incomes, with low paid workers receiving very little. Thus, marketisation has facilitated the rise of a 'dual welfare state' (Stebbing and Spies-Butcher, 2010). Rather than reducing the role of the state, marketisation can stratify access. Those on low incomes continue to access government payments and public services, while those on higher incomes often receive large tax concessions and rebates for private equivalents of the same payments and services. The largest concessions are related to savings, meaning the inequality generated is likely to grow over time (Spies-Butcher and Stebbing, 2011). Because support for private provision is less visible in the budget process it is often ignored, and attention instead focuses on payments to poor people, undermining social solidarity and potentially reinforcing paternalism.

Partisanship remains

The complexity of policy change during the period of neoliberalism partly explains the quite different interpretations of how social policy has developed. It has meant measured social spending has increased and has remained highly redistributive, but highly inequitable tax expenditures have also increased but remain uncounted. Most social programmes have remained in place, with some new schemes like Medicare and compulsory superannuation added. But new social spending was usually compensation for economic restructuring and lower wages, and changes to the nature of social spending have made it more paternalistic and more marketised. This potentially increases insecurity by undermining the ability of social policy to shield citizens from an increasingly unpredictable market.

Accounts of neoliberalism suggest another more fundamental change to the dynamic of social policy. International literature has largely accepted that the size and structure of the welfare state reflects partisanship (Baldwin, 1990; Esping-Andersen, 1990). Long periods of social democratic governance tend to increase the size of social spending and its redistributive effect. However, this has been brought into question since the 1980s with Labor governments in Australia and New Zealand implementing extensive market reforms, and by a broader literature critical of 'Third Way' governance (Frankel, 1997; Faux, 1999). Michael Pusey's 'economic rationalism' thesis (1990) suggests the change was bipartisan, driven by economic ideas in the central agencies within the bureaucracy, and so we might expect partisanship to matter less than in the past.

Yet on reflection important differences have remained. Labor governments have sought cooperation and consent from the union movement while Coalition governments have taken industrial deregulation, in particular, further, with significant consequences for inequality. Labor has continued to extend new social provisions, initially through Medicare and superannuation (both then opposed by the Coalition) and more recently through paid parental leave and an increase in the old age pension. And on family payments, where both sides have increased total spending, Labor has favoured payments to encourage women into work while the Coalition has given more to traditional breadwinner families (Brennan, 2007).

A particularly notable difference emerged over the policy response to the Global Financial Crisis. Here Labor explicitly endorsed a Keynesian strategy, based on highly redistributive and targeted social spending (Rudd, 2009). Substantial cash payments were made to those on low incomes (excluding unemployed people) and new investment went into schools and public housing. Evaluation of the impact of the crisis on poverty suggests that these payments were likely to have been effective, although poverty has now increased among unemployed people – those excluded from stimulus support and subjected to the greatest paternalism (Saunders and Wong, 2011). The stimulus was one of the largest in the OECD and the most targeted towards increased spending. It is generally considered effective in reducing the impact of the crisis on employment (OECD, 2009). In this sense it is consistent with the interpretation of social policy modestly refurbishing the older wage earner tradition.

The neoliberal thesis of bipartisanship is strongest in relation to support for the market and for paternalism. Both sides of politics have consistently advanced market reforms. Labor and the Coalition have privatised key assets. Both have liberalised trade and embraced marketisation within social policy. Labor promoted superannuation as a private pension scheme, reintroduced student fees and promoted competition policy. Likewise the Coalition introduced the Job Network, reintroduced private health insurance subsidies and expanded private school funding. Under Rudd and Gillard, Labor has been more willing to claw back social benefits from higher income earners

(Martin, 2013) although the effects remain relatively marginal. Perhaps more surprising is the lack of partisan difference over the paternalism of mutual obligation. Labor has extended income quarantining and mutual obligation to new groups and has resisted mounting pressure to raise the unemployment benefit (Lucas, 2013).

The complexity of this assessment helps to explain competing assessments of social policy in the period since market restructuring and the collapse of the older Settlement. These reforms, largely bipartisan in nature, have increased inequalities in market incomes. But alongside this, a number of renovations have contained overall inequality in some respects. This suggests that an earlier 'neoliberal thesis' may be too simplistic, but that the emerging critique of 'actually existing neoliberalism' remains helpful. Economic restructuring has not meant the end of the state, rather it has seen the role of the state transformed. The state remains a force for redistribution, but it is increasingly a 'hollowed out' form of social protection, one that leaves citizens less secure, and which increasingly marginalises those outside paid work. State support is less solidaristic, opening the door to greater stratification. This is not because the state has stepped away from supporting the middle class, but rather because it supports different social groups in different ways. Ensuring the political will to promote egalitarianism under these conditions will be an important challenge for governments of the future.

References

Atkinson, A. & A. Leigh (2007), 'The distribution of top incomes in Australia', *Economic Record*, 83, 247-261.

Baldwin, P. (1990), *The Politics of Social Solidarity: Class Bases of European Welfare States 1895–1975,* Cambridge: Cambridge University Press.

Beilharz, P. (2008), 'Australian settlements', *Thesis Eleven,* 95, 58–67.

Billings, P. (2011), 'Income management in Australia: Protecting the vulnerable and promoting human capital through welfare conditionality', *Journal of Social Security Law*, 18(4), 167-191.

Borland, J., B. Gregory and P. Sheehan (2001), 'Inequality and economic change', in Borland J, Gregory B and Sheehan P (eds) *Work Rich: Work Poor: Inequality and Economic Change in Australia*, Melbourne: Centre for Strategic Economic Studies, Victoria University.

Borland, J. and T. Tseng (2011), 'Does 'Work for the Dole' work?: an Australian perspective on work experience programmes', *Applied Economics*, 43, 4353-4368.

Braithwaite, J. (2008), *Regulatory Capitalism: How it Works, Ideas for Making it Better*, Edward Elgar, Cheltenham.

Brennan, D. (1998 [1994]), *The Politics of Australian Child Care: Philanthropy to Feminism and Beyond*, Melbourne: Cambridge University Press.

Brennan, D. (2007), 'Babies, budgets and birthrates: work/family policy in Australia 1996–2006', *Social Politics*, 14(1), 31–57.

Brenner, N. and N. Theodore (2002), 'Cities and the geographies of 'actually existing neoliberalism'', *Antipode*, 34(3), 349-379.

Bryson, L. and F. Verity (2009), 'Australia: From Wage-earners to Neo-liberal Welfare State', P. Alcock and G. Craig, eds. *International Social Policy: Welfare Regimes in the Developed World*, Basingstoke: Palgrave Macmillan.

Cahill, D. (2010), ''Actually existing neoliberalism' and the global economic crisis', *Labour and Industry*, 20(3), 298-316.

Castles, F.G. (1985). *The Working Class and Welfare: Reflections on the Political Development of the Welfare State in Australia and New Zealand, 1890–1980*, Sydney: Allen & Unwin.

Castles, F.G. (1994), 'The wage earners' welfare state revisited: refurbishing the established model of Australian social protection, 1983–1993', *Australian Journal of Social Issues*, 29(2), 120–145.

Castles, F.G. and I. Shirley (1996), 'Labour and social policy: Gravediggers or refurbishers of the welfare state?', in F. Castles, R. Gerritsen and J. Vowles (eds), *The Great Experiment: Labour Parties and Public Policy Transformation in Australia and New Zealand*, Auckland: Auckland University Press, 88-106.

Clarke, J., J. Newman, N. Smith, E. Vidler and L. Westmarland (2007), *Creating Citizen Consumers: Changing Publics and Changing Public Services*, Sage, London.

Davidson, B. (2009), 'For-profit organisations in managed markets for human services', in D. King and G. Meagher (eds), *Paid Care in Australia: profits, purposes and practices*, Sydney: Sydney University Press.

Eisenstein, H. (1995), 'The Australian femocratic experiment: a feminist case for bureaucracy', in M.M. Ferree and P. Yancey Martin (eds), *Feminist Organizations: Harvest of the New Women's Movement*, Philadelphia: Temple University Press, 69–83.

Esping-Andersen, G. (1990). *The Three Worlds of Welfare Capitalism*. Princeton, NJ: Princeton University Press.

Esping-Andersen, G. (1999), 'New risks in old welfare states', *Social Foundations of Post-Industrial Economies*, Oxford University Press, Oxford.

Faux, J. (1999), 'Lost on the Third Way', *Dissent*, 46(2), 67-76.

Fenna, A. and A. Tapper (2012), 'The Australian welfare state and the neoliberalism thesis', *Australian Journal of Political Science*, 47(2), 155-172.

Foster, M., P. Henman, J. Fleming, C. Tilse and R. Harrington (2012), 'The politics of entitlement and personalisation: Perspectives on a proposed National Disability Long-term Care and Support Scheme in Australia', *Social Policy and Society*, 11(3), 331-343.

Frankel, B. (1997), 'Beyond Labourism and Socialism: How the Australian Labor Party Developed the Model for "New Labour"', *New Left Review*, 221, Jan-Feb, 3-33.

Grahame, T. and G. Marston (2012), 'Welfare-to-work policies and the experience of employed single mothers on income support in Australia: Where are the benefits?', *Australian Social Work*, 65(1), 73-86.

Gray, G. (1991), *Federalism and Health Policy: The Development of Health Systems in Canada and Australia*, Toronto: University of Toronto Press.

Hacker, J. (2006), *The Great Risk Shift: The Assault on American Jobs, Families, Health Care and Retirement*, Polity Press: Cambridge.

Harding, A. (1997), 'The suffering middle: trends in income inequality in Australia, 1982 to 1993–94', *Australian Economic Review*, 30 (4), 341–58.

Jamrozik, A. (2009), *Social Policy in the Post-welfare State: Australian Society in a Changing World*. 3rd edn, Frenchs Forest: Longman.

Lantz, S. and G. Marston (2012), 'Policy, citizenship and governance: the case of disability and employment policy in Australia', *Disability & Society*, 26(7), 853-867.

Le Grand, J. & W. Bartlett (eds) (1993), *Quasi-Markets and Social Policy*, Macmillan, London.

Levi-Faur, D. & J. Jordana (2005), 'The making of a new regulatory order', *The ANNALS of the American Academy of Political and Social Science*, 598(4), 6-9.

Lucas, C. (2013), 'Unions call for $50 dole boost', *Sydney Morning Herald*, August 20.

Marston, G., J. Moss and J. Quiggin (eds) (2010), *Risk, Welfare and Work*, MUP, Melbourne

Martin, P. (2013), 'Focus', *Sydney Morning Herald*, March 14, 22-23.

McClure, P. (2000), *Participation Support for a More Equitable Society: Final Report of the Reference Group on Welfare Reform*, Department of Family and Community Services, Canberra.

Mead, L.M. (ed) (1997), *The New Paternalism: Supervisory Approaches to Poverty*, Washington, DC: Brookings Institution Press.

Mendes, P. (2009), 'Retrenching or renovating the Australian Welfare State: The paradox of the Howard Government's neo-liberalism'. *International Journal of Social Welfare*, 18, 102–10.

Mendes, P. (2012), 'Compulsory income management: A critical examination of the emergence of conditional welfare in Australia', *Australian Social Work*, 1-16.

Miletic, D. snf D. Harrison (2012), 'Single parents fear Newstart will set them back', *The Age*, 10 October. Available at: www.theage.com. au/opinion/political-news/single-parents-fear-newstart-will-set-them-back-20121009-27bas.html.

Mirowski, P. (2009), 'Postface: Defining neoliberalism', in P. Mirowski and D. Plehwe (eds) *The Road from Mont Pelerin: The Making of the Neoliberal Thought Collective*, Harvard University Press, Harvard, 417–55.

O'Connor, J., A. Orloff and S. Shaver (1999), *States, Markets, Families: Gender, Liberalism and Social Policy in Australia, Canada, Great Britain and the United States*, Cambridge University Press, Cambridge.

Organisation of Economic Cooperation and Development (OECD) (2009), 'The effectiveness and scope of fiscal stimulus', OECD Economic Outlook, Interim Report, March 2009.

Peck, J. (2000), *Workfare States*, Guilford Press, New York.

Pierson, P. (1995), *Dismantling the Welfare State? Reagan, Thatcher, and the Politics of Retrenchment*, New York: Cambridge University Press.

Pierson, P. (2001), *The New Politics of the Welfare State*, Oxford, Oxford University Press.

Productivity Commission (2013), *Trends in the Distribution of Income in Australia*, Working Paper, March.

Pusey, M. (1990), *Economic Rationalism in Canberra: A Nation Building State Changes Its Mind,* Cambridge: Cambridge University Press.

Quiggin, J. (2010), 'Risk shifts in Australia: Implications of the financial crisis', in G. Marston, J. Moss and J. Quiggin (eds), *Risk, Welfare and Work*, MUP, Melbourne, 3-23.

Ramia, G. and T. Carney (2001), 'Contractualism, managerialism and welfare: the Australian experiment with a marketised employment services network', *Policy & Politics*, 29(1), 59-80.

Rudd, K. (2009), 'Social democracy and the Global Financial Crisis' in R. Manne and D. McKnight (eds), *Goodbye to All That? On the Failure of Neoliberalism and the Urgency of Change,* Black Inc, Melbourne, 74-98.

Ryan, E. (1984), *Two-thirds of a Man: Women and Arbitration in New South Wales 1902–1908*, Hale & Ironmonger, Sydney.

Saunders, P. (2007), *The Government Giveth and the Government Taketh Away: Tax-Welfare Churning and the Case for Welfare State Opt-Outs*, Centre for Independent Studies, Sydney.

Saunders, P. and M. Wong (2011), 'The social impact of the global financial crisis in Australia', *Australian Journal of Social Issues*, 46(3): 291-309.

Sawer, M. (2003), 'The life and times of women's policy machinery in Australia', in S. Rai (ed) *Mainstreaming Gender, Democratizing the State? Institutional Mechanisms for the Advancement of Women,* Manchester University Press: New York.

Smyth, P. (1994), *Australian Social Policy: The Keynesian Chapter*, University of New South Wales Press, Sydney.

Smyth, P. (2006), 'Australian social policy in an international context', in A. McClelland and P. Smyth (eds), *Social Policy in Australia: Understanding for Action*, Melbourne: Oxford University Press.

Spies-Butcher, B. and A. Stebbing (2011), 'Population Ageing and Tax Reform in a Dual Welfare State', *The Economic and Labour Relations Review*, 22(3), 45-64.

Stebbing, A. and B. Spies-Butcher (2010), 'Universal welfare by 'other means'? Social tax expenditures and the Australian dual welfare state', *Journal of Social Policy*, 39(4): 585-606.

Stilwell, F. (1986), *The Accord – and Beyond: The Political Economy of the Labor Government*, Sydney: Pluto.

Stilwell, F. and K. Jordan (2007), *Who Gets What? Analysing Economic Inequality in Australia*, Port Melbourne: Cambridge University Press.

Surrey, S.S. and P.R. McDaniel (1985), *Tax Expenditures,* Cambridge, MA: Harvard University Press.

Wacquant, L. (2012), 'Three steps to a historical anthropology of actually existing neoliberalism', *Social Anthropology*, 20(1), 66-79.

Whiteford, P. (2012), 'Social security reform: The tax forum and beyond', *Economic Papers*, 31(1), 24-29.

Wilson, S., G. Meagher and K. Hermes (2012), 'The social division of welfare knowledge: policy stratification and perceptions of welfare reform in Australia', *Policy & Politics*, 40(3), 323-346.

Wilson, S., B. Spies-Butcher, A. Stebbing and S. St John (2013), 'Wage-earners' welfare after economic reform: refurbishing, retrenching or hollowing out social protection in Australia and New Zealand', *Social Policy and Administration*, 47(4), 623-646.

SIX

'Choice' and 'fairness': the hollow core in industrial relations policy

John Buchanan and Damian Oliver

Over the last 20 years, few policy areas in Australia have been contested as fiercely as industrial relations (IR). In 1993, the Keating Labor Government implemented the Industrial Relations Reform Act, which severed a 100-year Australian tradition of centralised wage fixing and state involvement through the conciliation and arbitration of industrial disputes. In its place was a new decentralised and deregulated regime, centred on enterprise bargaining.

Rather than establishing a new consensus, the effect of the Industrial Relations Reform Act has been to shift the parameter of IR policy further to the right. The Howard Coalition Government argued that the changes were not severe enough, and with its 1996 (Workplace Relations Act) and 2006 (Work Choices) interventions continued to dismantle what remained of a unique liberal collectivist experiment in IR. Labor's 2007 response, the Fair Work Act, remains true to the spirit of Keating's 1993 Act and keeps in place many of the reforms adopted by the Howard Government, intended to erode the collective institutions of IR policy. Consequently, the policy debate in IR has become one relating to a choice between an unregulated marketplace, where employers are free to set the terms, and a system where collective bargaining at the enterprise level is propped up by a residualist safety net. Neither option has the capacity to address rising insecurity in the labour market or the production and reproduction of skills, two of the biggest issues (in terms of economic and social costs) confronting the contemporary Australian labour market.

This chapter has four sections. First, we briefly summarise the changes that have occurred in the Australian labour market during the last 30 years. Next, we outline the fundamental policy questions in IR and how the main competing values frameworks attempt to answer them. Third, we review the foundations of IR policy in Australia, from the 1880s to the 1980s. Understanding how industrial relations evolved within a liberal collectivist framework, rather than a social democratic one, is key to explaining the neoliberal turn in IR policy since. Finally, we examine the transformation of IR policy since 1990 to a largely uncontested neoliberal terrain, built around the idea of the enterprise as a unitary whole, and the consequences for the Australian labour market.

A radically different Australian labour market

Starting around 1980, the Australian labour market underwent a dramatic transformation over a 20-year period, the result of changing economic and social conditions. Australia's exposure to international competition accelerated following the reduction of tariff barriers in automotive, textile and general manufacturing (ACIRRT, 1999: 14). International competition changed how businesses operated: a focus on short-term shareholder value eroded employers' willingness to make long-term investments in capital and in training and staff development (Watson et al, 2003: 194). Decline in agricultural and manufacturing employment was offset by growth in services, in the private sector (retail, hospitality, finance, property and business services) and the public and community sectors (education, health, care of older people and child care) (Watson et al, 2003: 51). Having been structured for so long around the 'Harvester man', the typical workers changed as women continued to enter the workforce (Watson et al, 2003: 136) and a significant student labour market emerged as school retention and higher education policies took effect. This influx of new workers had needs and expectations around when and how much they worked that conflicted with the prevailing Harvester man model of the standard, full-time 38 hour working week.

As a result of these demand and supply factors, the Australian labour market at the beginning of the 21st century was more precarious, more bifurcated and less equal than it had been 20 years earlier. The proportion of employees who were casual increased from under a fifth in 1988 to more than a quarter in 2001 (Watson et al, 2003: 68) and they were joined by growing numbers of 'non-employees': outworkers, contractors and agency workers (ACIRRT, 1999: 142). Divergent patterns of working hours created a group working too many hours, another group with too few, and a diminishing middle working the 'standard' 35–40 hour week (Watson et al, 2003: 86). These developments and others (such as the decentralisation of bargaining discussed later) led to a widening of income inequality (ACIRRT, 1999: 75). The role of IR policy over this period should be understood as facilitating the adjustment of the labour market to the new environment and the refashioning of existing values and standards to reflect the new reality.

Fundamental questions in IR policy and the responses of competing values frameworks

Any analysis of the role of values in shaping IR policy requires an understanding of the nature of IR as a domain of analytical and policy concern, the nature of 'values' and the nature of how policy emerges and evolves. IR is the domain of economic, political and cultural practice associated with the inherent complexities of the employment relation in market society. At the core of this is the treatment of human labour as a commodity. As Polanyi (1944) noted, this is a fiction. The absurdity of human labour as a commodity is that to constitute human activity as a good for sale is to sell life itself. There is no 'natural' state of labour in which it exists as a 'pre-given' entity independent of social relations. Narratives and allied practices emerge, however, which purport to specify how it will be managed and purchased as a component in the production of goods or the provision of services. In market societies the content of these narratives varies over time and between different nations at the same time (Beirnacki, 1995).

In thinking about developments in the last century or so, it is generally recognised in the IR, industrial sociology and labour process traditions that, while at law labour is formally treated as a 'commodity' for 'sale', this involves very peculiar social arrangements characterised by two very distinct inequalities (Fox, 1974: 289–90). The first is the inequality of bargaining power before the arrangement is settled. This arises because '[i]n all such disputes the masters can hold out much longer ... Many workermen could not subsist a week, few could subsist a month, and scarce any a year without employment' (Smith, 1930: 68). The other inequality surrounding any employment arrangement is the inequality of certainty: once hired, will the worker perform at a level and with a quality that will cover their costs of engagement? This inequality arises because what an employer hires is the potential of a person to perform, not a guarantee of their performance as such. This is known as the 'labour process problem' that stems from the open-ended nature of the employment relationship. This latter inequality of certainty can favour either the employer or the worker. We refer to the former as the external and the latter as the internal inequality associated with the employment relationship. IR policy and practice is concerned with how these inequalities of bargaining and uncertainty are managed. The inequality of uncertainty (internal) is primarily concerned with the value of 'efficiency'. The external inequality of bargaining power is primarily concerned with the value of 'fairness'. The bulk of labour law has been concerned with arrangements to redress inequality of bargaining power – not with rights to self-realisation at work.

In making sense of the evolution of IR policy and practice we draw on Fox's (1974) simple but profound insight that the labour contract is different from many others, because much of what is required to manage labour cannot be specified in contract. This leads to residual rights for employers to be able to manage, explicitly recognised in legal doctrines as the 'management prerogatives'. As Fox noted, while a free labour market was constructed around notions of 'freedom of contract' from the 18th century onwards, these notions of managerial prerogative preserved significant feudal privileges at the heart of modern-day capitalism because they carried over 'status' notions of relations between the parties beyond those specified in contract. Deakin and Wilkinson (2005) have taken Fox's argument further in the study of the evolution of labour law and labour market evolution in England. They show that a unified notion of the contract of employment only emerged with modern collective bargaining and the welfare state following the end of the Second World War.[1]

Fox has also noted that the balance between 'contract' and 'status' sources for governing relations at work are profoundly shaped by what he refers to as 'three frames of reference': the unitarist, the pluralist and the radical understanding of authority relations in the enterprise. Unitarists regard the firm or workplace as an organic, united entity controlled by owners who derive their authority from property relations. Contract is regarded as codifying 'common purpose' between the parties, not an outcome of 'bargaining'. Within the unitarist perspective, the role of the state is to defend the public interest and promote the assumed underlying harmony. Since workers' goals should be aligned with those of their employers, 'conflict and dissidence are regarded in pathological terms, as unnatural, aberrant and illegitimate' (Giles, 1989: 131). Traditionally the viewpoint favoured by political conservatives, the Australian example illustrates that it is also the natural starting point for a neoliberal agenda in IR.

The pluralist vision of the enterprise recognised that inequality of bargaining power across the labour market gives workers the right to form unions to redress it. Bargaining, primarily beyond the enterprise, ensures a fairer outcome than if individual workers had to bargain alone. As a matter of history, employers often recognised unions for the purposes of setting minimum standards across a sector, in return for unions explicitly recognising and respecting managerial prerogatives within the enterprise (Sisson, 1991; Wright, 1995). State power is directed towards establishing and enforcing a set of rules for the resolution of conflicts between competing groups (Giles, 1989: 136). As such, pluralists, and pluralist analysis, pay greater attention to rules than outcomes (Hyman, 1978). Although some pluralists would argue that the interventions of the state merely reflect the balance of power between two groups, there is an equally strong strain of pluralist thought that, for the IR system to work, it must be 'derived from the values [which] the nation judges and legitimises' (Flanders, 1965: 93). The radical frame of reference notes that inequality of power is pervasive and systemic and simply constituting unions does nothing to change this essential power imbalance. Fairness can only be achieved with a change in property relations – not tinkering with organisational rights within them.

Armed with these categories we can specify with some precision how values have shaped (or been embodied in) the evolution of IR policy. We do this in the Australian context in two parts. First, we examine the evolution of Australian IR policy for a century, from the late 19th century to the 1980s, within a predominant liberal collectivist framework. Second, we consider the period of rapid change in IR policy since the end of the Accord at the 1980s and the turn towards the neoliberal underpinning in the early 1990s.

The liberal collectivist foundations of IR policy in Australia

A distinctive Australian tradition of IR policy emerged in the late 19th century and early 20th century, in response to a prolonged period of disputes between employers and workers in agriculture, mining, and transport (Howe and Mitchell, 1999). Legislatures provided for the compulsory conciliation and arbitration of industrial disputes. Specialist tribunals were empowered to issue awards, which would set the terms and conditions of employment, to which named employers, employer associations, workers and their unions would be legally bound. Awards would generally cover a number of employers in the same industry or employing workers belonging to the same occupation. As a by-product of this system, industrial action was outlawed and unions' operations and governance of unions (and employer associations) became subject to oversight by the state.

Despite the novelty of the institutional framework and the emergence of an increasingly self-confident workers' movement at the time, compulsory arbitration and conciliation was entirely consistent with the liberal collectivist tradition then emerging in Australia (Macintyre, 1985) and the UK (Cutler, Williams and Williams, 1986). It was not predicated on any change in property relations and the bargain was commonly held to include acceptance of managerial prerogative in areas not otherwise dealt with in awards (Wright, 1995). It is therefore not surprising that its champions were the great Liberals of the Federation period, such as Isaac Isaacs and H.B. Higgins, rather than the first generation of Labor leaders.

Once adopted, compulsory conciliation and arbitration found fierce opposition from the Right, by employers (Plowman, 1989) and from the Left. Militant unions opposed the restrictions on industrial action (Gollan, 1975; Turner, 1979), the acceptance of managerial prerogative, and, in some cases, the solidaristic principle of comparative wage justice that kept industries in strongly organised industries and workplaces from outpacing weaker ones.

Following the Depression and the Second World War, the central role of arbitration became enmeshed within the framework of the Beveridge capitalist welfare state. In this period a broad consensus, including employers, acquiesced to a liberal collectivist notion of pluralist relations beyond the enterprise and respect of management prerogative within. Awards, which were the main method of establishing labour standards, operated in a universalistic fashion – linking all in the labour market. The setup provided security for workers and an ongoing institutional role for trade unions, and took wages out of competition for employers. Employer support for the system rested partly on the belief that the economic outcomes of arbitration varied little from what might have occurred under collective bargaining (Isaac, 2005: 2–3). Innovation was spurred by the dynamic links between the wages of the strong and weak through operation of collective bargaining, sector arbitration, national wage cases and 10 yearly productivity cases (Hughes, 1973; Fisher, 1983).

In the 1980s, following a turbulent period of recession, high inflation and high unemployment, the election of the Hawke Labor Government promised greater economic stability by coordinating an Accord between business and unions. The fundamentals of the Accord involved national wage bargaining buttressed by arbitration. Arguments around the need for wage restraint rested strongly on the macroeconomic justification of getting inflation under control. However, proponents of corporatism within the Government and the union movement also saw an opportunity for enhanced industrial democracy, greater rights for workers to be consulted around technology, change and redundancy (TCR) in the workplace, universal public health insurance (Medicare) and a stronger system of residualised social wages (including family assistance payments and expanded superannuation). Optimists from the labour movement saw in the Accord the potential vehicle to shift policy making towards a more social democratic model, something akin to a Scandinavia of the southern hemisphere, where unions were regarded as legitimate contributors to macroeconomic, industry and social policy as well as IR policy (Higgins, 1985; ACTU/TDCS, 1987).

However, the setting of national wage targets by political agreement between the parties weakened the role of arbitration. The agreement between the parties on the need for economic adjustment led to the Structural Efficiency Principle and the implicit endorsement of workplace negotiations around efficiency trade-offs. The Metal Trades Industry Association (MTIA) and the Australian Metal Workers Union (AMWU) led the call for more flexibility within the award system, as a means of accelerating the reform of award classifications and returning some of the productivity gains to workers as higher wages for the sector, which had been depressed as a result of wage restraint during the early years of the Accord. But beneath the policy changes that were under way during the 1980s, a fierce values debate was initiated by parts of the employer lobby and associated right-wing political groups. In 1989, the Business Council of Australia (BCA) was the first major employer association to break the liberal collectivist consensus with its commissioned report *Enterprise-based Bargaining Units: A Better Way of Working* (Hilmer et al, 1989). While the consensus between the MTIA and the AMWU around productivity-driven award restructuring provided political cover, it was the intervention of the BCA that would provide the neoliberal foundation for a radical recasting of Australian labour law.

1990s to present day: from liberal collectivism to neoliberalism

In its 1991 National Wage Case decision, the Industrial Relations Commission (IRC) rejected the submissions of the Government, the Australian Council of Trade Unions (ACTU) and most employer organisations to move away from centralised wage decisions and towards enterprise-level bargaining, claiming the parties were not sufficiently mature (Briggs and Buchanan, 2000). The furious response of all parties (including the Government) marked a decisive shift in values in IR policy towards a market inspired model of regulation. The Industrial Relations Reform Act 1993 reflected Prime Minister

Keating's commitment to a less regulated labour market (Keating, 1993). In his vision the workplace was conceived in isolated – but still pluralist – terms. By shifting the focus away from what workers had in common and instead embracing the classic liberal vision of the enterprise as an isolated unit of production, this legislation entrenched a neoliberal vision of labour and industry – a vision that underpins Australian labour law to this day.

The 1993 Act represented a radical departure from the Australian IR policy tradition up to that point, and laid the foundation for the three significant IR policy changes since then (the Workplace Relations Act 1996 and the Work Choices amendments in 2006 under the Howard Government, and the Fair Work Act 2009 under the Rudd–Gillard Labor Government). The primary objective of the 1993 Act was to shift bargaining from the industry to the enterprise level, and in so doing to weaken the role of the state (through industrial tribunals) and unions to influence the outcomes. The Act legitimated agreements between enterprises and their employees without the involvement of unions (the Enterprise Flexibility Agreements). It also introduced comprehensive unfair dismissal rights. Such initiatives marked a shift from a pluralist notion of labour law, where collectivities in civil society (namely unions and employer associations) were fostered to redress inequality of bargaining power. Instead, from 1993 the key social categories of interest were 'enterprises' for agreement making and 'individuals' newly empowered by antidiscrimination and unfair dismissal rights. At the core of this development has been the steady undermining of self-governing industrial organisations as the key players in setting and enforcing labour standards and the rise of enterprises and individuals directly reliant on the state as agencies for defining and enforcing fairness.

The Act had a dramatic impact on both policy and the behaviour of IR actors. From the 1990s onwards, we can observe a growing consensus from employers, both major political parties, and many unions on the enterprise as an island, independent of context and the site where gains in productivity and wealth are best achieved. The positive role of industry-wide bargaining to establish standards and spur innovation was forgotten, and the award and arbitration structure was left in place only as a residual structure to provide a safety net for those workers unfortunate enough not to share in the gains from enterprise bargaining. Instead, the enterprise was recognised as the most appropriate site for bargaining between employers and employees, and a series of legislative changes (the introduction of non-union Enterprise Flexibility Agreements (EFAs) in 1993, Australian

Workplace Agreements (AWAs) in 1996, and the transition from the arbitration and conciliation power to the corporations' power in 2006) have all emphasised the right of corporations to have a freer rein to pursue direct relations with their employees, while de-emphasising the fundamental disparity in bargaining power between employers and employees. The shift to enterprise bargaining also overwhelmed the resources of unions, reducing their members to economic units of the enterprise and severely diminishing the capacity of the union movement to influence IR policy, or economic, industry or social policy.

The prevailing legislative and policy framework does little to readjust the balance of power at the enterprise level. It might have been theoretically possible, and politically justifiable, to argue for a decentralised wage system, to promote productivity and reforms, but still insist on preserving and promoting collective bargaining and providing additional protections and rights of representation for workers. Such a system (which we could call 'enterprise pluralism') could not promote comparative wage justice between enterprises but would address disparities in bargaining power within them. This was certainly the rhetoric adopted by the Government, and the union movement, at the time. However, this was not the approach adopted by the Keating Government in 1993, which introduced non-union enterprise agreements for the first time. Subsequent changes to the IR legislative framework have continued to erode whatever protections for 'enterprise pluralism' did remain and the frontier of managerial prerogative continues to expand (Cooney, 2006; Peetz, 2006). Even where bargaining between employers and unions continued, employers found success in the courts and the Parliament in narrowly constructing the scope of what pertains to the employment relationship, restricting employees' rights to bargain over caps on casual and fixed-term employment, employment standards for contractors, union training, bargaining fees, and other matters.

The few iconic issues of policy disagreement that remain need to be understood in light of the broad swathe of uncontested values. In the federal sphere, statutory individual contracts first appeared as AWAs in the Workplace Relations Act 1996. Unions have remained opposed to them because they intentionally undermine the bargaining position of workers, not just for those participating in individual bargaining but also those workers who want to remain in collective bargaining. Research found that AWAs were not used to promote flexible working arrangements mutually beneficial to employer and employee, as the Act's authors claimed. Instead, template agreements were often used, resulting in identical AWAs and suggesting no real individual bargaining ever took place (Davis, 2007; Evesson et al, 2007). Wage outcomes for workers on AWAs were typically poorer than for similar employees on collective agreements, especially among women (Peetz and Preston, 2007). Following the 2006 Work Choices amendments, which decoupled AWAs from award conditions, research found widespread loss of penalty rates, loadings and allowances as well as control over working hours (Elton et al, 2007). Although Labor remained steadfast in its opposition to AWAs, it did include in its Fair Work legislation an Individual Transitional Employment Agreement (ITEA), as a concession to employers' demands for a statutory individual agreement. In the meantime, the principle of individual bargaining has a foothold in Australian workplaces, even those with collective agreements in place (van Wanrooy et al, 2007).

Another area of contest that remains is the scope of minimum labour standards and its relationship to other instruments. In order to pass the Workplace Relations Act in 1996, the Coalition were required to make a number of concessions to the Australian Democrats, who then held the balance of power in the Senate. The most important of these was the 'no disadvantage test', which was supposed to ensure that workers moving from an award to an AWA were not disadvantaged in terms of overall pay and conditions. The removal of the 'no disadvantage test' as part of the Work Choices amendments in 2006 prompted renewed interest in AWAs (and non-union collective agreements) from employers. Especially in the retail and hospitality industries, employers took advantage of the new arrangements to reduce costs by removing many conditions that remained in awards, including overtime and penalty rates and minimum shift lengths (Evesson et al, 2007). The latest guise of the 'no disadvantage test', the 'better off overall test' (BOOT) was reinstated by Labor in the Fair Work Act.

The scope and function of awards themselves remains another point of contest, but one in which Labor has ceded much more ground. The 1993 Act, while promoting enterprise bargaining, assumed that the role of awards would diminish over time. Howard's 1996 Workplace Relations Act took a more active approach to restricting the role of awards, limiting the content of awards to 20 allowable matters. In 2006, the Work Choices amendments went further again, removing even pay scales and classifications from awards and handing them over to the Australian Fair Pay Commission for determination. In its Fair Work Act, Labor retained the concept of a limited number of allowable award matters, essentially reverting to the requirements of the pre-2006 Workplace Relations Act. The Fair Work Act also gives the

Executive unprecedented influence over the determination of award contents, as it allows Ministers to issue the Commission with directives over how an award should be made and what factors it should take into consideration. So while the Coalition would prefer a system without any awards, Labor's commitment is to a system of modern awards, providing limited regulation of employment conditions (with the remainder set by managerial discretion) for a residual component of the workforce lacking the capacity to collectively bargain. To function effectively, however, a safety net of minimum standards requires an active inspectorate, an industrial climate where individual workers feel secure enough to raise objections, and a government with enough commitment to maintain minimum standards against international competition (Brown, 2005: 201).

Finally, there remains some contest between Labor and the Coalition over the institutional role of unions and the IRC (since 2012, the Fair Work Commission). In its Fair Work Act, Labor went part of the way to restoring some of the privileges of unions lost during the Howard Government, especially around right of entry. Work Choices was designed to sideline the role of the Commission, depriving it of its roles setting minimum wages and certifying collective agreements as well as removing its powers to make new awards and resolve disputes (except where both parties agreed). Labor restored the wage setting function and certification of agreements to the Commission, and has also moved to reinstate limited rights of the Commission to arbitrate disputes.

By the time Labor regained office in 2007, its response (Forward with Fairness and the Fair Work Act) adopted most of the framework put in place by the Howard Government. Labor values IR as a potent political issue and its institutional relationship with the trade union movement. Fundamentally, however, it remains comfortable with a labour market predominantly operating on neoliberal terms: labour as commodity and, by international standards, few collective rights and guarantees for labour. Consequently, Forward with Fairness may have addressed some of the more radical aspects of the Workplace Relations/Work Choices regime (abolishing formal individual agreements being the most prominent example) but not others (such as restoring the Commission's powers to settle disputes). Furthermore, all the fundamental changes of the 1993 Act remain. In the last 20 years, as the debate remained preoccupied with rules, rule setting, and formal rights of parties, policy has ignored and done nothing to address two serious long-term challenges for the Australian labour market: rising insecurity and a malfunctioning set of incentives for individuals and workplaces to invest in skills.

For more than a decade, the evidence has been accumulating that Australian employers are increasing their utilisation of labour through three trends: less secure employment relationships through casual employment; work intensification and a growth in the number of unpaid hours; and more flexibility in the range of tasks allocated to employees (Allan, O'Donnell, and Peetz, 1999; Watson, Buchanan, Campbell and Briggs, 2003). Casual employment, a distinctly Australian phenomenon, now comprises around quarter of the workforce, and their ranks are joined by growing numbers of 'independent contractors'. Unions have been unable to use enterprise bargaining to arrest this growth, estranging them from potential members. More broadly, all categories of Australian workers are being asked to assume a greater share of risk in managing their work, financial, family, education and health affairs (Rafferty and Yu, 2010) at the same time that they are capturing a declining share of the nation's wealth (Peetz, 2012).

In skills policy, the deterioration has been just as rapid, with developments in IR coalescing with neoliberal policies designed to create a market for training. During the transition out of the Accord, unions led by the AMWU saw value in working with employers to develop a new framework for skills and job classifications. However, the heavy focus on technical skills and the atomised nature of the competency-based training system that emerged served immediate employer objectives for a more functionally flexible workforce without providing workers with the career mobility that had been promised alongside it (Buchanan, Watson and Briggs, 2004: 199). The increase in nonstandard employment, contracting out and work intensification disturbed the balance in Australian workplaces between skills deployment and skills development (Buchanan and Jakubauskas, 2010). Employer policies to reduce the intake of apprentices and increase the utilisation of their existing workforce would rebound when ageing demographics and growing demand led to the claimed 'skill shortage crisis' of the mid 2000s (Richardson, 2009). The Government response – mainly an increase in subsidies for training to over $1.2 billion a year – has done nothing to resolve the underlying issue of how businesses can sustainably develop and deploy skills (McDowell, 2011). More recent developments, including the establishment of the Australian Workforce and Productivity Agency and the National Workforce Development Fund, are recognition of this, but these initiatives are largely disconnected from IR policy.

Conclusion

The turning point for IR policy in Australia occurred over 20 years ago, when a Labor Government abandoned a century-old regulated system of wage fixation and arbitration and conciliation to introduce a system built around enterprise bargaining. The Industrial Relations Reform Act 1993 reflects an underlying shift from a shared commitment to liberal collectivism to a more contested terrain of neoliberalism versus a restricted enterprise pluralism and residual safety net. Having accepted the centrality of enterprise bargaining, unions now find themselves in a perpetual argument to push back against unfettered management prerogative with an idea of enterprise pluralism. A system built around enterprise bargaining also requires a constant defence and justification of a comprehensive system of labour standards. Energy is expended by unions on maintaining current residual standards, with very limited means to extend or refashion standards or make a contribution on behalf of workers to other policy realms. For 20 years, Australian IR policy has pursued the neoliberal fantasy that labour is the same as any other commodity. The current challenges within the Australian labour market – especially the fragmentation of working arrangements and the transfer of risk to the worker on the supply side and the inability to reproduce the skills required on the labour demand side – are the unfortunate but predictable consequence.

Note

[1] In Australia the unified contract of employment emerged earlier due to arbitration (Howe and Mitchell, 1999). Before this time employment law was a blend of the old master and servant and contract law.

References

ACIRRT (1999) *Australia at Work*, Prentice Hall, Sydney

ACTU/Trade Development Council Secretariat (1987) *Australia Reconstructed*, AGPS, Canberra

Allan, C., O'Donnell, C. and Peetz, D. (1999) 'More tasks, less secure, working harder: Three dimensions of labour utilisation', *Journal of Industrial Relations*, 41(4): 519-535

Beirnacki, R. (1995) *The Fabrication of Labor: Germany and England, 1640–1914*, University of California Press, Berkeley

Briggs, C. and Buchanan, J. (2000) 'Australian labour market deregulation: A critical assessment', Department of the Parliamentary Library Research Paper, Canberra

Brown, W. (2005) 'Third party labour market intervention in open economies', in Isaac, J. & Lansbury, R. (eds) *Labour Market Deregulation: Rewriting the Rules*, Sydney: Federation Press, pp 191-203

Buchanan, J. & Jakubauskas, M. (2010) 'The Political Economy of Work and Skill in Australia: Insights from Recent Applied Research', in Bryson, J (ed) *Beyond Skills: Institutions, Organisations and Human Capability*, Basingstoke: Palgrave Macmillan, pp 32-57

Buchanan, J., Watson, I. and Briggs, C. (2004) 'Skill and the renewal of labour: The classical wage earner model and left productivism in Australia' in Warhurst, C., Grugulis, I. & Keep, E. *The Skills That Matter*, Basingstoke: Palgrave Macmillan, pp 186-206

Cooney, S. (2006) 'Command and control in the workplace: Agreement making under Work Choices', *Economic and Labour Relations Review*, 16(2), 147-62

Cutler, T., Williams, J. and Williams, K. (1986) *Keynes, Beveridge and Beyond*, London: Taylor and Francis

Davis, M. (2007) 'Revealed: how AWAs strip work rights', *Sydney Morning Herald*, April 17

Deakin, S. & Wilkinson, F. (2005) *The Law of the Labour Market: Industrialization, Employment, and Legal Evolution,* Oxford: Oxford University Press

Elton, J., Bailey, J., Baird, M., Charlesworth, S., Cooper R., Ellem B., Jefferson, T., MacDonald, F., Oliver, D., Pocock, B., Preston A. and Whitehouse, G. (2007) *Women and Work Choices: Impacts on the Low Pay Sector*, Adelaide: Centre for Work + Life, University of South Australia

Evesson, J., Buchanan, J., Bamberry, L., Frino, B. and Oliver, D. (2007) 'Lowering the Standards: From Awards to Work Choices in Retail and Hospitality Collective Agreements', report prepared for the New South Wales, Queensland and Victorian Governments. Available at: www.newtradeshall.com/ContentFiles/NewTradesHall/Documents/Lowering%20The%20Standards.pdf

Fisher, C. (1983) *Innovation and Australian Industrial Relations: Aspects of Arbitral Experience 1945– 980*, Canberra: Crom Helm

Flanders, A. (1965) *Industrial Relations: What is Wrong with the System?*, London: Faber

Fox, A. (1974) *Beyond Contract: Work, Power and Trust Relations.* London: Faber

Giles, A. (1989) 'Industrial relations theory, the state and politics', in Barbash, J. and Barbash, K. (eds) *Theories and concepts in comparative industrial relations*, Columbia SC: University of South Carolina Press, pp 123-154

Gollan, R. (1975) *Revolutionaries and Reformists. Communism and the Australian Labour Movement 1920–1955*, Richmond Publishing, Melbourne

Higgins, W. (1985) 'Political unionism and the Corporatist Thesis', *Economic and Industrial Democracy*, Vol 6b, No 3, pp 349 – 381

Hilmer, F., MacFarlane, D., Rose, J. and McLaughlan, P. (1989), *Enterprise-based Bargaining Units: A Better Way of Working*, Business Council of Australia

Howe, J. and Mitchell, R. (1999) 'The Evolution of the Contract of Employment in Australia', *Australian Journal of Labour Law*, 12(1): 113-30

Hughes, B. (1973) 'Wages of the strong and the weak', *Journal of Industrial Relations*, Vol 15, No 1, pp 1-24

Hyman, R. (1978) 'Pluralism, procedural consensus and collective bargaining', *British Journal of Industrial Relations*, 16(1): 16-40

Isaac, J. (2005) 'The deregulation of the Australian Labour Market', in Isaac, J. & Lansbury, R. (eds) *Labour Market Deregulation: Rewriting the Rules*, Sydney: Federation Press, pp 1-14

Keating, P. (1993) 'Speech to Australian Institute of Company Directors', 21 April

Macintyre, S. (1985) *Winners and Losers: The Pursuit of Social Justice in Australian History*, Allen and Unwin

McDowell, I. (Chair) (2011) *A Shared Responsibility: Apprenticeships for the 21st Century*, Final report of the Expert Panel prepared for the Australian Government, 31 January

Peetz, D. (2006) *Brave New Workplace: How Individual Contracts are Changing our Jobs*, Sydney: Allen and Unwin

Peetz, D. (2012) 'Does industrial relations policy affect productivity?', *Australian Bulletin of Labour*, 38(4), 268-292

Peetz, D. and Preston, A. (2007) *AWAs, Collective Agreements and Earnings: Beneath the Aggregate Data*, Report to Industrial Relations Victoria, Department of Innovation, Industry and Regional Development, Victoria, March

Plowman, D. (1989) *Holding the Line: Compulsory Arbitration and National Employer Coordination in Australia*, Cambridge University Press, Melbourne

Polanyi, K. (1944) *The Great Transformation*. New York: Farrar & Reinhart

Rafferty, M. and Yu, S. (2010) 'Shifting Risk Work and Working Life in Australia: A report for the Australian Council of Trade Unions', Workplace Research Centre, Sydney

Richardson, S. (2009) 'What is a skill shortage?', *Australian Bulletin of Labour*, 35(1), pp 326-54

Sisson, K. (1991) 'Employers and the structure of collective bargaining: Distinguishing cause from effect' in S Tolliday and J Zeitlin (eds) *The Power to Manage? Employers and Industrial Relations in Comparative-Historical Perspective*, Routledge, London, pp 256-72

Smith, A. (1930) *An Inquiry into the Nature and Causes of the Wealth of Nations*, 5th edn, Methuen & Co, London

Turner, I. (1979) *Industrial Labour And Politics: The Dynamics of the Labour Movement in Eastern Australia 1900–1921*, Hale and Iremonger (originally published 1965), Sydney

Van Wanrooy, B., Oxenbridge, S., Buchanan, J. & Jankubauskas, M. (2007) *Australia at Work: The Benchmark Report*, Sydney: Workplace Research Centre, University of Sydney

Watson, I., Buchanan, J., Campbell, I. and Briggs, C. (2003) *Fragmented Futures: New Challenges in Working Life*, Sydney: Allen and Unwin

Wright, C. (1995) *The Management of Labour: A History of Australian Employers*, Oxford: Oxford University Press

Part Three

CULTURE AND SOCIETY

SEVEN

Indigenous policy: Canberra consensus on a neoliberal project of improvement

Jon Altman

This chapter does four things. First it provides a brief history of Australian Indigenous policy in the modern era demarcated by the 1967 Constitutional Referendum. Next it looks at contemporary Indigenous policy – in particular, Closing the Gap strategies – and its unrelenting focus on a form of convergence and structural adjustment based on Western economic institutions and norms as measured by statistical indicators. Governments of all political persuasions favour such thinking. This particular form of governmentality justified by a neoliberal trope focused primarily on easily targeted and highly dependent segments of the Indigenous population living remotely is then outlined. Finally, alternatives better suited to diverse Indigenous circumstances and aspirations are articulated and defended.

A brief history of Indigenous policy

Indigenous affairs is a complex policy field because the Australian settler colonial state was largely built on a denial of Indigenous property rights or political and citizenship equality. It was only in the 1960s that Indigenous Australians became fully incorporated into the mainstream provisions of the Australian state and only in 1992 that the myth of *terra nullius* was legally buried by the Mabo High Court decision recognising native title at common law. Wolfe (2006) has theorised that Australian settler colonial society is predicated on a logic of elimination, the dissolution of native societies so as to gain access to territory. Thus settler colonisation is structural and ongoing – because both original settlers and later arrivals are here to stay; colonisation is not an historical event that can be limited to a particular time as in 1788, or particular place, like Sydney. Settler colonialism has negative and positive dimensions. Negatively, its forces strive for the dissolution of native societies. Positively, a new colonial society is created on the expropriated land base that members of native societies can eventually join as citizens if they meet certain criteria.

This possibility for integration was identified definitively over 50 years ago at what was called the Native Welfare Conference, where Indigenous policy was outlined in the following terms:

> The policy of assimilation means … that all aborigines and part-aborigines are expected eventually to attain the same manner of living as other Australians and to live as members of a single Australian community enjoying the same rights and privileges, accepting the same responsibilities, observing the same customs and influenced by the same beliefs, hopes and loyalties as other Australians. (Commonwealth of Australia, Parliamentary Debates [Hansard], House of Representatives, 20 April 1961, p 1051)

However, this approach was many things besides assimilationist: it was based on the then emerging modernisation paradigm and the view that progress was evolutionary.

By the 1970s assimilation was assessed as a failure and a new policy approach, 'self-determination', was adopted by the Whitlam Labor Government, elected with commitments to decolonisation and to dramatically enhance the Commonwealth's role in Indigenous affairs. The new government established a federal Department of Aboriginal Affairs in recognition of the still widespread neglect by mainstream service providers of Indigenous people, especially in rural and remote areas – where Indigenous people lived, and continue to live, disproportionately. And the widespread incorporation of Indigenous community organisations was encouraged to deliver services funded primarily from Indigenous-specific allocations that grew rapidly. Rowse (2002) has referred to these new institutions as 'the Indigenous sector'. This period also saw the passage of comprehensive land rights laws by the Commonwealth in the Northern Territory (which it administered) and the associated reoccupation of ancestral lands as a part of a homelands movement.

From 1972 a notable feature of policy practice in Commonwealth Indigenous affairs has been the high degree of similarity in the approaches of all governments; Indigenous policy delivered results albeit slowly according to social indicators reflecting the norms and values of the mainstream settler society (Table 7.1). However, the election of the Howard Coalition Government in 1996 with a 'For All of Us' platform saw the emergence of a concerted conservative critique

Table 7.1: Socioeconomic outcomes for Indigenous Australians, 1971–2011

Variable	1971	1981	1991	2001	2006	2011
Unemployment rate (% labour force)	9.0	24.6	30.8	20.0	15.6	17.1
Employment to population ratio (% adults)	42.0	35.7	37.1	41.7	46.0	44.2
Private sector employment (% adults)	29.7	17.2	20.5	n.a.	31.3	31.8
Labour force participation rate (% adults)	46.1	47.3	53.5	52.1	54.5	53.3
Median weekly personal income ($A2011)	n.a.	250	282	284	307	362
Household size	4.6	4.1	4.0	3.4	3.4	3.6
Median weekly household income ($A2011)	n.a.	903	872	1051	1235	1069
Home owner or purchasing (% population)	26.1	19.7	19.1	26.8	30.0	31.8
Never attended school (% adults)	22.7	10.7	5.1	3.2	2.7	1.8
Post-school qualification (% adults)	3.2	5.0	9.5	18.2	23.8	29.5
Degree or higher (% adults	n.a.	n.a.	n.a.	3.3	4.4	5.3
Attending educational institution (% 15–24 year olds)	n.a.	n.a.	n.a.	33.4	34.4	38.8
Population aged over 55 (%)	7.3	6.4	6..0	6.7	8.2	9.7

Note: 'n.a.' means that the data were not available in that year.

Source: ABS Census of Population and Housing 1971, 1981, 1991, 2001, 2006 and 2011

of the perceived lack of socioeconomic progress. In this context, the benefits of assimilation were re-emphasised. The Aboriginal and Torres Strait Islander Commission (ATSIC) – a unique Aboriginal organisation combining national and regional representation with administrative control of Indigenous-specific programmes totalling over one billion dollars – was dismantled from April 2004 with bipartisan support. A new mainstreaming approach sought to target Indigenous individuals rather than communities for advancement. This approach was driven in part by ascription to the neoliberal Thatcherite dictum that 'there is no such thing as society. There are individual men and women, and there are families'.

The Howard Government's assimilationist, mainstreaming approach was dramatically ramped up with the June 2007 announcement of a national emergency in remote Aboriginal communities in the Northern Territory. The impetus for this intervention was the latest of many reports outlining child sexual abuse in poverty-stricken and isolated communities. Deploying constitutional powers, Canberra was going to take over, using armed forces if necessary, to stabilise, normalise and then exit prescribed Aboriginal communities. A series of Northern Territory National Emergency Response laws targeted residents of prescribed communities with an unprecedented set of measures, including quarantining of welfare payments; enforced school attendance; compulsory takeover of land held 'inalienably' in fee simple; enhanced police powers; bans on alcohol, pornography and gambling readily available to other Australian citizens; and appointment of government business managers with supreme legally mandated authority (Hinkson, 2007). The Rudd Opposition supported these measures, which required the suspension of the Racial Discrimination Act.

The election of the Rudd Labor Government in 2007 saw some changes in Indigenous policy of a symbolic kind, but little in the way of practice. In February 2008, Prime Minister Rudd delivered a belated apology to Australia's Indigenous peoples in two parts. The first, very moving and compassionate, focused on the past, reflecting in particular on the mistreatment of those who were Stolen Generations – 'this blemished chapter in our nation's history' – and reminding Australia that such practice continued until the early 1970s. The Apology was widely acclaimed nationally and internationally. In switching from the symbolic to the practical, the second part of Rudd's speech moved to the generality of Indigenous Australians, and from the past to the present and future. Here the emphasis was on building a bridge between Indigenous and non-Indigenous Australians, a bridge based on a partnership to 'close the gap between Indigenous and non-Indigenous Australians in life expectancy, educational achievement and employment opportunities' (Rudd, 2008).

Such a convergence has a strong reference to assimilation. It assumes that adoption of Western economic institutions and norms will erase socioeconomic and health inequalities as measured by statistical social indicators that have been dominant in Indigenous policy thinking for 50 years. This view shapes the current paradigm in Indigenous policy variably termed the 'new' mainstreaming, integration, normalisation, and Closing the Gap.

The project of improvement

Since the Apology and the negotiation of a National Indigenous Reform Agreement (NIRA) between the Commonwealth and all States and Territories, the idea of Closing the Gap has become the dominant term shaping Indigenous policy. The term has become ubiquitous and is continually deployed to convey the national policy goal to reduce statistical disparities between Indigenous and other Australians (Council of Australian Governments, 2011). Arguably this has always been the aspirational goal of governments since five-yearly census data from 1971 allowed Indigenous people to be comprehensively identified. As information about disparities became available, government policy has sought to eliminate them. Closing the Gap has become so naturalised that critics of its questionable practical utility still need to engage with it or risk criticism of preferring disparity over equality. The now increasingly complex and convoluted assemblage of mainstream and Indigenous-specific programmes is conflated with an end point that will one day statistically describe outcomes in an imagined society with no statistical differences between Indigenous and other Australians.

The overarching goal to eliminate disparity is admirable in one of the world's richest countries, but just what it means in policy is difficult to determine. The definitional problem is partly a product of the late liberal state's obligations to Indigenous subjects both as citizens and as special citizens or First People – a notion that is gaining traction since Australia belatedly endorsed the United Nations Declaration on the Rights of Indigenous Peoples in April 2009. As citizens, Indigenous people should be able to access services on an equitable basis like other citizens. But as special citizens there have been a growing array of programmes over the past four decades that are Indigenous specific.

Compounding this problem of defining an Indigenous policy space are four features of the Indigenous population most recently documented in the 2011 Census: it is small, totalling an estimated 670,000 and constituting just 3% of the Australian population; it is far more geographically dispersed than the general population, with over 20% living in remote and very remote regions compared with less than 2% of the general population; a growing proportion (currently 50%) of partnered Indigenous Australians have a non-Indigenous partner, resulting in a high proportion of households of mixed ethnicity; and finally, less than 100,000 Indigenous people live in 1,200 discrete Indigenous communities, mainly in remote and very remote Australia, that are highly visible and the most materially impoverished (Figure 7.1).

The Closing the Gap paradigm does have some fundamental differences from early 'policy by numbers' attempts at convergence, of which Hawke's 1987 goal to achieve statistical equality in employment, education and income by the year 2000 and Howard's 1998 aspiration for practical reconciliation and a reduction in Indigenous disadvantage in health, housing, education and employment, are most notable. The Closing the Gap approach is far more technically precise in defining goals and time frames for achievement, although it also cleverly disguises the fact that four of its six goals are not about closing gaps (in the sense of eliminating them) but reducing them by 50%. Two others include the most difficult to achieve – life expectancy equality over

Figure 7.1: Indigenous lands, 2013, and discrete Indigenous communities, 2006

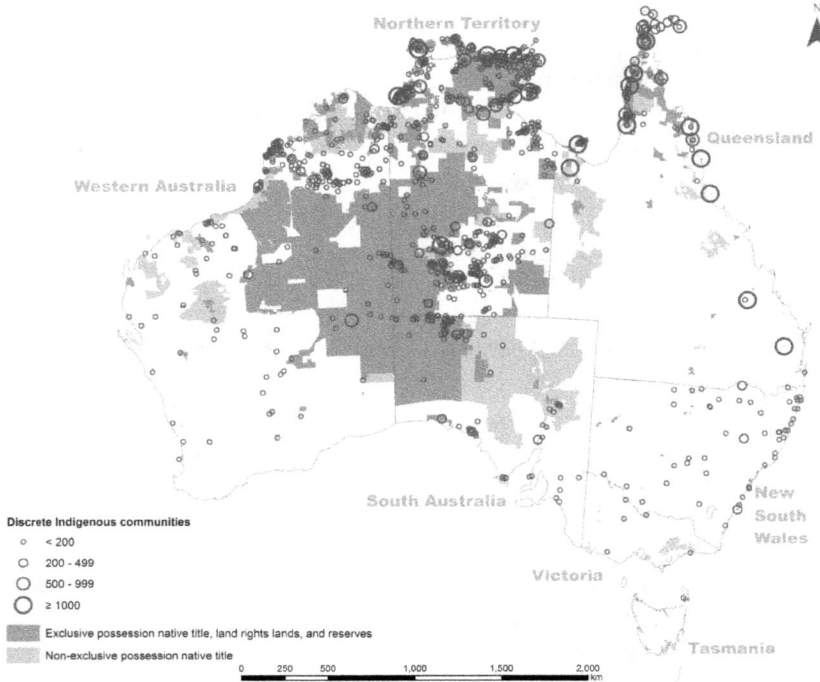

a loosely defined generation – and a goal focused very precisely on the access of four year olds to early childhood programmes, but only in remote communities and without a comparative non-Indigenous population.

In 2008 and 2009 the Rudd Government was able to lever bipartisan agreement on the Northern Territory Intervention to retain the narrative of emergency and to quickly implement unprecedented and enduring policy reform. This reform process was assisted in large measure by a political moment when there were coast-to-coast State Labor governments and a large national budget surplus available for commitment just before the Global Financial Crisis. Rudd orchestrated consensus within the Council of Australian Governments' (COAG) framework for an unprecedented intergovernmental approach in Indigenous policy to meet national statistical targets unilaterally set in Canberra. The elixir for this multi-year approach was a series of National Partnership Agreements, some of which extend for 10 years to 2018. Some of these have already been renewed, funded by a multi-billion dollar Commonwealth commitment.

The NIRA, as the foundation of current policy, was itself born of a particular trajectory of political convergence that has been labelled elsewhere 'the neoliberal turn' (Altman, 2010). Indigenous policy has always focused disproportionately on remote Australia, where need is perceived as greatest, although during the ATSIC years, 1990–2005, there was some attempt to redistribute Indigenous-specific funding on a more equitable nationwide basis. While economic rationalism and neoliberalism achieved greater policy influence in Australia from 1983 with the election of the Hawke Government with Paul Keating's dominant role as Treasurer, Indigenous policy retained a strong social democratic ethos born of recognition that politicostructural factors like historical neglect, cultural difference, discrimination and different demographics required a more nuanced approach. During an era when the idea of 'self-determination' was prevalent, there was what Sutton (2009) has termed a form of liberal consensus that alongside mainstream programmes there would also be a suite of Indigenous-specific programmes; this mixed approach retaining a social democratic inflection persisted longer for Indigenous than other Australians.

A variety of binary frames have been deployed to explain the recent history of Indigenous policy. Altman and Rowse (2005) identify approaches that focus on equality of outcomes favoured by economists who see socioeconomic differences as deficits and those favoured by anthropologists that focus on equity and choices to live differently as assets. Austin-Broos (2011) differentiates between those she identifies as separatists who see a strong role for Indigenous-specific approaches and anti-separatists who favour undifferentiated mainstreaming. And Rowse (2012) identifies approaches that focus on 'populations', where statistics might be deployed to assess relative socioeconomic status, and those that emphasise 'peoples', where issues of social justice and Indigenous rights might take priority. Each of these binaries can be understood as depicting a tension between policy approaches that emphasise self-determination and an accommodation of cultural differences and those that emphasise sameness and a requirement for fundamental sharing of Western norms; each interprets policy shifting from a weighting in favour of one or the other over time.

Sanders (2009) on the other hand traces dominant debates in Indigenous policy since the 1930s using a more complex framework that identifies three competing principles – equality, choice and guardianship – and a fourfold categorisation of left and right ideological tendencies – economically directive or liberal and socially directive or liberal – that interact with these principles. Sanders deploys his framework to explain cyclical aspects of change in Australian Indigenous policy.

In the view of this author a neoliberal framework better explains the forces shaping current policy, even if neoliberalism is a contested term with many manifestations. Harvey (2007) defines neoliberalism as a theory of political economic practice proposing that human wellbeing can be advanced by the maximisation of entrepreneurial freedoms within a state enabled institutional framework characterised by individualism, private property and unencumbered (free) markets. Harvey also focuses on neoliberalism as a class project redistributing wealth from labour to capital, from poor to rich. Wacquant (2012) focuses on neoliberalism as a political project. Neoliberal governmentality is the art of shaping populations and the self to conform to the free market, even if the free market might be miniscule or nonexistent, as in much of remote Australia: its institutional core consists of an articulation of the relationship between the state, the market and citizenship, harnessing the first to stamp the second on the third. Wacquant's framework of liberty for those at the top; punitive paternalism for those at the bottom; idleness as a perceived social problem for the 'unworthy unemployed'; ethnic disciplining and the communicative mission of projecting asserted sovereignty into previously undergoverned geographic regions, resonates strongly with what the state is looking to implement in remote Indigenous Australia. Wiegratz (2010) argues that the neoliberal development project is principally about the cultural conditioning of individuals. The goal of neoliberal states is to delegitimise and displace pre-existing norms, values, orientations and practices to ensure market society everywhere and so reshape existing moral economies with new norms and social institutions like individualism, self-interest, choice, wealth accumulation, and new forms of consumption.

Each of these forms, economic, political, cultural, has relevance in this context even if there might be debate over which has primacy, and whether governmentality is a means to an end or an end in itself (see Mark Davis, this volume). What is interesting to explore is what set of circumstances saw the hegemonic and belated infiltration of such an approach into Indigenous policy, a shifting from macroeconomic privatisation and deregulation, more market and less state, to the microeconomic and biopolitical focus on the Indigenous family and the individual (Lattas and Morris, 2010) and the attempts to marketise the delivery of services to remote living Indigenous communities.

Part of the answer is that neoliberal solutions to all perceived problems have been popular in Canberra since the 1980s, but it took the political ascendancy of the Howard Government, especially when it controlled both houses of the Australian Parliament from 2005, to extend them to Indigenous policy. Post-Intervention, a development approach for remote Australia has been in vogue that resonates with elements of the Washington Consensus – generally understood as a development approach for the Third World based on market fundamentalism favoured by powerful international financial institutions in the late 20th century – alongside social policy and welfare reform proposals to embed neoliberal values in remote living Indigenous subjects via a range of paternalistic measures.

What is termed by this author allegorically as 'the Canberra consensus' is not just a political bipartisanship given moral authority by some influential Indigenous spokespeople. It is also a consensus between political classes and dominant actors in the bureaucratic field, some of whom, like Peter Boxall (2012), who defined himself as an unabashed rationalist, were trained in Chicago School Economics. There is a now dominant view that Australia's long boom is linked to the rationality of modern Australian individuals, *homo economicus,* and to economic liberalism. Key actors are asking why such national success cannot be converted domestically to Australia's marginalised Indigenous populations so that they could share in Australia's boom from exported mineral commodities often extracted from Indigenous lands – if only they just adopted Western norms and institutions. Such views have been lent strong support by neoconservative think-tanks like the Centre for Independent Studies, and its prolific and highly influential senior fellow the late Helen Hughes, who had worked at the World Bank during its Washington Consensus heyday. Common themes among these 'unabashed rationalists', who all have direct access to political and bureaucratic elites, are the need for land individualisation and privatisation, enhanced investments in education to produce competitive human capital, welfare and labour market reforms, and the introduction of private housing on land held under common property regimes.

Simultaneously there has been an emerging view that Aboriginal culture was maladapted to late modernity and created a socially destructive cocktail when mixed with equitable access to social security. Influential Aboriginal activist and lawyer Noel Pearson (2000) most dramatically and evocatively highlighted the cost of welfare entrapment in Cape York communities in his treatise *Our Right to Take Responsibility*. With rhetorical flourish he catapulted terms like 'welfare poison', the 'gammon welfare economy' and the 'real economy' into public debate and policy discourse. And so he set about developing a comprehensive regional project, the Cape York Welfare Reform Trials, to restore norms, manage alcohol, enhance education and get people into real jobs. Pearson (2009) has quite explicitly sought to find a 'radical centre' where Aboriginal people could simultaneously engage with the real economy while morally restructuring what he identifies as dysfunctional social norms resulting from excessive welfare dependency, or 'welfare poison', and unrestricted access to alcohol. In doing so he has opportunistically engaged with neoliberal perspectives and has strategically aligned with dominant views in Canberra and so has managed to garner significant support for his vision for Cape York.

It has been a mix of politics, ideology and cultural critique that has driven the current policy project to neoliberalise geographically remote Aboriginal people so as to free them from a relational ontology that emphasises commitment to family and kin, ties to place, and obligations in ceremony. This is a culturalist project to 'creatively destroy' (to use Schumpeter's (1942) popularisation of Karl Marx's evocative term) existing institutions in the name of the individual and capitalist progress and replace them with Western ways – in other words, to inculcate new ways of schooling, working, spending, investing and home owning, the very values promulgated explicitly in NIRA.

The politics of delivery/non-delivery

Current Indigenous policy can thus be represented as combining the enduring goal of convergence with a new style neoliberal trope focused on individual responsibility alongside enhanced public spending that is closely monitored and constantly evaluated by new public sector management techniques. In making this representation, it is not suggested that it is uncontested. As Cris Shore (2011: 128) reminds us, the modern state is rarely a unified, homogeneous or monolithic actor. As has been noted elsewhere (Altman, 2010), deploying the Bourdieusian perspectives of Wacquant (2007), the bureaucratic field is fractured and unstable. And so while social democratic notions of justice and equity endure, they are today in a subordinate position in the power/knowledge discursive and policy struggles.

In the past it has been very difficult to assess the effectiveness of policy. But to some extent this has changed in recent years with the NIRA and extraordinary expenditures in the collection of statistics and the establishment of numerous new institutions for monitoring. Arguably, Indigenous policy in the 21st century has taken the notion of audit culture to unprecedented levels in Australian public policy

(Sullivan, 2011). Just as one example, a recently completed survey of the Northern Territory National Emergency Response Intervention evaluations between 2007 and 2012 enumerated 98 reports, and this did not include seven parliamentary inquiries and literally hundreds of submissions, much academic research and many evaluations undertaken at the subnational level (Altman and Russell, 2012).

This is not the place to undertake a systematic review of all the evaluations. However, the glossy 150-page *Closing the Gap Prime Minister's Report 2013* (Australian Government, 2013) indicates that it fails to provide evidence that gaps are closing in accord with the straight line trajectories made in NIRA in 2009 (COAG, 2011), irrespective of whether such abstract statistics have anything to do with improving people's lives. Similarly, the Productivity Commission in its latest *Overcoming Indigenous Disadvantage Key Indicators 2011* weighty report made the following summary statement:

> Across virtually all the indicators ... there are wide gaps in outcomes between Indigenous and other Australians ... in a few areas, the gaps are narrowing ... many indicators show that outcomes are not improving, or are even deteriorating. There is still a considerable way to go to achieve COAG's commitment to close the gap in Indigenous disadvantage (Productivity Commission, 2011: 4).

Suffice to say that there is no serious proposition in any government report as to when gaps might close, especially those that are diverging rather than converging. Nor is there analysis of whether the significant financial quantum committed by governments is sufficient, or whether it is hitting targets of need or merely propping up a complex administrative architecture. Most of the media spin focuses instead on the dollar expenditures and inputs, and where outcomes are reported this is usually for absolute improvements (Table 7.1), which are important, rather than relative improvement (Table 7.2), which is what gap closing is about. A few summary statistics are presented here, with the proviso that this author is increasingly sceptical about their utility because they turn people into numbers divorced from their social and cultural contexts, and all too often fail to recognise that these numbers are actually people demeaned by talk of gaps and deficiencies.

In Tables 7.1 and 7.2, information is provided on statistical disparities across a range of variables from 1971 to 2011. While some trends are in the right direction, there is little evidence that the period 2006 to 2011 – a best available proxy for the post-Apology period – is superior

Table 7.2: Ratio of Indigenous to non-Indigenous socioeconomic outcomes, 1971–2011

Variable	1971	1981	1991	2001	2006	2011
Unemployment rate (% labour force)	5.63	4.24	2.70	2.78	3.06	3.17
Employment to population ratio (% adults)	0.73	0.61	0.66	0.71	0.75	0.71
Private sector employment (% adults)	0.65	0.42	0.51	n.a.	0.61	0.62
Labour force participation rate (% adults)	0.78	0.77	0.84	0.82	0.84	0.81
Median weekly personal income ($A2011)	n.a.	0.55	0.62	0.56	0.58	0.62
Household size	1.35	1.32	1.3	1.31	1.31	1.32
Median weekly household income ($A2011)	n.a.	0.72	0.77	0.78	0.78	0.69
Home owner or purchasing (% population)	0.37	0.27	0.27	0.37	0.41	0.45
Never attended school (% adults)	37.83	15.29	5.10	3.20	3.00	2.00
Post-school qualification (% adults)	0.14	0.18	0.29	0.44	0.52	0.49
Degree or higher (% adults)	n.a.	n.a.	n.a.	0.23	0.24	0.24
Attending educational institution (% 15–24 year olds)	n.a.	n.a.	n.a.	0.61	0.62	0.67
Population aged over 55 (%)	0.43	0.34	0.32	0.31	0.33	0.37

Note: 'n.a.' means that the data were not available in that year.

Source: ABS Census of Population and Housing 1971, 1981, 1991, 2001, 2006 and 2011

to earlier intercensal periods. This is something that was predicted in 2008 using 1971 to 2006 trend analysis even as the Closing the Gap targets were announced (Altman, Biddle and Hunter, 2008). But the observation that prospects for convergence based on past trends will take a very long time, 100 years plus, went unheeded. The national Closing the Gap approach appears to be poorly designed to address the needs and aspirations of Indigenous Australians living across a diversity of circumstances, ranging north to south, from inner Sydney to remote Arnhem Land, or east to west, from Brisbane to the Pilbara. In so far as policy should be addressing a complex 'wicked' development problem such a critique is hardly surprising; it replicates that made of the Washington Consensus by numerous commentators (Stiglitz, 2002).

The current policy paradigm can be seen benignly as an attempt to address the unintended consequences of the belated incorporation of Indigenous Australians into the mainstream provisions of the welfare state. There is no question that Indigenous people are highly dependent on welfare and that intergenerational inactivity is socially corrosive. But the policy response to this is to seek to change the norms and values of welfare beneficiaries rather than the form of welfare institutions designed for an earlier Keynesian–Fordist economic system in urban Australia. These institutions are most destructive in remote Australia because capitalist economy is most absent there and yet it is here that the greatest effort is being made to alter persistent noncapitalist norms, values, orientations and practices. This project of moral restructuring and socioeconomic improvement is mainly targeting the 1,200 discrete Indigenous communities in remote Australia and mainly located on Aboriginal-owned lands (Figure 7.1). The state is deploying the powerful metaphor of Closing the Gap as a development framework for these places, promising to deliver a gap-free existence, a quest for equality that sounds like common sense, Indigenous people should share in the national wealth; it is just that they will need to be a new and different kind of citizen adopting Western neoliberal norms.

This project appears to be destined to fail owing to profound policy incoherence, as illustrated in the following three examples. First, this project is a geographic paradox. It is increasingly targeting remote discrete Indigenous communities because these communities are the poorest; they can also be targeted because of their 'discreteness' in marked contrast to Indigenous people residing in urban situations. However, remote places are also the most difficult situations in which to address socioeconomic disparities, and there is little in policy that provides either guidance or assistance about what form economic development might take to reduce dependence on government and welfare, and certainly no exploration of alternate approaches that might promote livelihoods. The NIRA is focusing most effort on the less than 25% of the Indigenous population where gaps are least likely to close, while focusing too little on the other 75% of the population where gaps are also clearly evident.

Second, there is the paradox of cultural norms. Since the 1970s, under first land rights and then native title laws, traditional owners have been able to claim back their land if they can prove continuity of customs and traditions and physical connection to their lands since settler colonisation. In Figure 7.1 the continental extent of Indigenous lands is shown – over 30% is now held under exclusive or nonexclusive (shared) possession. The paradox is that having had their claims recognised, Indigenous landowners are expected to engage in the capitalist economy, including as fly in/fly out or drive in/drive out workers in nearby mines that they might have opposed on cultural and environmental grounds. There is a fundamental mismatch of frames here between the aspirations of many landowners to reclaim and live on their land and policy dogma to use the land to close gaps.

Third, there is an emerging view that the Government's top down and paternalistic approach focused on deficits is not working, although the Canberra consensus is far from broken on this. This critical view is emerging from Indigenous communities, organisations and regions, some of whom, like the Noongar Nation in Western Australia, are negotiating their own forms of self-government. State governments, too, like New South Wales (NSW), are developing policy frameworks that emphasise assets and partnership rather than deficits. There are also agencies within the bureaucratic field that seek to empower regions with alternate development opportunities based on land occupation and management that undermine the dominant project to close statistical gaps. Finally, new institutions like the Closing the Gap Clearing House are advising the Government that a fundamentally different consultative set of approaches would be more productive in addressing the diversity of Indigenous circumstances.

Indigenous Australians as special citizens

This chapter began by asking how Indigenous Australians might be treated as Australian citizens, gaining access in an equitable way to the mainstream provisions of the Australian state, while at the same time being treated differently, as a First Peoples with special needs born of cultural difference and diversity and of historical trauma, marginalisation and neglect. In the present there is a dominant view that there needs to be a fundamental shift from a focus on structural rights as citizens to one on agency and individual responsibility without adequate analysis of whether entitlements are being equitably delivered. Arguably, late liberal democracy combined with particular forms of fiscal federalism deliver poor outcomes for marginalised groups in Australian society. Indigenous Australians face a triple jeopardy: they constitute a small, dispersed and highly fragmented population and so lack effective political representation; there is an absence of recognition in the broader society of the different norms that might inform Indigenous aspirations; and a form of national blindness to the damage wrought by historical legacy persists, resulting in an absence of just redistribution. These three issues, recognition, redistribution and representation, conform to Fraser's (2009) holistic 'scales of justice' framework.

Australia's policy response in the 21st century has shifted to deploy a mix of reconstituted colonial paternalism and 'neoliberal' market mentalities in an attempt to recolonise Aboriginal spaces and promulgate a new project of improvement. At once the Indigenous problem is seen as requiring welfare reform and enhanced market engagement alongside a need to address past neglect and to recalibrate norms and values. Even according to the normative criteria of the dominant paradigm this approach is failing to deliver adequate results. This is especially the case for remote-living people for whom a pathway to integration is being charted by distant political and bureaucratic players via imagined wealth creation and accumulation. These 'untrustworthy trustees', to use Tania Murray Li's (2007) terminology, who always promise and rarely deliver, seek to render deep development problems technical, choosing to turn a blind eye to past and present failures as the ideological rationales for improvement schemes become entangled with the real world (Ferguson, 1994). What is being observed can be interpreted as a messy political struggle to reshape norms and values away from the perceived failed communal or community fix to the market fix, except that no-one in power really seems to know what the market fix might look like and what people might actually do for livelihoods. Instead we see continuing ideological promotion of what Wiegratz (2010) calls 'fake capitalism' or 'pseudo development' – an imagined 'real' economy.

What alternative visions for development might be reasonably put forward? Three possibilities are canvassed here. First, James Ferguson (2009: 183), researching in Africa and drawing on the metaphor of *bricolage*, 'a piecing together of something new out of scavenged parts originally intended for some other purpose', suggests that governmental techniques can be repurposed or refigured to serve local livelihood and political projects. After all, much neoliberal discourse promotes the view that individuals should be allowed to make their own choices. Such choices that are not contingent on forgoing citizenship entitlements could prove productive.

Second, linking such options to mainstream social democratic institutions will require the activation or re-activation of local and regional Indigenous political activism to challenge destructive forms of state or corporate economisms which local practice in many situations continues to resist and subvert (Scott, 2009). This is not something that will happen everywhere, but policy needs to be structured so as to empower local communities to mould forms of hybrid economy that recognise distinct norms and values that matter to them. Hybrid economy theory recognises that where custom has to be legally proven it usually exists and that everything in the production, distribution and consumption realms is intermingled with the customary. The hybrid economy project advocates for development thinking beyond the market/customary (or any other) binary. Rather, it encompasses articulations between interdependent market, state and customary sectors while recognising tensions as well as accommodations between capitalist and noncapitalist values and norms (Altman, 2010).

Third, Indigenous interests must discursively engage with the dominant paradigm of Closing the Gap to highlight its shortcomings and advocate for alternatives. Indigenous political institutions like the National Congress of Australia's First Peoples could play an important role here championing principles of self-determination and social justice as outlined in the United Nations Declaration on the Rights of Indigenous Peoples. As Fraser (2009) highlights, issues of social justice are not just played out within nation states, but increasingly need to defer to higher supranational power, or 'inter-mestic' politics. Such linkages might provide productive avenues for Indigenous actors who want to advocate for a different policy approach.

In *Envisioning Real Utopias* Erik Olin Wright (2010) notes that the adverse impacts of late capitalism are well documented and yet in Australia the Closing the Gap paradigm is only looking to integrate Indigenous people into late market capitalism as if there is no alternative. It is questionable if such a risky strategy is warranted at a time of post-Fordist uncertainty and when there is a growing national dependence on Aboriginal lands for mineral extraction and biodiversity conservation. It is possible, of course, that relative gaps between Indigenous and other Australians will be closed as much by mainstream decline as by Indigenous socioeconomic improvement. Surely such possibility requires responsible policy to canvass alternatives to the currently fashionable one-size-fits-all Canberra consensus?

Acknowledgements
I would like to thank Francis Markham for his comments and for producing Figure 7.1; Nicholas Biddle for compiling Tables 7.1 and 7.2 from Australian Bureau of Statistics (ABS) material; and Melinda Hinkson, Lionel Orchard, Chris Miller and various book authors for constructive feedback.

References
Altman, J.C. (2010) 'What future for remote Indigenous Australia?: Economic hybridity and the neoliberal turn', in J.C. Altman and M. Hinkson (eds) *Culture Crisis: Anthropology and politics in Aboriginal Australia*, Sydney: UNSW Press, pp 259–280

Altman, J.C., Biddle, N. and Hunter, B. (2008) 'How realistic are the prospects for Closing the Gaps in socio-economic outcomes for Indigenous Australians?' *CAEPR Discussion Paper 287. Available at:* http://caepr.anu.edu.au/sites/default/files/Publications/DP/2008_DP287.pdf.

Altman, J.C. and Rowse, T. (2005) 'Indigenous affairs', in P. Saunders and J. Walter (eds) *Ideas and Influence: Social science and public policy in Australia*, Sydney: UNSW Press, pp 159–77

Altman, J.C. and Russell, S. (2012) 'Too Much "Dreaming": Evaluations of the Northern Territory National Emergency Response Intervention 2007–2012', *Evidence Base*, Issue 3. Available at http://journal.anzsog.edu.au/userfiles/files/2012Issue3Final.pdf.

Austin-Broos, D. (2011) *A Different Inequality: The Politics of Debate about Remote Aboriginal Australia*, Sydney: Allen & Unwin

Australian Government (2013) *Closing the Gap, Prime Minister'sReport 2013*. Available at: www.fahcsia.gov.au/sites/default/files/documents/02_2013/00313-ctg-report_fa1.pdf.

Boxall, P. (2012) Reflections of an 'unabashed rationalist', in J. Wanna, S. Vincent and A. Podger (eds) *With the Benefit of Hindsight: Valedictory Reflections from Departmental Secretaries, 2004–2011*, Canberra: ANU E Press, pp 107–116

Council of Australian Governments (2011) National Indigenous Reform Agreement (Closing the Gap), Revised February 2011. Available at: www.federalfinancialrelations.gov.au/content/npa/health_indigenous/indigenous-reform/national-agreement_sept_12.pdf

Ferguson, J. (1994) *The Anti-Politics Machine: 'Development', Depoliticization and Bureaucratic Power in Lesotho*, Minneapolis: University of Minnesota Press

Ferguson, J. (2009) 'The uses of neoliberalism', *Antipode* vol 41, pp 166–184

Fraser, N. (2009) *Scales of Justice: Reimagining Political Space in a Globalizing World*, New York: Columbia University Press

Harvey, D. (2007) 'Neoliberalism as creative destruction', *The ANNALS of the American Academy of Political and Social Science*, vol 610, no 1, pp 22–44

Hinkson, M. (2007) 'Introduction: In the name of the child', in J.C. Altman and M. Hinkson (eds) *Coercive Reconciliation: Stabilise, Normalise, Exit Aboriginal Australia*, Melbourne: Arena Publications, pp 1–12

Lattas, A. and Morris, B. (2010) 'The politics of suffering and the politics of anthropology', in J.C. Altman and M. Hinkson (eds) *Culture Crisis: Anthropology and Politics in Aboriginal Australia*, Sydney: UNSW Press, pp 61–87

Li, T.M. (2007) *The Will to Improve: Governmentality, development and the practice of politics*, Durham: Duke University Press

Pearson, N. (2000) *Our Right to Take Responsibility*, Cairns: Noel Pearson and Associates

Pearson, N. (2009) *Up from the Mission: Selected Writings*, Melbourne: Black Inc.

Productivity Commission (2011) *Overcoming Indigenous Disadvantage: Key Indicators 2011*, Canberra: Productivity Commission

Rowse, T. (2002) *Indigenous futures: Choice and Development for Aboriginal and Islander Australia*, Sydney: UNSW Press

Rowse, T. (2012) *Rethinking social Justice: From 'Peoples' to 'Populations'*, Canberra: Aboriginal Studies Press

Rudd, K. (2008) Apology to Australia's Indigenous peoples, Prime Minister's speech, 13 April. Available at: www.dfat.gov.au/indigenous/apology-to-stolen-generations/rudd_speech.html.

Sanders, W. (2009) 'Ideology, evidence and competing principles in Australian Indigenous affairs: From Brough to Rudd via Pearson and the NTER', *CAEPR Discussion Paper 289*. Available at: caepr.anu.edu.au/sites/default/files/Publications/DP/2009_DP289.pdf.

Schumpeter, J.A. (1942) *Capitalism, Socialism and Democracy*, New York: Harper and Brothers

Scott, J.C. (2009) *The art of not being governed: An anarchist history of upland South-east Asia*, New Haven: Yale University Press

Shore, C. (2011) 'Introduction: Policy as a window onto the modern state', in C. Shore, S. Wright and D. Però (eds), *Policy Worlds: Anthropology and the Analysis of Contemporary Power*, Oxford: Berghahn, pp 125–129

Stiglitz, J.E. (2002) *Globalization and its Discontents*, New York: W.W. Norton

Sullivan, P. (2011) *Belong Together: Dealing with the Politics of Disenchantment in Australian Policy*, Canberra: Aboriginal Studies Press

Sutton, P. (2009) *The Politics of Suffering: Indigenous Australia and the End of the Liberal Consensus*, Melbourne: Melbourne University Press

Wacquant, L. (2007) *Punishing the Poor: The neoliberal government of social insecurity*, Durham: Duke University Press

Wacquant, L. (2012) 'Three steps to a historical anthropology of actually existing neoliberalism', *Social Anthropology*, vol 20, no 1, pp 66–70

Wiegratz, J. (2010) 'Fake capitalism? The dynamics of neoliberal moral restructuring and pseudo-development: the case of Uganda', *Review of African Political Economy*, vol 37, no 124, pp 123–37

Wolfe, P. (2006) 'Settler colonialism and the elimination of the native', *Journal of Genocidal Research*, vol 8 no 4, pp 387–409

Wright, E.O. (2010) *Envisioning Real Utopias*, London: Verso

EIGHT

Culture and diversity

George Crowder

According to one leading writer, 'we are all multiculturalists now' (Glazer, 1997). This claim would be warmly endorsed by many Australians but hotly disputed by many others.[1] It would be fair to say that most Australians acknowledge that they live in a 'multicultural' society – that is, a society that does in fact contain a diversity of cultures. But whether that fact is something to be celebrated and encouraged as a matter of public policy – whether, that is, Australia should embrace multicultural*ism* – is a much more contentious question. Along with countries such as Canada, the United Kingdom, the Netherlands and New Zealand, Australia has historically been a leader in the field of multiculturalist policy – although one should note immediately that the background and actual experience of multiculturalist policy has varied considerably among these different countries. But criticism has intensified over the years since the policy's beginnings in the 1970s, to the extent that many observers now claim that in Australia, as elsewhere, multiculturalism is in retreat (Joppke, 2004).[2]

However, this picture of decline should not be exaggerated. For one thing, Australian multiculturalism still has vigorous defenders, such as the former Minister of Immigration, Chris Bowen (Bowen, 2011). Moreover, even if support for multiculturalism has declined since its inception, the decline may not be as steep as is sometimes claimed. As Geoffrey Levey writes, 'if we are witnessing a retreat from "multiculturalism", it appears to be a measured one' (Levey, 2008: 19). Undeniably, opinions are now more divided than they were in the 1970s and 1980s, or perhaps it would be truer to say that the opposition to multiculturalism is more insistent and articulate now than it was then. However, at time of writing multiculturalism remains the official policy of Australia, although there is no longer a federal Minister of Multicultural Affairs.[3] Perhaps the rhetoric has changed more than the actual policies.

In this chapter I consider the arguments for and against multiculturalism, with special reference to Australia, leaning ultimately towards a qualified defence. I begin by trying to answer some salient issues of definition. This leads me, in the second section, to examine some questions of philosophical justification. How multiculturalism is justified will, again, determine what kind of multiculturalism we are talking about. At this point I shall be in a position to consider a selection of standard objections to multiculturalism, the topic of the third section.

What is multiculturalism?

Might it be that at least some of the prevalent disagreement over multiculturalism stems from confusion over what the term means? As Geoff Levey writes, 'it is striking how much of the criticism focuses on the word and its perceived connotations, rather than on the various policies of minority inclusion and equal opportunity for which the word stands in the Australian context' (Levey, 2008: 19). One gets the strong sense that the 'multiculturalism' that some critics attack is only the most radical and least defensible version. Similarly, some supporters insist on describing as central to multiculturalism positions that are at best one form among others.

First, is Australian multiculturalism a description of existing patterns of diversity or a prescription for change? Brian Galligan and Winsome Roberts have argued that Australian multiculturalism is 'a conceptual muddle' between the two (Galligan and Roberts, 2004: 96). The policy is sometimes justified as merely reflecting contemporary realities. To this Galligan and Roberts reply that in the Australian context multiculturalist claims of existing cultural distinctions are exaggerated, the truth being that immigrants integrate rapidly into a common Australian identity. Full-blown multiculturalism goes beyond mere description, a role it plays poorly, and it really presents a vision of something quite different from what we have.

On the other hand, Galligan and Roberts continue, the prescription itself is confused. The Australian policy began as a way of integrating new migrants more effectively but ended by emphasising the separateness of their cultural backgrounds. These are very different goals, and they deserve very different assessments. In its integrationist form multiculturalism should be hailed 'as a humane policy for accommodating migrants from non-English speaking backgrounds, and also as a cultural policy for enhancing the richness and variety of Australian life' (Galligan and Roberts, 2004: 75). But as a vision of a new form of national identity, dwelling on differences rather than similarities, multiculturalism 'has been used to hollow out what it means to be and to become an Australian citizen, depriving citizenship of its cultural base in a distinctive Australian nationality' (Galligan and Roberts, 2004: 80). Reduced to a set of abstract liberal-democratic principles, citizenship loses its power to win and retain people's visceral allegiance. Instead we have multiculturalism, which 'includes everyone but engages no one'.

Finally, there is ambiguity at a more philosophical level – that of approaches to justification. Galligan and Roberts do not pick this up, but they hint at it when they describe multiculturalism as sometimes the view that all cultural groups 'are of equal value' and at other times an 'equity tool' (Galligan and Roberts, 2004: 83, 82). This suggests a key distinction between relativist and universalist moral argument. On the one hand, the judgement that all cultures are morally equal is often based on cultural relativism, the idea that moral claims are never universally true but only locally valid from the perspective of a particular culture. On this view each culture is its own moral authority, so all must be equals. This approach implies a strong or unqualified form of multiculturalism that regards liberal democracy as only one cultural form among others. On the other hand, the notion of multiculturalism as an 'equity tool' suggests that it may be valuable as a means to justice conceived universally. That lets in the possibility that all cultures are not moral equals in every respect because not all are equally hospitable to multiculturalism. Such a possibility points towards a more moderate or qualified kind of multiculturalism, such as the liberal multiculturalism examined later.

Despite these ambiguities and conflicts, it is possible to sketch a working definition of multiculturalism in three parts in order to frame the discussion.

1. Multiculturalism includes the empirical claim that most contemporary societies are 'multicultural' – that is, they do in fact contain multiple cultures.
2. More distinctively, multiculturalists respond to that fact as something to approve of rather than oppose or merely tolerate.
3. More distinctively still, multiculturalists argue that the multiplicity of cultures within a single society should be not only generally approved but given positive recognition in the public policy and public institutions of the society.

Note that, on this account, Australian multiculturalism is essentially a normative rather than purely descriptive idea. It includes the empirical claim that Australia contains a diversity of cultures (item 1), but goes beyond that claim to a response of approval (item 2). Items (1) and

(2) together are enough for 'multiculturalism' in the broadest sense. However, it is only when we arrive at (3) that we have multiculturalism in its most distinctive sense This last sense of multiculturalism provides the focus for the remainder of the chapter.

The three components of the multiculturalist view require some brief expansion. First, multiculturalists accept that under contemporary conditions any single political society is likely to contain more than one culture. But what is a 'culture'? This concept is itself a major crux of debate, but there is general agreement that a culture is a common set of beliefs and values that identify a group.[4]

However, there are many kinds or levels of 'group', and consequently culture, and depending on which of these is the focus 'cultural recognition' can produce a variety of political outcomes. At one end of the scale we might conceivably be talking about the 'microcultures' of firms, clubs or associations, although these are seldom discussed in the multiculturalist literature. More commonly the emphasis is on the claims of identity groups such as women or gays and lesbians, connecting with the 'identity politics' championed by writers such as Iris Marion Young (1990). At the macro end of the scale are cultures, often based on religions, that have global reach: the subjects of Samuel Huntington's famous 'clash of civilisations' thesis (Huntington, 1996). Usually, however, multiculturalist theory and practice address the claims of either or both of two kinds of cultural minority: on the one hand immigrant groups, and on the other 'national' minorities, which include Indigenous peoples and minority nationalities such as the Quebecois in Canada. Cultures of these kinds are the primary concern here. I shall return to the different circumstances of these distinct kinds of group, and to the different cases that can be made for their recognition.

Given this preliminary understanding of culture, the next step is to observe that, for the multiculturalist, nearly all modern societies contain multiple cultures as a matter of fact. There is a sense in which Australia has always been multicultural because of the presence of the Indigenous peoples alongside the settler society. Add to that the fact that, as in other developed countries, levels of migration have increased enormously since 1945 as a result of the influx of refugees from war zones, economic migration in the aftermath of decolonisation, and to some extent the freer movement of people under economic and technological globalisation.[5] Successive waves of migrants have arrived from the United Kingdom, Europe, Asia, the Middle East and Africa. The upshot has been the creation of very substantial minority communities within Australian society and, as a result, the reshaping of that society.

It is important to note that the multicultural character of Australia is taken here to embrace the coexistence of the two quite different kinds of minority mentioned earlier: namely, immigrant and Indigenous groups. It may be that multiculturalism requires different kinds of accommodation or recognition depending on which sort of minority is being discussed. Indeed, Australian Indigenous peoples have sometimes objected to having their claims considered under the heading of multiculturalism at all, since they see that as out of keeping with their special status as 'first' peoples. This distinction between immigrant and Indigenous claims is a feature of the work of the multiculturalist theorist Will Kymlicka, and I return to it later.

But multiculturalism requires more than the presence in a society of multiple cultures; it requires, at a minimum, the second step mentioned above, from fact to approval. Historically, the great majority of responses to cultural diversity within a society have fallen short of approval. Even where cultural difference has not provoked outright violence, many societies have pursued policies and practices of 'assimilation': the more or less coercive subsuming of minority groups into a dominant national identity. In Australia this is typified by the past policy of resettling Aboriginal children with white families – the 'stolen generations'. This is not to say that all assimilation is coercive, since sometimes it is very much desired by those assimilated – by immigrants, for example (Kukathas, 2003: 154). But where assimilation is a goal of public policy, or even where it is backed informally by public sentiment, an element of coercion is often present.

Another possibility, often overlapping assimilation, is 'toleration'. Here minority cultures are not approved but neither are they actively discouraged or assimilated: the policy is basically one of noninterference. This is essentially the classical liberal approach to cultural diversity, dominant in liberal democracies, including Australia, before the advent of multiculturalism. The principle is one of the 'privatisation' of culture: minorities are not prevented from maintaining their own languages, traditions and so forth in the privacy of their own homes and associations, but there is no public recognition of these groups as having special legal rights or political status. Crucially, toleration requires no element of approval or even respect for the beliefs or practices tolerated. Indeed, toleration implies noninterference despite disapproval.

Multiculturalism proper requires the addition of the third element of my definition. Beyond the idea of cultural diversity as a fact to be registered, or a situation to be tolerated, beyond even the celebration of cultural diversity as in general a good thing, multiculturalism requires that multiple cultures within the same polity be given positive recognition at an official or public level. Conceivably, there could be a society in which minority cultures are widely admired but receive no official support from the state. Such a society is more accurately described as multicultural rather than truly multiculturalist. Multiculturalism requires, most distinctively, that the value of cultural diversity be recognised in public policy, the political voice of the society as a whole.

Public recognition of the value of cultural diversity may take various forms. At its weakest, recognition may be purely rhetorical or inspirational. This may involve no more than an assertion that the presence of minority cultures in the society is desirable or that certain minorities, usually Indigenous, have a special place in a country's history and identity. Such declarations can be quite powerful, however, especially when they enter into the institutional symbolism of the society – its 'official emblems, anthems, flags, public holidays, and the like' (Levey, 2008: 16) – or when they take the form of special one-off government announcements. An example of the latter is the Australian Government's official apology to the Aboriginal and Torres Strait Islander peoples delivered by Prime Minister, Kevin Rudd, in the Australian Parliament in 2008.

Beyond symbolism, multiculturalism may take the form of the use of public resources to support cultural minorities in various ways, such as the funding of events or institutions. One example is the establishment by the Fraser Government in the 1970s of the Special Broadcasting Service (SBS), Australia's multicultural and multilingual broadcaster, recognising the presence and contribution of minority ethnic groups in Australian society. Public recognition of minority cultures may also involve adjustments to the law. One common form of cultural recognition is exemption from legal obligation: members of a group may be exempt from a law that applies to everyone else. An Australian example is the practice in some states of exempting Indigenous groups from compliance with laws prohibiting the hunting or fishing of endangered species.

A stronger form of minority recognition is the provision by the state of various kinds of special opportunity not available to other citizens. These special rights are typically justified not as superior privileges but as compensation for certain kinds of disadvantage. For example, in Australia people from Indigenous backgrounds are entitled to special university scholarships ('Abstudy') not open to others, on the ground that Indigenous people have historically received fewer such opportunities than other Australian citizens.

Finally, the strongest form of special minority accommodation is group self-determination. In some countries, certain minority groups, usually Indigenous peoples, are recognised as having the right to govern themselves, in accordance with their traditional norms, within some designated jurisdiction. Self-determination itself can take several forms, ranging from (at the weaker end) advisory institutions such as the Australian Indigenous Council, to semi-sovereign polities like the Canadian Inuit and Native American nations. Beyond 'accommodation' altogether there is the possibility of complete secession, where the self-determining group forms a state of its own.

How is multiculturalism justified?

Among the reasons why multiculturalist policy has taken such a variety of forms is the variety of justifications that have been offered for it. One dimension of variation is between the circumstances of 'settler' societies such as Australia, Canada and the United States, and 'traditional' societies such as the United Kingdom and the Netherlands. In the latter case multiculturalism is directed more to the integration of migrants from former colonies; in settler societies multiculturalist policies embrace both immigrants, often needed for either labour or professional expertise, and Indigenous peoples.

There is also a range of arguments at a more philosophical level. Four leading arguments advanced by multiculturalist advocates are considered here: relativist, compensatory, protective, and polyglot.[6] How far do these arguments succeed in justifying multiculturalism?

The relativist justification of multiculturalism was noted earlier in connection with the claim of Galligan and Roberts that multiculturalists see all cultures as being 'of equal value'. Recall that cultural relativism is the idea that each culture possesses its own unique and authoritative moral perspective. If that is so, then it is a short step to holding that all cultures must be respected equally within a single polity and none must be dominant. All should receive the same level of public recognition. Thus Paul Scheffer writes that 'multicultural thinking represents a continuation of cultural relativism by other means' (Scheffer, 2011: 197).

It was also noted that the relativist starting point leads to a quite radical form of multiculturalism, since even the basic principles of liberal democracy would then be seen as expressing merely one cultural perspective among others. On this basis multiculturalist thinking would need to press beyond the framework of liberal democracy towards some 'higher level of philosophical abstraction' which was more thoroughly inclusive of the full range of cultural difference (Parekh, 2006: 14). This approach is in line with the 'curriculum multiculturalism' that informs some current educational practice, especially in the United States, which strives to go beyond the supposed limitations and biases of 'Western civilisation'.[7]

By and large, however, the relativist approach goes well beyond current political practice in Australia and elsewhere, and it is not strongly supported by current political theory. Even among those political theorists at the more radical end of the multiculturalist spectrum — that is, those most willing to question the liberal-democratic framework — there are very few leading thinkers who accept an unqualified cultural relativism.

The reason is that cultural relativism suffers from a number of philosophical difficulties that are so serious as to be disabling.[8] The most obvious problem is that if we accept cultural relativism then we must also accept as morally justified whatever practices a culture may endorse. Historically, this category has included every conceivable outrage against humanity: racism, sexism, imperialism, homophobia, and so on. This 'anything goes' problem is what opponents of multiculturalism such as Scheffer often seem to have in mind, assuming that multiculturalism is the same thing as cultural relativism. If that were true they would have a strong point.

However, multiculturalism is not the same thing as cultural relativism — or at least, cultural relativism is cited as the basis for only the most radical kind of multiculturalism. Indeed, even that link is philosophically dubious because relativism is a poor basis for any political position. In the case of multiculturalism, the values that multiculturalists typically advocate — toleration, mutual respect, the positive valuation of other ways of life — are themselves goods that may or may not be supported by a given culture. Hence, the values of multiculturalism may or may not be defended in a given cultural setting under relativism.

Let us assume, then, that a sensible multiculturalism will not be relativist but rather qualified by a concern for universal values such as human rights. The leading justifications along these lines are broadly liberal, framing multicultural policies within a commitment to individual rights and liberties, toleration, equal treatment, limits on the authority of government, and private property rights. In turn, liberal arguments for multiculturalism can be divided into three main varieties: compensatory, protective and 'polyglot'.

The basic idea of the compensatory argument is that public recognition is needed to compensate a minority group for unjust treatment in the past. In Australia this is most obviously applicable to Indigenous groups whose lands were taken and whose cultures were suppressed by 19th-century colonisers. The remedies sought include the return of land, concessions to traditional practices such as the hunting and fishing of species that are otherwise protected, and rights of self-determination.

There are a number of problems with claims of this kind. Sometimes it is difficult to demonstrate that the alleged past mistreatment occurred or that there is a sufficient link between those bringing the claim and those who suffered the past injustice. Even where such a link can be established, the question is often raised, as it was by John Howard during his time as Australian Prime Minister, whether the current majority can be held responsible for the behaviour of its forebears. Further, it may be argued that, whatever past injustice may have occurred, this has by now been 'superseded' by the efforts of the majority in the intervening generations (Waldron, 1992).

On the other hand, it is not obvious that the problems always trump the claims. In the Australian experience the High Court's landmark decision in the Mabo case, in which the colonial doctrine of *terra nullius* was rejected and Indigenous land rights recognised, is a strong example of compensatory policy. While there are ongoing difficulties in resolving particular claims, the mechanisms and institutions created to deal with them are now well established and woven into the fabric of Indigenous cultural recognition.

The protective line of argument addresses not what happened in the past but the disadvantages a cultural group allegedly suffers from in the present. Here public recognition is recommended to protect cultural minorities from oppressive treatment or even just unwitting marginalisation by the majority. What form the recognition should take will depend on the nature of the oppression or disadvantage in a particular case.

The leading multiculturalist thinker along these lines is the Canadian philosopher Will Kymlicka (1989, 1995a).[9] In his earlier work Kymlicka argued that all cultural minorities are entitled to redress through public recognition because simply to be in a minority is to suffer disadvantage through inequality. The majority has its culture sustained for free, as it were, because its norms are by definition those of the society's official culture – as reflected, for example, in the state's official language and public holidays. Minorities, by contrast, have to work harder to maintain their culture. Immigrant groups who want to retain their native language usually have to do so outside of the mainstream education system, and Indigenous groups have to 'bid' against competitors for control of resources, such as land, that are both essential to the group's cultural identity and commercially valuable to others.

To this it might be replied that not every disadvantage is unfair. Laws requiring people to keep left on the roads disadvantage those who would rather drive on the right, but no one thinks that is unjust. Kymlicka himself eventually distinguished between two kinds of minority disadvantage corresponding to two different sorts of minority. On the one hand, immigrants ('ethnic' groups) have chosen to come to the host country, and in doing so have implicitly agreed to accept the conditions prevalent there. Although they may wish to preserve aspects of their culture, such as language, they accept the host's institutions – its political, legal and education systems, and so on. They are still entitled to special consideration in order to assist their integration, but that kind of public recognition does not extend to the reconstruction of their full 'societal', or institutionalised, culture.[10]

On the other hand, 'national' groups, such as Indigenous peoples or the French-Canadian Québécois, have been subsumed into larger political societies without their consent, often violently. They have never agreed to surrender their societal institutions and usually struggle to maintain them. In these cases, Kymlicka argues, much stronger forms of public recognition are appropriate, including various levels of self-determination.

Thus far Kymlicka's case for multicultural recognition is based on an ideal of equal treatment among cultural groups, but he also has an argument grounded in individual liberty. For Kymlicka, the maintenance of cultures, whether majority or minority, should be important to liberals because it is essential to the enjoyment of the central liberal value of personal autonomy, or the capacity to choose one's own way of life. To be able to choose how to live presupposes a cultural context that makes sense of the options that confront the individual and that suggests a way of resolving conflicts among alternatives. Cultures are like maps for navigating our way through life. Consequently, if we value individual autonomy, as liberals say we should, we should value the culture that provides us with a necessary context for autonomy.

But what if the culture in question is not liberal or contains illiberal norms and practices? From a liberal–feminist perspective Susan Okin objects that multicultural recognition is a licence for the protection of the patriarchy characteristic of virtually all traditional cultures (Okin,

1999). Kymlicka's response is that the liberal state should not simply exclude such cultures but instead offer them the appropriate kind of assistance while at the same time trying to liberalise them. This proposal has in turn been criticised as, in effect, giving with one hand and taking with the other – pretending to preserve cultural groups but really transforming them in the image of liberals like Kymlicka (Kukathas, 1992). He is himself uneasy on this point, rightly insisting that a liberal state must in principle be entitled to protect the rights and liberties of individual citizens, against their own groups if need be, but also aware that excessively heavy-handed forms of intervention may be counterproductive. In the Australian context the Northern Territory intervention of 2007 has raised similar issues.

Someone may also question how far Kymlicka's argument justifies multiculturalism, since it appears at first sight to be consistent with a monoculturalist nationalism too. If what is important is a cultural context for individual autonomy, then why could such a context not be provided by a single dominant, even assimilationist national culture rather than the recognition of multiple minority cultures? Kymlicka's reply is that few people can move easily from one culture to another, so for most people it is the culture they are brought up in that must be their context for autonomy. Given the fact that under modern conditions the citizens of any developed state come from many different cultural backgrounds, a case for the state recognition of many such cultures follows.

However, this argument provokes a further objection. As Jeremy Waldron puts it, 'we need culture, but we do not need cultural integrity' (Waldron, 1995: 108). Granting Kymlicka's point that in order to make sense of their autonomy people need a cultural context, it does not follow that they must be immersed in a single national or religious culture that governs their lives comprehensively. Rather, they can construct a perfectly satisfactory life and identity by borrowing from all sorts of cultural influences – the life of the 'cosmopolitan' individual.

To this Kymlicka responds that even cosmopolitans live in a societal culture, it is just that this is an internally diverse, complex culture that borrows from many sources (Kymlicka, 1995b). That is a reasonable reply but it lets in a different kind of argument for multiculturalism from the protective argument Kymlicka favours – namely, the 'polyglot' argument outlined by Robert Goodin (2006). The basic idea is that public recognition of multiple cultures is desirable not because it serves the interests of vulnerable minorities by protecting them, but because it benefits the whole society, including the majority, by giving people a greater range of cultural options from which to select when they are choosing how to live.

Kymlicka considers this line but regards it as having limited utility because people seldom exchange one cultural affiliation for another. We do not choose cultures as if from a supermarket shelf. But Waldron's point is that people can borrow from many different cultures without living in any of them comprehensively or exclusively. The point is effectively conceded by Kymlicka when he allows that a societal culture can borrow from many sources.

Moreover, it could be argued, if the conditions for individual autonomy are valuable, among these is the existence of an adequate range of options from which to choose (Raz, 1986). Multicultural recognition is desirable because it helps to maintain or increase the range of a society's cultural options. No one has to immerse herself in any one way of life in order to enjoy the benefits of their availability. This argument goes back to John Stuart Mill and his idea of multiple 'experiments of living' that provide people with examples either to embrace or reject as they see fit (Mill, 1859 [1974]: 120).

Do the benefits outweigh the costs?

The foregoing arguments suggest that, with allowances for the critical difficulties that accompany any justificatory claim, multiculturalist recognition is capable of being beneficial to a political society in several ways: it can provide minority groups with redress for past injustice; it can protect such groups from unfair disadvantage; it can maintain the cultural context necessary for personal autonomy; and it can expand the range of choices in a society in a way that benefits not only minorities but the majority as well.

But even if all these arguments are accepted, the case for multiculturalism is not complete. That is because the anticipated benefits of the policy may be outweighed by its costs. Three areas of cost are especially salient in the critical literature: political, economic, and solidaristic.

Politically, the worry is that multiculturalist policies will generate a divisive competition for public resources at various levels: between rival minorities, between minorities and the mainstream, and even within minority groups (Kukathas, 1997: 147–9). This objection is likely to be pressed, in particular, by public choice theorists, who are always on the lookout for the way systems of governance can be exploited by self-interested, 'rent-seeking' behaviour. What this kind of analysis tends to miss is that people's motives are often mixed, and that the merits of policies cannot be reduced to their motivations. As for the association of multiculturalism with divisive competition, conflict is inescapably the stuff of politics.

Brian Barry (2001) is prominent in his stress on the economic costs of multiculturalism, complaining that cultural recognition distracts egalitarians from the economic redistribution that ought to be their primary goal. For example, policies aimed at sustaining a minority language may have the effect of preventing people from pursuing opportunities for mainstream employment. One response to this objection is Nancy Fraser's argument that redistribution and recognition are both important policies, pursuing equally legitimate and important goals (Fraser, 2008). Fraser is wary of merely 'affirmative' recognition that perpetuates existing hierarchies, but that is not the kind of recognition that Kymlicka and other liberal multiculturalists would defend.

Finally, concerns about the costs of special group recognition to national solidarity take us back to the claim by Galligan and Roberts that multiculturalism 'has been used to hollow out' Australian citizenship. One of the most frequent complaints against multiculturalism is that it emphasises the differences between people at the expense of what they have in common, and in this connection the notion of a shared national identity is often singled out as an especially significant casualty. In a large, impersonal world, it is argued, where the individual's place is often made uncertain by a volatile global economy, nationality is more important than ever in providing people with a sense of belonging. Yet this is undermined by what seems to be the multiculturalist invitation to place minority identity ahead of patriotism.

Tim Soutphommasane (2012) advances an interesting response to this worry. Soutphommasane agrees with the nationalists that modern citizenship requires more than a purely 'civic' identification with the abstract principles of liberal democracy. Rather, it depends on 'pre-political sources of trust and solidarity', and these, in turn, are 'difficult to divorce from historical national communities' (Soutphommasane, 2012: 65, 67). Citizenship, that is, involves a commitment to a shared national identity, or 'patriotism'. But this need not be undermined by multiculturalism as long as all parties are open to a continuing public dialogue. In such a dialogue, national identity is subject to constant reinterpretation, in the course of which both majority and minority cultures must be willing to reflect on their own demands and norms. A combination of liberal nationalism and deliberative democracy, Soutphommasane's proposal aims to reassert the value of patriotism and national culture but in a form that does not exclude cultural minorities.

Regardless of how well justified multiculturalism may be at the level of philosophical argument, it is hard to deny that the lived experience of multiculturalism can be disturbing and disorienting for many people, the source of a complex of anxieties and resentments, whether rational or not. In Australia this was shown by the rise of Pauline Hanson and her One Nation party in the 1990s. Behind much of the criticism of multiculturalism is a visceral sense of the 'host' as being 'swamped' by 'others'. To some extent this is a question of numbers: small numbers matter little because the effect on the majority's way of life is minimal, but large numbers change things. Allied to this is the question of proximity: to what extent do the 'others' look like and behave like the majority? The less they do the more challenging the task. There is also an issue of whether minorities express a desire to live like the majority or whether they wish to establish their own cultural practices in the majority's midst. More challenging still is the case where a minority expects (or is perceived as expecting) the majority to change its behaviour and conform to the norms of the minority. All these issues have a historical dimension to the extent that people tend to compare current difficulties with what they once knew or imagined to be the norm. These aspects of multiculturalism 'on the streets' are often what make the politics in this area so fraught. Such concerns should not be ignored or belittled. On the other hand they should not be allowed to drown out those voices that speak for the beneficial aspects of multiculturalism, and that are prepared to defend the idea in a properly balanced form.

Conclusion

The first step to reaching a sensible judgement on multiculturalism is to be clear about which variety is being discussed. What many of the opponents of the idea take to be the whole of multiculturalism may be really just the radical version that takes cultural relativism as its starting point. This interpretation the critics are justified in rejecting as ethically objectionable, politically unrealistic and philosophically incoherent.

But a liberal form of multiculturalism, such as Kymlicka's, is another matter. Qualified by a concern for human rights and personal autonomy, this is a natural outgrowth of liberal-democratic thinking. The liberal tradition, emerging from the movement towards religious toleration in early modern Europe, has always been concerned with the accommodation of difference. To this the multiculturalist wing of the tradition adds an interest in redress for past injustice and present disadvantage suffered by members of cultural minorities, and, more positively, a desire to expand the range of cultural choice for all citizens.[11]

This is not to deny that, even in its liberal form, multiculturalism raises issues of genuine concern – for example, the rent-seeking behaviour of some minorities and their leaders, the possibility of a conflict between recognition and redistribution in some cases, the tension between minority and shared identities, and the persistence of popular anxieties. However, it is far from obvious that these problems need be fatal to a reasoned and moderate version of the multiculturalist project overall.

Notes

[1] For the history of Australian debate over multicultural policy, see Lopez (2000), Galligan and Roberts (2004): ch. 4, Levey (2008).

[2] See also Joppke and Morawska (2003) for the alleged retreat of multiculturalism in countries other than Australia.

[3] The current federal policy document is *The People of Australia: Australia's Multicultural Policy*: see Department of Immigration and Citizenship (2011). In the Abbott Coalition Government that took office after the 2013 federal election, Multicultural Affairs has been downgraded from a Cabinet portfolio to part of the brief for the Parliamentary Secretary for Social Services.

[4] For discussion of the idea of 'culture', see Carrithers (1992), Jenks (2004), Lawson (2006).

[5] According to the federal government's official policy document, 'since 1945, seven million people have migrated to Australia. Today, one in four of Australia's 22 million people were [sic] born overseas, 44 per cent were born overseas or have a parent who was and four million speak a language other than English. We speak over 260 languages and identify with more than 270 ancestries. Australia is and will remain a multicultural society' (Department of Immigration and Citizenship, 2011: 2).

[6] Critical discussions of the justificatory arguments for multiculturalism include Joppke and Lukes (1999), Laden and Owen (2007), Modood (2007), Murphy (2012), Rattansi (2012), and Crowder (2013).

[7] For the American debate on this issue see Schlesinger (1992); Hughes (1993); Friedman and Narveson (1995).

147

[8] Critical discussions of cultural relativism include Williams (1972), Ladd (1973), Levy (2002), Wong (1993), Lukes (2008).

[9] See also Taylor (1994), Raz (1995).

[10] 'Integration', where a minority culture is included within a larger society but without losing its own character entirely, is distinguished from assimilation by Kymlicka (1995a: 78).

[11] Compare Garton Ash (2012), who argues that multiculturalism contains nothing of value that was not already in mainstream liberalism.

References

Barry, B. (2001) *Culture and Equality*, Cambridge: Polity

Bowen, C. (2011) 'Address to the Sydney Institute – The Genius of Multiculturalism' http://www.chrisbowen.net/media-centre/speeches.do?newsId=4154

Carrithers, M. (1992) *Why Humans Have Cultures: Explaining Anthropology and Social Diversity*, Oxford: Oxford University Press

Crowder, G. (2013) *Theories of Multiculturalism: An Introduction*, Cambridge: Polity

Department of Immigration and Citizenship (2011) 'The People of Australia: Australia's Multicultural Policy. Available at: http://www.gov.au/living-in-australia/a-multicultural-australia

Fraser, N. (2008) 'From Redistribution to Recognition? Dilemmas of Justice in a "Postsocialist" Age', in Kevin Olson (ed.), *Adding Insult to Injury: Nancy Fraser Debates Her Critics*, London: Verso

Friedman, M., and J. Narveson (1995) *Political Correctness: For and Against*, Lanham, MD: Rowman & Littlefield

Galligan, B. and W. Roberts (2004) *Australian Citizenship*, Melbourne: Melbourne University Press

Garton Ash, T. (2012) 'Freedom and Diversity: A Liberal Pentagram for Living Together', *New York Review of Books*, 22 November

Glazer, N. (1997) *We Are All Multiculturalists Now*. Harvard University Press, Cambridge, Mass

Goodin, R. (2006) 'Liberal Multiculturalism: Protective and Polyglot', *Political Theory* 34 (3): 289-303

Hughes, R. (1993) *Culture of Complaint: The Fraying of America*, New York: Oxford University Press

Huntington, S. (1996) *The Clash of Civilizations and the Remaking of World Order*, New York: Simon & Schuster

Jenks, C. (2004) *Culture*, London: Routledge

Joppke, C. (2004) 'The Retreat of Multiculturalism in the Liberal State: Theory and Policy', *British Journal of Sociology* 55 (2): 237-257

Joppke, C. and S. Lukes (eds) (1999) *Multicultural Questions*, Oxford : Oxford University Press

Joppke, C. and E. Morawska (eds) (2003) *Toward Assimilation and Citizenship: Immigrants in Liberal Nation-States*, Basingstoke: Palgrave Macmillan,

Kukathas, C. (1992) 'Are There Any Cultural Rights?, *Political Theory* 20 (1): 105-139

Kukathas, C. (1997) 'Liberalism, Multiculturalism and Oppression', in Andrew Vincent (ed.) *Political Theory: Tradition and Diversity*, Cambridge: Cambridge University Press

Kukathas, C. (2003) *The Liberal Archipelago*, Oxford : Oxford University Press

Kymlicka, W. (1989) *Liberalism, Community, and Culture*, Oxford : Oxford University Press

Kymlicka, W. (1995a) *Multicultural Citizenship: A Liberal Theory of Minority Rights*, Oxford : Oxford University Press

Kymlicka, W. (1995b) 'Introduction' to W. Kymlicka (ed.), *The Rights of Minority Cultures*, Oxford : Oxford University Press

Ladd, J. (ed.) (1973) *Ethical Relativism*, Belmont, CA: Wadsworth

Laden, A.S. and D. Owen (eds) (2007) *Multiculturalism and Political Theory*, Cambridge: Cambridge University Press

Lawson, S. (2006) *Culture and Context in World Politics*, Basingstoke: Palgrave Macmillan

Levey, G.B. (2008) 'Multicultural Political Thought in Australian Perspective', in G.B. Levey (ed.), *Political Theory and Australian Multiculturalism*, New York: Berghahn Books

Levy, N. (2002) *Moral Relativism: A Short Introduction*, Oxford: Oneworld

Lopez, M. (2000) *The Origins of Multiculturalism in Australian Politics, 1945–75*, Melbourne: Melbourne University Press

Lukes, S. (2008) *Moral Relativism*, New York: Picador

Mill, J.S. (1859 [1974]) *On Liberty*, ed. G. Himmelfarb, Harmondsworth, Penguin

Modood, T. (2007) *Multiculturalism*, Cambridge: Polity

Murphy, M. (2012) *Multiculturalism: A Critical Introduction*, London and New York, Routledge

Okin, S. (1999) *Is Multiculturalism Bad for Women?* (with respondents), ed. J. Cohen, M. Howard and M. Nussbaum, Princeton: Princeton University Press

Parekh, B. (2006) *Rethinking Multiculturalism: Cultural Diversity and Political Theory*, 2nd edn, London: Palgrave

Rattansi, A. (2011) *Multiculturalism: A Very Short Introduction*, Oxford: Oxford University Press

Raz, J. (1986) *The Morality of Freedom*, Oxford: Clarendon Press

Raz, J. (1995) 'Multiculturalism: A Liberal Perspective', in *Ethics in the Public Domain*, Oxford: Clarendon Press

Scheffer, P. (2011) *Immigrant Nations*, trans. L. Waters, Cambridge,:Polity

Schlesinger, A.M. (1992) *The Disuniting of America: Reflections on a Multicultural Society*, New York: Norton

Soutphommasane, T. (2012) *The Virtuous Citizen: Patriotism in a Multicultural Society*, Cambridge: Cambridge University Press

Taylor, C. (1994) 'The Politics of Recognition', in A. Gutmann, (ed.), *Multiculturalism: Examining the Politics of Recognition*, Princeton, Princeton University Press

Waldron, J. (1992) 'Superseding Historic Injustice', *Ethics* 103, 2: 4-28

Waldron, J. (1995) 'Minority Cultures and Cosmopolitan Alternatives', in W. Kymlicka (ed.) *The Rights of Minority Cultures*, Oxford: Oxford University Press

Williams, B. (1972) *Morality*, Cambridge: Cambridge University Press

Wong, D. (1993) 'Relativism', in P. Singer (ed.) *A Companion to Ethics*, Oxford: Blackwell

Young, I.M. (1990) *Justice and the Politics of Difference*, Princeton: Princeton University Press

NINE

The business of care: Australia's experiment with the marketisation of childcare

Deborah Brennan[1]

Introduction

The care and education of young children has been subject to 'a surge of policy attention' since the 1990s (OECD, 2006). According to some policy experts, high quality education and care services are 'the centrepiece of progressive institution-building in the early 21st century' (Pearce and Paxton, 2005: xxi). Early childhood education and care (ECEC) can contribute to multiple goals: facilitating the labour force participation of mothers, boosting children's educational and social development and providing a platform for a more equitable division of labour between men and women. Once the domain of philanthropists, feminists and progressive educators, early childhood education has attracted the attention of economists, human capital theorists and brain scientists. The notion that expenditure on high quality early education is a form of investment, producing measurable returns through reduced expenditure on remedial education, juvenile justice and unemployment benefits in the later years, has captured the imagination of politicians and policy makers around the world.

Yet, as ECEC assumed its place on national policy agendas, many countries experienced a 'turn to the market' in human service provision (Brennan et al., 2012). Governments in English speaking liberal welfare states, in particular, and in Europe to a lesser extent (Plantenga, 2012) began to withdraw from, or reduce, direct funding of services and to introduce supply-side strategies such as vouchers that enable those seeking care to purchase services in a competitive market. Private investors responded with enthusiasm: childcare is now big business. But reorienting childcare from a nonprofit community service to a commodity to be bought and sold involves more than a simple change in the mode of delivery. As political philosopher

Michael Sandel observes, '... markets don't only allocate goods; they also express and promote certain attitudes towards the goods being exchanged' (Sandel, 2012, p 9).

This chapter examines the shift in Australia from a nonprofit childcare sector to one that is heavily marketised. It considers the impact of this shift on the broader social purposes of childcare and, in particular, the tension between official claims of *social* investment in the early years and the reality of a system in which most providers are driven by the imperatives of *private* investment and profit. The chapter is organised in three sections. The first outlines the nature of early care and education provision, the level of expenditure and trends in maternal labour force participation. The second section looks at the shift from community-based provision to a market in childcare and the rapid growth of stock market listed childcare providers. This section traces the growth of ABC Learning, an Australian company that became the world's largest listed childcare company and explains the business model it adopted before its spectacular collapse in 2008. The third section examines the efforts of Labor Governments (2007–13) to implement a human capital framework for ECEC through the regulation of quality standards. The central argument of the chapter is that Australia's system of market-based provision exists in uneasy tension with the goal of quality service provision. Of even deeper significance, the marketisation of ECEC in recent decades has focused public attention and debate on a narrow set of 'outcomes' and 'targets'. Technocratic debates of this kind divert attention from the deeper political and ethical issues at stake in the organisation of care and education for young children.

Early childhood education and care in Australia

Policy and funding responsibility for ECEC is shared between the Commonwealth, State and Territory governments. Services are delivered through a mixed market of government, private for-profit, nonprofit and community-based providers (PWC, 2011, p 14). Despite measures to bring care and education closer together and to encourage the development of a unified 'early childhood education and care' sector, entrenched differences exist between childcare and preschools (known as kindergartens in some states). The Commonwealth targets the bulk of its childcare expenditure towards services such as long day care,[2] family day care[3] and in-home care[4] that support parental labour force participation. Such services typically cater for children from birth to school age and are open throughout the year. In contrast, preschools and kindergartens, largely funded by state governments, only accept children in the year or two before school and offer either half-day sessions or short days (9am to 3pm) during school terms only, thus limiting their potential to support workforce participation. Preschool is provided free or at negligible cost in several states, while childcare fees can amount to hundreds of dollars per week, even after Commonwealth subsidies (described later) are taken into account.

Government expenditure on early childhood services has risen rapidly in recent years, in line with broader Organisation for Economic Cooperation and Development (OECD) trends (Jensen, 2009). The Australian, state and territory governments spent approximately $6 billion on ECEC in 2011–12, which was a real increase of almost 63% on 2007–08 expenditure. Around 80% of this is Commonwealth spending on demand-side measures such as fee subsidies and rebates for childcare. Since 2010, additional Commonwealth funds have gone to the states under an agreement to increase access to early childhood education. The states spend $1.3 billion, almost all of which funds the supply of preschool (Productivity Commission, 2013). Preschools have not been subjected to the market pressures discussed in this chapter.

Childcare – including out-of-school-hours services for primary-school-aged children – is a normal part of life for many Australian children. However, there are significant variations in usage depending on the demographic and social characteristics of families, notably whether or not mothers are employed. The labour force participation of Australian mothers in both single parent and couple families has increased markedly in recent decades. In 2011, 57% of single parent mothers and 68% of mothers in couple families were employed, compared with 44% and 57% in 1993. Although single mothers' rate of employment is lower than that of mothers in couple families, single mothers have increased their rate of participation more quickly than mothers in couples (Baxter, 2013: 9). Part-time work is a strong feature of mothers' employment, especially when children are very young. This is reflected in the average weekly hours of childcare participation: 27 hours in long day care, 22 hours in family day care and in-home care and 9 hours in out-of-school-hours care (Productivity Commission, 2013).

The number of children using formal care has grown since the early 1990s, while the use of informal care has fallen. There has been particularly strong growth in the use of formal care by 0–2 year old children with employed mothers; interestingly, formal care usage has also grown for children whose mothers are not employed. This is partly explained by the fact that the category of 'mother not employed' includes mothers who are on various forms of leave, including parental leave. However, the data also suggest that the use of formal care is becoming more common in Australia (Table 9.1).

Family income plays a crucial role in mediating access to childcare. In families with a combined weekly income of $2,500 or above, 34% of 0–12 year old children regularly participate in formal childcare, compared with 16% of children in families with a weekly income of $1,000 or less. Family income also affects the likelihood of *informal* care being used. While more than 44% of children in families where parents' weekly income exceeds $2,500 use informal care, only 23% of children in families earning less than $1,000 per week do so. These differences may reflect the fact that higher income families are more likely to be in work, or to be engaged in relatively long hours of work, and thus need more care for work-related purposes. However, the relative lack of participation of low-income children in childcare may mean less engagement with peers and other adults and fewer opportunities for access to educational and developmental resources. There is also a strong 'social gradient' in access to outside school hours care, with children from more affluent areas far more likely to

Table 9.1: Participation in formal/informal childcare or Early Childhood Education, by age of child and mother's employment status, 1993 and 2011

	Mother employed		Mother not employed	
	1993	2011	1993	2011
	%	%	%	%
Child aged 0–2 years				
Any care	76.0	82.2	36.5	32.8
Formal care	29.7	54.6	10.1	16.9
Informal care	59.8	49.3	29.9	20.1
Child aged 3–5 years				
Any care	80.2	82.7	58.4	61.0
Formal care/ECE*	55.0	71.2	43.1	51.3
Informal care	55.0	41.4	30.4	20.0
Children aged 6–11 years				
Any care	51.6	43.4	23.4	20.2
Formal care	9.9	19.7	1.5	5.0
Informal care	45.9	30.3	22.3	16.7

* Early childhood education

Notes: more than one type of care could be nominated. Mothers who were employed but away from work were counted as 'not employed'.

Source: Adapted from Baxter, 2013, p.9

access formal services than their peers from poorer areas (Cassells and Miranti, 2012).

The Australian Government has identified participation by children from particular groups as a target for services such as long day care, family day care and in-home care, where children from these groups are under-represented in Commonwealth approved childcare. Children from non-English speaking backgrounds make up almost 19% of 0–12 year old children in the community, for example, but less than 14% of enrolments in approved childcare services. Children from Aboriginal and Torres Strait Islander backgrounds represent 4.7% of this age group, but only 2% of children in approved care. Children with disabilities make up 6.6% of 0–12 year olds but only 2.6% of those attending Commonwealth approved care. Children from both regional and remote parts of Australia are also under-represented (Productivity Commission, 2013, Table 3.4).

Marketisation and the growth of corporate childcare

Australian childcare was firmly embedded in the philanthropic and nonprofit domain until the 1990s. Delivery through community-based services ensured diversity of provision, since auspice bodies were locally based and closely connected with the communities they served. Services received a mix of operational funding and 'fee relief' from the Commonwealth Government but, under the Child Care Act 1972, only nonprofit services were eligible for public subsidies. As increased women's labour force participation fuelled the demand for childcare, private operators lobbied for funding to be extended to the users of their services. This shift in direction was fiercely resisted by advocates of the community-based sector, who pointed to evidence of lower standards in the for-profit centres and argued that childcare should be a public responsibility rather than an opportunity for private profit (Brennan, 1998).

In 1991, in response to sustained pressure from private operators and Treasury concern about the growing cost to government of new services, the Hawke Government extended childcare assistance to for-profit centres and began to wind back capital expenditure on the community-based services. Since then, both Labor and the Coalition have tacitly agreed that markets are the appropriate way to deliver childcare services. As in the UK, 'there was no moment when government explicitly argued the case for a market approach … no policy document where different options were considered and the market option justified; no parliamentary or public debate on the subject; no national evaluation of the experiment in marketisation and privatisation' (Moss, 2012, p 200). Both parties accept markets unquestioningly as the appropriate vehicle for expansion and provision.

The impetus for marketisation in Australia was different from that in the UK, where New Labour promoted the importance of parental 'choice' in a market-driven system. In Australia, diversity was the hallmark of community-based provision and it would not have been credible to suggest that 'choice' was a factor. Two main arguments were advanced in favour of marketisation. The first was that the cost to government of childcare was becoming unsustainable and that new players needed to be brought in to share the burden. The second argument, vigorously pursued by Hawke's Finance Minister Peter Walsh, was that market-based provision would impose wage discipline on childcare workers. In Walsh's view, turning to the market would weaken the alliance between childcare workers and (nonprofit) providers, thus putting a brake on wage growth in the sector. The government, he believed, should limit the small advances that had been made towards increasing the qualifications and improving the professional status of childcare workers. Walsh argued that efforts to improve the pay and conditions of these staff were simply rent seeking. Such measures were designed 'to make even softer the nests of bachelors of early childhood education and their middle-class well-feathered friends'. He and his supporters accused childcare workers of crippling the system with 'creeping credentialism'. Keeping wage costs as low as possible was thus a major reason for Labor's support for the marketisation of childcare (Brennan, 1998).

The centre-right government of Prime Minister John Howard (1996–2007) intensified the marketisation of childcare. As part of the introduction of a new tax system and the reorganisation of family benefits in 2000, the government introduced a new approach to subsidising childcare fees. Child Care Benefit (CCB) provided more financial assistance than the system it replaced and families could claim more hours of subsidised care, but it had a higher income threshold for eligibility. Working parents were eligible for up to 50 hours of CCB per week and non-working parents 20 hours (later extended to 24 hours). Parents could direct their CCB entitlement to the service of their choice and pay reduced fees, or pay the full fee and claim CCB at a later date. Not surprisingly, the vast majority chose to direct CCB to their service. Not only did this system have clear benefits for parents, it dramatically improved the cash flow position of providers and reduced the likelihood of bad debts. As one provider observed, 'The child care business is the best business I've ever seen in my life. The government pays subsidies, the parents pay you two weeks in advance and property prices keep going up' (Kirby, 2003).

Although CCB was structured in a progressive way, with the highest subsidies going to families with the lowest incomes, it was (and continues to be) overlaid on a market system in which providers are free to set their own fees and parents pay the gap between their CCB entitlement and the fee charged. At the high end of the income scale, some families received very little CCB and a few were excluded. In 2004, the Howard Government introduced an additional subsidy, Child Care Tax Rebate, to cover 30% of out-of-pocket expenses up to a ceiling amount.[5] The structure of the Child Care Rebate (CCR) reduced the incentive for providers to restrain fee rises. CCR is a very 'market-friendly' subsidy; effectively, it guarantees that government will pick up half of any fee increases (up to a ceiling) for high-income parents. Given the shortage of places in many parts of Australia, parents may be willing to pay very high fees, which will automatically increase government subsidies (Brennan, 2007a, 2007b).

ABC Learning

In 2001, ABC Learning, a Queensland company, became the first publicly listed childcare corporation in Australia. Others followed soon afterwards and, within a few years, Australia had experienced not merely an expansion of for-profit childcare at the expense of nonprofit provision, but a shift towards *corporate* care, that is, care provided by companies whose shares are traded on the stock exchange (Brennan, 2007a; Sumsion, 2012). ABC Learning expanded rapidly and aggressively, taking over services run by community-based, nonprofit groups as well as those owned by individual owner-operators. Within a few years, it had absorbed most of its corporate rivals, as well as hundreds of individual centres, and had become the dominant player in Australian long day care (Ellis, 2009). At the height of the company's success, its CEO was Australia's richest person under 40 (Farouque, 2006). ABC also became a major player in international childcare markets, expanding into the US, the UK and New Zealand (see Table 9.2), and acquiring franchises in Hong Kong, Indonesia and the Philippines. In 2006 it was the largest listed childcare company in the world (Gottliebsen, 2006).

ABC separated the real estate, or property, element of its business from the day-to-day operation of childcare centres. It sold the real estate (childcare centres) to a property investment company and leased them back. The cash flow generated from the sale of the sites enabled

Table 9.2: Growth in number of ABC Learning childcare centres 2001–07

	Australia	New Zealand	United States	United Kingdom	Total
Year (June)					
2001	43				
2002	94				94
2003	187				187
2004	327				327
2005	660				660
2006	905	28	324		1,257
2007	1,084	104	1,015	35	2,238
2007 (December)	1,095	116	1,000	112	2,323

Source: Newberry and Brennan (2013)

ABC to finance its rapid expansion. ABC raised additional funds from shareholders on the basis of claims in its annual reports that the value of its licences was escalating (Newberry and Brennan, 2013). In fact, as noted in a Senate inquiry into the provision of childcare, licences have no trading value and are nontransferable (Australian Senate, 2009, p 19).

The demand–side subsidies paid by Australian governments fed directly into this model. As noted earlier, the CCR covered 30% (now 50%) of parents' 'out-of-pocket' expenses up to a ceiling. This meant that subsidies increased automatically as fees rose. Childcare prices rose far more quickly than the cost of living, with each new measure seeming to lead to another hike in the price of childcare. Government had trapped itself into an endless game of 'catch up' (Figure 9.1).

Despite its meteoric rise on the share market, ABC's strategy of continuous growth and expansion was unsustainable. At the beginning of 2008, its profit slumped and its share price began to slide, triggering margin calls on its directors. ABC's share price continued to plunge and in August 2008 it was suspended from trading. A few months later, the company went into receivership. At this time, ABC owned approximately 25% of the long day care services in Australia. These catered for 120,000 children and employed 16,000 staff (Ellis, 2009). Fifty-five centres closed immediately and the government spent $24 million keeping the remainder open while their viability was assessed (Sumsion, 2012). In December 2009, four of Australia's largest charities, working in conjunction with Social Ventures Australia, formed a new consortium called Goodstart in order to purchase more than 650 former ABC centres from the receivers. A nonprofit organisation, Goodstart's expressed purpose is to operate

Figure 9.1: Cost of childcare, 1982–2008 – Child Care Index vs Consumer Price Index

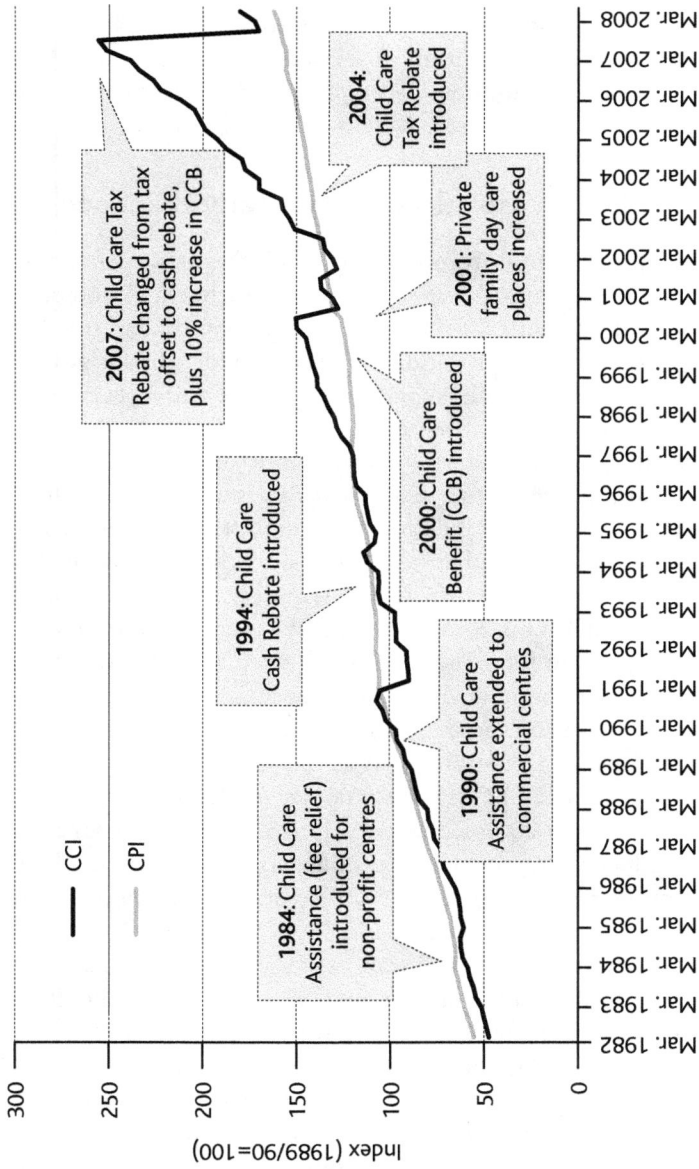

for 'social purpose' and it is committed to reinvesting any surplus into improvements in the quality of services across the sector. As a result of the Goodstart purchase, the proportion of services run by for-profit organisations fell from 88% to 66% (DEEWR, 2010).

Labor's 'human capital' agenda for early childhood

While in opposition from 1996 to 2007, the Labor Party turned its attention to the human capital framing of early childhood education. In the lead-up to the 2007 election, the party promised that 'the early years' would become a national priority under a Labor government. It cited 'brain research' suggesting that the early years are critical for future cognitive development as well as social and emotional functioning. It also referred to the work of Nobel Laureate James Heckman, showing that early learning sets the scene for future educational success, 'Childhood is a multistage process where early investments feed into later investments. Skill begets skill. Learning begets learning' (Heckman, 2007). Labor sought to reposition early childhood education, recognising that it has the potential to contribute to children's development in the short term as well as to longer-term social and economic goals – productivity, labour force participation, skills formation and social inclusion. It also acknowledged reports from international organisations such as the OECD that rated Australia's performance in ECEC relatively poorly (OECD, 2001).

Following the 2007 federal election, the new government moved to introduce more integrated administrative arrangements for ECEC. Reflecting this, it established an Office of Early Childhood Education and Child Care within the Department of Education, Employment and Workplace Relations. The location of the office within a department focused on education and employment was also symbolic. Previously, responsibility for children's services had been based in an office of 'child care' located in the social welfare department. Importantly, Labor did not challenge the heavily marketised environment of ECEC or the dominance of the for-profit sector. This was despite its commitment to 'evidence based policy' and the existence of a strong body of research demonstrating that better outcomes for children are more likely in state-based or nonprofit settings than in private for-profit ones.

Labor's strategy built on work done as part of the Council of Australian Governments' (COAGs') human capital and productivity agenda. In 2006, COAG had stated that, 'High quality and integrated early childhood education and care services ... are critical to increasing the proportion of children entering school with the basic skills for life and learning' (COAG, 2006). Labor introduced a suite of measures intended to improve quality through regulation, to make standards consistent across service types and across the country and to improve outcomes for children. The first initiative was the development of an overarching *National Early Childhood Development Strategy – Investing in the Early Years* agreed between all Australian jurisdictions. This articulated a range of measures in education and care, health, child protection, family support and housing, intended to reduce inequalities in outcomes between groups of children aged 0 to 8 years (COAG, 2009a). Labor also introduced a government-funded paid parental leave scheme, providing 18 weeks at the minimum wage to eligible parents and an additional two weeks 'Dad and partner' pay if the second parent took leave.

In the domain of early childhood, several initiatives followed the national strategy *Investing in the Early Years*. These included:

• A *National Partnership Agreement on Early Childhood Education* which aimed to ensure that every child gained access to a quality early childhood education programme delivered by a qualified early childhood teacher for 15 hours a week, 40 weeks a year, in the year before school (COAG, 2009b; AIHW, 2012).
• A *National Indigenous Reform Agreement*, which included a target that all Indigenous 4 year olds in remote communities should have access to early childhood education by 2013 (COAG, 2009c).
• A *National Partnership Agreement on the National Quality Agenda for Early Childhood Education and Care*. This included a *National Quality Framework (NQF)* and a *National Quality Standard* to ensure consistent early childhood education and care standards across Australia. The quality agenda included streamlined regulatory approaches, a unified assessment and rating system, an *Early Years Learning Framework* and a *Framework for School Age Care* (COAG, 2009d).

All elements of the ECEC reform agenda have caused vigorous public debate, but easily the most contentious aspect has been the National Quality Framework (NQF). Under the NQF, from 2014, all staff employed in preschools and long day care services are required to have, or be working towards, a two-year vocational diploma in children's services; the remaining staff are required to have, or be working towards, a vocational Certificate III level ECEC qualification (a 6-month entry level qualification) or equivalent. A university-qualified early childhood teacher is required in most long day care centres and preschools licensed for 25 or more children. Some long day care centres and some service types, including Indigenous services and in-home care, were initially excluded from NQF. According to some private, for-profit providers, the quality agenda is too burdensome for them and too expensive for parents (Karvelas, 2013).

In most states and territories, the new quality standard requires a significant upgrading of staff skills and qualifications (Fenech, Guigni and Bown, 2012). However, despite the stated goal of 'national consistency', the new national regulations do not apply equally to all services. Requirements concerning the employment of university qualified teachers, for example, vary according to the size of the service. The requirement to employ at least one early childhood teacher only applies to centres licensed to enrol 25 or more children. Centres licensed for fewer than 25 children are only required to have access to an early childhood teacher for 20% of their operating hours. Additionally, teacher requirements continue to vary across states and territories due to protected standards that reflect past regulations. In New South Wales, for example, due to these 'grandfathering' provisions, centres licensed for 40–59 children require two teachers, centres licensed for 60–79 children require three teachers, and centres licensed for 80 or more children require four teachers. Given the difference university-qualified teachers can make to the quality of early learning programmes (Siraj-Blatchford and Manni, 2007) it is highly problematic that children's access to a quality centre will remain tied, at least for a period, to where they live and the licensed capacity of the service they attend.

The quality agenda depends, at least in part, upon the willingness of educators to increase their skills and remain in the sector. However, although the federal government has provided funding to assist ECEC staff to upgrade their qualifications, it has not provided the additional funding needed by services to raise salaries in line with these enhanced qualifications. ECEC remains a highly feminised, poorly paid occupation and around 180 educators leave the sector each week (United Voice, 2013, p 4). Commenting on the federal Government's workforce initiatives, United Voice observed that 'these measures fall short of addressing the lack of career structures and wage incentives needed to encourage workers to remain in the sector and to undertake further study or training' (United Voice, 2012, p 8). The Productivity Commission has also identified low pay as an underlying cause of the labour shortages in ECEC: 'While the policy landscape now recognises the trends towards a more highly skilled workforce, the industrial landscape has not kept pace. [There is a] mismatch ... between the pay and conditions available in the sector on the one hand and the work skills and qualifications on the other' (Productivity Commission, 2011, p 5).

In addition to the controversy surrounding the NQF and the resources required to implement it, Labor came under pressure to introduce more flexible forms of childcare that would cater to the needs of parents working outside the 'standard' nine-to-five working day. In response to this, the Government initiated 'flexibility trials' to explore ways of extending the hours of subsidised childcare within a quality regulated context. The trials included extending family day care to provide overnight care for the children of police officers and nurses, providing additional hours at some 'regular' childcare centres and extending the hours of operation of out-of-school-hours care services.

The Liberal agenda for ECEC: 'flexibility' and 'affordability'

The Liberal Party's flagship programme in the work and family domain is a paid parental leave (PPL) scheme that will provide full wage replacement for six months for mothers earning up to $150,000 per year. The focus on PPL effectively sidelined ECEC during the 2013 federal election, although some commentators noted that the major challenge for mothers re-entering the workforce is not paid parental leave but the availability and cost of childcare (Sloan, 2013).

Before the election, the Coalition parties flagged their intention to establish a Productivity Commission inquiry on how the childcare system can be made 'more flexible, affordable and accessible' (LPA, 2013). This would almost certainly result in watering down or delaying the implementation of the NQF. Expanding 'choice', especially through the promotion of in-home care (such as nannies) is high on the Coalition's agenda. Part of the Productivity Commission inquiry will be to develop 'options ... for enhancing the choices available to Australian families as to how they receive child care support'. This could mean offering tax concessions to families to enable them to employ home-based caregivers. Such an interpretation is given impetus by the fact that the Productivity Commission will be asked to develop options 'within the existing funding envelope' (LPA, 2013, p 4). Tax concessions could become an option under new arrangements – especially if the Coalition limits the payment of direct subsidies to higher income families. Tax concessions are not regarded as expenditure, but rather as 'revenue foregone'.

Conclusion

Between the early 1990s and 2013, services for young children expanded significantly in Australia. The Rudd and Gillard Labor Governments (2007–13) embarked on an ambitious reform agenda which, if adequately funded and resourced, had the capacity to improve the quality of ECEC provision and make a significant difference to the lives of young Australians. However, Labor's initiatives built upon, rather than challenged, the notion of childcare as a commodity. Policy debate is dominated by a narrow agenda centred on 'targets', 'goals' and 'outcomes', while much public discussion focuses on practical issues such as access and affordability. There is very little space for consideration of the deeper political and ethical issues at stake in framing arrangements for children's care and education (Moss, 2009, p 5). All indications are that the Coalition Government will intensify the market focus of the programme, while diluting quality requirements and sidelining the critical issue of improved wages and conditions for educators in children's services.

Notes

[1] Research for this chapter was supported under the Australian Research Council's *Linkage Projects* scheme (LP100200297) Families at the Centre: Negotiating Australia's Mixed Market in Early Education and Care.

[2] The term used in Australia for day nurseries or crèches.

[3] Regulated care provided in the homes of trained carers. state and territory government laws determine the number of children each carer can have in their home.

[4] In-home care is similar to family day care but the carer works in the child's home. In-home care is not widely available and usually only an option where other forms of care are not suitable, e.g. when the child or parent has a disability, when there are several children under school age or where the family lives in a remote or isolated area.

[5] Later, the Rudd Labor Government increased the Child Care Rebate to cover 50% of out-of-pocket expenses up to a ceiling of $15,000.

References

AIHW (Australian Institute of Health and Welfare) (2012) *A Picture of Australia's Children,* Cat. no. PHE 167. Canberra: AIHW

Australian Senate (2009) *Inquiry into the Provision of Child Care,* Education, Employment and Workplace Relations References Committee, Canberra

Baxter, J. (2013) *Parents working out work,* Australian Family Trends No. 1, Melbourne: Australian Institute of Family Studies

Brennan, D. (1998) *The Politics of Australian Child Care: Philanthropy to Feminism,* Cambridge: Cambridge University Press

Brennan, D. (2007a) 'Babies, Budgets and Birthrates: Work/Family Policy in Australia 1996–2006', *Social Politics: International Studies in Gender, State and Society,* 14 (1), 31-57

Brennan, D. (2007b) 'The ABC of Child Care Politics', *Australian Journal of Social Issues,* 42 (2), 213-225

Brennan, D., Cass, B., Himmelweit, S. and Szebehely M. (2012) 'The marketization of care: Rationales and consequences in Nordic and liberal care regimes', *Journal of European Social Policy,* 22 (4), 377-391

Buckingham J. (2008) *Child Care and the Labour Supply,* Sydney: The Centre for Independent Studies

Cassells, R. and Miranti, R. (2012) *Outside School Hours Care: Social Gradients and Patterns of Use,* Sydney: UnitingCare

COAG (Council of Australian Governments) (2006) 'Human capital reform: report by the COAG National Reform Initiative Working Group', Canberra

COAG (Council of Australian Governments) (2009a) *Investing in the early years: A national childhood development strategy,* Canberra

COAG (Council of Australian Governments) (2009b) *National partnership agreement on the national quality agenda for early childhood education and care,* Canberra

COAG (Council of Australian Governments) (2009c) *National Indigenous Reform Agreement (Closing the Gap),* Canberra

COAG (Council of Australian Governments) (2009d) *National Partnership for Early Childhood Education,* Canberra

DEEWR (Department of Education, Employment and Workplace Relations) (2010) *State of Child Care in Australia,* Canberra: Office of Early Childhood Education and Child Care

Ellis, K. (2009) *Ministerial Statement – The Future of ABC Learning,* 15 September

Farouque, F. (2006) 'The other Eddy everywhere', *The Age,* 8 April

Fenech, M., Giugni, M. and Bown, K. (2012) 'A critical analysis of the National Quality Framework: Mobilising for a vision for children beyond minimum standards', *Australasian Journal of Early Childhood*, 12(4), 5-14

Gottliebsen, R. (2006) 'The building blocks of a global empire', *Weekend Australian*, 21-22 October

Heckman, J. (2007) *The economics, technology and neuroscience of human capability formation, Discussion Paper No. 2875*, Bonn: Institute for the Study of Labor (IZA)

Jensen, C. (2009) 'Institutions and the politics of childcare services', *Journal of European Social Policy*, 19(1), 7-18

Karvelas, P. (2013) 'Kindy staff too busy reporting to care', *The Australian*, 6 July.

Kirby, J. (2003) 'Playgrounds for profit', *Business Review Weekly*, 13-19 November, 32-37

LPA (Liberal Party of Australia) (2013) *The Coalition's Policy for Better Child Care and Early Learning*, Sydney

Moss, P. (2009) *There are alternatives! Markets and democratic experimentalism in early childhood education and care*, Working Paper No 53, The Hague, The Netherlands: Bernard van Leer Foundation and Bertelsmann Stiftung.

Moss, P. (2012) 'Need markets be the only show in town?', in E. Lloyd and H. Penn (eds) *Childcare markets: Can they deliver an equitable service?* Bristol: Policy Press, pp 191-208

Newberry, S. and Brennan, D. (2013) 'The marketisation of early childhood education and care (ECEC) in Australia: A structured response, *Financial Accountability & Management*, 29 (3), 227-245

OECD (Organisation for Economic Cooperation and Development) (2001), *OECD country note: Early childhood education and care policy in Australia,* Paris: OECD

OECD (Organisation for Economic Cooperation and Development) (2006), *Starting Strong II*, Paris: OECD

Pearce, N. and W. Paxton (eds) (2005) *Social Justice: Building a Fairer Britain*, London: Institute for Public Policy Research

Plantenga, J. (2012) 'Local providers and loyal parents: competition and consumer choice in the Dutch childcare market', in E. Lloyd and H. Penn (eds), *Childcare Markets: Can they Deliver an Equitable Service?* Bristol: Policy Press, pp 63-77

Productivity Commission. (2011) *Early Childhood Development Workforce, Research Report*, Melbourne

Productivity Commission (2013) *Report on Government Services,* Canberra

PWC (PriceWaterhouseCooper) (2011), A practical vision for early childhood education and care, Melbourne: PWC

Sandel, M. (2012) *What Money Can't Buy: The Moral Limits of Markets*, New York: Farrar, Straus and Giroux

Siraj-Blatchford, I., and Manni, L. (2007) *Effective leadership in the early years sector (ELEYS) study*, London: Institute of Education, University of London

Sloan, J. (2013) 'Too dear, too wasteful: drop it for daycare', *Australian*, 19 August

Sumsion, J. (2012) 'ABC Learning and Australian early childhood education and care: A retrospective audit of a radical experiment', in E. Lloyd and H. Penn (eds) *Childcare Markets: Can they Deliver an Equitable Service?*, Bristol: Policy Press, pp 209-26

Tayler, C. (2011) 'Changing policy, changing culture: Steps toward early learning quality improvement in Australia', *International Journal of Early Childhood*, 43, 211-25

United Voice (2012) *Professional Wages Proposal for Early Childhood Education and Care*, United Voice 2013 ECC Federal Budget Submission

TEN

Mixed messages in the new politics of education

Louise Watson and Charlotte Liu

The neoliberal approach to education policy is to understate education's social value, valorise its economic role and emphasise the private returns to individuals who 'invest' in it. Employing such a narrow set of assumptions makes it easier to attack the efficiency of public education institutions and champion market-based mechanisms for distributing funding (Chubb and Moe, 1990; Norton, 2012). In contrast, social democratic perspectives, while acknowledging its economic value both to individuals and to nations, also emphasise education's social role in 'civilising humanity' and are concerned about the fair distribution of educational opportunities and outcomes (Nussbaum, 1997; Dreze and Sen, 2003). The narrow assumptions of the neoliberal consensus have now gained such ascendancy, that few politicians have the courage to defend their education policies in social terms alone. As a result, agendas are invariably framed in terms of both economic objectives and social goals, conveying a 'hybrid mix of the neo-liberal with social democratic aspirations' (Lingard, 2010, p 1) that lead to apparent contradictions in policy and practice.

This chapter explores how the Australian Labor Government accommodated the neoliberal consensus in its national education policies between 2007 and 2013. The chapter focuses on federal education policy initiatives in schooling and higher education as these two sectors are primary vehicles for social and economic mobility (Ball, 2003). However, it is acknowledged that Australia's vocational education and training (VET) sector has also been the target of extensive neoliberal reform which has diminished its capacity to contribute to social outcomes (Smith and Keating, 1997; Wheelahan, 2007). The concluding section discusses how education policy needs to change to address the social and economic challenges of the 21st century.

Structural inequalities in higher education

Today, in spite of 150 years of public funding, access to Australian universities remains unequal. Although the total number of domestic undergraduate students more than trebled over the 35 years from 1974 to 2009, the proportion of higher education students from the bottom socioeconomic quartile (i.e. the bottom 25%) has remained, since 1989, at 15% (Bradley et al, 2008, p 12). In 2007, men with a university-educated father in Australia were still 2.8 times more likely to have graduated from university than other men, while women with a university-educated father were 3.7 times more likely to have graduated than other women (Chesters and Watson, 2012). This structural inequality is perpetuated by universities' influence over senior secondary assessment, their institutional habits that deter low socioeconomic status (SES) students from aspiring to higher education and the often inadequate systems of support for students during their first year of study (Teese, 2000; Naylor et al, 2013).

As Education Minister in the Federal Labor Government, from 2007, Julia Gillard delivered a higher education policy that emphasised both economic and redistributive goals. Arguing that Australia needed a more highly educated workforce to fuel economic growth, Gillard removed the quota or 'cap' on funded undergraduate places. This decision, which proved a considerable drain on the Commonwealth budget, was advocated by the elite 'Group of Eight' universities, who lobby for a more 'market-driven' approach to funding higher education places (Group of Eight, 2011). This policy was accompanied by an 'economic' target of having 40% of 25 to 34 year olds holding a bachelor degree or higher by 2025 (from the 2008 level of 32%). At the same time, Gillard announced a participation target with a redistributive goal: to raise the proportion of students from the lowest SES quartile attending universities from 15% to 20% by 2020 (Australian Government, 2009).

To support its low SES participation target, the government introduced a Higher Education Participation and Partnerships (HEPP) Program (Australian Government, 2013a). The 'Participation' element provided a loading for each low SES student enrolled that gave universities a financial incentive to broaden their undergraduate intakes. In response, most 'Group of Eight' universities introduced or extended programmes to modify their admissions processes by making an adjustment to low SES students' tertiary entrance rank. The 'Partnerships' element of the programme encouraged universities to engage more proactively with schools serving low SES communities (Lomax-Smith et al, 2011; McKenzie et al, 2013). This initiative was based on evidence that young people's decisions about their post-school options are influenced by their socioeconomic status and are formed in the early years of secondary school (Cardak and Ryan, 2009; Tieben and Wolbers, 2009).

While it is difficult to evaluate the success of the HEPP Program in the short term, since 2007, the proportion of total university students from postcodes in the lowest socioeconomic quartile has increased slightly from 16.09% in 2007 to 16.76% in 2011, leading to some pessimism about the likelihood of achieving the target of 20% by 2020 (Naylor et al, 2013). The 'economic' target to have 40% of 25 to 34 year olds holding a bachelor degree or higher by 2025 appears likely to be met. Gillard's proactive policy to improve the low SES participation rate was in stark contrast to the more complacent policies of previous federal governments of both political persuasions. Yet by lifting the cap on funded places she also initiated a quasi-market for higher education, which was firmly within the boundaries of the neoliberal consensus.

The achievement gap in schooling

Since the 1980s, there has been a growing policy interest in the 'performance' of schools, which has led to new standards for monitoring the performance of teachers, standards for curriculum and benchmarks for student achievement (Watson, 1996; Elmore, 2004) Although the 'standards-based reform' movement has been used to support neoliberal political agendas (Gardner, 1983), it has also been driven by teachers' professional associations and education systems (Watson, 2005) and is consistent with worldwide trends in public sector management reform focused on improving accountability (OECD, 1995)

Traditionally, education authorities assumed that best practice in teaching simply needed to be disseminated widely in order to be taken up in classrooms. Education policy was therefore focused on promoting innovation in pedagogy and curriculum, experimenting with new school structures and delivery and revising curriculum, and while there were incentives for teachers and schools to innovate and experiment, there was very little measurement of the impact of any reforms (Fullan, 2009). Once education systems began to collect data on student achievement on a consistent basis, education researchers noticed a large and persistent gap in the achievement levels between children from different socioeconomic backgrounds (Lamb, 1997; Teese et al, 2007).

It has long been recognised that the educational level of a child's parents has significant effects on the child's educational attainment and that this is established well before the commencement of schooling (Melhuish et al, 2008; Rodriguez and Tamis-La Monda, 2011). Data on children's literacy and numeracy achievement suggests that schooling has little or no impact in reducing these effects. Children at the bottom of the distribution for achievement at the end of their first year of school continue to be ranked low in successive years, while children ranked highly when they are young remain at the top of the scale. The longer a child attends school, the wider the achievement gap becomes, suggesting that the experience of schooling exacerbates, rather than ameliorates inequalities in the distribution of educational outcomes (Rothman and McMillan, 2003; Teese et al, 2007).

The collection of system-wide data on literacy and numeracy achievement also enabled researchers to identify some schools that appeared to have a positive impact on student achievement, particularly among low SES students. Studies investigating these schools concluded that teachers and principals play a critical role in influencing students' educational outcomes and effective teaching can raise the educational achievement levels of low SES students. Studies of teacher effectiveness suggest that students placed with high-performing teachers will progress three times as fast as those placed with low performing teachers, while students placed with low performing teachers for several years in a row suffer an educational loss that is largely irreversible (Reeves, 2008). These studies highlight the importance of teacher expertise in areas such as content, pedagogical and curriculum knowledge as well as classroom management and communication skills, which allow both sophisticated planning before lessons and a rich improvisational repertoire during class (Yates, 2005). Also emphasised are teachers' social-emotional competencies, such as compassion, empathy, reflectivity and resilience, as a strong predictor of their performance (Jennings and Greenberg, 2009; Kirby and Dipaola, 2011). Studies of school leadership suggest that the skill, knowledge and behaviour of school principals also has an influence on student learning, and thus on overall school performance (Robinson et al, 2008)

Challenging the complacent assumption that teachers and principals are no more than 'potted plants, decorating a school with good intentions while demographic destiny marches onward' (Reeves, 2008), education research now investigates how to better prepare teachers and principals to have a positive impact on student learning. School authorities are also more focused on holding schools to account for educational outcomes, particularly schools serving high proportions of students from lower socioeconomic groups. Research on what schools and systems can do to improve educational outcomes in schools serving low SES communities identifies policies and practices such as: increasing the focus on educational attainment; raising expectations among students, teachers and parents; making teaching more student-centred and responsive to individual learner needs; and delivering education in partnership with other service providers and with the school's external community. These findings have implications for school staffing, school assessment practices, staff training and development and school leadership (Department for Education and Skills, 2007; McKinsey and Company, 2007; Butt and Lowe, 2012).

On the assumption that schools should make a difference to students' educational outcomes, school systems are now being called to account. In 2007, the New South Wales Auditor-General criticised the NSW education system for making little progress since 1999 in improving the educational outcomes of socioeconomically disadvantaged students. (Department of Education and Training/the Audit Office, 2008). Two years later, the Victorian Auditor-General criticised Victoria's expenditure on literacy programmes, pointing out that the Department could not demonstrate any impact of targeted expenditure on reducing the gap in literacy outcomes between advantaged and disadvantaged students (Victorian Auditor-General, 2009).

Literacy and numeracy are not the only outcomes of schooling and teachers should never be expected to focus all their efforts on the narrow goal of achieving high scores in system-wide tests. Nevertheless, data collected in such tests has provided evidence of widespread inequality in the distribution of learning outcomes, implying that the way in which government resources are allocated to schools could be improved. Federal Labor, and Gillard especially in her role first as Education Minister and then Prime Minister, used this evidence to underpin a national school improvement policy agenda, which commenced with National Partnership Agreements in 2007 and culminated in the Australian Education Act of 2013, which introduced a new national funding system for all schools. While Gillard frequently portrayed the persistence of a wide gap in achievement between schools serving different socioeconomic groups as evidence of ineffective teaching, poor school leadership and policy failure, she also justified her policies in terms of Australia remaining 'competitive' in international league tables of student performance (Gillard, 2008a). This led to confusion about the intentions of the federal government's school reforms, particularly when the mass media chose to emphasise the policy details that were more consistent with the accepted neoliberal consensus.

A National Plan for School Improvement

In 2007 the Federal Labor Government used strengthened intergovernmental processes (Painter, 1998) to forge a National Education Agreement aiming to improve Australian schooling, by allocating resources towards building the capacities of teachers and school leaders, particularly in schools serving low SES communities (Council of Australian Governments, 2009). The Council of Australian Governments' (COAG) communiqué emphasised education's economic value as well as its social role, stating 'reform in the way education and training is delivered is critical to driving our future productivity and increasing social inclusion' (Council of Australian Governments, 2008, p 19). COAG endorsed five agreed outcomes for schooling that echoed both neoliberal and social democratic sentiments:

1. all children are engaged in, and benefit from schooling;
2. young people meet basic literacy and numeracy standards and levels of achievement are improving;
3. Australian students excel by international standards;
4. schooling promotes social inclusion and reduces the educational disadvantage of children, especially indigenous children;
5. young people make a successful transition from school to work and further study.

(Ministerial Council on Education, Employment, Training and Youth Affairs, 2008, p 12)

National Partnership Agreements

The National Education Agreement resulted in three National Partnership (NP) Agreements, negotiated bilaterally with each state or territory, worth more than $2.5 billion. Under the Agreements, state and territory governments were expected to allocate additional funding to designated schools (in both the government and non-government sectors), to support specified activities in six agreed reform areas. Systems were also expected to evaluate the impact of these activities and report publicly on their effectiveness, both for accountability purposes and to inform future policy (Ministerial Council on Education, Employment, Training and Youth Affairs,

Attachment B, 2008, p 12*)*. Targets were set and a proportion of funding was held back to 'reward' states that delivered on nationally significant reforms (Council of Australian Governments, 2008).

The first NP Agreement, on Literacy and Numeracy, controversially mandated the establishment of the Australian Curriculum and Assessment Reporting Authority (ACARA) and the publication of all schools' National Assessment Program in Literacy and Numeracy (NAPLAN) test results along with information about the socioeconomic status of school student populations, on a national MySchool website. Gillard defended the website as providing '... the best possible information as the basis for our decisions ... not for the production of crude league tables but to inform a real program to address disadvantage. And we need all of this information in the public domain to inform parents and teachers in their efforts' (Gillard, 2008b).

The then Prime Minister, Kevin Rudd, more explicitly invoked the neoliberal concept of parental choice in defending the website, when he remarked, 'if some [parents] walk with their feet [in response to the publication of performance data] that is exactly what the system is designed to do' (Rudd, 2008).

Under the second NP, for Low Socio-Economic Status School Communities, some $1.5 billion (from 2008–09 to 2014–15) was allocated to low SES schools (Australian Government, 2012) for the introduction of significant and far-reaching reforms based on school improvement research (Council of Australian Governments, 2008). Many of the reforms had industrial implications, such as: affording principals greater autonomy over managing teacher performance, including performance pay; providing financial incentives to attract high-performing principals and teachers to disadvantaged schools; and funding to support partnerships between schools and their communities (Council of Australian Governments, 2009). While state and territory governments implemented the reforms in different ways, low SES schools targeted under the NP received significant injections of additional funding – often in the order of millions of dollars – to employ specialised staff to help implement the agreed programmes of school improvement (NSW Department of Education and Communities, 2011, p 5).

The third NP, on Quality Teaching, funded initiatives to improve teacher effectiveness, through measures that research suggested could have an impact on teacher quality, satisfaction and retention (Watson, 2005). The Federal Government established the Australian Institute of Teaching and School Leadership (AITSL) to develop national professional standards for teachers and school principals (Australian

Government, 2012). It also funded an alternative teacher education initiative – *Teach for Australia*. Modelled on a controversial North American programme called *Teach for America*, and a similar programme in the UK, the initiative recruits graduates from selected universities to undergo a six-week, fast-tracked teacher training before the 'associates' are assigned with a two-year position in the public school system, which then leads to a formal teaching certification (Teach for Australia, 2013).

By providing a substantial, yet targeted, increase in funding, and in holding schools and systems to account for improving educational outcomes, particularly among low SES students, these reforms represented a radical and hard-edged approach to addressing inequality in Australian schooling. Yet although Gillard frequently stated her concern about the gap in achievement between students from different socioeconomic groups, she also referenced neoliberal concepts such as Australia's (declining) competitiveness in international league tables, which were more commonly reported in the mass media.

Reform of private school funding

Once the NP Agreements were in place, the Federal Labor Government embarked on an ambitious project to overhaul Australia's system of funding private schools, which had always been controversial (Anderson, 1993; Buckingham, 2000; Watson and Ryan, 2010). Calls for reform of the system had been ignored by major political parties in fear of reopening the divisive state aid debate (Hogan, 1984; Watson, 1998). In 2001, the Howard Government introduced a new SES-based funding scheme that delivered significant funding increases to well-resourced private schools (Watson, 2004). On winning office in 2007, Labor extended the existing funding arrangements until 2013 and in 2010, after extensive consultation, established a six-member review panel, chaired by businessperson David Gonksi, charged with 'achieving a funding system for the period beyond 2013 which is transparent, fair, financially sustainable and effective in promoting excellent educational outcomes for all Australian students' (Gonski et al, 2011, p 225).

The Gonski review's recommendations, largely adopted by the Federal Government, proposed an overall increase in funding under a new system that would apply to both public and private schools. All schools would be eligible for a relatively small core amount per student, supplemented by larger amounts allocated on the basis of student characteristics. Under the Gonski plan, funding for private schools would be the responsibility of state and territory governments within the nationally agreed funding system, based on School Improvement Plans (Gonski et al, 2011). The approach had been trialled, in part, during in Labor's first term, when a dozen federal schools funding programmes were rolled into NP Agreements. From 2009, money which had previously been distributed to private schools by the Commonwealth Government was now distributed by state and territory governments under NP Agreements. This represented a first step in dismantling the direct funding relationship between private school stakeholders and the Federal Government. The passage of the Australian Education Act in 2013 marked the end of the relationship, with the largest federal private schools funding programme – the recurrent grants programme – rolled into the National School Improvement Plans from 2014 (Australian Government, 2013b).

Inequality in resources between public and private schools has been a contested issue since federal funding for private schools was introduced five decades ago. Policies aiming to equalise resource levels by reducing funding to selected private schools, such as those proposed by Labor leader Mark Latham in 2004 and the Hawke Labor Government in 1983, provoked intense opposition and were never implemented. Throughout the Gonski review process, the Gillard Government repeatedly reassured private school stakeholders that no school would receive less funding under the new scheme. When Gillard discussed her intention to reform private schools funding in 2010, she did not focus on inequalities in resource levels between public and private schools. Instead, she justified her policy direction in terms of improving school performance, including addressing the achievement gap. In a speech to the Sydney Institute on 15 April 2010, Gillard said that the NP Agreements had 'changed the politics of education', by making 'high expectations the central feature of education policy in this country – high expectations for every student, regardless of their background, the type of school they go to, or the barriers that they might face to educational achievement' (Gillard, 2010, p 3). Gillard acknowledged the historical divisiveness of the private schools funding issue, but distanced herself from it, saying that 'Australia's educational future is too important to allow it to be dominated by ideological questions that exercise only a small minority' (Gillard, 2010, p 1). Throughout the address, she referred to data illustrating the achievement gap and emphasised her determination to 'reject the orthodoxies that say it is too hard to educate some children effectively' (Gillard, 2010).

The Australian Education Act 2013 was a significant milestone in the history of schools funding because it ended five decades of direct federal funding of private schools and promised an unprecedented increase in resources to all schools. Yet the most prominent public justification for this reform was the argument that Australia needed to address its poor standing in international league tables of student performance. The government's initial discussion paper for the Gonski review cited Program of International Student Assessment (PISA) results indicating that 'between 2003 and 2006, Australian student performance declined in both absolute and relative terms in reading literacy' while also noting that 'this decline is partly the result of students from disadvantaged backgrounds performing relatively poorly. Socioeconomic factors play a stronger role in determining student outcomes and life chances than they should ...' (Australian Government, 2010, p 6). During 2013, when the Federal Labor Government was negotiating with state and territory governments to secure agreement to the new Plan, Australia's ranking on international league tables of student achievement became linked to its economic performance. The Government argued that its Better Schools Plan would 'take Australian schools into the top 5 in the world by 2025', noting 'our performance has been declining by international standards and the gap between the highest and lowest performing students has widened'. (Australian Government, 2013b). The state and territory governments that prevaricated in signing the agreement were portrayed as 'jeopardising Australia's international competitiveness' (Shorten, 2013). Thus a national reform of considerable significance was reduced to an instrument for making schools more 'competitive' in terms of narrow international benchmarks of student achievement, which placed it comfortably within the boundaries of the neoliberal consensus.

From 2010, Gillard ensured that the total level of resources received by every school, from both public and private sources, was published annually on the MySchool website, in the interests of transparency and accountability (Gillard, 2010). Thus the disparities in resources between public and private schools are now available for all to see, although addressing these disparities is not, as yet, the explicit objective of any government policy.

Contemporary challenges

Human capital theorists have long argued that investment in education delivers a net national benefit in terms of economic growth (Becker, 1964) and the level of global economic integration achieved through the application of new technologies has further increased the value of educational qualifications (Ryan and Watson, 2003). While social democrats readily acknowledge education's economic value as well as its broader social role, the neoliberal tendency to ignore education's social value, while focusing on economic benefits alone, threatens to impoverish education policy.

The power of educational qualifications to deliver lifetime economic security to individuals in the 21st century compounds the disadvantage faced by individuals who are less 'successful' in terms of educational achievement. The growth of new jobs in professional and managerial occupations contrasts starkly with the disappearance of full-time employment in lower-level occupations (Saunders et al, 2008). Until education policy is refocused squarely on engaging learners – of all ages –at risk of low educational attainment, Australia's education system will fail to address the needs of its 'small chaotic, disadvantaged underclass, which consumes massive resources' (McTernan, 2013, p 13;).

A barrier to developing a more inclusive education system is the historical legacy that directs the bulk of public funding to institutions in the traditional sectors of schooling, training and higher education, which were designed to 'track' individuals into categories of employment reflecting the social conditions of earlier times (Fooks, 1994; Wheelahan, 2007). Public funding for learners outside of these three 'formal' sectors remains haphazard and uncoordinated, even though education providers within the 'informal' adult and community education (ACE) sector are more likely to engage learners at risk of social exclusion (Crowley, 1997; Watson, Wheelahan and Chapman, 2002).

An inclusive education system would also deliver appropriate education and training to vulnerable children and their families during the years prior to formal schooling. Educational support for families with vulnerable young children during the first years of life increases parental competence, reduces social and environmental risks and contributes to improved educational, social and economic outcomes in the long term (Heckman, 2006). Yet there is scant public education provision for vulnerable young children and their families prior to formal schooling (Hayes, Gray and Edwards, 2008; Corlin et al, 2009). While in some jurisdictions, early childhood education services are now integrated with school education services, it remains a challenge to bridge the gap between the education sector and the community services sector in meeting the educational needs of vulnerable young children between birth and five years of age (Taylor and Giugni, 2012).

Australia's 19th-century public education system remains ill equipped to assist individuals who have the least capacity – socially, financially, physically or psychologically – to engage in education to the extent now necessary for full participation in society. To address the deepening social and economic divide between people who are well educated and those who are not, we need new ways of conceptualising public expenditure on education, free of nostalgic attachments to traditional institutions and sectors. This task is more difficult when it is assumed that education's primary role is to fuel economic growth, and educational institutions are portrayed as vehicles for delivering high financial rewards to individuals in return for a largely private investment.

Conclusion

This chapter has explored recent developments in Australian education policy, illustrating how the ascendancy of neoliberalism, which emphasises the economic and private benefits of education as well as the value of markets, competition and individual choice in the delivery of education services, renders it difficult for education policies to be defended in terms of their social or redistributive value. Labor's coupling of social democratic objectives with neoliberal concerns led to apparent contradictions in national education policies, but may have been successful in silencing its potential critics, both on the Opposition benches and in sections of the mass media. This strategy also contributed to the invisibility of social democratic perspectives in education policy debates at a time when Australia desperately needs a new social democratic vision.

A social democratic vision for education policy, while concerned with the equitable distribution of educational outcomes, would also acknowledge education's role in shaping society. It would champion the intrinsic value of encouraging critical thinking and open inquiry and would argue that publicly funded institutions should perform this role in a robust democracy. It would also validate the role of education in questioning contemporary orthodoxies, such as the assumed value of material consumption and economic growth. It would argue for public investment in education to deliver innovations for the benefit of society as a whole, as distinct from private benefits to individuals or corporations. It would aim to measure the performance of education systems against these broad goals, while also monitoring the distribution of educational outcomes between social groups. A social democratic vision of education that recognises the value of qualifications has a responsibility to ensure that the benefits of publicly funded education services are equally enjoyed by all members of society. In the face of a neoliberal consensus that seeks to measure education's value solely in terms of student 'achievement', international 'competitiveness' and the acquisition of formal qualifications, it remains a challenge to fashion education policies that reflect complex objectives and less tangible outcomes.

Education's role in creating and supporting a sustainable society must be affirmed if we are to achieve a social democratic vision that addresses the complex needs of educationally dispossessed people, including vulnerable young children and their families in home and community settings. In the absence of such a vision, the contemporary neoliberal consensus that portrays education primarily as a good for private consumption, best delivered via market mechanisms, albeit with substantial public funding, will gain further legitimacy.

References

Anderson, D.S. (1993) 'Education and the Social Order: The effect of the private sector' in Najman J.M. and Western J.S. (eds), *A Sociology of Australian Society,* Melbourne: Macmillan, pp 255-73

Australian Government (2009) *Transforming Australia's Higher Education System,* Canberra: Commonwealth of Australia

Australian Government (2010) *Review of Funding for Schooling – Discussion Paper and Draft Terms of Reference,* Canberra: Commonwealth of Australia

Australian Government (2012) *Smarter Schools Website.* Department of Education, Employment and Workplace Relations: http://smarterschools.gov.au

Australian Government (2013a) *Higher Education Participation and Partnerships Program.* Available at: www.innovation.gov.au/highereducation/Equity/HigherEducationParticipationAndPartnershipsProgram/Pages/default.aspx

Australian Government (2013b) *Better Schools Website,* Department of Education, Employment and Workplace Relations: http://betterschools.gov.au

Ball, S.J. (2003) *ClassStrategies and the Education Market: The Middle Classes and Social Advantage,* London: Routledge

Becker, G. (1964) *Human Capital: A Theoretical and Empirical Analysis, with special reference to Education,* New York: NBER & Columbia University Press

Bradley, D., Noonan, P., Nugent, H. and Scales, B. (2008) *Review of Higher Education in Australia – Final Report*, Canberra: Australian Government

Buckingham, J. (2000) 'School funding for all: making sense of the debate over dollars', Issue Analysis Paper No. 17, Centre for Independent Studies, 12 October

Butt, R. and Lowe, K. (2012) 'Teaching assistants and class teachers: Differing perceptions, role confusion and the benefits of skills-based training', *International Journal of Inclusive Education*, vol 16, no 2, pp 207-19

Cardak, B.A. and Ryan, C. (2009) 'Participation in higher education in Australia: Equity and access', *Economic Record*, vol 85, no 271, pp 433–48.

Chesters, J. and Watson, L. (2012) 'Understanding the persistence of inequality in higher education: evidence from Australia', *Journal of Education Policy* vol 28, no 2

Chubb, J. and Moe, T. (1990) *Politics, Markets and America's schools,* Washington DC: Brookings Institution

Corlin, N., Katz, I. and Patulny, R. (2009) 'Engaging hard-to-reach families and children: Stronger families and communities strategy 2004–2009', Occasional Paper No 26, Department of Families, Housing, Community Services and Indigenous Affairs

Council of Australian Governments (2008) *Intergovernmental Agreements,* COAG Meeting, 29 November 2008, Attachment B – Productivity Agenda, Council of Australian Governments

Council of Australian Governments (2009) National Education Agreement, Council of Australian Governments. Available at: www.coag.gov.au/intergov_agreements/federal_financial_relations/index.cfm

Crowley, R. (1997) *Beyond Cinderella: Towards a Learning Society: A Report of the Senate Employment, Education and Training References Committee,* Canberra: the Committee

Department for Education and Skills (2007) *Every Parent Matters.* London: Department for Education and Skills

Department of Education and Training/The Audit Office (2008) *Improving Literacy and Numeracy in NSW Public Schools,* Audit Office of New South Wales

Dreze, J. and Sen, A. (2003) 'Basic education as a political issue', in Tilak, J.B.G. *Education, Society and Development: National and International Perspectives, 3 – Empowerment,* New Delhi, National Institution of Educational Planning and Administration, pp 3-48

Elmore, R.F. (2004) *School Reform from the Inside Out: Policy, Practice and Performance,* Harvard Education Press

Fooks, D. (1994) 'The life and times of Cinderella' in Kearns, P. and Hall, W. (eds), *Kangan: 20 Years On*, South Australia, National Centre for Vocational Education Research

Fullan, M. (2009) 'Large-scale reform comes of age', *Journal of Educational Change* vol 10, pp 101-13

Gardner, D.P. (1983) *A Nation at Risk: The Imperative for Educational Reform, A Report to the Nation and the Secretary of Education by the National Commission on Excellence in Education*, D.P Gardner (Chair) April

Gillard, J. (2008a) Address to the Education, Employment and Social Inclusion Symposium, Northern Community Summit, Melbourne, 21 August. Available at: www.unisa.edu.au/northernsummit/resources/symposiumspeech.asp

Gillard, J. (2008b) 'A new progressive reform agenda for Australian schools', 2008 Fraser Lecture

Gillard, J. (2010) 'A future fair for all – school funding in Australia', Address to the Sydney Institute, 15 April

Gonski, D., Boston, K., Greiner, K., Lawrence, C., Scales, B. and Tannock, P. (2011) *Review of Funding for Schooling – Final Report*, December, Canberra: Australian Government

Group of Eight (2011) 'Submission to the Review of Higher Education Base Funding', April. Available at: www.deewr.gov.au/HigherEducation/Policy/BaseReview/Submissions/AtoF/Pages/Submissions.aspx

Hayes, A. Gray, M. and Edwards, B. (2008) *Social Inclusion: Origins, Concepts and Key Themes,* Department of Prime Minister and Cabinet, Social Inclusion Unit

Heckman, J.J. (2006) 'Skill formation and the economics of investing in disadvantaged children', *Science,* no 312, pp 1900-1902

Hogan, M.C. (1984) *Public versus Private Schools, Funding and Directions in Australia*, Penguin Books

Jennings, P.A. and Greenberg, M.T. (2009) 'The prosocial classroom: teacher social and emotional competence in relation to student and classroom outcomes', *Review of Educational Research*, vol 79 no 1, pp 491-525

Kirby, M. and Dipaola, M. (2011) 'Academic optimism and community engagement in urban schools', *Journal of Educational Administration,* vol 49, no 5, pp 542-62

Lamb, S. (1997) 'Access to level of mathematics study in high school: social area and school differences', *Conference Proceedings of the 20th Mathematics Education Research Group of Australasia, Vol 1*, pp 286-93

Lingard, B. (2010) 'Policy borrowing, policy learning: Testing times in Australian schooling', *Critical Studies in Education*, vol 51 no 2, pp 129-147

Lomax-Smith, J., Watson, L. and Webster, B. (2011) *Higher Education Base Funding Review – Final Report* October, Canberra: Australian Government

McKenzie, L., Crawford, N. and Jacquet, A. (2013) 'Transitions to tertiary education; Measuring and minimizing inequality between private and public school students in a university outreach program' *Journal of Academic Language and Learning*, vol 7, no 1, pp 40–60

McKinsey and Company (2007) *How the World's Best-Performing School Systems Come Out on Top*, September

McTernan, J. (2013) 'Shadow-boxing', *The Monthly*, no 92, August pp 48–50

Melhuish, E.C., Phan, M.B., Sylva, K., Sammons, P., Siraj-Blatchford, I. and Taggart, B. (2008) 'Effects of home learning environment and pre-school centre experience on literacy and numeracy development in early primary school', *Journal of Social Issues*, vol 64, no 1, pp 95-114

Ministerial Council on Education, Employment, Training and Youth Affairs. (2008) *Communique,* 22nd MCEETYA Meeting, Melbourne, 18 April. Available at: www.mceecdya.edu.au/mceecdya/meetings,11402.html

Naylor, R., Baik, C. and James, R. (2013) *Developing a Critical Interventions Framework for Advancing Equity in Australian Higher Education,* Melbourne: Centre for the Study of Higher Education, The University of Melbourne, April

Norton, A. (2012) *Graduate Winners. Assessing the Public and Private Benefits of Higher Education*, The Grattan Institute, August. Available at: http://grattan.edu.au/publications/reports

NSW Department of Education and Communities (2011) *Low Socio-Economic Status School Communities National Partnership; Information Package for Reform Extension Initiative Schools,* July, Sydney: NSW DEC

Nussbaum, M.C. (1997) *Cultivating Humanity: A Classical Defense of Reform in Liberal Education*, Harvard University Press

Organisation for Economic Co-operation and Development, (1995). *Governance in Transition, Public Management Reforms in OECD Countries*, Paris: OECD

Painter, M. (1998). *Collaborative Federalism: Economic Reform in Australia in the 1990s*, Cambridge University Press

Reeves, D.B. (2008). 'Leadership and Learning', The William Walker Oration, delivered on 1 October, 2008, Melbourne on behalf of the Australian Council for Educational Leaders (ACEL)

Robinson, V.M., Lloyd, C.A. and Rowe, K.J. (2008) 'The impact of leadership on student outcomes: An analysis of the differential effects of leadership types', *Educational Administration Quarterly*, vol 44, no 5, pp 635-74

Rodriguez, E.T. and Tamis-La Monda, C.S. (2011) 'Trajectories of the home learning environment across the first 5 years: Associations with children's vocabulary and literacy skills at prekindergarten', *Child Development*, vol 82, no 4, pp 1058-75

Rothman, S. and McMillan, J. (2003) *Influences on Achievement in Literacy and Numeracy, Longitudinal Surveys of Australian Youth*, Research Report No 36, Australian Council for Educational Research, October

Rudd, K. (2008) Questions and Answers, National Press Club, Press Conference, 27 August, Canberra. Available at: www.pm.gov.au/node/5620

Ryan, C. and Watson, L. (2003) *Skills at Work: Lifelong Learning and Changes in the Labour Market*, Canberra: Department of Education, Science and Training

Saunders, P. Naidoo, Y. and Griffiths, M. (2008) 'Towards new indicators of disadvantage: Deprivation and social exclusion in Australia', *Australian Journal of Social Issues*, vol 43, no 2, Winter pp 175-94

Shorten, B. (2013) 'Transcript of Minister Bill Shorten, Doorstop, Brisbane Adventist College, 6 August 2013'. Available at: http://billshorten.com.au/doorstop-brisbane-adventist-college

Smith, E. and Keating, J. (1997) 'Making sense of training reform and competency based training', Adelaide: National Centre for Vocational Education Research

Taylor, A. and Giugni, M. (2012) 'Common worlds: Reconceptualising inclusion in early childhood communities', *Contemporary Issues in Early Childhood*, vol 13, no 2, pp 108-19

Teach for Australia (2013), www.teachforaustralia.org/content/graduate-program-overview.

Teese, R. (2000). *Academic Success and Social Power*, Melbourne University Press

Teese, R., Lamb, S.P. and Duru-Bellat, M. (eds) (2007) *International Studies in Educational Inequality, Theory and Policy*, Springer

Tieben, N. and Wolbers, M.H.J. (2009) 'Transitions to post-secondary and tertiary education in the Netherlands: a trend analysis of unconditional and conditional socio-economic background effects', *Higher Education: The International Journal of Higher Education and Educational Planning*, published online 15 November

Victorian Auditor-General (2009) *Literacy and Numeracy Achievement*, Victorian Government Printing Office

Watson, L. (1996) 'Public accountability or fiscal control? Benchmarks of performance in Australian schooling', *Australian Journal of Education*, vol 40, no 1, pp 104-123

Watson, L. (1998) *Intentions, Opportunities and Outcomes, The impact of Commonwealth involvement in Australian schooling*, Unpublished PhD thesis, Australian National University, November

Watson, L. (2004) 'Don't throw out the baby with the bathwater: The case for a reformed SES funding scheme', *Australian Journal of Education*, vol 48, no 3, pp 227-38

Watson, L. (2005) *Quality Teaching and School Leadership*, Canberra: Teaching Australia

Watson, L. and Ryan, C. (2010) 'Choosers and losers: the impact of government subsidies on Australian secondary schools', *Australian Journal of Education*, vol 54, no 1, pp 86-107

Watson, L., Wheelahan, L. and Chapman, B. (2002) *A Cross-Sectoral Funding Model: Is it Fair and Feasible?*, Adelaide, SA: National Centre for Vocational Education Research

Wheelahan, L. (2007) 'How competency-based training locks the working class out of powerful knowledge: A modified Bernsteinian analysis', *British Journal of Sociology of Education*, vol 28, no 5, pp 637-51

Yates, G.C.R. (2005) '"How obvious": personal reflections on the database of educational psychology and effective teaching research', *Educational Psychology*, vol 25, no 6, pp 681-700

ELEVEN

The accidental logic of health policy in Australia

Fran Baum and Judith Dwyer

Introduction

Health policy debates reflect 'a strife of interests' (Sax, 1984). They are usually fraught, dealing as they do with matters of life and death, our hopes for long healthy life and our fears of pain, grief and loss of capacity. The Australian health system delivers essential care and enacts public health policy and programmes designed to keep us healthy. It is also a major industry with ever expanding capacity to diagnose and treat. It is one of Australia's largest employers (ABS, 2013), consistently delivering better than average wage growth for its professional workforce, and supporting strong growth in the pharmaceutical and medical technology sectors. Health policy can also act against powerful commercial interests and through concerted and sustained attention can effectively change the daily habits of the population (Scollo and Winstanley, 2012).

National health systems have many common features, but each is differentiated by what Tuohy describes as the 'accidental logics' of history and culture, structural and institutional parameters, and the interactions of the many actors in health policy and the health system. Structurally, power and influence are distributed between the state, capital and the health professions. The institutional dimension is the mix of instruments of control – hierarchy, market and professional collegiality – and the interacting patterns and pathways of their use over time (Tuohy, 1999, pp 6–7). Thus health policy and health systems develop with at least a degree of internal consistency as the various elements, shaped by circumstance, interests and compromise, influence each other to produce something that works in practice. In this chapter we argue that contemporary health policy in Australia is shaped by its response to three fundamental challenges: how to maximise health outcomes; how to ensure equity in access to health care; and how to operate an effective health care delivery system within constrained resources.

Maximising health outcomes: health is 'produced' in everyday life

The noise and heat in health policy debates is often driven by the question of who gets what health care at what price and standard. But if the underlying goal is healthy life, a focus on prevention offers a more direct route to health gain. In comparison with other Organization for Economic Co-operation and Development (OECD) countries, Australians on average enjoy relatively long lives (Figure 11.1). While the health system is partly responsible for this relatively reassuring picture the broader 'social determinants of health' have a greater impact (Baum, 2008; CSDH, 2008).

The 'social determinants' of health is an umbrella term for the underlying factors impacting on people's chances of a healthy life. These include the distribution of wealth, income and political power and the conditions of everyday life (access to health care, education, housing, working conditions and the natural and built environment (CSDH, 2008, p 1). It has long been understood that such resources are unevenly distributed, roughly but not exactly in accordance with the distribution of wealth. There is evidence too that it is not absolute levels of wealth (above a certain baseline), but rather disparities in its distribution that matter for health (Wilkinson and Pickett, 2009). It is also clear that other public policies (such as universal access to education, and relative equality for women) can counteract the health effects of relative poverty (CSDH, 2008; Raphael, 2012). Such policies, together with a strong primary health care sector, enabled relatively poor countries such as Cuba, China, Sri Lanka and Kerala state in India to achieve good health at a low cost (Werner and Sanders, 1997) and more recently Bangladesh, Thailand, Ethiopia, Kyrgzstan, and the Indian State of Tamil Nadu (Balabanova et al, 2013).

Public health has a central role in disease prevention and health promotion by its focus on such social determinants. Over time, public health has broadened its mandate to include the prevention of noncommunicable disease to a more general consideration of wellbeing. 'New public health' (Baum, 2008) has involved assessing the health impacts of other policy domains (for instance urban development and international trade agreements) and subsequently advancing more integrated public policy, such as the Healthy Cities

Figure 11.1: Life expectancy at birth, in years, females and males, 2010[1]

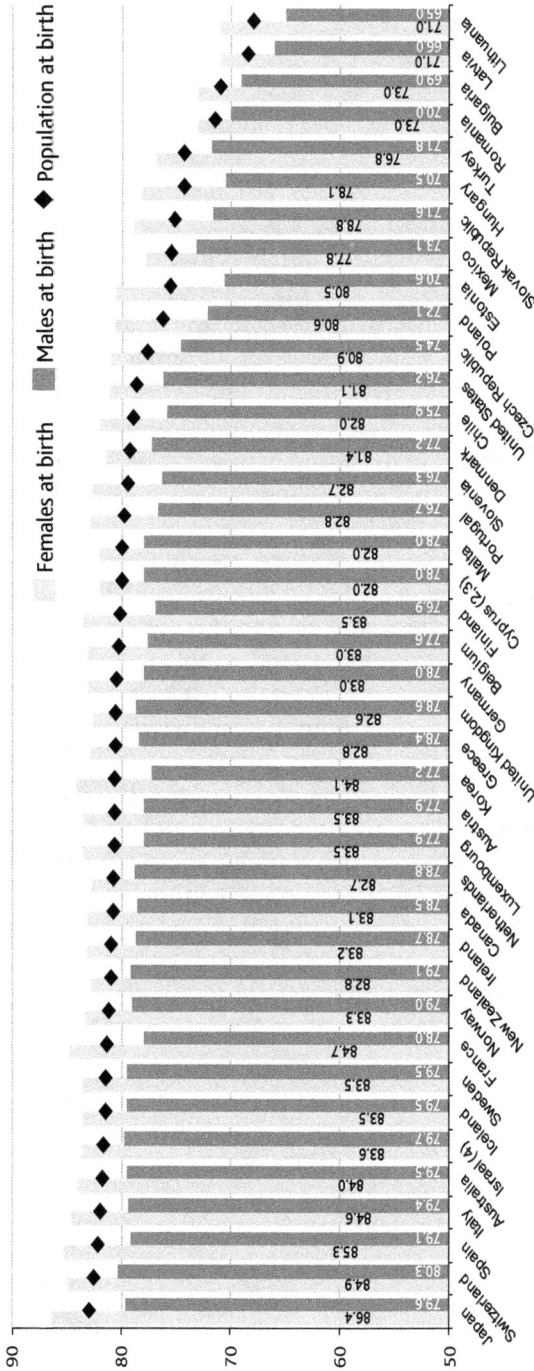

Legend: Females at birth | Males at birth | ◆ Population at birth

Notes: Countries sorted by life expectancy of total population at birth; 1) Data refers to 2007 for non-OECD EU countries, 2008 for Canada, and 2009 for Italy; 2) Footnote by Turkey: The information in this document with reference to 'Cyprus' relates to the southern part of the Island. There is no single authority representing both Turkish and Greek Cypriot people on the Island. Turkey recognizes the Turkish Republic of Northern Cyprus (TRNC). Until a lasting and equitable solution is found within the context of United Nations, Turkey shall preserve its position concerning the 'Cyprus issue'; 3) Footnote by all the European Union Member States of the OECD and the European Commission: The Republic of Cyprus is recognised by all members of the United Nations with the exception of Turkey. The information in this document relates to the area under the effective control of the Government of the Republic of Cyprus; 4) The data for Israel are supplied by and under the responsibility of the relevant Israeli authorities. The use of such data by the OECD is without prejudice to the status of the Golan Heights, East Jerusalem and Israeli settlements in the West Bank under the terms of international law.

Source: OECD (2010) Family Database CO1.2 Life Expectancy at Birth, p2. At: www.oecd.org/social/family/database

initiative (Baum, Jolley et al, 2006; WHO, 2013) and Health in All Policies (Baum, Ollila et al, 2013).

The Commission on the Social Determinants of Health reported on the evidence for change in public policy aimed at improving the underlying conditions and resources for health and the equity of their distribution (CSDH, 2008). It argued that the unequal distribution of health-promoting resources 'is the result of a toxic combination of poor social policies and programs, unfair economic conditions and bad politics' (CSDH, 2008, p 1). It suggested that the health sector could have a central role in providing leadership and stewardship on the social determinants of health. However, resource redistribution is both politically and technically difficult. Thus governments tend to focus on intermediate factors (behavioural and lifestyle aspects like quitting smoking, exercising more and eating less fat and sugar) even though there is little evidence that change at the individual level will make a difference (Popay et al, 2010).

Baum and Fisher (2013) suggest three reasons for this. They see neoliberalism as promoting a philosophy of individualism that offers little space to support a view that chances for health are primarily the product of the systems within which people live, including the dominant economic structure (Navarro, 2009). The biomedical model of disease and treatment further reinforces individualism and means most health spending is on medical services (Lantz et al, 2007).

A focus on individual behaviours and lifestyles has an appealing directness to it, whereas changing the policies and structures which constrain people's capacity to make healthy choices is more difficult. For example, the dramatic increase in obesity in the past two decades is largely a result of increased consumption of high fat and high sugar foods (Egger and Swinburn, 2010). It is *easier*, but not necessarily *as effective*, for policy makers to inform the population about this link than it is to change the conditions that make healthy choices harder (for example by regulating the size of sugary drink bottles, requiring prominent labelling of sugar, fat and salt content of foods; or reducing the exposure of children to marketing of unhealthy foods) (Gortmarker et al, 2011; Swinburn et al, 2011). Corporations (including many health sector businesses) have powerful incentives to keep the focus on behaviour change and treating illnesses because this detracts attention from the underlying social and economic drivers of ill health and health inequities.

Health policy is often also dominated by the needs of the professions and the acute care sector. A recent study involving 20 former federal, state and territory health ministers (Baum, Laris et al,

2013) demonstrated the hold the medical profession has over health policy and the ways in which consideration of health care, especially hospital services, crowds out policies and programmes concerned with keeping people well. Thus the politics of health, and the interests of the principal actors in health policy, tend to keep the focus away from the social determinants of health, and capacity to prevent health problems before they occur is compromised as a result.

Policy focuses on secondary prevention of chronic disease

The major preventive effort is directed to the secondary prevention of chronic disease (i.e. minimising its progress and impact) (Baum and Fisher, 2011). In 2011, the Australian National Preventive Health Agency (ANPHA) was established, following the report of the National Preventive Health Taskforce which aimed to 'provide a blueprint for tackling the burden of chronic disease currently caused by obesity, tobacco, and excessive consumption of alcohol' (National Preventative Health Taskforce, 2009, p 287). While the Taskforce did address the challenge of health equity and took account of evidence on inequities in chronic disease and associated risk factors, its terms of reference limited its capacity to address the social determinants of health, and the limitation continues in the work of the ANPHA.

There are exceptions to the general failure to focus on the 'upstream' determinants, as illustrated by South Australia's Health in All Policies initiative. Directed by the Department of Premier and Cabinet, it focuses on Health Lens Analysis, examining policy areas such as literacy, urban planning, cycling and Aboriginal road safety in order to identify ways in which policies can maximise their positive impact on health (Baum, Lawless et al, 2013). In another positive move, the Senate Standing Committee on Community Affairs reported in March 2013 on an Inquiry into Australia's domestic response to the Commission on Social Determinants of Health report and recommended that Australia formally accept its recommendations and commit to addressing the social determinants of health relevant to the Australian context. It further recommended that the government place responsibility for addressing social determinants of health within one agency, with a mandate to address issues across portfolios and ensure consideration of the social determinants in all relevant policy development activities, particularly in relation to education, employment, housing, family and social security policy. However in mid-2014 no follow-up action had been taken and the Abbott Coalition Government elected in

September 2013 has shown no interest in disease prevention or health promotion as policy priorities.

While there is currently little sign of major policy change there are other ways in which the Australian community and its institutions act on policy matters relevant to health. For example, the formation of the Royal Commission on Child Sexual Abuse, the result of sustained advocacy by survivors and their allies, seeks to protect the lives and health of children (Levy, 2012). There is a long history of such action by citizens and community organisations on matters of public health, and they continue to play an important role in advocating for the conditions for better health, on local, regional and national issues from neighbourhood safety to local disaster response capability to family violence. Similarly the National Disability Insurance Scheme – DisabilityCare Australia – will improve living conditions for people with disabilities. Tuohy's (1999) model does not directly include community action as a structural force in health policy and the relative weakness of the community has long been recognised (Alford, 1975), but it is in relation to action on social determinants that it is perhaps strongest.

The health of Australia's First Peoples

The relatively poor health status of Aboriginal and Torres Strait Islander people (as measured by life expectancy and burden of disease) is Australia's most significant health challenge. In December 2007 the Council of Australian Governments (COAG) agreed to a partnership between both levels of government to work with Aboriginal and Torres Strait Islander peoples to address several important 'gaps' between the life and health chances of Australia's First Peoples and the rest of the population. For 2005–07 the gap in life expectancy was estimated at 11.5 years for males and 9.7 years for females (ABS, 2011).

The strategy incorporates attention to the determinants of health, including increasing employment and education participation, reducing Aboriginal smoking rates and improving housing conditions. It aims to improve health system performance for Aboriginal people by better chronic disease detection and management, and improving access and acceptability of health services.

While progress is patchy at best, there are signs in the health indicators of improvement, for example a reported 48% reduction in young child mortality between 1991 and 2010 (Australian Government, 2012, p 17). The 2012 report concluded that progress is tracking well to halve the gap in under-five mortality rates by 2018. We note that this and other health indicator improvements cannot be confidently attributed to recent government policy; and that the expiry of COAG funding in 2013 created uncertainty about the continuation of several programmes, despite bipartisan support (see Altman, this volume, for an account of the neoliberal foundations of the Close the Gap (CtG) strategies). We suggest that the health gap will not be closed without national determination to overcome the well-documented mistrust (Reconciliation Australia, 2013) and exclusion that impede relationships between Indigenous and non-Indigenous people. This will involve finding effective ways to work with and engage with Aboriginal people and organisations. The Aboriginal Community Controlled Health sector constitutes a critical network of more than 150 primary health care (PHC) organisations, providing PHC services to between one third and one half of the Aboriginal population (NHHRC, 2009, p 87; NACCHO, 2009, pp 2–3) in rural, remote and urban settings, through approximately 2.5 million episodes of care in 2010–11 (AIHW, 2012a). The sector provides an important base for advocacy and engagement with the mainstream health system, assisting efforts to provide access to quality care for Aboriginal people. Together with the National Congress of Australia's First Peoples, the Aboriginal Community Controlled Health Services (ACCHS) sector offers a base for effective engagement in health between Indigenous and non-Indigenous Australia.

Delivering equitable benefits: access and quality

The second major challenge shaping health policy is how to deliver access to good quality health care equitably. To do so requires both the financing of the health care system and its operations – the way the many complex components work together to deliver care at the right levels in the right settings (or not) – to be designed to meet the goal of equitable access to good quality care for everyone.

There is strong evidence in favour of universal access and public funding of health care. For example, Australia, Canada, New Zealand and Britain, all of which have longer average life expectancy than America, where access to health care is largely determined by insurance status, spend less on their predominantly publicly funded systems. (Figure 11.2)

Health systems based on the principle of universal coverage achieved through public financing are generally cheaper, more efficient and more equitable (Gilson et al, 2007). This finding runs counter to the general belief that production and distribution of services is more efficient in the private sector, based on market principles. The reasons

Figure 11.2: Health spending and life expectancy

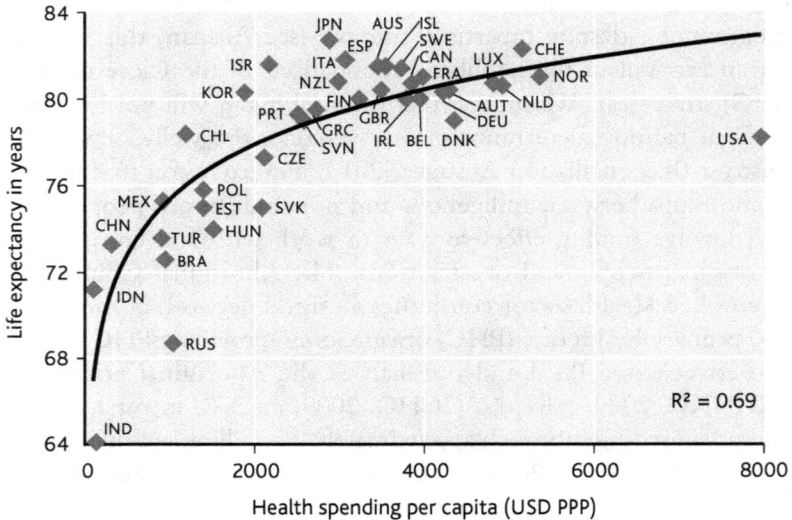

Source: Health at a Glance 2011: OECD Indicators 1.1 Life expectancy at birth

for this are complex, but arise from the fact that health is essentially a public good, where market principles do not work (Duckett and Wilcox, 2011, pp 43–5).

However, there is considerable concern about the growing costs of health care. In 2010/11, Australia spent just over $130 billion, or 9.3% of Gross Domestic Product (GDP), on all health expenditures, compared to 8.2% a decade earlier (AIHW, 2012b, p 8). Figure 11.3 shows the growth in health care expenditure as a proportion of GDP from 1960–61 until 2005–06 and demonstrates the sustained long-term increase.

The strongest growth has been in public and private hospital costs, followed by dental services and medicines (AIHW, 2012b, p 45). However, Australia's total health expenditure is in the lower end of the range of selected OECD countries (see Figure 11.4). So while the cost of Australia's health system is neither 'out of control' nor unusually high, there is no reason to believe the sustained upwards pressure of the last 50 years will stop, and significant effort to contain costs will need to continue.

Australia's system of funding health care is a good example of the outworking of accidental logics, with a complex layering of elements. It is derived from a unique mix of the competing principles of universal coverage and the choice to insure privately against the costs of private

Figure 11.3: Historical health spending

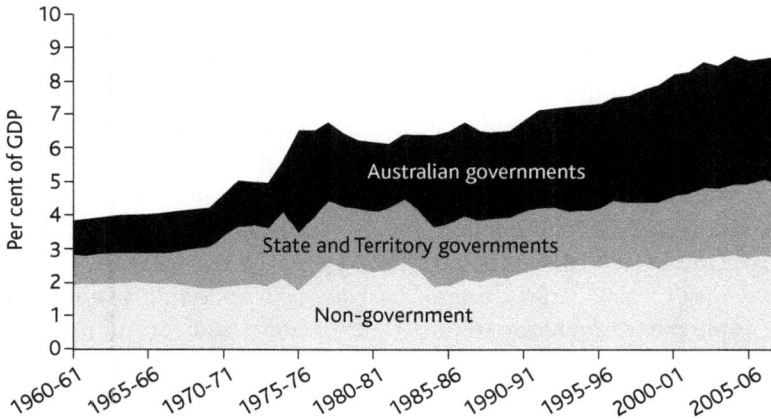

Source: Australian Institute of Health and Welfare Expenditure Data – National Health Expenditure, http://www.aihw.gov.au/expenditure-data/

Figure 11.4: Comparative spending on health in OECD countries

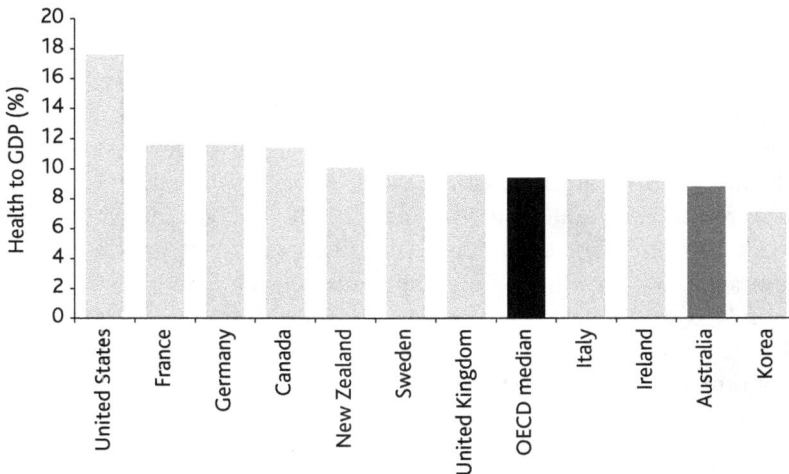

Source: AIHW (2012). Health Expenditure in Australia 2010-11. Health and Welfare Expenditure Series No 47. Cat no. HWE 56. Canberra

health care; of public and private sector provision; and of payments by government and private health insurers, as well as some direct cash costs for patients. Overall, governments are the largest payers of the costs of care provided by both public and private sectors. Not only are there multiple sources of funding, and types of providers, the system is also funded and regulated by both levels of government. The relative roles of national and jurisdictional levels are somewhat differentiated. For example, most occasions of service paid for by the Australian Government are delivered in the private sector; while most funding for public health care providers comes from state governments (including some funding transferred from national to state governments).

Regardless of the party in power at federal level, the balance in the system moves within a relatively narrow range. Conservative governments tend to focus more on choice and increases in private provision (for example the highly inefficient tax subsidies for private health insurance) (Menadue and McAuley, 2012). Labor gives emphasis to equity of access and shifting the balance to public provision (for example the introduction of public sector home and community care services). Yet the range of movement is relatively small because the principles of both universal access and choice have strong community support.

As a consequence of this complex funding, policy advocates and vested interests can argue on the basis of hypothesised effects that are logical, but often misleading. For example, the Howard Government argued that subsidies for private health insurance would reduce pressure on the public hospital system and thereby on the public purse. However, the 'new joiners' tended to be younger (Walker et al, 2005) and healthier and were not using public hospital services in any numbers. Impact on demand for public hospital care was limited, and was the result of the Lifetime Health Cover policy (introduced 18 months later and involving no cost to taxpayers) rather than the 30% rebate (Menadue and McAuley, 2012). The combined policies work to the extent that many Australians took out private health insurance, but have been very expensive and inefficient because the subsidy is paid to everyone with private health insurance, including the majority who made no change in their insurance status. The Abbott Coalition Government has made it clear through a number of statements that it sees benefits in privatising aspects of the Australian health system such as allowing private health insurance to cover GP visits and outsourcing the management of public hospitals to private companies.

The challenge for Australian health policy is to maintain the (often competing) principles of universal access and choice, under continuing pressure of growing demand and growing costs. While it is taking time for the Coalition Government's health policy agenda to emerge, the signals indicate a significant move to the choice side of this balance. Such a move is likely to increase total costs while reducing access for those who are dependent on the public health system. This brings us to the related challenge of designing a system in which the providers can work together to deliver the right services at the right time in the right place to meet the needs of patients and the community at least cost and good quality.

System design for access and quality

Universal access to essential health care addresses a fundamental access barrier but others include out-of-pocket costs, shortage of supply of needed services, complex eligibility requirements, distance and lack of transport, and reluctance to engage because of experiences of discrimination or judgmental responses. There are two major design problems that impact on both access and quality – the relative weakness of the primary health care system and the split responsibility among levels of government.

There is widespread policy consensus that health systems should be built on the basis of a strong comprehensive primary health care (PHC) system. The World Health Organization has advocated for this approach since 1978 with the adoption of the 'Health for All by the Year 2000' strategy and reiterated this in 2008 (WHO, 2008). An important time series comparison among 18 wealthy OECD countries found that a strong primary care system was associated with lower mortality and reduced deaths from respiratory and heart diseases (Macinko et al, 2003). The components of PHC are shown in Box 11.1.

Box 11.1: Characteristics of comprehensive primary health care (WHO, 2008)

- Community-based services including first-level care (provided by general medical practitioners, nurses, and allied health professionals); specialised community services like maternal and child health care, mental health care; related services like pharmacy and radiology.
- Care for illness, rehabilitation from injury or illness, preventative services and services to promote health and wellbeing.
- Whole of population service planning.
- Community involvement in setting priorities and evaluating service quality.

In Australia general medical practitioners provide primary health care in private practices that are predominantly funded by Medicare. State governments also provide community health services including parent and child health, community mental health, and drug and alcohol services. Despite its importance, primary health care receives a very small slice of the health budget. General practice is firmly rooted in the fee-for-service model that focuses mainly on curative services to individuals (Fry and Furler, 2000). This method of funding is essentially episodic and GP services lack continuity and coordination, especially for chronic diseases such as diabetes and asthma. Improving the operation of general practice and PHC more generally has been a central focus of reform for more than 20 years. Divisions of General Practice, introduced in the mid-1990s, gave GPs the opportunity to develop a range of preventive programmes and to take a more population-based approach. However, the strategy missed an opportunity to encourage multidisciplinary teamwork needed to improve continuity and coordination (Baum, 2008).

The emergence of the Divisions of General Practice did lead to some changes. For the first time GPs were encouraged to come together and respond to the health problems confronting whole communities, not just individual patients; and opportunities to integrate more effectively with hospitals and community-based health services were enhanced. Furthermore, GPs were offered a chance to move away from an exclusive focus on fee-for-service, if they wished. The introduction of 61 Medicare Locals by the Gillard Labor Government was an attempt to continue these benefits while increasing integration and a more coordinated sector being less dominated by general practitioners. The Abbott Coalition Government has embarked on a review of the Medicare Locals which is predicted to result in a reduction of their number or even their abolition and a move back to more control by GPs. Additionally, some state governments have now withdrawn from, or reduced provision of, health promotion and other community health services. In Queensland significant cuts were made to community nutrition programmes and other health promotion services (Sweet, 2012). South Australia has accepted recommendations to cut a range of community health services on the basis that the Medicare Locals would replace them (Hughes, 2013). This is unlikely, given that the Medicare Locals have primarily a coordination role, and relatively small budgets with targeted priorities; and the cuts are likely to increase demand for more costly hospital services (Australian Medicare Locals Alliance, 2012).

PHC reform that focused on improved service integration and coordination has also been pursued by state and territory governments. In Victoria, Primary Care Partnerships (PCPs) aim to engage consumers, carers, and communities in the planning and evaluation of services; improve health promotion, early intervention, and continuity of care; and reduce the use of hospital services; all underpinned by a social model of health that begins to address social determinants. Community health plans, based on population needs, identify the strategic objectives, map the partnerships that need to be forged, and the service systems and infrastructure that need to be better integrated. In 2012 there were 31 PCPs linking 1,200 organisations, resulting in a more integrated and coordinated sector (Victorian Department of Health, 2010).

Overall, compared to 20 years ago, and despite the uneven development in different jurisdictions, Australia's PHC sector is now more coordinated and better resourced. The Medicare Locals have great potential to be the basis of a more coordinated and systematic PHC system. The initial priorities set by the Federal Government are to improve access to after-hours medical care, community mental health and the coordination of services. They have also been given a mandate to address the social determinants of health but exactly what this might mean is not clear. Investment is needed so that the PHC sector can develop as a planned and coordinated system with prompt, reliable access for patients to the needed range of services. A strengthened, more effective PHC sector should result in fewer demands on the acute care system and so reduce cost pressures over the medium term.

Fragmented governance and funding of the system also contributes to difficulties in providing access to good quality services. This problem is most well known as 'cost-and-blame shifting' between governments, and has long been the focus of concern (NHHRC, 2008, 2009). But while regulators prevent or contain creative responses by health care providers to complex funding rules, the more fundamental concern is the way in which patient care is broken up into fundable chunks. A person with a chronic disease will effectively cross the border between state and federal funding several times in a major episode of care, with serious risk of loss of continuity of care (and of health gain) at each crossing. Attempts to improve access and quality while containing costs have generally failed to address this problem (Dwyer, 2004). The health system, and its funding arrangements, were designed to deal with acute illness, and are not suitable for chronic disease. Reform and restructuring have continued unabated since the late 1980s, with neither convincing resolution nor rest for the change-weary workforce.

Health reform entered a new era in the early 2010s, based loosely on the work of the National Health and Hospitals Reform Commission

(2009). The Commission sought to untangle the relative roles of federal and jurisdictional governments, but its recommendations have been compromised in negotiations at the COAG and elsewhere. Real change has occurred in several important areas under the terms of the National Health Reform Agreement (COAG, 2011), all of which are building blocks towards the development of a national approach to health care, such as the Independent Hospital Pricing Authority (Commonwealth of Australia, 2012a) and the National Health Performance Authority (Commonwealth of Australia, 2012b). However, the fundamental split remains, and the design of convincing ways of working around it so that neither care nor efficiency is compromised has proven elusive. Table 11.1 compares the proposed and agreed division of responsibilities, with problem areas highlighted in grey.

The problem of split responsibilities and overlapping roles has proved intractable and is unlikely to be resolved with the attention of reformers now looking for 'smart' ways to smooth the patient journey without

Table 11.1: Commonwealth and state/territory roles (grey = gap or overlap problem areas)

Sector of health system	Proposed single level of government (2009)	Actual levels of government 2013	
		Commonwealth	State/territory
Primary health care (including GPs and community health)	Commonwealth	GPs; Medicare Locals; Aboriginal Health; Private Allied Health and Diagnostics	Community Health; Aboriginal Health; Public Allied Health
Public hospitals	State	Funding mostly to state governments; + provision for direct funding	Own, fund and operate public hospitals
Mental health	State	Fund private medical and community-based programmes	Own, fund and operate public services
Dental health	Commonwealth	Selective funding programmes for public and private dental care	Own, fund and operate restricted public services
Public health	State	Fund some programmes and activities	Fund and sometimes operate; some states withdrawing
Care of older people	Commonwealth	Fund residential and community-based care of older people	Fund some in-home services
Illness prevention	Commonwealth	Fund and/or provide some programmes	Fund and provide some services

constitutional change or structural reform at government level. The general perception of fragmentation, waste and duplication remains strong among providers, and cost-and-blame shifting continues.

Operating a sustainable and effective health care delivery service

The third challenge is to provide an effective and sustainable health care system despite increased demand, and the availability of more diagnosis and treatment technologies, within constrained resources. There is controversy about what drives health care costs. Hospitals, dental services, medicines and doctor consultations are all growing as a proportion of the health budget (AIHW, 2012b), at the expense of community-based and preventive activities. Underlying factors include the ever expanding range of screening, diagnostic and treatment options; health workforce above average salary increases; population growth; and the rising numbers living with chronic diseases (National Health and Hospitals Reform Commission, 2009).

There have been significant productivity gains by health care providers such as the reduction in the average time patients spend in hospitals. These have been made possible by increasing use of day surgery and other day treatment options and by the changed incentives, as payments to hospitals have shifted to a per admission rather than a per day basis. There are still significant gains to be made in technical efficiency – such as reduction of waste and duplication through improved data about individual patient illnesses and interventions; and improvements in the 'patient care journey' (i.e. reducing the opportunity cost and re-work arising from failure to properly coordinate a patient's care package). However, there is also an argument for an improvement in allocative efficiency, in the decisions that are made about what services will be paid for and in what settings they should be provided. The current shift from residential to home-based care for frail older people is an important example. Most people prefer home-based care and it is more effective and cheaper to provide. Growth in home care 'packages' continues, but it is still not available at a level that would approach meeting demand (Productivity Commission, 2011) For this to occur, there must be not only clear benefits in the acceptability and costs of care, and no loss in effectiveness, but also sustained and determined policy action and professional leadership. Since the 1990s, a series of National Mental Health Plans have guided the dismantling of asylums for people with serious mental illness in favour of community-based services. This was made possible by mounting pressure of demand for care; increasing evidence of the benefits of a shift in the settings and modes of care; strong professional leadership; destigmatisation of mental illness; and concerted sustained policy momentum at national level (Savy and Sawyer, 2009).

Timely access to public hospitals remains a public priority. Problems occur because public hospitals cannot act like other sectors that tailor activities to manage their budgets (such as home care providers operating waiting lists for new clients). Public hospitals are required to respond to all in need, at any time, regardless of whether they are working at or beyond capacity (as measured by staff and beds) and in spite of capped budgets. Governments have responded to problems of waiting lists and long waits in emergency departments with a range of measures, including performance indicators and incentives, and a tendency to centralise operational control (Dwyer, 2004; Rix et al, 2005), in spite of considerable evidence that local operational autonomy is required for innovation and performance (Carlfjord et al, 2010; Exworthy et al, 2010). Staff concerns, voiced around the country in 2009 during a 'listening tour' conducted by the Prime Minister and Minister for Health and Ageing (Commonwealth of Australia, 2010, p 10) led to the establishment of Local Hospital Networks (Commonwealth of Australia, 2010) designed to return some degree of autonomy to hospitals and reduce the impact of 'long and rusty' chains of command.

Two other factors will shape health care delivery in the coming decades: the revolution in information technology and more assertive consumers. Advances in communication technology will enable improved coordination of care but the potential benefits for patients and budgets are yet to be realised, as the changes require further significant health provider and policy maker changes. New technologies have revolutionised consumer access to information with profound implications for the relationships between health care providers and patients. There are real gains in both the quality of care and in cost reduction that will depend on sensitive policy attention to a more active and informed consumer preference for care, and the development of models of care tailored to the information age.

Conclusion

Health policy continues to be conducted as a 'strife of interests', involving powerful professional and industry groups. Governments, constrained by the accidental logics of a complex, finely balanced health system, struggle to control outcomes or create innovative policies. Medicare remains as one of the strengths of the health system, providing affordable and effective care for most Australians. Health inequities remain and these reflect the distribution of the social determinants of health, including access to health care. For the future special efforts need to be made to close the gap in life expectancy between Indigenous and non-Indigenous Australians, strengthen primary health care and reshape health care delivery so that it can be sustainable, efficient and effective. Maintaining a strong universal public health system will require resistance to the pressures to privatise health systems which are being strongly considered by the Australian government in 2014.

References

ABS (Australian Bureau of Statistics) (2011) *The Health and Welfare of Australia's Aboriginal and Torres Strait Islander Peoples.* Oct 2010, Cat. No 4704.0. Available at: www.abs.gov.au/AUSSTATS/abs@.nsf/lookup/4704.0Chapter3550ct+2010

ABS (2013) *6306.0 – Employee Earnings and Hours, Australia, May 2012.* www.abs.gov.au/ausstats/abs@.nsf/mf/6306.0/

Alford, R. (1975) *Health Care Politics: Ideological and Interest Group Barriers to Reform,* University of Chicago Press: New York

Australian Government (2012) *Closing the Gap – Prime Minister's Report 2012,* Australian Government: Canberra.

Australian Medicare Locals Alliance (2012), www.amlalliance.com.au/about-us/medicare-local

Australian Institute of Health and Welfare (2012a) *Aboriginal and Torres Strait Islander Health Services Report: OATSIH Services Reporting – Key Results.* Canberra: AIHW. IHW 79, p viii.

Australian Institute of Health and Welfare (2012b) *Health Expenditure Australia 2010–11,* Canberra: AIHW.

Balabanova, D., Mills, A. et al (2013) 'Good Health at Low Cost 25 Years On: Lessons for the future of health systems strengthening'. *The Lancet,* vol 381, no 9883, pp 2118-33

Baum, F. (2008) *The New Public Health,* Oxford University Press: South Melbourne

Baum, F. and Fisher, M. (2011) 'Are the national preventive health initiatives likely to reduce health inequities?', *Australian Journal of Primary Health,* vol 17, no 4, pp 320-6

Baum, F. and Fisher, M. (2013) 'The appeal of behavioural health promotion despite its limitations in reducing health inequities', *Sociology of Health and Illness,* forthcoming.

Baum, F., G. Jolley, et al (2006) 'What makes for sustainable Healthy Cities initiatives: A review of the evidence from Noarlunga, Australia after 18 years'. *Health Promotion International*, vol 21, no 4, pp 259-65

Baum, F., Laris, P. et al (2013) 'Never mind the logic, give me the numbers': former Australian health ministers' perspectives on the social determinants of health', *Social Science & Medicine*, Jun, No 87, pp 138-46

Baum, F., Lawless, A. et al (2013) 'Health in All Policies from international ideas to local implementation: policies, systems and organizations', in Clavier, C. and de Leeuw, E. (eds) *Health Promotion and the Policy Process: Practical and Critical Theories*, Oxford University Press, forthcoming

Baum, F., Ollila, E. et al (2013) 'A History of Health in All Policies' in Leppo, K. Ollila, E, Cook, S and Peña, S. (eds) *Health in All Policies, Seizing Opportunities, Implementing Policies*, Helsinki: Ministry of Social Affairs and Health

Carlfjord, S., Lindberg, M. et al (2010) 'Key factors influencing adoption of an innovation in PHC', *BMC Family Practice*, vol 11, no 60, doi:10.1186/1471-2296-11-60

Commonwealth of Australia (2010) *A National Health and Hospitals Network for Australia's Future.* Australian Government: Canberra

Commonwealth of Australia (2012a) *Independent Hospital Pricing Authority Annual Report 2011–12*, IHPA, Sydney

Commonwealth of Australia (2012b) *National Health Performance Authority Annual Report 2011–12*, NHPA: Canberra

Council of Australian Governments (2011) *National Health Reform Agreement*, COAG: Canberra

CSDH (Commission on the Social Determinants of Health) (2008) *Closing the Gap in a Generation: Health Equity through Action on the Social Determinants of Health: Final Report of the Commission on Social Determinants of Health*, World Health Organization: Geneva

Duckett, S. and Wilcox, S. (2011). *The Australian Health Care System*, (3rd edn), Oxford University Press: Melbourne

Dwyer, J. (2004), 'Australian health system restructuring: what problem is being solved?', *Australia and New Zealand Health Policy*, vol 1, no 6. Available at: www.anzhealthpolicy.com/content/1/1/6

Egger, G. and Swinburn, B. (2010) *Planet Obesity*. Allen & Unwin: Sydney.

Exworthy, M., Frosini, F. et al (2010) *Decentralisation and Performance: Autonomy and Incentives in Local Health Economies*, Research report produced for the National Institute for Health Research Service Delivery and Organisation programme Queen's Printer and Controller of HMSO: London

Fry, D. and Furler, J. (2000) 'General practice, primary health care and population health interface', *General Practice in Australia 2000*, Commonwealth Department of Health and Aged Care: Canberra

Gilson, L, Doherty, J. et al (2007) *Challenging Inequities through Health Systems: Final Report of the Knowledge Network on Health Systems*, WHO Commission on the Social Determinants of Health. Available at: www.who.int/social_determinants/resources/csdh_media/hskn_final_2007_en.pdf

Gortmaker, S., Swinburn, B. et al (2011) 'Changing the future of obesity: science, policy and action', *The Lancet*, vol 378, pp 838–47

Hughes, M. (2013) 'Cuts to community –based health services short-sighted', *Croakey: the Crikey health blog*, 27 March. Available at: http://blogs.crikey.com.au/croakey/2013/03/27/cuts-to-community-based-health-services-short-sighted/

Lantz, P. Lichtenstein, R. et al (2007) 'Health policy approaches to population health: The limits of medicalization', *Health Affairs*, vol 26, no 5,pp 1253–7

Levy, M. (2012) 'Satisfied whistleblower weighs future in the force', *The Sydney Morning Herald*, 14 November, pp 10

Macinko, J., Starfield, B. et al (2003) *Health Services Research*, vol 38, no 3, pp 831–864

McAuley, I. (2011) 'PHI: costs for public, private the same, so they should compete for funds'. *Crikey*, 16 August. Available at: www.crikey.com.au/2011/08/16/phi-costs-for-public-private-the-same-so-they-should-compete-for-funds/

Mendadue, J. and McAuley, I. (2012) *Private Health Insurance: High in Cost and Low in Equity*, Centre for Policy Development: Sydney

NACCHO (National Aboriginal Community Controlled Health Organisation) (2009) 'Towards a National primary health care strategy: fulfilling Aboriginal people's aspirations to close the gap', *Submission to the National Primary Health Care Strategy*. Available at: www.naccho.org.au/Files/Documents/PHC%20Strategy%20NACCHO%20submission%202009%20FINAL.pdf

National Health and Hospitals Reform Commission (2008) *Beyond the Blame Game: Accountability and Performance Benchmarks for the next Australian Health Care Agreements*, NHHRC: Canberra

National Health and Hospitals Reform Commission (2009) *A Healthier Future for all Australians – Final Report June 2009*, NHHRC: Canberra

National Preventative Health Taskforce (2009) *Australia: The Healthiest Country by 2020National Preventative Health Strategy – the roadmap for action,* Commonwealth of Australia: Canberra

Navarro, V. (2009) 'What we mean by social determinants of health'. *International Journal of Health Services,* vol 39, no 3, pp 423-41

OECD (2010) *Family Database CO1.2 Life Expectancy at Birth,* p 2, www.oecd.org/social/family/database

Popay, J., Whitehead, M. et al (2010) 'Injustice is killing people on a large scale – but what is to be done about it?', *Journal of Public Health,* vol 32, no 2, pp 148-9

Productivity Commission (2011) *Caring for Older Australians: Enquiry Report,* Productivity Commission: Sydney

Raphael, D. (ed) (2012) *Tackling Health Inequalities in Canada: Lessons from International Experiences,* Canadian Scholars Press Inc: Toronto

Reconciliation Australia (2013) *Australian Reconciliation Barometer 2012: An Overview,* Reconciliation Australia: Canberra

Rix, M., Owen, A. et al (2005) '(Re)form with Substance? Restructuring and governance in the Australian health system 2004/05', *Australia and New Zealand Health Policy,* vol 2, no 19, doi:10.1186/1743-8462-2-19

Savy, P. and Sawyer, A. (2009) 'Mental Illness: Understanding, Experience and service provision' in Germov, J. (ed) *Second Opinion: An Introduction to Health Sociology,* Melbourne: Oxford University Press

Sax, S. (1984) *A Strife of Interests: Politics and Policies in Australian health Services,* Allen & Unwin: Sydney

Scollo, M. and Winstanley, M. (2012) *Tobacco in Australia: Facts and Issues,* 4th edn, Melbourne: Cancer Council Victoria

Sweet, M. (2012) 'Overview of Qld Health changes, including the "historic" dismantling of public and preventative health services', *Croakey: the Crikey health blog,* 11 September. Available at: http://blogs.crikey.com.au/croakey/2012/09/11/overview-of-qld-health-changes-including-the-historic-dismantling-of-public-and-preventative-health-services/

Swinburn, B., Sacks, G., et al (2011) 'The global obesity pandemic: shaped by global drivers and local environments', *The Lancet,* vol 377, pp 804-814

Tuohy, C.H. (1999) *Accidental Logics: The Dynamics of Change in the Health Care Arena in the United States, Britain and Canada.* Oxford University Press: New York

Victorian Department of Health (2010) *Primary Care Partnerships: Achievements 2000–2010*, Victorian Department of Health: Melbourne

Walker, A., Percival, R. et al (2005). 'Distributional impact of recent changes to private health insurance policies', *Australian Health Review*, vol 29, no 2, pp 167-177

Werner, D. and D. Sanders (1997). *Questioning the Solution: The Politics of Primary Health Care and Child Survival*, Health Rights: Palo Alto, CA

Wilkinson, R. and K. Pickett (2009). *The Spirit Level: Why More Equal Societies almost always do Better*, Penguin Books: London

World Health Organization (2008) *The World Health Report 2008 – Primary Health Care Now More Than Ever*, WHO: Geneva

World Health Organization (2013) *Healthy City Checklist*. Available at: www.euro.who.int/en/what-we-do/health-topics/environment-and-health/urban-health/activities/healthy-cities/who-european-healthy-cities-network/what-is-a-healthy-city/healthy-city-checklist.

TWELVE

Loose moorings: debate and directions in Australian housing policy

Lionel Orchard

Housing preferences and options in Australian society are dominated for better or worse by private markets. Public and social housing, with some variation between Australian states, plays a marginal role. In 2011, the housing tenure split comprised, in percentage terms, 67/25/5 between home ownership, private rental housing and public/social housing respectively, with 3% in other tenures. Home ownership was itself split 32/35 between outright and mortgaged ownership in 2011, a significant change from 2001 when it was 40/27. Significantly, the foundations of the Australian housing system are increasingly shaky across all housing tenures – ownership and rental, private and public. The character of the housing policy debate – always conflicted and unsettled – is turbulent given ongoing economic, social and environmental change and uncertainties. The moorings of the housing system and the policies and programmes shaping it continue to be in flux, with the existing framework unable to deal adequately with maintaining good equitable access to housing for all.

Different and complex elements and perspectives are evident in any policy field and this is so in housing policy. This chapter is premised on the view that it is important to reflect on first principles entailed in that complexity while recognising that we do not start from a blank sheet. Key themes in current debates about Australian housing policy are examined against the backdrop of recent history and the ideas and debates that have shaped housing policy. The chapter argues that while neoliberal ideas and frameworks are increasingly influential, the debate about progressive responses to contemporary housing problems reflects an uneasy reconciliation of libertarian, communitarian and social democratic values. An assessment of progressive agendas concludes the chapter.

Thought and practice in Australian housing policy: a brief history

The establishment of public housing agencies at state government level in the 1920s and 1930s registered the public priority of housing issues in both low income home ownership and public rental housing even if the effort took a little while to gain momentum and impact. That impact was augmented by work of the Commonwealth Housing Commission (CHC) in the 1940s, undertaken as part of the post-war reconstruction effort. The CHC developed an integrated vision for urban planning and increased housing supply, in particular public housing. However, the Commonwealth-State Housing Agreement (CSHA), first negotiated in 1945, was the main ongoing outcome of the CHC's work. The CSHA was perhaps the longest standing intergovernmental agreement in Australian federalism directing Commonwealth and State funds to a specific area of economic and social policy. Renegotiated every few years to the early 2000s, the CSHA provided one of the key foundations for Australian housing policy and programmes. These agreements reflected a changing balance between investment in public and private housing that saw a small but important public housing system develop (Troy, 2012). During the period 1950–70 Australia experienced economic and employment stability and, combined with public effort shaped by the CSHA and coherent regulation of the banks, saw the growth of home ownership as the dominant housing tenure which rose from 50% to 70% of all Australian housing.

From the mid-1970s, Australian housing policy has been the subject of relentless and turbulent debate, when major shifts in thinking began to emerge. New problems in the management of private housing markets and growing demands and problems in the public housing system were increasingly influenced by emergent reform ideas from both the Right and the Left. Debate began with the so-called *Great Housing Debate* of the 1970s and early 1980s, in which a range of views were articulated in response to new economic and social challenges. This was one of the earliest expressions of the intellectual contest in Australian public policy, and which continues to resonate, between economic rationalist/neoliberal and social democratic views. Left libertarian and socialist views added to the mix.

At the most general level, economists led by John Paterson argued that Australians overconsumed housing as a result of government policies and subsidies and defended the greater use of market disciplines and principles to counter this. He argued that distributional questions in housing should be dealt with through welfare and income support rather than directly through housing provision (Paterson, 1975). Other economists, including Ronald Henderson and Judith Yates, outlined the economic case for more careful attention to the distribution of direct and indirect public subsidies in the housing system and the inefficiencies and inequities they produced (Henderson, 1978; Yates, 1982). Left libertarians like Brian Howe were concerned about the ways in which mainstream public housing provision, citing in particular Melbourne's high rise public housing, limited and constrained the housing choices of lower income people (Howe, 1974). Social democrats, in particular Hugh Stretton, highlighted the success of the more ambitious public housing experience in South Australia under the South Australian Housing Trust, and the positive economic and social contribution that home ownership can make so long as strong efforts are made to equalise class access to it. Stretton challenged the neoliberal overconsumption view, arguing that the productive activity that goes on within the household, domestic sphere needs strong support through policy intervention. He defended a practical and flexible orientation towards the multiple principles and factors that must be reconciled in good housing policy – the complexities, virtues and limits of the various housing tenures and the impacts on them through economic and social change (Stretton, 1974). The socialist critique, associated primarily with Jim Kemeny, argued that the social democratic defence of a mixed housing system worked against more sober consideration of the ways in which the Australian emphasis on home ownership reinforced social divisions and inequities, while the cost and choice benefits that greater levels of public housing could bring were downplayed (Kemeny, 1978, 1983).

The general differences between these views are familiar. They ascribe quite different meanings to ideas about individualism, freedom, choice, diversity and equity. Mainstream economists think that freedom and choice are essentially individual matters and that private markets and direct income distribution are much better enablers than government provision of services like housing. While left libertarians and socialists understand that freedom and choice are defined socially, they too think that the individual's capacity to choose from a diversity of options was not well served by mainstream housing policy. Nor was equity.

Social democrats, on the other hand, argue that freedom and liberty are shaped by a mixed structure of market, public and social institutions. While markets may be good at facilitating choice, variety and freedom, they often fail to address collective and social consequences, are never unbiased, and may produce outcomes that need to be checked and shaped by public institutions. In response to the socialist critique, some social democrats highlighted the role of home ownership in enabling investment and saving through the ownership of an important asset, while facilitating choices in the productive but undervalued domestic sphere, in key respects an early expression of the now common centre-left stakeholding and asset equity arguments (Stretton, 1976; see Mok and Lee, 2013 for a recent statement of the asset/stakeholding argument as it relates to home ownership).

Overall, at this general level, left and right libertarians, sceptical about the role of government, confront social democrats and socialists who, while aware of the dangers in the abuse of public power, argue that direct public involvement in the regulation and provision of housing provides for important needs and acts as an essential counter to the more serious dangers posed by unchecked private markets (King and Oxley, 2000). Differences about the balance between private and public options separate the social democrats and the socialists. When expressed more directly in the debate about policy directions, the differences between the various positions focused on four main issues – the significance of housing tenure, the meaning and policy implications of tenure 'neutrality', the role of income and housing services as vehicles for redistribution, and the question of the role and reform of the Australian public housing system.

On housing tenure, social democrats have been relatively comfortable about the strong emphasis on cross-class access to home ownership, balanced with some attention to the role of public housing agencies at the lower ends of the market. They were less disposed to private rental housing, given both the unequal and often exploitative relations between landlords and tenants and weaker influence and control enjoyed by tenants in this sector. They worried too about the impact of higher cost thresholds in the home ownership and public housing tenures that were beginning to emerge in the 1970s, but stressed the need to deal with those problems without losing focus on the strengths and weaknesses of the different housing tenures. On the other hand, economists, left libertarians and socialists argued that the existing tenure system had a negative social and economic influence on Australian society – albeit for quite different reasons. They argued that the emphasis on home ownership and the minor role for public housing expressed fundamental imbalances and inequities that only wholesale change that ignored housing tenure would improve. For analysts on both the Right and the Left, the idea of a 'tenure neutral' housing policy was required to correct existing imbalances, particularly in economic and subsidy flows benefiting home ownership over both public and private rental tenures.

On tenure neutrality, Left and Right meanings of the term were evident. On the Right, economists wanted to 'level down' the subsidies flowing to home ownership and public housing, to those applying to private renters, limiting public assistance to income support schemes. The Left wanted to 'level up' the status of public and private renting, so that people in those tenures could enjoy about the same public assistance and economic advantages enjoyed by homeowners. While the Left and the Right embraced tenure neutrality in theory, in practice they were strongly committed to particular tenure outcomes, defending views about which should grow and which should decline – the Left less home ownership and much greater public housing, the Right private housing options – home ownership and private rental housing – over public options.

On the relations between social and housing policy, economic rationalists and left libertarians argued that the issues should be separately considered if equity objectives are to be properly served. Social policy should emphasise income redistribution while housing policy should focus on efficient housing production. The idea of creating housing allowance and voucher schemes as vehicles to look after the income redistribution side were prominent. On the other hand, social democrats argued that equity in housing policy will only ever be addressed if the production of housing, particularly public housing, pays attention to ensuring a good, efficient housing supply, centrally linked to the social question of who gets what housing, where, and at what cost.

Finally, on public housing, social democrats and socialists strongly defended tenure on both economic and social grounds and wanted to extend it, while acknowledging the need for reform to cater for more diverse needs and to facilitate greater tenant participation in its management. On the other hand, right and left libertarian critics argued that public housing provision as it was organised in Australia – through state-based housing authorities mainly in large housing estates of both low density and high rise kinds – had failed. Public housing should be replaced either by housing allowances and increased private supply of rental housing or through the growth of the community and not-for-profit sector – housing associations and cooperatives.

Change in housing policy from the late 1970s has been slow and incremental. Shifts in priority giving expression to various aspects of the policy debate, in particular libertarian priorities, have been evident. For example, the CSHAs of the late 1970s and 1980s began to shift priority away from direct investment in public housing supply and management towards income support for public and private tenants. The Australian financial system was deregulated in the early 1980s, with major consequences for mortgage finance for home ownership, in particular much higher interest rates in the period immediately after deregulation. This, together with major changes in the structure of the economy and less secure employment, began to make access to home ownership more precarious for those entering the market for the first time.

From the late 1980s, ongoing housing problems have been accompanied by successive waves of housing policy review. During the middle Hawke/Keating years, the National Housing Policy Review (1988–89) and the National Housing Strategy (1990–92) produced many reports on the problems. Sophisticated analysis was undertaken about subsidy flows in the housing system, the contest between service and income models of assistance to poorer renters, debate about housing allowances versus ongoing investment in public housing supply, and the sustainability of home ownership in the face of ongoing economic and social change.

During the Howard years (1996–2007), housing problems fell down the list of policy priorities, but the issue of higher house prices and worsening affordability problems gained prominence, with the Productivity Commission conducting a major review of access to first home ownership (Productivity Commission, 2004). Shared ownership and income contingent 'loan' schemes to assist low income households gained greater policy attention (Gans and King, 2004).

The Rudd Government elected in 2007 took action to replace the CSHA with a new National Affordable Housing Agreement (NAHA) and made large one-off investments in social housing as part of its response to the Global Financial Crisis (GFC). The National Rental Affordability Scheme (NRAS) was established in 2008 to provide tax offsets or direct payments to investors in private rental housing, as long as the housing attracting these benefits is rented to eligible tenants at rates at least 20% below market rents. The NRAS aims to provide 50,000 housing units by 2016 and just over 9,000 units had been supported under the scheme to late 2012. The equity impacts of the scheme have recently been questioned and it is now under review by the Abbott Government.

From the early 2000s, research on Australia's housing problems has highlighted the growing inequities between generations evident in the home ownership tenure (Badcock and Beer, 2000) while the Australian Housing and Urban Research Institute (AHURI) has sponsored research on housing futures, the flow of housing subsidies through the tax system, the crumbling economic and social foundations of state-based public housing, and more nuanced analysis of the housing needs of particular social groups (AHURI, 2010). In general, housing policy development has become increasingly targeted to particular needs – for example, homelessness and the housing needs of those facing complex problems. Grappling with the larger forces shaping the housing system is proving more difficult.

The sense of crisis about housing affordability and the structure of the Australian housing system grows. Mobilisation around the issues continues, for example through the Australians for Affordable Housing group, launched in 2011, bringing together a coalition of 60 national housing, welfare and community bodies to advocate on the issues (AAH, 2011). The problems have become worse and less tractable to the point where ways forward are increasingly difficult, producing policy stasis in the housing system in the face of social and economic change, an incapacity of public investment and government action to deal adequately with either indirect (income) and direct (housing) demands, and a general inability to robustly reconcile equity, efficiency and sustainability principles in the system.

Current debates

Recent thinking about Australian housing policy reflects an important shift in the terms of debate. There has been an almost complete waning of older social democratic ideas about the structure and direction of the housing system. Likewise the ways in which the style of public intervention and market regulation from the latter 1940s to the early 1980s achieved some measure of cross–class access to home ownership and a serviceable if flawed and inadequate public housing system. Social democratic views about public intervention as countervailing private power in housing markets and socialist ideas about decommodification and cost rental in housing policy reform enjoy much less influence than they once did. Recent thinking rather reflects the continuing influence of the left and right libertarian perspectives outlined earlier. Neoliberal orthodoxies about markets run alongside third way and new centre left arguments for policy intervention in interesting ways.

Some argue that these shifts are mostly driven by underlying structural changes in Australian political economy and society – economic restructuring, financial deregulation, innovation in production processes, social diversity, and demographic shifts – as they relate to housing (Berry, 1999). Others lay more importance on the framing of policy choices, limitations in state capacity and political leadership, and weaknesses in civil society alliance building in shaping change (Dalton, 2009). Clearly all of these aspects are important. The key questions for housing policy are: what is the scope for action to respond to the dilemmas and challenges, how much of the right and left libertarian orthodoxy is now so ingrained that they are beyond significant change, and what hope is there that other views will register politically? Contemporary challenges and problems centre on at least five major and often interconnected issues: high housing costs and prices and associated issues of housing affordability; the impact of taxation policies – including negative gearing and the tax treatment of home ownership – in worsening price threshold and equity problems; the management and regulation of housing markets, particularly in relation to the adequacy of supply of new housing; the linkages between social change and diversity, environmental sustainability and housing preferences; and the corrosion of the public housing sector.

The problems of rising housing costs and prices and housing affordability are stark. House price thresholds have been worsening dramatically in recent times, as Yates explains:

> Between 1995 and 2005, real house prices in Australia increased by more than 6% per year ... This was well above the average annual increase in the 20 years to 1995 of just 1.1% and the 50-year average (from 1960 to 2010) of 2.5% per year. These data ... contrast with the significantly slower growth in GDP per capita and average earnings over much of the period (Yates, 2011, p 263)

Given these trends, access to home ownership, particularly for younger households entering the market for the first time, is increasingly difficult. Price thresholds and the costs of finance are beyond the capacity of many on low to middle incomes to service the levels of mortgage debt required, especially given the employment volatility in the economy. As a result, younger people facing frustration in gaining access to home ownership do not place the emphasis on the tenure that older generations did (Hurley, 2012a; Whitty, 2013). The longstanding role of home ownership as a way of investing in an important asset over the life course, thereby lessening demands on the welfare state in retirement, can no longer be relied upon, given the difficulties facing the younger generations in accessing the tenure (Yates and Bradbury, 2010).

One important area of debate centres on the subsidy and tax treatment of private housing tenures. As outlined earlier, this debate has been long standing. Advocacy of policy change in this area continues without much political traction, reflected most recently in the failure of the Rudd Government to take up recommendations made by the 2010 Henry Tax Review. 'Negative gearing' is the scheme whereby investors in private rental housing can write off the costs of financing and maintaining a rental property against rental and other income and thereby lessen the tax paid on that income. The tax losses under the scheme in 2010–11 were over $13 billion. Negative gearing is seen as inequitable, expensive and as fuelling price inflation in private housing markets to the cost of appropriate housing access for low income households (Eslake, 2011a). The Rudd Government's NRAS dealt with some of the inequities but not the basic market distortions.

The subsidy and tax treatment of home ownership also attracts criticism. First homeowner grants, involving subsidies in the billions, increase demand for housing without attention to adequate supply and thereby exacerbate house price inflation. The evidence is that these grants do not do much to facilitate access of younger people into home ownership (Eslake, 2011b). Exemptions of homeowners from capital gains taxation, land tax on the sale of a property and as a means-tested asset for access to the old age pension are also seen as encouraging excessive investment in this tenure and thereby inflating house prices. For some, these arrangements 'kill home ownership with kindness' (Disney, 2010).

Policy thinking to improve the affordability of private housing also centres on questions of market regulation and housing supply. Consistent with neoliberal policy directions, much emphasis has been placed on deregulating urban planning instruments to help deal with housing affordability problems. Quicker development approval processes aim to facilitate the supply of more appropriate and affordable housing in a timely way. 'User pays' policies to meet the costs of infrastructure – pipes, wires, road, and so on – thereby adding to the costs of new housing for individual households – are another expression of the prevalence of market principles. Increasing housing densities through urban consolidation and urban growth boundaries, curtailing the outward growth of low-density suburban development while not allied exclusively to neoliberal policy directions, nevertheless do shape housing options in new ways. These policies are strongly pursued but are seen by some as allowing government 'to sidestep the problem' of ensuring affordable and appropriate housing for all (Beer et al, 2007).

Concern about the adequacy of supply of new housing has gathered steam in recent years. The ways people adapt to changing conditions in the housing market lie at the heart of this debate. The Rudd Government established the National Housing Supply Council in 2008 to monitor and report on this issue. The Council was abolished by the Abbott Government in late 2013. In 2012, the Council estimated that there was an undersupply of new houses of some 228,000 units, although this figure and its basis have been contested. Some argue that increasing supply to meet unmet demand is only one way to look at the problem. Demand is also changeable in the face of high price thresholds. Household formation may be postponed, renting might become the new norm in the face of affordability barriers to ownership, and medium and higher density housing seem to be emerging as real options in response to higher housing prices (Hurley, 2012b; Harley, 2013; NHSC, 2013).

The debate about demographic change, housing preferences and housing supply – the so-called 'mismatch' debate – is also longstanding (Maher, 1995). The emphasis in Australian cities on low-density house and garden in far-flung and poorly serviced suburbs is a source of concern for a range of reasons – economic (too expensive), social (too isolating) and environmental (too car dependent and unsustainable). Demographic change is bringing with it a more complex pattern of smaller households with new kinds of housing priorities and needs (Beer, 2008). Recent surveys suggest that housing preferences for more diverse and denser housing are growing, even if the mismatch between declining household size and increasing average house size continues (Kelly, Weidmann and Walsh, 2011). Better neighbourhood planning might help achieve a more mixed range of housing types, well integrated with community facilities and linked to wider urban services (Kelly, Breadon and Reichl, 2011). Others argue that the mismatch problem will be exacerbated as the Australian population ages. Older single-person households comprising outright homeowners occupying large three bedroom houses in larger numbers is inefficient but nevertheless encouraged by favourable economic (taxation) policies if these householders remain in houses no longer suitable for them. Nevertheless, policy intervention to disrupt established preferences needs to be handled carefully, especially given the emphasis in policies for care of older people on 'ageing in place' (Mares, 2013).

Despite complexities about the adequacy or otherwise of existing housing in Australian cities, most agree that there is a need for attention to building more low income housing, particularly for rental. Much thought with a 'third way' pedigree has been given to creating housing bond and related schemes using public investment to leverage greater levels of private investment in this kind of housing. Many schemes have been broached drawing on international models, particularly European. Much energy has and is being expended on this but without much pay-off so far (Berry, 2003; Lawson, Milligan and Yates, 2012). Given urban consolidation policies, debates about the supply of new housing takes place in markets shaped by basic limits to the availability of new urban land. Urban growth boundaries encourage these limits. New housing will be smaller, denser and more often built in brown field locations. Yet land prices will inflate as a consequence of these trends and thereby add to price thresholds in housing markets. In response, some argue that new housing supply requires closer attention to decentralised urban development, even if this proves difficult to achieve in practice (Disney, 2006).

The last major area of concern is the shape of the social housing system and its reform. The social housing system comprises public, community and Indigenous housing together with crisis accommodation. Public housing in the hands of State housing authorities increased from about 273,500 units in 1985 to 388,600 in 1995 but has since declined to just under 331,000 units in June 2012. However, over the period 1996–2012, the community housing sector has more than tripled in size from 16,500 units to 60,000. When Indigenous and crisis accommodation dwellings in public hands are added, the overall social housing system has grown slightly over the period since the mid-1990s (McIntosh, 1997; AIHW, 2013). Nevertheless, major cracks are visible and advocacy for change grows more insistent. Waiting lists for access to public housing stood at 200,000 households in June 2012, not much below the level of the early 1990s. Much of the public housing stock is older, of poor quality and in need to significant upgrading. The operating and investment deficits in the system are substantial. Redevelopment through privatisation has been the chosen response to renewal of older public housing estates. The public system also faces major issues in the management of tenants with higher needs and less capacity to pay than in the past. In many respects, tenure is largely being left to wither (Jacobs, Berry and Dalton, 2013). Given these trends and the unwillingness of governments to make the necessary investment to support tenure, many argue the need to break it up through wholesale transfer of public stock into housing cooperatives, housing associations and smaller social housing corporations (Gilmour and Milligan, 2012). Such arguments draw upon international, particularly British experience (Pawson and Gilmour, 2010). These directions have been supported by the move from the CSHA to the

NAHA under the Rudd Government. The NAHA now directs more capital funding to the newer community-based tenures. Similarly, the Rudd Government's GFC funding injections mainly went in social and community housing directions. The left libertarian and related communitarian perspectives outlined earlier underpin many of the arguments for change. Yet some who support these directions worry about the capacity and scale of social housing models to address the demand and need for housing of public and social kinds while others see the priority setting involved as deeply flawed (Lennon, 2008; Troy, 2012). Mark Davis's argument (see Chapter 2) about the impact of neoliberalism in hollowing out the public sphere – 'running down public systems creates incentives to abandon them' – certainly applies to the Australian public housing system.

Conclusion

While neoliberal, pro-market views shape general directions in Australian housing policy, the debate about how the centre left should respond reflects a contest between older and newer frameworks. Recent thinking is based on the view that the defence of the traditional tenure structure – priority to home ownership and public housing over private rental – and policies to support these priorities are now exhausted. For some, the affordability problem in home ownership has been ignored for so long that it is now too late to do much to respond, especially given the ongoing failure to curtail taxation and other policies encouraging over-investment and major inequities that have emerged in access to tenure (Yates, 2011). Public housing has always been marginal in Australia and is increasingly so. In any case, the tenure is based on an outdated and inflexible management model that we would do well to replace with smaller-scale, more inclusive community-based approaches. Social, economic and environmental change – smaller, more diverse households, deregulated finance, the need for more flexible and responsive housing options in the face of sustainability pressures, the absence of strong government – all imply the need for what Maryann Wulff called some time ago a 'new social settlement' in housing (Wulff, 2001).

Drawing on Duncan Maclennan's criteria for a 'modern' housing policy – that it should be system-wide; multilevel and joined up, involving government and nongovernment actors; need and client focused; and attend to longer-term equity issues through greater supply-side investment – some argue that housing policy, particularly through the period of the Rudd/Gillard Governments, reflects more responsive and appropriate directions. Yet the scale of the response has been limited, particularly the funding commitment, and the problems facing access and equity in home ownership remain (Milligan and Pinnegar, 2010).

Through all of this, insights from more mainstream social democratic views continue to demand attention. Housing markets are economically and socially inefficient – 'private investors rarely supply new houses to the bottom quarter or third of the market' (Stretton, 2005, 121). Direct and indirect public policies for the production of low-priced housing are required at greater levels than currently:

> ... the richer we get, the longer our queues for public housing grow, and the higher the prices rise of a stock of market housing that grows more slowly than the numbers wanting it ... we have a serious failure of supply and no current program, public or private, to correct it (Stretton, 2005, 123)

Stretton's reflections on the dilemmas surrounding the design of policy responses are worth summarising. On institutions, he asks what level and kind of government responsibility and institutional design are required to deliver effective housing programmes? Australian federalism produces complications but the CSHA experience suggests that these problems are not insurmountable. Partnership models also raise questions of accountability and balance between principles of general access for all to housing services at times of need and the targeting or tailoring of housing institutions to specific needs. On urban locations for new housing investment, Stretton suggests that addressing areas of demand is likely to concentrate attention in the big cities and add to the cost and density problems they face. Thus better urban planning and decentralisation would seem essential. On priority setting, he asks who should come first, 'paying' or 'subsidised' housing customers? Ideas about housing bonds aid the 'paying' component of housing supply while public housing transfer policies may segment the social housing system into higher quality and residual sectors, especially in the absence of a flow of public funds to support 'subsidised' supply. On housing density, he argues issues of preference and choice must be faced, but mixed medium density across cities should be pursued. Stretton acknowledges that while policies like 'negative gearing' are dysfunctional for reasons outlined earlier, bringing them to an end is difficult for two main reasons – the entrenchment of the policy and the political breach of promise in making changes, and the detrimental impact on housing supply that abandoning such policies might bring (Stretton, 2005, 124–7).

Ways forward responding to the basic problems confronting the Australian housing system will necessarily entail blending perspectives and adapting priorities to contemporary times. One assessment might go as follows. Home ownership is a good thing if everyone has equal and affordable access to it. It remains perhaps the most important expression of the value of individual (household) asset ownership in the modern democracies. This is not to say that major problems, in particular inequity and exclusion, do not accompany the tenure. We need to make basic policy changes to facilitate equitable access to it. This requires much closer attention to the large subsidy and taxation distortions that the economists are so concerned about. They should be replaced over time with better ways of augmenting housing supply. Mainstream social democratic methods and third way partnerships, or Stretton's 'dual' market entailing 'two kinds of ownership and capital risk' – 'price-restrained' and 'market-priced' – can make contributions to that task but the decisive social democratic response at arm's length for private housing markets based on a flow of subsidised public finance should not always play second fiddle. On public and social housing, we need to recognise the virtues of the traditional case for public housing on cost and choice grounds, choice here built upon the principle of impartial treatment of clients through (respectful and inclusive) bureaucratic means. The ambitions for social housing shaped by communitarian and libertarian principles are important but they are, by design, selective and targeted. They should not be allowed to create new schisms and divisions in what, at least in Australia, are marginal tenures serving important needs. Government should face up to the ongoing need for greater investment in public and social tenures, but in ways that do not leave older public housing in decline. New housing investment should also be better reconciled with social and environmental objectives through more conscious thought about the appropriate mixture of housing densities and types in our cities. This will challenge the longstanding preference for traditional low-density house and garden but the trend away from those is already firmly in train. Overall, while private choices in our housing system should continue to be facilitated those choices are never fully independent and need to be better balanced with public choices. This essentially social democratic insight and the policy anchors it provides seem more firmly and broadly based than any alternative perspective.

References

Australians for Affordable Housing (2011) *Australia's Broken Housing System*. Available at: http://housingstressed.org.au/wp-content/uploads/2011/09/Australias_Broken_Housing_System.pdf

Australian Housing and Urban Research Institute (2010) *AHURI's Contribution to the Cumulative Evidence Base to inform the national Housing Reform Agenda*, AHURI, Melbourne

Australian Institute of Health and Welfare (2013) *Housing Assistance in Australia 2013*, Cat. No. HOU 271, AIHW, Canberra

Badcock, B. and Beer, A. (2000) *Home Truths: Property Ownership and Housing Wealth in Australia*, Melbourne University Press

Beer, A. (2008) *Housing: Mirror and Mould for Australian Society?*, Occasional Paper 5/2008 Census Series # 3, Academy of the Social Sciences in Australia, Canberra

Beer, A., Kearins, B. and Pieters, H. (2007) 'Housing Affordability and Planning in Australia: The Challenge of Policy under Neo-Liberalism', *Housing Studies*, vol 22, no 1, pp 11-24

Berry, M. (1999) 'Unravelling the 'Australian Housing Solution': the Post-War Years', *Housing, Theory and Society*, vol 16, pp 106-23

Berry, M. (2003) 'Why is it Important to Boost the Supply of Affordable Housing in Australia – and How Can We Do it?', *Urban Policy and Research*, vol 21, no 4, pp 413-35

Dalton, T. (2009) 'Housing Policy Retrenchment: Australia and Canada Compared', *Urban Studies*, vol 46, no 1, pp 63-91

Disney, J. (2006) 'Over Our Heads: Housing Costs & Australian Families', *AQ*, March-April, pp 4-11

Disney, J. (2010) 'PM dumps the chance to fix housing', *Age*, 4 May, p 11

Eslake, S. (2011a) 'Crunch time for negative gearing', *Insight* (VCOSS), no 4, pp 22-4

Eslake, S. (2011b) 'Doling out cash to first-home buyers hasn't made more of us home owners', *Sydney Morning Herald Business*, 16 March, p 6

Gans, J. and King. S. (2004) 'The Housing Lifeline: A Housing Affordability Policy', *Agenda*, vol 11, no 2, pp 143-55

Gilmour, T. and Milligan, V. (2012) 'Let a Hundred Flowers Bloom: Innovation and Diversity in Australian Not-for Profit Housing Organisations', *Housing Studies*, vol 27, no 4, pp 476-94

Harley, R. (2013) 'Housing: a nation of renters', *Australian Financial Review Weekend*, 2-3 March, pp 1-7

Henderson, R. (1978) 'Housing Policy and the Poor', *Australian Economic Review*, vol 41, pp 34-9

Howe, B. (1974), 'Fitzroy Ecumenical Centre Annual Conference 1974', *Ekstasis: A Quarterly of the Centre for Urban Research and Action*, 10, pp 1-5

Hurley, B. (2012a) 'Neither a borrower nor a home owner be', *Australian Financial Review*, 30 August, p 51

Hurley, B. (2012b) 'Forget undersupply, we've got too many houses', *Australian Financial Review*, 7 July, p 7

Jacobs, K., Berry, M. and Dalton, T. (2013) 'A dead and broken system?: "insider" views of the future role of Australian public housing', *International Journal of Housing Policy*, DOI:10.1080/14616718. 2013.785716

Kelly, J-F., Breadon, P. and Reichl, J. (2011) *Getting the Housing We Want*, Grattan Institute, Melbourne

Kelly, J-F., Weidmann, B. and Walsh, M. (2011) *The Housing We'd Choose*, Grattan Institute, Melbourne

Kemeny, J. (1978), 'From Welfare Housing to Cost Renting', *Australian Quarterly*, vol 50, no 4, pp 67-73

Kemeny, J. (1983), *The Great Australian Nightmare: a critique of the home-ownership ideology*, Georgian House, Melbourne

King, P. and Oxley, M. (2000) *Housing: Who Decides?* Macmillan, Basingstoke

Lawson, J., Milligan, V. and Yates, J. (2012), 'Towards cost effective private financing of affordable rental housing', *Housing Finance International*, Summer, pp 25-31

Lennon, M. (2008) 'Australia', in J. Cowans and D. Maclennan (eds), *Visions for Social Housing: International Perspectives*, Smith Institute, London

Maher, C. (1995), 'Housing Need and Residential Mobility: The Mismatch Debate in Perspective', *Urban Policy and Research*, vol 13, no 1, pp 7-19

Mares, P. (2013), 'The rising costs of the great Australian Dream', *Inside Story*. Available at: http://inside.org.au/the-rising-costs-of-the-great-australian-dream/

McIntosh, G. (1997) *Reforming Public Housing*, Current Issues Brief No. 31, 1996–97, Canberra: Department of the Parliamentary Library

Milligan, V. and Pinnegar, S. (2010), 'The Comeback of National Housing Policy in Australia: First Reflections', *International Journal of Housing Policy* vol 10, no 3, pp 325-44

Mok, F. and Lee, J. (2013) 'Just Housing Policy: Is There a Moral Foundation for a Homeownership Policy?', *Housing Studies*, DOI: 10.1080/02673037.2013.771153

National Housing Supply Council (NHSC) (2013), *Housing Supply and Affordability Issues 2012–13*, Commonwealth of Australia, Canberra

Paterson, J. (1975) 'Home Owning, Home Renting and Income Redistribution', *Australian Quarterly*, vol 47, no 4, pp 28-36

Pawson, H. and Gilmour, T. (2010), 'Transforming Australia's Social Housing: Pointers from the British Stock Transfer Experience', *Urban Policy and Research*, vol 28, no 3, pp 241-60

Productivity Commission, (2004), *First Home Ownership*, Report No. 28, Melbourne

Stretton, H. (1974) *Housing and Government: 1974 Boyer Lectures*, ABC, Sydney

Stretton, H. (1976), 'Ownership and Alienation', in Stretton, H. *Capitalism, Socialism and the Environment*, Cambridge University Press, pp 183-206

Stretton, H. (2005) *Australia Fair*, UNSW Press, Sydney

Troy, P. (2012) *Accommodating Australians: Commonwealth Government Involvement in Housing*, Federation Press, Sydney

Whitty, T. (2013) 'Sick and tired of chasing dreams of finding a home', *The Age*, 5 April, p 31

Wulff, M. (2001) 'Out with the old and in with the new? Housing's role in the new social settlement' in Hancock, L., Howe, B., Frere, M. and O'Donnell, A., *Future Directions in Australian Social Policy: New Ways of Preventing Risk*, Growth No. 49, Committee for Economic Development of Australia, Melbourne, pp 57-65

Yates, J. (1982) 'Tenure choice and the distribution of income: implications for housing policy', *Australian Quarterly*, vol 54, no 1, pp 63-75

Yates, J. (2011) 'Housing in Australia in the 2000s: On the Agenda Too Late?' in H. Gerald and J. Kearns (eds), *The Australian Economy in the 2000s: Proceedings of a Conference,* Reserve Bank of Australia, Sydney

Yates, J. and Bradbury, B. (2010) 'Home ownership as a (crumbling) fourth pillar of social insurance in Australia', *Journal of Housing and the Built Environment* vol 25, no 2, pp 193-211

Part Four

ENVIRONMENT, POPULATION
AND CITIES

THIRTEEN

Population policy

Ian Lowe

Introduction

While it is given relatively little attention, population policy is extremely important. Decisions taken now will have economic, social and environmental consequences for many decades. So policy decisions should be given very high priority. A consequence of federalism is that most decisions about population policy are made by the national government, for whom growth is at least a short-term benefit, whereas the social and economic costs of that growth are largely borne by state and territory governments. Refugees are a small fraction of the migrants coming to Australia and refugee policy is largely driven by international treaty obligations rather than government policies, but the heated debate about the treatment of 'boat people' has confused the broader issue of population. There is a broad consensus between the major Australian political parties that supports a high rate of population growth, mainly because of the belief that it has economic benefits. The consensus covers both explicit and implicit population policies. The differences at the margin only concern some relatively minor issues. Underpinning the consensus are shared values about the primacy of economic management over social and environmental considerations. While the Green Party differs significantly from the Australian Labor Party (ALP) and the coalition parties on those fundamentals, its policies still support a growing population (Lowe, 2012).

There are significant groups opposed to population growth entirely. The organisation Sustainable Population Australia has for many years campaigned vigorously for a goal of stabilising the population (SPA, 2013), as have prominent authors (O'Connor and Lines, 2008), while other interest groups have actively opposed non-European migration (McCormack, 1996). Australians Against Further Immigration (AAFI) was for several years a registered political party and ran candidates on an anti-immigration platform. The 2013 federal election saw the emergence of the Stable Population Party as a single-issue group campaigning on this issue (SPP, 2013). While the party did not achieve its goal of Senate representation, its existence has put the issue of population on the political agenda. This could prove to be temporary, as with previous single-issue groups, like the Nuclear Disarmament Party, or it could represent a turning point in the public debate about population.

This chapter analyses the economic, social and environmental issues associated with population policy before drawing some conclusions about alternative futures for Australia. These issues have been explored in recent books about the population debate (Lowe, 2012; O'Connor, Hartwich and Brown, 2013). The critical point is that decisions being made now have implications many decades into the future, leading one worried observer to conclude that Australia's implicit commitment to unlimited population growth is effectively 'sleepwalking to catastrophe' (Heinrichs, 2012).

The broad consensus: explicit policies

The 'natural increase' in the Australian population, the number of births minus the number of deaths, was relatively stable from 1970 to 2000 at about 120,000 a year. Widespread availability of effective contraception and women's consequent control of their fertility led to a steady decline in the average number of children per adult woman. The average number of children per adult woman is now less than the replacement rate of two, leading to some simplistic and uninformed comment that "we are not replacing ourselves" or "the population would be declining if we weren't bringing in migrants". In fact, the number of adult women is still growing as a result of the birthrate in earlier decades and immigration, so there remains a significant excess of births over deaths. This effect is known as 'demographic inertia': the population continues to grow for several decades after the birthrate drops below the replacement level. As the women of Australia age, this natural increase will decline.

Examining those trends in the early years of this century, demographers concluded that the Australian population could stabilise in the 2030s and the average age would inevitably increase (Hugo, 1984). The Howard Government was so alarmed by this prospect that it introduced the so-called 'baby bonus', a financial incentive to women to have more children. It was famously launched by Treasurer Peter Costello with the facile slogan that women should have three children: 'one for mum, one for dad and one for the country', as if it were self-evident that the nation would benefit from a higher birthrate. The natural increase has risen since the introduction of the financial incentive to about 150,000 a year, but there is still a debate about whether the rise has been caused by the bonus or if the association is simply a coincidence. Minor changes to the policy have been made since its introduction and, as this chapter was being written, the concession was abolished in the 2013–14 Budget (for a more detailed discussion see the chapter by Pocock et al in this volume). The natural increase remains significant; if there were no net migration to Australia, the population would be increasing by about a million every seven years.

While that 'natural increase' has been relatively steady for nearly 50 years, the level of net migration has varied between about 20,000 a year and over 300,000, with government decisions each year setting both the overall number and the allocation to the various categories of migrants accepted: refugees, skilled workers, family reunions, business migrants, students et cetera (Lowe, 2012). The level of migration has typically been a reflection of economic circumstances, larger numbers in times of rapid economic growth and relatively modest levels at times of high unemployment. Again, there has effectively been unquestioned support in the major political parties for high levels of migration in general, mainly on the grounds of the economic benefits that are widely believed to result. Examining the data does not reveal any significant difference between ALP and Coalition Governments in the setting of overall migration targets. A very small number of elected politicians have publicly questioned such assumptions about economic benefits and consequently the migration levels.

With growing public unease about the overall levels of migration or other aspects of the migration programme in particular, some prominent politicians have calibrated their public utterances. One of the most egregious examples is Scott Morrison, who was at the time of writing Opposition spokesperson on immigration. In one published article, Morrison (2010) boasted that the Howard Government had increased net inward migration to nearly a quarter of a million people in its last year in office. He said the policy was designed to achieve positive economic outcomes and so it demonstrated the superior economic management of coalition governments. In the very same article, he attacked the Labor Government for allowing similar levels of migration, accusing it of being out of touch with community opinion. It takes some flexibility and chutzpah to attack the Government for its migration policy while boasting for having taken an identical approach when his party was in power, but that has consistently been Morrison's approach. On the latter point, he was right; this author has written elsewhere that a political insider said "the focus groups went ballistic" in their angry response when Prime Minister Rudd said that he believed in "a big Australia". While clearly supporting high levels of migration because of its supposed economic benefits, Morrison taps into community disquiet about those levels of migration as a means of attacking the government. He has also refined the 'dog-whistling' introduced to Australian mainstream politics by John Howard, as discussed below.

When Julia Gillard replaced Kevin Rudd as Prime Minister in 2010, she was quick to distance herself from what were seen as his less popular policy stances: his support for a tax on the most profitable mining ventures and his championing rapid population growth. Where Rudd had appointed a Minister for Population, Gillard went a step further and rebadged Tony Burke as Minister for Sustainable Population. While this was presumably intended to signal a less enthusiastic approach to high levels of net inward migration, the interpretation within Canberra circles was that the portfolio encompassed the distribution of the migrants as well as their numbers. This could have been an indication that decentralisation, a topic of political discussion several decades ago, was back on the agenda. However, three years after the renaming of the office, there had been no sign of action to influence where migrants go when they arrive in Australia. While the labour needs of the mining industry are often advanced as a justification for high levels of migration, few migrants move to the regions where mining is conducted. Most new migrants understandably settle in the largest cities where they are likely to find communities in which they feel comfortable. It is possible in principle to attach conditions to visas for skilled migrants, precluding them from working in the major cities, but this approach has not been adopted by recent Australian governments. After the return of Rudd as Prime Minister there was a more careful approach to the issue of population with the appointment of Tony Burke, who had been Minister for Sustainable Population, to Minister for Immigration; this meant that the job was for a short time occupied by someone who understood that the distribution of migrants is as important as the overall numbers.

Implicit population policy

J.K. Galbraith (1971) argued that the development of the modern industrial state has led almost inevitably to a situation in which politics is seen as synonymous with economic management. The reaction to the Global Financial Crisis was a clear demonstration of this effect;

social, environmental and even broader economic considerations were swept aside by the urgency of stabilising the financial system and restoring growth. Growth is seen by most decision makers as the overwhelming priority. Politicians and pundits are puzzled when governments lose office despite economic prosperity, so entrenched is the view that voters judge governments mainly on their economic performance.

Since politicians generally believe that population growth is good for the economy, there is an implicit population policy underpinning public statements: effectively it is 'the more the better', in words once used by Bob Hawke when he was Prime Minister. At a superficial level, it is clearly true that a larger population requires more food, more housing, more clothes and more transport, so the growing population increases the overall level of economic activity. However, the economic question is not that simple. A growing population requires increasing investment in infrastructure: housing, power and water, waste management, transport services and so on. Some studies have concluded that there is a small net benefit, all things being considered, while others show a net cost to the community of population growth. The second issue is that individuals are only better off on average if the rate of economic growth is higher than the rate of population growth, increasing wealth per person. It is also clear that there are social costs and benefits associated with the scale and nature of population growth, as well as environmental questions. The population debate is often confused because of the conflation of all those issues: social, environmental and economic, with quite radically different legitimate perspectives in each area.

Economic dimensions of population policy

There has been widespread support for the assumption that economic considerations demand growth since the Great Depression of the 1930s, an economic slump that only ended with the massive public spending of World War II. Earlier economic thinkers such as J.S. Mill (1848) had argued for a steady-state economy, a view also developed in the 20th century by Herman Daly as a professor and then official of the World Bank (Daly, 1996). His writings had little impact on the economics profession, with a belief in the necessity of growth being almost universal. This is perfectly understandable, since debt financing of development implicitly requires growth to enable the repayments to be made; periods of low growth or recession cause serious economic problems as a result, so few question the need for economic growth.

Since the simplest way to increase the overall scale of the economy is to have more people buying the goods and services produced, it is usually assumed that population growth is both inevitable and beneficial.

There are dissenting views. *Managing Without Growth* begins with a confession: having supported economic growth in the belief that it would end unemployment, eliminate poverty and enable us to solve our environmental problems, the author was forced to admit that growth had not achieved any of those goals (Victor, 2008). Victor used a model similar to that of the Canadian Treasury to explore alternative futures for that country's economy. He found that attempting to pursue growth as a goal would lead to the disastrous outcomes nationally that *Limits to Growth* projected for the world as a whole: social, environmental and economic collapse (Meadows et al, 1972). He also found that stopping growth immediately would be equally disruptive. The only future which appeared sustainable was one in which both population increase and economic growth were gradually slowed until a steady state was achieved, combined with policies to reduce inequality, share work and reduce environmental impacts of production. Victor concluded that economic growth is politically essential if the population is growing, because otherwise wealth per person declines. Stabilising the population enables subsequent stabilising of the scale of the economy and opens up the prospect of a sustainable future. Lester Thurow (1986) had earlier questioned the impacts on public spending of rapid growth, arguing that it would prove impossible to provide the infrastructure needs without selling public assets or trying to develop public–private partnerships. Jane O'Sullivan (2012) refined this approach and did detailed calculations on the economic impacts of growing populations in Australian cities, concluding that each extra citizen requires public spending of about a quarter of a million dollars to provide electricity, water, transport, waste management and other essential services. So a situation of rapid population growth requires very large public investments to provide that infrastructure. Critics view this as a subsidy to those sections of the private economy that benefit, most obviously land development, housing and the retail sector.

The present author's analysis of the economic costs and benefits of population growth endorses such conclusions (Lowe, 2012). An increasing population clearly adds to the sales revenue and profitability of some sections of the economy, most obviously housing and retail, but it adds significantly to the need for public investment. The overall size of the economy grows, but it is doubtful whether people are wealthier on average. Studies aimed explicitly at justifying the recent rapid growth usually show a small net benefit. Queensland Government (2010) published before its 2012 Growth Management Summit two pieces of research conducted by the State Treasury. The first analysed the contributions to the state's economic growth from population increase, higher levels of participation and improving productivity. It calculated that the average contributions of the three components to the 3% growth rate for the previous decade had been 0.2%, 0.6% and 2.2%. So the economy had been growing at a rate of 3.0% with rapid population growth, whereas it would have grown at 2.8% with no increase in population. A prospective study concluded that wealth per person would increase significantly if population growth were 'heavily restricted' and grow rather more if there were no restrictions. The quantitative forecasts were that economic output per person in southeast Queensland would grow from $50,000 to about $65,000 if growth were curbed drastically and to about $69,000 if unrestricted growth were to continue. Assuming these figures to be valid, they could be the basis for a rational argument about the extent to which the extra wealth would be seen as an overall benefit, given that some of the consequences of growth are negative for the existing population: more crowded buses and trains, more traffic on roads, restricted access to recreational facilities and so on. The overall consideration of costs and benefits does not take place in the modern political climate, in which it is taken as axiomatic that population growth is beneficial.

Gittins (2010) argued that 'immigration adds little or nothing to the material living standards of the existing population' because the new arrivals and their families need capital investment in the form of housing and support services, without which living standards and quality of life decline. O'Sullivan (2012) expressed the same argument in quantitative terms. If the average life of built infrastructure is about 50 years, the normal annual replacement bill is about 2% of the total capital investment. If the population grows by 2%, the replacement bill of 2% is supplemented by the extra 2% for the new arrivals. So the infrastructure bill is doubled, but the revenue base has only increased by 2%, leading to an inevitable crisis of public finance. She asked,

> How is the extra revenue from 2% more taxpayers expected to cover 100% more infrastructure construction, 50% more university places, 30% more buses and more besides? The fact that it doesn't is why the Queensland government, at the height of the mining boom, feels compelled to sell public assets to balance its books (O'Sullivan, 2012).

State governments along the eastern coast all lost office during the time of writing this chapter, at least partly because of public perceptions that infrastructure provision was not keeping pace with growing demand, despite the unpopular sale of some public assets.

It is sometimes argued that increasing the workforce is necessary to meet the demands of the economy. At the overall level, Birrell et al (2011) have shown that this is a circular argument. If you assume rapid population growth, you inevitably conclude that more workers are needed to meet the needs of the growing population. If you begin with the alternative hypothesis of a stable population or one that is growing slowly, the equally inevitable conclusion is that the main challenge is providing jobs for those who wish to work. At the time of writing, it was accepted that about 5% of the workforce would be unemployed and a larger group underemployed, but large numbers of people were being brought into Australia because of shortages of skilled workers, real or perceived. It is certainly true in Australia, as in many other countries, that recent migrants do jobs that members of the local population are reluctant to do, for one reason or another. From a local policy perspective, it is much less expensive to lure trained doctors and nurses from poor countries than to train them ourselves, but the practice has certainly caused resentment in some of those countries (Kanck, 2012).

The overall conclusion is that rapid population growth clearly benefits some sectors of the economy and makes a small contribution to average wealth per person, but it also imposes on the community significant financial costs. It certainly makes the overall size of the economy larger, a factor which is generally welcomed by policy makers.

Social dimensions of population policy

The scale and balance of the population have a range of social effects. There are social opportunities in large cities that do not exist in smaller settlements, causing a steady migration of young people away from country areas to the major cities. When I left my small country town to move to Sydney in the 1950s, my main motivation was the chance of more interesting work than was available where my parents lived. I quickly noticed that the city had more options for eating and drinking, a wider range of entertainment and higher levels of performance in sport. Some of those opportunities were simply a function of scale, but others were related to the degree of diversity. Country towns in the 1950s were overwhelmingly Anglo–Celtic, but the cities were receiving significant numbers of migrants from a wide range of backgrounds and becoming more diverse. The city offered a degree of anonymity and tolerance of diversity not found in a small town. Many can find this liberating, but at another level, large cities can lack the sense of community found in smaller settlements. Those cities that work socially tend to function as a series of urban villages, within which people can feel a sense of community. While small towns usually have a sense of community, they can also have a uniformity of values that makes newcomers feel unwelcome. I witnessed tensions in small country towns when migrants behaved in ways that were perfectly normal in their home countries, but aroused antagonism because the behaviour was not consistent with the values of 1950s rural Australia.

It makes a big difference whether growth is due to the birthrate or migration. Since babies join existing households at age zero, their impacts on the social fabric and age structure of the population are very different from the effects of adult migrants arriving. Most local authorities support growth, whether through the birthrate or migration, for the increased rate of income and the greater number of households to share the cost of basic infrastructure. A motivation for amalgamating local authorities in recent years has been the perception that those with small populations have difficulty providing the range of services that the modern community expects. In an interesting move back to earlier times, the citizens of Noosa recently voted to leave the amalgamated Sunshine Coast Regional Council, apparently feeling that the loss of identity was not justified by the financial benefits of joining a larger polity.

There has been widespread discussion, much of it poorly informed, about the age structure of the population and the impacts of an ageing society. This has created a widespread impression that Australia has a problem of an unusually high proportion of ageing people who will inevitably put increasing pressure on the medical system. There are two components of this impression, both of them questionable. The fundamental perception is just wrong. The age structure of Australia is not unusual for an economically advanced country; Australia ranks 43rd in the world in a league table of the average age (UN Statistical Division, 2010). In those terms Australia is a much younger society than most European countries and affluent Asian nations like Japan. Whereas western European countries typically have almost twice as many people over 65 as those under 15, in Australia those two groups are of roughly equal numbers (UN Statistical Division, 2010).

The second contentious belief is that an older population inevitably means soaring medical bills. The basic reason people are living longer is that they are healthier. I am not unusual in being alive and productive at an age by which my father, my grandfathers and all my male direct ancestors were already dead. While it is true that medical bills tend to rise in the last few years of life, the demographic change of recent years has simply shifted that burden into a higher age bracket, rather than increasing the scale of the problem: 70 is the new 50! In terms of the workforce, having young, physically fit people was important when there were many jobs requiring strength and endurance, but technology has dramatically changed those demands. As the extreme example, agriculture employed about 600,000 people 100 years ago, most of them fit young men; by the 1980s the agricultural workforce had declined to about 100,000 because technology allowed each worker to achieve much more (Jones, 1982). Those sectors traditionally requiring physical strength, such as farming, mining and stevedoring, are now more likely to require experience and judgement than brute strength. So there is no longer such a strong economic requirement for a young workforce.

As mentioned earlier, population growth based mainly on migration affects the diversity and social cohesion of a society. The Australian population has become much more diverse since the introduction of mass migration in the 1940s. The early waves of migration were predominantly from Western Europe, when what was explicitly referred to as the 'white Australia policy' was used to discriminate against migrants from Asia or Africa. As the explicit racism of this stance became embarrassing, it was replaced by the more nuanced, Restrictive Immigration policy. That in turn unravelled, initially when the Fraser Government accepted some responsibility for the casualties of the situation created by the USA in Vietnam, and more dramatically when the Hawke Government allowed thousands of Chinese people to stay in Australia after the Tienanmen Square massacre. The present author has argued elsewhere about the possible education scam, under which hundreds of thousands of international students, primarily from Asian countries, have effectively been granted migration to Australia on the pretext of taking courses in such areas as cooking or hairdressing (Lowe, 2012). The largest group of migrants each year is now from Asia, with significant numbers also from Africa. That in turn makes migrants much more visible. There is now serious tension in parts of the larger cities as a result of the different lifestyles, different expectations and different cultural traditions of relatively recent migrants. These tensions can be exploited by opportunistic politicians.

As Prime Minister, John Howard developed a technique which has become known as 'dog-whistling', hinting to older Australians that he shared their concern about non-European migrants, while maintaining a policy of high levels of migration and discriminating only against those migrants who arrived in unauthorised boats.

In public policy terms, there was from 1970 to 2000 effectively bipartisan agreement between the Coalition and the ALP, both to support large-scale immigration in the belief that it was good for the economy and to eschew discrimination. Malcolm Fraser as Liberal Prime Minister dismissed Glen Sheil from his ministerial post for championing the apartheid regime in South Africa. Pauline Hanson, having been preselected by the Liberal Party to contest the Queensland seat of Oxley, had her endorsement withdrawn for making openly racist comments; she then successfully stood as an independent candidate and subsequently formed the One Nation Party. For a brief period it was a significant minority in the Queensland Parliament, before falling apart in a welter of recrimination and personal attacks. Its agenda openly blamed Asian migrants and Indigenous people for the problems of modern society. For a few years the group AAFI was registered as a political party and ran candidates in national elections; its former spokesperson and political candidate, Denis McCormack, continues to circulate material attacking Asian, African and Muslim migrants. He advocates a campaign to encourage voters to write, 'reduce immigration' on ballot papers. Because the campaign would be perceived as discriminatory the approach was endorsed by neither Sustainable Population Australia nor the Australian Conservation Foundation, both of which advocate stabilising the population.

That raises a more general social issue as the current population debate defies simple explanations (Lowe, 2012). As one example, some humanitarians argue for very generous treatment of refugees, effectively an open door policy, on the grounds that those people would inevitably be better off in Australia than in the countries they are fleeing. So, they argue, it is Australia's responsibility to be generous to those wanting to go there. Other, equally fervent, humanitarians believe that Australia cannot solve the refugee problem and argue for more generous aid to give desperate people a better life in their own countries. Some of those who welcome the social diversity produced by migration in general terms are uneasy about particular groups of recent migrants, such as Muslims. Some who are concerned about the overall level of migration worry that the recent emphasis on Asian migrants has produced a new situation. If migrants are predominantly Asian, slowing migration could be perceived as a return to earlier policies which discriminated against non-Europeans. The media attention to the arrivals of boatloads of asylum seekers has led to an especially confused debate, with many recent arrivals sharing the view of some politicians that these people are 'jumping the queue'. The critical point is that the total number of refugees is a very small fraction of the annual migrant intake, so the scale of arrivals is not significant in terms of population policy. As discussed earlier, in 2012 the Stable Population Party was formed, with a policy of stabilising the population, which is less likely to alienate voters than the explicit targeting of immigration, even though it would inevitably require reducing immigration levels substantially.

Ecological consequences of population policy

The first independent national report on the state of the Australian environment identified a range of problems that need to be addressed to live sustainably (SoEAC, 1996). It said explicitly that there are no simple causes of these problems, which are the combined consequence of the growth and distribution of the population, lifestyle choices and technologies used. Three subsequent reports at five-year intervals have said that all those problems are getting worse as the population continues to grow and consumption per person also increases, putting compounding pressure on natural systems (SoEC, 2011). The Australian Conservation Foundation made a submission in the 2011 round of considering threats to endangered ecological systems under the Environmental Protection and Biodiversity Conservation Act, identifying the growth in the human population as a process threatening coastal wetlands and other biological communities such as heathlands (Lowe, 2012). The clear conclusion is that environmental degradation will continue unless impact per person is reduced faster that the population grows.

It is certainly possible in principle to reduce greatly the environmental impact of the existing population. The National Framework for Energy Efficiency (NFEE) found that carbon dioxide emissions could be reduced by 30% using cost-effective existing technology (Australian Government, 2003). A report published by the United Nations Environment Program (UNEP) *Resource Efficiency and Economic Outlook for the Asia-Pacific Region* (REEO) called for 'a new industrial revolution' in which people's needs are met using 25% of the resources now employed (UNEP, 2011). There is, however, no sign of the political will to implement even the modest NFEE changes, let alone the sweeping changes proposed by the REEO report. Most people who see population growth as desirable also see increasing per capita consumption as a sign of progress, so those dominant values implicitly support increasing pressure on natural systems.

Humans are not exempt from general ecological laws. No species can expand without limit in a closed system. In his book *Collapse*, Jared Diamond (2005) argued that human societies naturally expand until they reach a limit of one kind or another: food, water, energy or other resources, or relations with neighbours. Whether the society survives, Diamond argued, depends on whether they are able to change their approach to get back into balance, or continue their old ways until the inevitable collapse. In a chapter devoted specifically to Australia, Diamond noted that it has a comparatively small population but limited resources, as the driest inhabited continent with old, nutrient-poor soils. He concluded that the most likely future for Australia would be steadily declining quality of life with an increasingly degraded environment. When the current author pointed this out to a conference in Sydney, the person chairing the session interrupted to conduct a snap audience poll, asking if they agreed with that description of life in contemporary Sydney. The overwhelming majority raised their hands, supporting Diamond's analysis. Rightly or wrongly, they perceive their material quality of life to be declining as the city grows larger and they observe environmental problems getting worse. While there is no simple link between the scale of the population and their impact on the environment, the only way an increasing population could improve environmental outcomes is if the economic benefits were to provide extra resources to handle the impacts of growing consumption. Up to the point of writing, this has not happened.

Conclusion: alternative futures for Australia

In *Bigger or Better?*, alternative futures for the Australian population were explored (Lowe, 2012). A strategic decision to stabilise the population at some level is one possibility. Demographic studies show that net annual migration levels between zero and about 70,000 are consistent with that strategic goal. The population is currently increasing by about a million every three years; it would be increasing by about a million every seven years if there were no net migration. As the adult population ages, the 'natural increase' between births and deaths will gradually decline. With no net migration, the population would stabilise in the 2030s at about 28 million. With migration levels up to about 70,000 the population stabilises later at a higher level. At the current rate of migration, the 2050 population will be over 40 million and growing more rapidly than now. So the decisions taken in the next decade about migration levels will, all other things being equal, determine whether the population stabilises below 30 million, stabilises later at a higher level, or continues to increase until constrained by such physical limits as food, water and energy supply. Of course, government policies in this area are not taken in a vacuum and need to take into account relations with Australia's neighbours. Some of those who support the current approach of setting high migration levels argue that other countries in the region would not find it credible for an affluent country with a relatively small population to say that it cannot take more, so such a policy would be a source of tension with those neighbours.

The federal system of government is a serious complication for public policy in the area of population. As discussed earlier, the principal explicit policies have been the previous financial incentive to have children and the annual migration quota, both in the hands of the national government. The infrastructure costs of the growing population are almost entirely the responsibility of state and territory governments, who are also partly responsible for managing the social and environmental consequences of growth. From the viewpoint of the national government, a growing population means the overall size of the economy increases and so the government can claim to be presiding over a wealthier society. From the viewpoint of the state or territory government, the improvements in economic output and public revenues are offset by the burden of increasing infrastructure costs. Though the Rudd and Gillard Governments sought to share the load by investing in urban public transport, this remains a contentious political issue; then Leader of the Opposition, Tony Abbott said that he would oppose funding to improve the Melbourne rail network, even though his Coalition colleagues in the Victorian Government first proposed this.

The current overall approach is to encourage continued expansion for the foreseeable future. An obvious problem in terms of public policy is that the time horizon of politicians is the three-year electoral cycle, but the timescale of changes is very long. A decision to aim at stabilisation would take decades to implement. If serious problems occur as there are attempts to support an increasing population, the growth pattern that is established will ensure that the problem will continue to worsen for decades. So population policy deserves to be a high priority. It arguably has greater economic impact than decisions about public spending, fiscal stimulus or interest rates. Its effect on the age structure, health care budgets and social cohesion is immense, as is its impact on the capacity to manage Australia's unique and fragile environment. Decisions being made now, often based on short-term political expediency, have enormous long-term consequences.

References

Australian Government (2003) *Towards a National Framework for Energy Efficiency,* Energy Efficiency and Greenhouse Working Group, Melbourne

Birrell, R., Healy, E., Betts, K. and Smith F. (2011) *Immigration and the Resources Boom Mark 2,* Centre for Population and Urban Research, Monash University, Clayton

Daly, H. (1996) *Beyond Growth: The Economics of Sustainable Development,* Beacon Press, Boston

Diamond, J. (2005) *Collapse: How Societies Choose to Fail or Succeed,* Viking Books, New York

Galbraith, J.K. (1971) *The New Industrial State,* Houghton Mifflin, Boston

Gittins, R. (2010) 'Stop beating around the bush and talk about a big Australia', *Sydney Morning Herald* 4 August. Available at: www.brisbanetimes.com.au/federal-politics/stop-beating-about-the-bush-and-talk-about-big-australia-20100803-115bg.html#ixzz2ZCZPFi9x

Heinrichs, F. (2012) *Sleepwalking to Catastrophe.* E-book available at: www.fionaheinrichs.com

Hugo, G. (1984) *Ageing of the Australian Population: Changing Distribution and Characteristics of the Aged Population,* Department of Immigration and Ethnic Affairs, Belconnen

Jones, B.O. (1982) *Sleepers, Wake!,* Oxford University Press, Melbourne

Kanck, S. (2011), pers.com quoted in Lowe, I. (2012), op. cit. p. 133

Lowe, I. (2012) *Bigger or Better? Australia's Population Debate,* University of Queensland Press, St Lucia

McCormack, D.M. (1996) 'The Asianisation of Australia: race, place and power', Paper presented to Asian Studies Association conference, LaTrobe University, cited in Current House, Hansard, 1996, p 5926 et seq

Meadows, D.H., Meadows, G., Randers, J. and Behrens, W.W. III (1972) *The Limits to Growth,* Universe Books, New York

Mill, J.S. (1848) *Principles of Political Economy with some of their Applications to Social Philosophy,* Longmans, Green & Co. London

Morrison, S. (2010) 'Migration and Population', *Australian Mosaic* vol 25, pp 15-17

O'Connor, M., Hartwich, O. and Brown, J. (2013) *Why vs Why: Australia's Big Population Conundrum*, Pantera Press, Sydney

O'Connor, M. & Lines, W.J. (2008) *Overloading Australia*, Envirobook, Canterbury

O'Sullivan, J.N. (2012) 'The Burden of Durable Asset Construction in Growing Populations', *Economic Affairs* vol 32, no 1, pp 31-7

Queensland Government (2010) *Opportunities, Challenges and Choices*, Growth Management Summit Background Paper, Queensland Government, Brisbane

SoEAC (State of Environment Advisory Council) (1996) *State of the Environment Australia*, CSIRO Publishing, Melbourne

SoEC (State of Environment Committee) (2011) *State of the Environment Australia 2011*

Sustainable Population Australia (2012), www.population.org.au

Stable Population Party (2013), www.populationparty.org.au

Thurow, L.C. (1986) 'Why the Ultimate Size of the World's Population Doesn't Matter', *Technology Review* vol 89, no 6, pp 22-9

United Nations Statistical Division (2010) *Population and Vital Statistics Report*, UN, New York

UNEP (2011) *Resource Efficiency: Economics and Outlook for Asia-and the Pacific*, UNEP, Nairobi

Victor, P.A. (2008) *Managing Without Growth*, Edward Elgar, London

FOURTEEN

Australian cities: in pursuit of a national urban policy

Paul Burton and Jago Dodson

Introduction

Cities are the places where many of the problems to which Australian public policy responds are most evident and indeed concentrated: health inequalities, unemployment, housing affordability, congestion, crime and violence and environmental quality. In the sense that where we live has some impact on how we live, cities are important places because most Australians live in cities and have always done so (Davison, 1995). While it is not always easy to define cities with any degree of clarity and consistency over time and between countries, most definitions include some combination of population size and density as well as historical recognition and function (OECD, 2012). The Major Cities Unit (MCU) of the Australian Government's Department of Infrastructure and Transport recognises 18 major cities, each with a population of over 100,000, including the all state and territory capital cities and an increasingly important set of non-capital cities such as the Gold Coast, Newcastle and Wollongong. These major cities now hold three quarters of the nation's private housing stock and the majority of jobs (DITMCU, 2013).

Many of the major policy challenges in Australia have a distinctly urban dimension and attempts to resolve them have impacts throughout the wider urban system. However, while Australian cities are affected by any number of policies, there has not until recently been a national policy *about* cities in the sense of proposing, for example, a hierarchy of cities in which anticipated growth in its various forms might be channelled towards particular types of city. Indeed, federal governments have typically eschewed any role in the planning of cities and have not often expressed a policy position about the role of cities in the development of the nation. All the major cities of Australia experience some problems of growth management that might be one of attracting, accommodating and locating growth. Most also typically proclaim their ambitions to become world cities, new world cities, more liveable cities, knowledge cities, smart cities, and so on. In other words, while cities themselves prepare plans for the stimulation and management of growth or the promotion of liveability *within* their boundaries, and similar plans are prepared for some wider metropolitan regions, there has never been a national plan for cities. Nor has there been a national plan for accommodating growth with an explicit spatial dimension, apart from periodic suggestions that rural and regional areas would benefit from more growth (DSEWPC, 2011).

The publication of the Commonwealth Government's National Urban Policy in 2011 marked, therefore, an important step in this direction, offering for the first time an outline of the '... overarching goals and priorities for the nation's cities and how we [the Australian Government] will play a role in making them more productive, sustainable and liveable' (DIT, 2011). In this chapter we critically review the development of policy for Australian cities that culminated in this important initiative. However, we begin by considering the theoretical and conceptual underpinnings of urban policy in developed countries before tracing the historical pattern of policy debate about cities in Australia. We conclude by reflecting on the prospects for urban policy and ask whether Australia is on the verge of having a coherent national urban policy with the potential to address the many problems experienced by the vast majority of Australians living in cities.

Theoretical and conceptual underpinnings of urban policy

From a theoretical and conceptual perspective, what do we understand by policy for cities or urban policy, and indeed can the two be treated as synonymous? Atkinson and Moon (1994, 20) referred some time ago to British urban policy as 'a chaotic conception' while Cochrane notes in his critical review of urban policy that '... assessing quite why one particular form of policy intervention attracts the soubriquet "urban", while another does not, simply adds to the difficulties' (2007, 1).

If urban policy in general appears to be a chaotic conception that at the same time displays a globally familiar set of orthodoxies and instruments, is urban policy in Australia any different? It would appear not, at least in any substantial and systematic way, even if the day-to-day practices of urban planning in Australian cities may be different from those in European or North American cities, and are certainly different from those in the emerging cities of China and India. But to present a more detailed and rigorous assessment of the historical trajectory of what has constituted Australian urban policy, we need to take a more conceptual and theoretical approach in considering the question: what factors, both ideological and material, require responses from governments in the form of urban policy?

We can approach these questions through any number of theoretical lenses, but two are used here, albeit in simplified and truncated forms: Keynesian or social democratic and critical. While the social democratic tradition offers a theoretical account of, and justification for, government intervention in cities, critical approaches are more often focused on critique than on prescription, not least because the number of 'actually existing' cases of urban policy intervention based on principles other than social democratic ones are increasingly rare, especially since the demise of the Soviet Union and the collapse of communism.

Social democratic or Keynesian approaches to urban policy are by far the most common form of intervention found in practice in developed countries. They are premised on a belief in the essential plausibility of both markets and government intervention in response to occasional market failure. They often involve an area-based approach in which particular parts of cities, or in some cases wider metropolitan regions, are designated for policy intervention, with this intervention often managed by special agencies set up specifically for this purpose. The complexity and interconnectedness of the urban problems encountered in these designated places means that particular emphasis is usually given to partnership working, to the importance of community engagement in policy development, implementation and delivery, and to the need for relatively long-term policy commitments. Urban policy interventions of this type are often established as 'demonstration projects', partly to emphasise their experimental nature and to signal a desire to learn incrementally from experience, and partly because this approach is inevitably cheaper than a fully blown, nationally applicable policy. Policy failure is typically framed and explained as the result of lack of coordination, lack of engagement and the imposition of time frames that do not allow major changes to be realised, rather than as a result of any underlying structural problems or contradictions that can only be addressed by radical systemic change. Peck, Theodore and Brenner speak of a depressingly familiar reaction to these failures in cities around the world, including '... more social state retrenchment and paternalist-penal state expansion, more privatisation and deregulation, more subjection of urban development decisions to market logics, a continued delinking of land-use systems from relays of popular-democratic control and public accountability [and] more courting of mobile events, investment and elite consumers ...' (2013, 1092).

Critical conceptions of urban policy drew initially on Marxist frames of analysis and developed primarily as critiques of social democratic or Keynesian measures and rarely if ever became the basis of alternative policy prescriptions in capitalist settings. These critiques begin with the assumption that the state in capitalist societies exists to serve the interests of a dominant class of capitalists and in particular to support the creation of surplus value in processes of urban development. Variations on this basic analytical theme take more or less account of the existence of different fractions of capital and of possible conflicts between landowners, developers, construction firms and the suppliers of development finance. Some attempt also to account theoretically for the emergence of apparently contradictory pressures on the state to prepare and implement long-term plans and to give free rein to market forces so long as they remain within the framework of law. Attempts to translate an often powerful critique into principles for an alternative set of policy prescriptions tend to hinge on the extent to which the protagonists believe in the possibility of reform through working 'in and against the state' or whether they see the overthrow of the capitalist mode of production and its state apparatus as a necessary precondition for change or indeed as the ultimate goal.

In recent years an alternative critique has emerged which takes as its starting point the transformation of the social democratic approach to urban policy in the face of neoliberalising processes. While this has sometimes followed the more traditional Marxist belief that neoliberalism as a form of capitalism will eventually succumb to its own instabilities and internal contradictions, many current formulations of the critique recognise the constantly evolving nature of 'the neoliberal project' and its capacity to withstand crises, including those with a distinctly urban dimension. This critical approach includes a view of urban policy as inextricably linked with pernicious processes of neoliberalisation, as seen in Peck et al's quote earlier, but in some cases takes a more accommodating stance, as in Healey's (2004) more positive interpretation of New Labour's urban policy measures in the UK as having the potential for achieving progressive outcomes and achieving what Amin and Thrift (2002) refer to as 'an urbanism of hope'. In the remainder of this chapter we explore the emergence of urban policy in Australia, review this process of policy development through these competing theoretical and conceptual lenses and conclude by addressing the question of whether Australian cities need a reinvigorated national urban policy in order to see any improvement in their circumstances and prospects.

A brief history of urban policy in Australia

For what is one of the world's most urbanised nations, Australian politicians and policy makers have displayed a surprisingly low level of interest in urban conditions and their contribution to national prospects and have mostly eschewed any kind of explicit national policy for cities. Australia's first formal, systematic and self-conscious national urban policy was only released in 2011, some 223 years after the founding of the first European settlement on the continent on what was then *Terra Australis*, and more than a century since federation formally constituted Australia as a unitary nation. Perhaps our public policy making reflects an uneasy and often paradoxical cultural attitude towards cities from the outset, celebrating the pioneering spirit of the outback while living a more mundane suburban existence. European settlement was in part a response to the pressures of domestic urbanisation as the teeming industrialising cities of Britain produced a surplus and transportable population. Yet some of those despatched by colonial authorities to oversee the settlement of Australia also brought with them Enlightenment notions of the possibility of human improvement through planning and a growing belief in the potential for the regulation of urban development to bring social order and a better quality of urban life. While we should not conflate or confuse the wide range of principles, movements and measures used in the planning of cities in Australia with a coherent, explicit and national urban policy, it is worth sketching briefly some of the more significant developments in these measures and movements over the last 200 years.

In 1788 Governor Phillip, upon founding the settlement at Sydney Cove, initiated the first attempt at what might be termed a planning policy in Australia, when he wrote to his superiors in Britain describing his plans for a new town. These included specifying the width of streets and requiring that no more than one house should be built on each allotment to avoid the 'inconveniences' that might otherwise arise (Freestone, 2010). In 1810 Governor Macquarie sought to regulate the materials used to construct dwellings and their dimensions, all in the interest of civic standards and safety (Marsden, 2000). There is scant evidence that these early regulations were strenuously adhered to by those building houses, and to the extent that planning policy had any purchase on early Australian settlement it came via the surveyor's mark which delineated the plot and street layout rather than as a result of the Governor's planning decree.

For most of the early decades of European settlement the pace of urban development was relatively slow as the Australian colonies were risky venues for investment, remote from European markets. With unclear economic purpose, they struggled to attract capital with which to build and grow. The development of agriculture and the wider colonial economy by the mid-19th century permitted much more rapid urban development and yet regulation remained light, partly because of the lack of institutions, such as municipal councils, through which it might be applied. Although local governments were established from the 1840s onwards they remained weak and often ineffective in managing urban problems, particularly in the face of rapid growth and at scale. Melbourne, for example, saw extraordinarily rapid population growth in the mid-19th century, with 90,000 settlers estimated to have arrived between 1838 and 1851 (Priestley, 1991, 227). This influx, in the context of minimal civic oversight, led to 'periodic outcries against piles of refuse, builders' rubbish, putrefying animal carcasses, from horses to cats, and general filth' (Priestley, 1991, 220) and regular flooding from inadequate drainage mingled with growing volumes of informally disposed sewage and the effluent produced by such noxious activities as slaughterhouses, tanneries and wool scours (Davison, 1978). That said, the founding of the City of Sydney in 1843 largely arose from to the need to secure and manage an improved public water supply (Hector, 2011).

A major institutional change for Australia occurred with federation of the colonies into states in 1901 and the establishment of the Commonwealth Government, but this shift had little immediate effect on the conception of anything resembling urban policy, as under the new constitution territorial affairs such as land development were left to the states to manage. In practical terms, therefore, federation brought little innovation in urban policy, as the states continued an incremental approach to managing the processes and consequences of urbanisation. Despite the suburban rush from the 1880s onwards, the core areas of Australian cities remained crowded and often degraded. In the early decades of the 20th century the nascent global town planning movement acquired Australian advocates. The competition to design Canberra as the new national capital, plus other concerns about urban sanitary hygiene and moral order, served as a spur to the development of various policy responses. Attempts were made to establish the institutions and principles of town planning at the metropolitan scale, through, for example, the 1929 Victorian

Royal Commission into Melbourne's metropolitan planning and the amalgamation of Brisbane's individual boroughs into a unitary metropolitan council in 1925, which remains the only amalgamated council serving a state capital.

The period after World War II saw new Commonwealth intervention into urban affairs, particularly housing. The main vehicle for this was the Commonwealth-State Housing Agreement (CSHA), through which federal monies were made available to support the expansion of state government housing stock (Winter and Bryson, 1998; Berry, 1999). The focus initially was on mass rental housing but this soon shifted to providing for owner occupation, primarily via suburban expansion. Largely as a result of this policy, Australia's housing tenure structure shifted dramatically; whereas in 1947 just 52% of households were owner-occupiers, by 1971 this figure had reached 70%, an extraordinary shift in the social distribution of housing ownership and wealth (Badcock, 2000). The Commonwealth hoped that these housing reforms would be accompanied by more metropolitan scale planning of and for Australian cities, but while some efforts were made, such as the 1948 County of Cumberland plan for Sydney and Melbourne's 1954 Metropolitan Plan, these had at best only modest impact on substantive planning outcomes. Meanwhile, the extraordinary pace of suburbanisation during the boom years of the 1950s and 1960s stretched the capacity of suburban local governments to provide local infrastructure and services to meet the needs of this growing population.

By the 1970s the consequences of weak planning policy implementation had become increasingly visible and difficult to ignore as large tracts of Sydney and Melbourne remained unsewered and concern mounted about suburban isolation in all of the major cities. It was at this point that the pioneering Whitlam Government launched what was Australia's first significant attempt at developing a national urban policy, under the political direction of the Minister for Urban and Regional Development, Tom Uren, and the intellectual stimulation of Patrick Troy and Max Neutze of the Urban Research Unit at the Australian National University (Lloyd and Troy, 1981). The establishment of the Department of Urban and Regional Development (DURD) and the articulation of an urban policy that combined measures to address the spatial concentration of poverty within cities with 'a bold program of decentralisation, attempting to direct settlement growth into newly designated regional centres' (Gleeson and Low, 2000, 33) represented not only the first but perhaps also the high-point of Australian urban policy, at least in practice. Following

251

the dismissal of the Whitlam Government in 1975 these institutions and policy measures were abandoned, and as Stretton (1989, xiii) notes in his review of government and the cities, '... most of his urban initiatives ... came to be remembered – or slandered – as extravagant follies which had helped him to fall'. However, Orchard's (1999) more systematic review of the shifting visions of post-war national urban policy captures the variety of outcomes of this short-lived initiative, from the practical benefits of dealing with Sydney's massive sewerage backlog to the failure of the land commissions and regional growth centre programmes. His review also demonstrates clearly how the Whitlam/Uren urban policy experience set the tone for subsequent academic and policy debate, revealing to some the scale and even the futility of this particular social democratic project and to others a clear set of principles for how to progress more effectively in the future.

While the Conservative governments that followed Whitlam were resolute in denying the need for urban policy as anything other than a relatively parochial set of town planning measures, the Hawke Labor Government formed after the 1983 election heralded a period of renewed debate about the nature of urban policy in general and the particular case for its reformulation and reintroduction. In terms uncannily similar to those used by Prime Minister Rudd in the last days of the 2013 election campaign, Prime Minister Hawke, Treasurer Keating and Minister for Social Security Brian Howe began to make a case for a major programme of investment in urban infrastructure, especially in outer suburban rather than city centre locations, all in pursuit of a more sustainable urban form and a more efficiently functioning Australian city. This thinking eventually manifested itself in Keating's Building Better Cities (BBC) programme, that combined a degree of spatial targeting with the principle of the demonstration project. While many see a positive legacy from the programme (for example Simons, 2011), others have observed how difficult it was to measure with any precision the impact of BBC-funded local initiatives because of their breadth and depth as well as their local specificity (Baragwanath, 1996). Orchard suggests a number of problems associated with the initiative, including the tendency for a sense of 'suffocating closure' (1999, 207), in debate about the possibilities of urban policy and a retreat to what Kirwan (1990, 90) referred to as 'reluctant pragmatism' as the only way forward.

The election of the Howard Government in 1996 saw a return, predictably, to the conservative orthodoxy of abandoning urban policy as a national imperative, and although some saw this as storing up political trouble as conditions in cities inevitably worsened, there appears to have been a continuing, albeit reluctant, public acceptance of the chronic problems facing cities, rather than any sign of a radical response to an acute urban crisis. Nevertheless, under the Rudd/Gillard Governments from late 2007 onwards, the case for a national urban policy was again taken up by the Federal Government and in intergovernmental bodies such as the Council of Australian Governments (COAG).

Towards a national urban policy?

Since 2007 the Rudd/Gillard Governments pursued a programme of national urban policy development that produced a substantial volume of analytical material accompanied by a large programme of major project infrastructure investment. This new National Urban Policy (NUP) can be distinguished from previous attempts at national intervention in terms of both its content and strategic approach. For the first time national urban policy was articulated via the governance capabilities provided by the federal–state hierarchy rather than in face of opposition from them. Yet despite its ambitious objectives and methods, the NUP had a number of weaknesses that limited its impact on the trajectory of Australian cities and their ever-evolving patterns of urbanisation.

Although its internal management was institutionally complex, the NUP programme recognised that the Australian federal system limits the capacities of each level of government. The commonwealth level of government possesses strong taxation and revenue raising powers with income, company and consumption taxation among the most significant, yet the areas in which this level may intervene are limited constitutionally to those of a national scope. These include the critical responsibilities of immigration control, which regulates population flows and thus urban growth rates, as well as interest rate settings, which influence aggregate business and household investment, particularly in commercial development and housing. Territorial matters, including land and urban development, are typically state responsibilities, for which there is no direct commonwealth role. Conversely, the states have responsibility for the territorial delivery of an array of services and infrastructure, including strategic urban planning and development regulation and the provision of most physical urban infrastructure, such as water, electricity, sewerage, roads and rail. Yet the states have weak taxation powers with which to fund such services and infrastructure. With the key levers of urban development – population and capital flows – held by the Commonwealth, the states face major planning and infrastructure coordination problems. Although the costs of water, electricity and sewerage provision can be almost entirely covered by user charges, this is more difficult for road and rail networks, whose benefits are more diffuse. While states are responsible for planning in their major cities this task is often either delegated to comparatively weak local governments or undertaken by state agencies with limited purchase at the metropolitan scale. Thus urban planning is subject to a classic Australian constitutional policy tension between a well-resourced Commonwealth with limited leverage on direct service provision and capable states with limited funds to resource their urban planning ambitions and to deliver metropolitan infrastructure.

Prior to the 2007 federal election, the Australian Labor Party put forward an extensive platform of urban policy measures (ALP, 2007) relating to housing affordability, infrastructure investment and metropolitan strategic planning, all presented as part of a wider platform of 'nation building' measures. The process for developing a national framework was initially the responsibility of the COAG Reform Council as a part of broader national agenda of institutional and policy reform. The COAG identified a set of shared principles for urban planning, focusing on strategic metropolitan planning as the most important policy scale for such principles to be applied. The COAG then audited the metropolitan strategies of each of the eight state or territory capital cities to test their adherence or lack thereof to the agreed principles (COAG, 2012) and in its next phase invited each state to revise its relevant metropolitan strategy to align it with these national policy principles.

This model contrasts with previous commonwealth urban policy efforts. There is no dedicated delivery agency, *à la* DURD; rather, the MCU, as the key policy development entity, sits within the Department of Infrastructure and Transport, but has few programme implementation powers. While the wider urban policy framework involves infrastructure investment, it is very different from that developed under Keating's BBC programme, in that it is a long-term framework for commonwealth investment and currently does not include urban renewal projects, as did the BBC. In essence the NUP seeks to establish a clear policy rationale for a commonwealth interest in cities and then use the federal system as a mechanism for applying this policy within each state or territory jurisdiction, via a largely cooperative model. Within the Commonwealth there has been some effort to establish a longer lasting interest in urban affairs than was the case with a standalone department such as DURD, however the later risks conflict with other agencies and is easily abolished along with any policy measures associated with it. Likewise, the NUP process differs from a project based spending programme, such as the Better Cities programme, which effectively ended once the budget was cut, and thus had little longer term impact on policy. A substantial institutional architecture of department, interdepartmental committee, statutory agency, advisory unit, and standing intergovernmental advisory committee has been established to integrate the activities of the Department of Infrastructure and Transport, its MCU, Infrastructure Australia and the Standing Council on Transport and Infrastructure (SCOTI) plus some other less significant agencies and committees.

Part of the intent of these arrangements is to embed urban questions, and particularly infrastructure considerations, in a wider array of institutional sites than just a single programme within an agency. This could in theory make it harder for urban issues to fall off the policy agenda of a future government, although the Coalition has shown little commitment to keeping the institutional architecture of urban policy established by Labor. The Coalition's 2013 election platform made only passing reference to the significance and importance of cities, noting that 'congestion is an increasing problem in our cities' and proposing a programme of investment in urban roads and national highways '… because people who are stuck in traffic jams, moving around our cities or moving between our regional centres, are obviously far less productive than they should be' (Abbott, 2013). The Liberals' Coalition partners, the Nationals, focus their attention on issues important to people living outside of the capital cities and define themselves as the only party 'dedicated to regional Australia' (Truss, 2013). Their interest in urban policy was not especially evident, apart from supporting the development of policies that would help unemployed city residents move to regional areas where there are unfilled jobs.

In the last week of the 2013 election campaign, the then Prime Minister announced that if a Labor government were to be re-elected a Minister for Cities would be appointed, because '… it was about time that the 80 per cent of Australians who live in cities get a look in' (Hall, 2013). The Planning Institute of Australia and its partners in 'The Urban Coalition' welcomed this announcement as the culmination of many years of lobbying, but called in vain for the Coalition to make a similar commitment. It would seem, therefore, that national urban policy remains something that divides the two main parties, at least in symbolic terms: concrete proposals seem to emerge only from Labor governments, while Coalition governments eschew them, even if they continue to support in practice a number of specific measures that typically exist under the banner of a national urban policy.

A final pertinent question to ask of Labor's recent NUP programme is whether it made an appreciable difference to metropolitan planning outcomes, or indeed to the quality of life in Australia's cities over the last six years. Certainly the infrastructure investment element of the programme ensured a number of major transport infrastructure projects, particularly public transport schemes such as the Gold Coast Rapid Transit light rail project, commenced when they might not otherwise have proceeded. Nevertheless, other proposals for major infrastructure investment, including a second airport for Sydney and the construction of a high-speed rail link between Melbourne and Brisbane, have failed to attract a cross-party consensus. It remains to be seen whether the new Prime Minister, Tony Abbott, will succeed in his ambition to be renowned for being 'an infrastructure prime minister', and if so whether this will have an especially urban dimension or extend beyond road building.

Labor's NUP was ambitious, but a reasonable concern can be raised over whether the content necessary to provide a national degree of oversight, plus the need to cooperate with rather than dictate to the states, left the policy as earnest in intent but weak in application. The very long time frames established for national level planning principles to filter through state reviews of metropolitan strategic plans amplified this concern, particularly where some new state governments claimed a mandate to weaken metropolitan level planning as part of their programme of cutting 'red tape'. In July 2013 the Government published its fourth *State of Australian Cities* report (DITMCU, 2013), which as well as providing a snapshot of conditions in the 18 major cities also reported on progress in the implementation of the NUP first articulated in *Our Cities, Our Future* (DIT, 2011). Along with the creation of the MCU, the establishment of the advisory National Urban Forum and the roll-out of the capital cities planning framework, a $70 million Liveable Cities programme was introduced to demonstrate good practice in urban design. However, it is difficult to conclude that this represented a strong and clear national policy framework for guiding the development of Australia's major cities in ways that they would not have otherwise grown. While it is widely recognised that substantial and fundamental change in the form, function and liveability of cities must be measured in decades rather than years, there is no obvious sign that problems of congestion, housing affordability, differential access to essential services and liveability are changing for the better.

Conclusions

We began by pointing to the highly urbanised nature of Australia and hence to the fact that many if not most of the problems faced by Australians are experienced in cities or other urban settings. We say 'other urban settings' because the definition of cities is not clear-cut, and while federal government has defined 'major cities' a variety of terms is used to describe these other urban places, including small cities, regional cities and midi-cities. But leaving aside these imprecisions of nomenclature, the nature of policy for cities or urban areas is also unclear in its focus, rationale and content. Using a loose definition, Australian urban policy initiatives over the decades have ranged from the renewal of inner city neighbourhoods, through broad programmes to stimulate social and economic change, to proposals for the building of new cities. Most, though, fall into the category of measures to improve matters within cities, and there is relatively little policy debate about location of growth at a national scale, apart from very general proposals to encourage more growth in rural and regional areas and in the north of the country.

It is not obvious that the either of the major parties have a clear and firmly held policy agenda for cities. This is not to say that they do not recognise the importance and significance of cities, simply that major policy proposals do not have a clear urban or spatial dimension. But does this indicate a problem or a serious lacuna in the policy armoury of governments of any political colour? Would Australia be better served if a clear, detailed and comprehensive policy for cities existed? To begin to answer this we need to revisit and apply the theoretical lenses outlined earlier. We find that most programmes and initiatives that could be described as 'urban policy' have been framed within a broadly Keynesian or social democratic tradition. As Jones (1979) observed of Whitlam's urban policies of over 30 years ago, it would be presumptuous to call them radical as they were remarkably conservative and showed a strong faith in the capacity of bureaucracies to solve problems. Former Prime Minister Rudd's belief that the creation of a Minister for Cities represented a significant policy innovation betrayed a similar stance. In this respect little appears to have changed since Whitlam's experiments of the 1970s, but since then a wide-ranging academic critique of urban policy has developed, initially drawing explicitly on Marxist principles and categories but more recently claiming to be 'critical'. This ever growing body of critical work has never served as a platform for policy development, and probably was never intended to, but an alternative basis for urban policy has emerged in recent years from the other end of the political spectrum. Although riddled with contradictions in the eyes of critical theorists, a neoliberal approach is being developed and, even more importantly, increasingly put into effect by sympathetic state governments and metropolitan or city councils across Australia.

Baeten and Tasan-Kok (2012) have pointed out the existential flaws in the very idea of 'neoliberal planning' and to some extent these apply also to conceptions of neoliberal urban policy. However, bearing in mind that an important part of the 'neoliberal project' has always been to reframe issues and problems in ways best suited to particular forms of state intervention, the proposals for neoliberal planning put forward by Queensland lawyer, Wright (2012) typify an approach to city-scale planning that is becoming increasingly common in cities and is fostered by many state governments. By removing 'unnecessary' regulations, creating streamlined planned regimes designed to quickly approve development proposals and even providing what might otherwise be considered Keynesian subsidies in the form of 'construction kick-start' packages and infrastructure charge exemptions, a number of impediments to neoliberal urban growth have been removed. From a traditional Marxist perspective this creates the conditions for a crisis of legitimacy if an unfettered and indeed subsidised urban development market fails to deliver on promised jobs, affordable homes and iconic cultural facilities. However, more recent critical frameworks point to the enduring capacity of contemporary capitalism to withstand what appear to be systemic crises.

Perhaps the most significant conclusion to draw about the past, present and future of urban policy in Australia is that it has had only a marginal impact on the state of Australian cities. While Marxist and neoliberal perspectives are both critical of the capacity and potential of state intervention, albeit from very different political and analytical standpoints, the social democratic or Keynesian tradition continues to put its faith in the potential of policy even while it espouses a commitment to evidence-based policy making (Burton, 1997). While it is notoriously difficult to design and conduct rigorous assessments of the impact of urban policy (Robson, Bradford and Deas, 1994), even when conceived as a series of limited spatially targeted programmes, there is little evidence in Australia or indeed elsewhere of major rather than marginal transformations in the development trajectories of our cities as a result of urban policy interventions. While neoliberal enthusiasts pursue minimalist urban policy programmes of regulatory reform and reduction alongside public subsidy of selected forms of infrastructure, critical perspectives such as those of Peck, Theodore and Brenner ask, '... why is it that mainstream late neoliberal urban policy formulations appear to be so tired, so prosaic, so anaemic, and yet still continue to represent the doxic 'common sense' of urban policy makers around the world?' (2013, 1095).

Meanwhile, those who retain some faith in the possibilities of social democratic state intervention struggle to imagine national urban policy that successfully combines Whitlam's political ambition with greater capacity to deliver tangible improvements to Australian cities, although recent attempts have been made. (see for example Albanese, 2013; Hunt, 2013; Kelly, 2013; Ludlam, 2013) It is difficult, therefore, to avoid the pessimistic conclusion that despite small pockets of innovative local intervention that often create tangible improvements, Australian cities as a whole will continue to lumber forward, struggling to cope with housing shortages, jobs located away from major centres of population and ever increasing congestion. The prospects of imaginative, well-designed, properly resourced urban policy with sufficient bipartisan support to survive for decades, looks as distant as ever in contemporary Australia.

References

Abbott, T. (2013), 'New accountability on infrastructure and major project delivery', *Liberal Party Media Release*, 12 August, www.liberal. org.au/latest-news/2013/08/12/tony-abbott-new-accountability-infrastructure-and-major-project-delivery

Albanese, A. (2013), 'Urban Policy and Research (2013): Our Cities, Our Future', Urban Policy and Research, DOI: 10.1080/08111146.2013.832843

Amin, A. and Thrift, N. (2002) *Cities: Reimagining the Urban*, Cambridge: Polity

Atkinson, R. and Moon, G. (1994) *Urban Policy in Britain: The City, the State and the Market*, London: Macmillan

Australian Labor Party. (2007) *National Platform and Constitution*, Sydney, ALP

Badcock, B. (2000) 'Home Ownership and the Illusion of Egalitarianism', in P. Troy (ed) *A History of European Housing in Australia*, Cambridge, UK: Cambridge University Press, pp 254-68

Baeten, G. and Tasan-Kok, T. (eds) (2012) *Contradictions of Neoliberal Planning*, New York, Springer

Baragwanath, C. (1996) *Building Better Cities: A Joint Government Approach to Urban Development*, Special Report No 45, Melbourne, Auditor-General of Victoria

Berry, M. (1999), 'Unravelling the "Australian Housing Solution": the Post-War Years', *Housing Theory and Society* 16, 106-123

Burton, P. (1997) 'Urban Policy and the Myth of Progress', *Policy & Politics*, 25, 4, 421-436

Council of Australian Governments (COAG) (2012) *Review of Capital City Strategic Planning Systems*, Canberra, COAG

Cochrane, A. (2007) *Understanding Urban Policy: A Critical Approach*, Oxford: Blackwell Publishing

Davison, G. (1978) *The Rise and Fall of Marvellous Melbourne*, Melbourne University Press

Davison, G. (1995) 'Australia: The first suburban nation?', *Journal of Urban History* 21, 1, 40-74

Department of Infrastructure and Transport (DIT) (2011) *Our Cities, Our Future: A National Urban Policy for a Productive, Sustainable and Liveable Future*, Canberra, Commonwealth of Australia

Department of Infrastructure and Transport, Major Cities Unit (DITMCU) (2013) *State of Australian Cities 2013*, Canberra, Commonwealth of Australia

Department of Sustainability Environment Water Population and Communities (DSEWPC) (2011) *Sustainable Australia – Sustainable Communities: A Sustainable Population Strategy for Australia.* Canberra, Australian Government

Freestone, R. (2010) *Urban Nation: Australia's Planning Heritage*, Melbourne, CSIRO Publishing

Gleeson and Low (2000) *Australian Urban Planning: New Challenges, New Agendas*, St Leonards, NSW, Allen and Unwin

Hall, B. (2013) 'States don't get it on reforming our cities, says Kevin Rudd', *Brisbane Times*, 30 August, www.brisbanetimes.com. au/federal-politics/federal-election-2013/states-dont-get-it-on-reforming-our-cities-says-kevin-rudd-20130830-2sv1j.html

Healey, P. (2004) 'Towards a "social democratic" policy agenda for cities', in C. Johnstone and M. Whitehead (eds) *New Horizons in British Urban Policy: Perspectives on New Labour's Urban Renaissance*, Aldershot: Ashgate

Hector, D. (2011) 'Sydney's Water Sewerage and Drainage System', *Journal & Proceedings of the Royal Society of New South Wales*, 144, 3-25

Hunt, G. (2013), 'Urban Policy and Research (2013): Achieving the 30- and 50-Year Plans for Our Cities', *Urban Policy and Research*, DOI: 10.1080/08111146.2013.832844

Jones, M. (1979) Review Article: 'Australian Urban Policy', *Politics*, 14, 2, 295-303

Kelly, K. (2013) 'Urban Policy and Research (2013): National Urban Policy', Urban Policy and Research, DOI: 10.1080/08111146.2013. 832845

Kirwan, R. (1990) 'Planning our urban futures', in D. Wilmoth *Towards an Agenda for Australian Cities – conference papers*, Canberra: AGPS

Lloyd, C. and P. Troy (1981) *Innovation and Reaction: The Life and Death of the Federal Department of Urban and Regional Development*, Sydney: George Allen and Unwin

Ludlam, S. (2013) 'Urban Policy and Research (2013): Whether or Not Australia Needs a National Urban Policy', *Urban Policy and Research*, DOI: 10.1080/08111146.2013.832846

Marsden, S. (2000) 'The Introduction of Order', in P. Troy (ed) *A History of European Housing in Australia*, Cambridge, UK: Cambridge University Press, pp 26-40

OECD (2012) *Cities in Europe: The New OECD-EC Definition.* Available at: http://ec.europa.eu/regional_policy/sources/docgener/ focus/2012_01_city.pdf

Orchard, L. (1999) 'Shifting Visions in National Urban and Regional Policy 2', *Australian Planner*, 34, 4, 200-209

Peck, J, Theodore, N. and Brenner, N. (2013) 'Neoliberal Urbanism Redux?', *International Journal of Urban and Regional Research*, 37, 3, 1091-9

Priestley, S. (1991) 'Melbourne: A Kangaroo Advance', in P. Statham (ed) *The Origins of Australia's Capital Cities*, Cambridge University Press

Robson, B., Bradford, M.A. and Deas, I. (1994) *Assessing the Impact of Urban Policy*, London: HMSO

Simons, M. (2011) 'Who should look after the cities?' *Inside Story*, 2 June, http://inside.org.au

Stretton, H. (1989) *Ideas for Australian Cities*, 3rd edn, Sydney: Transit Australia Publishing

Truss, W. (2013) *The Coalition's 2030 Vision for Developing Northern Australia*, Barton, ACT: The National Party

Winter, I. and L. Bryson (1998) 'Economic restructuring and state intervention in Holdenist suburbia: Understanding urban poverty in Australia', *International Journal of Urban and Regional Research* 22, 1): 60-75

Wright, I. (2012) *Reinvigorating Planning and the Planning Pystem in Queensland: A Neoliberal Perspective*, Brisbane: Herbert Geer

FIFTEEN

Natural resource management: steering not rowing against the current in the Murray-Darling Basin

Daniel Connell

At the centre of the long history of policy development in the Murray-Darling Basin is a complex debate about the role of governments. During recent decades there has been a pull back from the highly interventionist role that all Australian governments – state and Commonwealth – played in the economy and society during the first 150 years of European settlement. Indeed, during the past 20 or so years thinking worldwide about the delivery of government services has shifted. The resulting transformations have involved many variations, but common is increasing emphasis on market-orientated arrangements such as purchaser–provider contracts with payments tightly linked to milestones and targets. In essence the call is for governments to become umpires between competing interests, addressing market failures, removing bureaucratic impediments, identifying options and disseminating information so that entrepreneurial non-government actors can develop innovative responses. Described as 'steering not rowing', this is based on a vision of a stable, settled society in which mature, confident citizens are to be allowed to work out what is best for them. It is in stark contrast with the conception of government as the leader and driver of change. This chapter argues, however, that 'government as umpire' is an inadequate response to the challenge of our times. Worldwide and in the Murray-Darling Basin (MDB), there is a need to move to policies and management systems that will halt declining resource security and environmental conditions. To steer towards sustainability is to push back against the powerful forces driving economic growth and consumption. Yet steering will not be enough. A source of energy to support reform is also needed.

The Australian context

In Australia this worldwide change in thinking about the delivery of government services has come together with the evolution of the nation's federal system. As was recognised early in the history of the Australian federation by the constitutional drafter and Prime Minister, Alfred Deakin, the process of allocating powers between the national government and the states resulted in a division of responsibilities that left the national government with most of the growth taxes. This meant that over the course of the 20th century the redistribution of tax revenues from the national commonwealth government to the states has emerged as a major component of the federal political process. Added to this have been High Court decisions that have given the national government wide discretion in the way reallocated funds can be directed to the states through what are known as 'tied grants'. To go the small extra step of redistributing these funds through highly prescriptive purchaser–provider contracts, a process now given added justification by the 'steering not rowing' literature, must have seemed a natural progression to the federal politicians and administrators managing the process through the 1990s and 2000s. As the central organising principle of the Commonwealth Water Act 2007 it is now the dominant institutional model for the MDB.

In addition to the international philosophical influences, in the MDB there were a number of other concerns that fuelled demands for fundamental change in the way governments develop and implement policy. They too push in the direction of 'government as umpire between competing interests' as opposed to driver of change. It is now widely agreed that water in the MDB is over-allocated and only greater efficiency will allow continued economic growth. Existing management systems appear unable to halt environmental decline and the erosion of resource security. There is also the complexity created by the growing recognition in recent decades of additional stakeholders that need to be taken into account by water managers. These include interest groups associated with plantation forestry, non-irrigation based agriculture and animal husbandry, all of which have major impacts on catchment processes, tourism, urban consumers, mining, Indigenous peoples and a number of other issues that were previously outside the water policy sphere. In relation to water management, no longer do governments only have to look after irrigators, they now have to manage competing demands. Government as lead developer is no longer appropriate.

At the same time pressure to maximise the autonomy of producers and minimise bureaucratic discretionary decision making is causing a move away from direct management by the public servants that previously ran regional water delivery systems. In part this is coming from confident actors who resent government 'interference', but many government officials also want to pull back, albeit for different reasons. After a century of water infrastructure development the cost of renewal and further development should be carried by the direct beneficiaries, irrigation-based industries. All this means that there is broad-based agreement that in relation to water policy and management in the MDB governments should set the rules that shape interactions between stakeholders and then as much as possible remove themselves from direct decision making. In the MDB the most overt manifestations of a change in philosophy about the best way to manage the region have been the water reforms linked to National Competition Policy approved by the Council of Australian Governments in 1994 and in more detail in the National Water Initiative in 2004. Subsequently, in somewhat modified form, these agreements were incorporated into Commonwealth Government legislation in the Water Act 2007.

The Murray-Darling Basin

Working out the potential impacts of climate change that will need to be managed is a challenging task given the complexity of the region. The MDB is just over a million square kilometres in size and has a diverse range of landscapes, ecosystems, land uses, and climates ranging from the subtropical north to the temperate south with its long dry summers, wet winters and snowfields (although most of the Basin is naturally semi-arid). It contains the watersheds of two major rivers – the Darling and the Murray – along with their many tributaries. The Basin includes over 30,000 wetlands, of which 11 are listed under the Ramsar Convention of Wetlands of International Importance. Adding to the social, economic and environmental complexity is an overlay of jurisdictions whose borders reflect 19th century British colonial priorities. As a result the MDB is divided between five jurisdictions: New South Wales (NSW), Victoria, South Australia (SA), Queensland and the Australian Capital Territory (ACT), with the national Commonwealth Government having overall responsibility. The region is also home to just under two million people, supplies much of the water used by another million in SA, and generates approximately 40% of the gross value of Australia's agriculture and pastoral production. Those three million people and various industrial activities use about

4% of the water diverted from the region's rivers. The other 96% is used by irrigated agriculture and constitutes about two thirds of national rural and urban usage. Compared with other major river systems in the world, the Murray-Darling is a low energy system with little capacity to purge itself of salts and sediments. Much of the salt mobilised into streams is not flushed out of the Murray Mouth but is redistributed elsewhere in the Basin to what were previously fertile low lying areas or onto floodplains of high environmental value, often over state borders. In broad terms the challenges facing the region can be divided into the need to manage overdevelopment and also prepare for the predicted impacts of climate change which will require additional reforms.

Competing approaches to managing intergovernmental relations in the federal system

The influence of two very different models or approaches to organising relations between governments in a federal system can be discerned in the MDB. The first approach, as already outlined, is that of the national Commonwealth Government acting as purchaser with the state governments as providers. This is combined with an array of market orientated arrangements. The second can be described as the collective approach that involves governments at both the national and state levels sharing responsibility for both purchasing and providing. The two models have been identifiable in varying strengths as powerful conflicting political currents shaping events ever since debates about cross border management of the River Murray first became serious in the late 19th century. The term 'collective' is not meant to suggest that the main actors are driven by altruistic or benign motives that cause them to take a basin-wide or whole-of-society perspective. Collective decision making is usually the product of institutional pressures that induce governments to make compromises, often reluctantly.

Between the implementation of the River Murray Waters Agreement in 1914/15 and the Commonwealth Water Act 2007, the collective approach was dominant. However, elements of what we would now call the purchaser–provider approach or fiscal federalism were clearly present in many early policy episodes. This combination with its tensions has worked well in a rough and ready way on many occasions, but since the passing of the Water Act 2007, the purchaser–provider approach has become dominant to the detriment of efforts to manage environmental and resource issues from the perspective of what is best for society-as-a-whole, particularly in relation to issues such as climate change.

When the Australian states federated in 1901 two changes strongly increased the pressure on the three states in the River Murray Basin to act collectively. One was a new legal environment in which the water rights of upper and lower states were not clear. There were and are a number of dramatically different legal doctrines that can be applied to disputes between river states with potentially very different outcomes. What the new national High Court would do was quite unpredictable. For each of the three states with territory in the MDB, NSW, Victoria and South Australia, there was a real risk that a court decision could cause it to lose badly. The other change was in the relationships between the colonies which had now become state governments. Suddenly South Australia had access to a shared parliament through which it could exert significant pressure on the upriver states. After considering all the alternatives the three states reluctantly agreed in principle to cooperate.

Negotiations dragged on for well over a decade, however, and numerous reports into different options were commissioned. The deadlock was broken in 1913 when the Commonwealth External Affairs Minister, South Australian Patrick McMahon Glynn, persuaded his Prime Minister, Joseph Cook, to offer one million pounds if the three states stopped procrastinating and signed the River Murray Water Agreement, which they did. This sizeable sum was more than enough to pay for the construction of the first version of Hume Dam (about half the current size). The agreement was incorporated into identical legislation passed in parallel in all four parliaments the Commonwealth, NSW, Victoria and SA. Subsequently, money directed through the River Murray Commission, most of it from the Commonwealth, funded a large portfolio of infrastructure which included enlargement of Lake Victoria, a network of weirs and locks, the barrages at the Murray Mouth and, through the 1940s, '50s and '60s, water piped to most of the towns and cities of SA.

The largest controversy during this period was caused by SA's plan to construct a dam at Chowilla near Renmark, just inside the border with the two upriver states (to be funded largely by the Commonwealth). It would have been a large, shallow dam in a region with high evaporation and, in retrospect, a major environmental disaster. The alternative was Dartmouth Dam, on a much better site, upstream of Lake Hume in Victoria. The Chowilla proposal was eventually blocked by the other states and the Commonwealth acting through the River Murray Commission who insisted that the choice had to be made from a whole-of-basin perspective. The South Australian Commissioner defied his premier and voted for Dartmouth. Central to resolution of the Chowilla saga was Commonwealth pressure on SA that the issue be decided through a collective process (with funds from the national government being available to support whatever was the joint decision). This involved the use of Commonwealth financial power, not to take over responsibility for deciding which dam should be built, but rather to shape the institutional framework within which the choice was made by the three state governments.

Similarly, it was Commonwealth Government pressure that eventually led to major institutional reforms in the mid-1980s in response to South Australian concerns about growing salinisation of the river due to irrigation development upstream. In principle the new arrangements, based on identical legislation passed in all jurisdictions, allowed for integrated policy development and management in respect of any issue upon which all jurisdictions agreed to cooperate. The limits were those imposed by what was possible in terms of politics, economics and implementation capacity rather than any restriction resulting from lack of constitutional power. Despite this, however, the early years of the new arrangements were marked by widespread enthusiasm and considerable achievements such as the Salinity and Drainage Strategy implemented in 1989, which significantly improved water quality in the lower reaches of the Murray, and the 'cap' on further increases in extractions in 1995, which reflected agreement by all governments that the Basin's water resources were overcommitted.

But by the mid-2000s, with the passing of the generation of policy makers who had introduced the reforms from the late 1980s, and continuing environmental problems exacerbated by one of the most severe droughts in Australia's recorded history, the water reform process stalled. The drought required unprecedented reductions in irrigators' water allocations and created pressures for new levels of integration. An indication of even more stress in the future was provided by a Commonwealth Scientific and Industrial Research Organisation (CSIRO) study commissioned by the MDB Ministerial Council. It predicted major reductions in inflows into the Murray system and of the volumes of water that would be available for irrigation and towns in future years because of the increasing impact of factors such as climate change, farm dams, forest plantations, and reduced leakages due to delivery systems upgrades (Van Dijk et al, 2006). Significantly, all these threats were outside of the previously agreed list of responsibilities of the Murray-Darling Basin Ministerial Council (MDBMC) (which required unanimous agreement for any additions).

As a result of such studies it was widely thought that the confederate model for cross-border water management in the MDB, which had been in place for nearly 90 years, was not an adequate institutional framework within which to expand the policy agenda. The eventual result was the Commonwealth Water Act 2007, through which for the first time the national government took direct control of high level policy which the states would have to implement (if they wanted to gain access to Commonwealth funds).

Shift in Commonwealth approach

The *Water Act 2007* was the end product of a range of policies going back to the early 1990s introduced under the umbrella of National Competition Policy, the primary focus for the Council of Australian Governments (COAG) during this period. One of these policies was the water reform package approved by COAG in 1994. It reflected concerns about the environment and climate change as well as economic efficiency and a desire for a smaller or at least a more discreet role for governments. First, levels of extraction were to be pulled back to what was needed to ensure sustainability. Second, water trading across state boundaries and between uses was to be promoted to gain the best economic results from the water that remained after sustainability had been defined and protected. Third, irrigators and other entitlement holders were to be given more legally robust and clearly defined water entitlements separate from land titles that would be suitable for water trading. The fourth was a requirement that entitlement holders should take on responsibility for future maintenance and development of the regional delivery systems. In addition, they, and not governments, would also be responsible for dealing with the future impacts of climate change and drought that were to become part of the risks involved in operating their businesses. Subsequently, these principles were given more detailed form in the National Water Initiative approved by COAG in 2004, particularly in regard to managing drought and the impacts of climate change, which were to be the responsibility of water entitlement holders.

Having agreed on the 1994 water reforms and the National Water Initiative in 2004, the challenge for the governments in the COAG was to implement the full package and prevent water entitlement holders taking the benefits and rejecting the costs. Their success has been very mixed. In January 2007 the then Prime Minister, John Howard, on behalf of his Conservative coalition, announced a $10 billion package (later more than $12 billion) to support implementation of the National Water Initiative. Nearly $6 billion was assigned to infrastructure upgrades to assist communities to adapt to climate change. This was despite the earlier COAG stipulations that entitlement holders would have prime responsibility for dealing with the impacts of climate change.

The Commonwealth Water Act 2007 provides a good example of the neoliberal, market-orientated, new public management model promoted by COAG's National Competition Policy. The pre-Water Act 2007 confederate model for running the MDB had serious problems, especially in its final years, but it was effective in keeping all governments engaged in the basin-wide governance process. Despite its failings it could have been reformed in ways that retained its inclusive character. The most obvious reform would have been to replace unanimous voting in the MDB Ministerial Council with, say, four out of five majorities (leaving aside the ACT). Under those conditions any government that wanted to block a decision would have needed the support of at least one other government. That would have changed the decision making dynamics very substantially. Instead there is the Water Act 2007, which allows the Commonwealth to blame failure on bad implementation by the states. Against this, the states can respond that the real problem was bad policy developed by the Commonwealth.

Under the purchaser–provider model set up by the Water Act 2007 the Murray-Darling Basin Authority has prepared the high level Basin Plan, approved by the National Parliament in December 2012. This requires the states to develop implementation plans for their sections of the Basin. If they comply they will then be able to access the $6 billion fund set aside by the Commonwealth for infrastructure projects. It is quite likely, however, that the Basin Plan will not be implemented as envisaged in the Water Act 2007. Implementation will depend on a very high degree of support from the Basin states, which have most of the detailed knowledge and on-ground administrative capacity that will be needed. In addition, preparation of the implementation plans will probably be even more controversial than that of the Basin Plan, because it will involve translation of its general principles into details that will have direct consequences for irrigation communities. The Water Act 2007 gives the Commonwealth the legal power to prepare implementation plans if states fail to do so. But whether it has this capacity in practice against community and state agency opposition is a very open question.

It is also doubtful that the Commonwealth Government can exclude a non-compliant state from accessing the $6 billion infrastructure fund if there is a protracted dispute. One of the inherent weaknesses in the purchaser–provider approach, as applied in a federal political system, is that it assumes that purchaser and provider are substantially different entities and that one is in a position to exert real pressure on the other. However, politicians in both state and national governments are elected by state-based electorates. If a national government seriously attempted to punish a state for non-compliance it would have to confront the significant number of representatives from that state within its own ranks. Driven by concern about the electoral consequences they could not afford to appear complicit in actions by a national government which appear to harm the interests of their voters. In other words, at one remove purchaser and provider are essentially the same. Much of the discussion about interjurisdictional water management in the MDB gives the misleading impression that interaction between the Commonwealth and states is highly structured, but the reality is more elusive. It is possible in the short term and at a superficial level for a commonwealth government minister or agency to put pressure on state government ministers and officials to comply with a contract, but if an issue becomes significantly contentious the distinction between purchaser and provider rapidly collapses.

For observers, and possibly participants, COAG provides a striking example of the blurring of the appearance and reality of power. Ostensibly, COAG is a collective decision making body which produces agreements between governments but allows dissenting states to opt out. (As Western Australia and Tasmania did initially from the National Water Initiative in 2004.) That, however, excludes them from the funds that the Commonwealth provides to support implementation of the COAG agreements. This is the purchaser–provider dynamic in action. It belies the officially promoted appearance of collegiality. But behind this level of activity is yet another layer of reality. Almost invariably, after the theatre of defiance has played itself out, a process of intense bargaining ensues which frequently results in the Commonwealth making concessions to the states that held out. To counter this risk the Commonwealth tries to reward those states that sign on early. Because detailed implementation varies according to the particular circumstances of each state, it is often not easy to tell which one benefits the most. Working out where power and advantage really lie in these situations is a difficult analytical task.

The MDB's policy environment is volatile. At any given time, a large number of enterprises (individuals, businesses, associations, industry groups, governments, and so on) are interacting and influencing its policy process in many different ways. In practice, decisions are not made from the top down but emerge from cycles of interaction in which the participants have varying degrees of influence. No single voice is dominant. The apparently independent centres of power provided by the Commonwealth and state jurisdictions create focal points in a polycentric governance arrangement around which contending interest groups arrange themselves, moving from one to the other as their members make strategic decisions about alliances and how best to promote their goals or block those of others. In addition, many apparently national government conflicts with state governments are really manifestations of the way competing state based interest groups use federal government agencies against each other.

In such a context it is often very difficult for policy reformers to maintain support for their original vision. The COAG water reform process provides a striking example of these political processes in action. One of the infrastructure projects that are being funded from the allocated $6 billion is the Food Bowl Modernisation (FBM) project in central northern Victoria. It is estimated that it will eventually cost approximately $2 billion. The irrigation community in that region (which should have been the sole funder according to the COAG 1994 rural water reforms and the 2004 National Water Initiative (NWI)) is contributing $100 million of the $2 billon. In this case, even though the risk that it might be difficult to require local community responsibility for such investment had been foreseen and apparently dealt in the 1994 COAG and 2004 NWI reforms, that effort was not sufficient to ensure the integrity and commitment to this principle subsequently.

Linked to the FBM project is the construction of the desalination plant in Melbourne. As part of the process of making the government investment in the FBM scheme acceptable to the wider public it was originally intended that the water saved by the infrastructure improvements would be divided equally between irrigation, the environment and the city of Melbourne, a short distance outside the MDB catchment to the south. The water that would be diverted to Melbourne from the MDB as a result of the FBM project was a small proportion of the water annually extracted for irrigation in the central Victorian section of the MDB but it would have been enough to transform the water security situation of the state capital, Australia's second largest city. Despite this, the transfer to Melbourne was successfully blocked by communities in central Victoria. After it was completed the connecting pipeline was closed down by the newly elected Victorian state government after it gained power in early 2011.

To cover the water supply shortfall that could have been met by the pipeline the Victorian Government is now building a 150 gigalitre desalination plant for Melbourne which it is estimated could end up costing nearly $6 billion net present value over the 30 year life of the project. There is a similar story to be told about Adelaide in SA, which is building a 100 gigalitre desalination plant. In both cases the water could have been acquired from the MDB at much less cost by either savings through investment in infrastructure or, even better, water trading. Desalination plants are a useful option to diversify sources of supply for both cities but they do not need to be this large. The extra costs of these very large plants are the direct result of policy capture in defiance of the original COAG reform programme. The fact that they could be incurred is indicative of low public knowledge of both the particular details and the principles underpinning the water reform programme as originally developed through the COAG in 1994 and 2004. A significant factor in the debates about these projects has been a shift in the way public debates are assessed by participants and the public. It is much harder now than in the 1990s to argue that issues should be assessed on their whole-of-society benefits. Of course it would be foolish to think that policy actors working within a collective decision-making framework are likely to act with greater concern for the common good than is the case when they are working within a market-orientated environment. What the latter does, however, is to provide strong arguments for self-interested behaviour and against working for the common good not previously available.

Neoliberalism and sustainability

Has new public management, neoliberalism and the increasing role assigned to market forces increased the capacity of Australian society to manage the predicted stresses of climate change in the Murray-Darling Basin? The answer is complex. On the one hand, water markets have allowed individual irrigators much greater flexibility and provided new incentives to extract maximum financial benefit from every drop of water. This has increased awareness of the value of water and encouraged innovation in crops and irrigation practices. It has also reduced water logging and irrigation-induced salinisation. The benefits of the water market at the level of the individual and the overall economy were demonstrated dramatically during the Millennium Drought that affected the MDB for a number of years in the 2000s. Although water availability was much lower than normal in what was the worst drought since records began to be kept in the

1890s, economic returns for irrigation-based activity stayed at round about pre-drought levels. This was because water trading allowed the movement of water away from low value to high value activities where producers were willing to pay higher prices.

On the other hand, the stronger focus on water use efficiency reduced what are now termed return flows to the river system, a previously poorly documented but large contributor to the volumes of water available to downstream users and the environment. The water market also created a new incentive to sell any water than would not be used. Previously, such water would have remained in the river, providing significant benefits to the environment. The water market has also created new stresses between irrigators and their communities where previously there was a strong sense of shared destiny. In communities that were originally created as irrigation settlements, of which there are many in the southern basin, or which in many parts of the northern basin have expanded largely because of irrigation, the movement of water entitlements out of the district can threaten businesses and activities dependent on the size of the town. In this situation non-irrigators get none of the benefits from the money paid for the water entitlements. What impact does this have on the social cohesion of such communities?

Perhaps surprisingly, for the environment there have been significant benefits from the introduction of water markets. Since the 1980s there have been a number of determined efforts to shift water from agricultural production back to the rivers. But until the emphasis on water purchases those efforts have had little success. For the first time, as a result of the decision to source environmental water through the water market at commercial prices from willing sellers, a way has been found to reclaim a substantial percentage for the environment. That decision caused angst amongst those who resented governments paying large sums for water assets that had been handed out almost free of cost to irrigators a few decades earlier in the form of water licences. But without that change in strategy it would probably not have been politically possible to regain much water for the environment.

The existence of the Basin Plan, the first attempt at comprehensive management, can also be attributed at least in part to a movement to the purchaser–provider model of policy development. The change made it easier to develop an overall plan that did not need the agreement of all jurisdictions in the MDB, as was the situation before. The Basin Plan not only aims to take account of all pressures on the riverine system, it also contains within it processes to allow resetting the balance between irrigation and the environment every ten years, an essential requirement to allow adjustment to climate change. The mere existence of such provisions does not of course mean that they will be used. Both the cap on extractions introduced in the mid-1990s and the River Murray First Step programme introduced in 2004 by the COAG explicitly recognised the need for further increases in environmental water. In both cases the foreshadowed increases did not eventuate because of political opposition.

For individuals and commercial businesses these institutional innovations with their neoliberal market-style attributes have made adaptation to climate change much easier. They allowed a degree of flexibility and creativity in adaptation that it would be hard to envisage in the earlier period, dominated by government water agency decision makers and the need for unanimity between all MDB governments. The movement away from collective decision making has also made it easier for the Commonwealth to unilaterally broaden the MDB water policy framework and produce a Basin Plan which is more comprehensive than anything likely to be approved by the MDB Ministerial Council, abolished by the Water Act 2007. However, it will also probably be easier under the Basin Plan framework for governments to reject or deviate from the priorities assigned to their respective jurisdictions than it would have been under the pre Water Act 2007 arrangements, where policies were the product of collective decisions. From a more general perspective the neoliberal, market orientated reforms of the past 20 years, by inducing changes in cultural values, may have reduced capacity to make decisions in the public interest in the MDB. For example, is the contrast between the refusal by basin communities to allow Melbourne and Adelaide to buy extra water at commercial rates on the water market rather than build desalination plants in the 2000s and the decisions by the Commonwealth and three state governments of the Murray Basin acting through the River Murray Commission to supply water to most South Australian cities and towns in the 1950s and 60s, indicative of a decline in society's capacity to consider the benefits to society as a whole? It is hard to say definitively but it seems so.

Conclusion

It is easy to be cynical about arguments that concern for the public good should be a significant part of the policy process. Nevertheless, adapting to climate change involves challenging decisions about sharing the costs of change that are difficult to negotiate in an environment in which self-interest has become a socially respectable goal rather than a necessary evil to be a managed. Purchaser–provider contracts and market style arrangements encourage people to get the best deal possible and not pay more or do more than is necessary. Almost by definition competition does not encourage concern for others. The underlying assumption is that the general good is best promoted by each person looking after their own self-interest. From this perspective, generosity and cooperation appear weak and out of touch with the 'real world'. In this management environment the search for clear performance indicators favours economic values numerically defined rather than non-material goals that require more complex forms of measurement. 'If you can't measure and cost it, you can't manage it' has become the dominant call. The stress on deliverables also prioritises short term goals achievable within the funding cycle. This is backed by the increasing use of discount rates for investment in environment related projects which quickly renders longer term benefits irrelevant. Rarely discussed is how the use of a discount rate can be reconciled with the sustainability imperative to restrain consumption in the present to protect future options. The alternative view is that scarcity and increasing need will lift prices and stimulate innovation in ways that can be assumed but which are currently unknown.

Behind these arguments there has been a substantial shift in the cultural values that shape people's perceptions of how debates about public policy should be assessed. Earlier in the chapter it was suggested that, when political pressure becomes intense, purchaser–provider arrangements between governments in the same political system are likely to collapse. So why is the popularity of that approach in Australian natural resource management such a problem? The answer is that while institutional frameworks force people and governments back to collective decision making processes, the result is often deadlock because discussions are more likely to be dominated by concerns for self-interest rather than the needs of society as a whole. That has been the fate of climate change policy in Australia ever since governments started pulling back from the bold commitments of the early 1990s. Individuals and organisations that were likely to lose out were always going to argue against any reforms. What has made their arguments so effective is that the cultural values that influence public thinking are now much more sympathetic to the underlying theme of self-interest than was the case in previous decades. Within the complex policy environment in the Murray-Darling Basin there needs to be a much stronger defence of the now embattled concept of the public good. Developing that is a political process but its expression and pursuit will require a much more active role for government than just steering.

Bibliography

Australian Government (2007) Water Act 2007, Canberra

Connell, D. (2007) *Water Politics in the Murray-Darling Basin*, Federation Press, Sydney

Connell, D. and Grafton, R.Q. (2011), *Basin Futures: Water Reform in the Murray-Darling Basin*, ANU-E Press, Canberra

Council of Australian Governments (1994) *Attachment A: A Water Resource Policy*, Canberra

Council of Australian Governments (2004) *Intergovernmental Agreement on a National Water Initiative*, Canberra

Crase, L. (2008) *Water Policy in Australia*, Resources for the Future, Washington DC, USA

Osborne, D. and Gaebler, T. (1992) *Reinventing Government: How the Entrepreneurial Spirit is Transforming the Public Sector*, Addison-Wesley, Boston, USA

Painter, M. (1998), *Collaborative Federalism: Economic Reform in Australia in the 1990s*, Cambridge University Press, Cambridge

Powell, J. M. (1989) *Watering the Garden State: Water, Land and Community in Victoria 1834–988*, Allen & Unwin, Sydney

Sinclair, P. (2001), *The Murray: A River and its People*, Melbourne University Press, Melbourne

Van Dijk, A., Evans, R., Hairsine, P., Khan, S., Nathan, R., Payday. Z., Viney, N., and Zhang, L. (2006) 'Risks to the shared water resources of the Murray-Darling Basin', Murray-Darling Basin Report, Canberra

SIXTEEN

International perspectives: low carbon urban Australia in a time of transition

Ralph Horne and Colin Fudge

Introduction

Australia may be regarded as successful in many ways. Across the Organisation for Economic Co-operation and Development (OECD), it has been one of the best-performing economies over the past two decades. Although productivity has slowed this century, the commodities boom ensured the impact of the global recession has been less severe than in most other OECD countries – an outcome also partly attributed to regulatory reform (OECD, 2010). In this chapter, we draw on such passing comparisons with the OECD, especially the US and the UK, and consider the prospects for urban Australia in a time of transition.

As Burton and Dodson point out (Chapter 14, this volume), Australia is one of the most urbanised countries. Moreover, Australian cities are also often regarded as successful. In August 2013, Melbourne was ranked the world's most liveable city for the third year running in 'The Economist Intelligence Unit Survey'. It received perfect scores for health care, education and infrastructure, and was joined in the top ten by Adelaide, Sydney and Perth. Wellbeing, seemingly, is another reason to applaud Australia. According to the World Health Organization Better Life Index (WHO, 2013), 'Australia performs exceptionally well in measures of well-being'. It does this particularly, according to WHO measures, in safety, health and, perhaps surprisingly given the long-running affordability crisis, in housing and civic engagement. The Index includes housing, income, jobs, community, education, environment, civic engagement, health, life satisfaction, safety and work–life balance. Such measures are always partial but nevertheless the Index puts Australia ahead of the US and the UK on most measures, exceptions including housing and income.

If we look more closely we find that Australia is at the wrong end of the spectrum on work–life balance, and is rather middle ranking in the OECD on community and civil engagement – well behind the UK. Moreover, the critiques of liveability indices are shrill and telling. Behind 'The Economist Intelligence Unit Survey' index, in a similar way to the Mercer liveability index, is a rationale more about the salary-loading calculations for global executives than it is about how life is for the majority. In Melbourne, the top 20% of the population earn six times as much as the bottom 20%, and 21% of men work very long hours, compared to the OECD average of 9% of people in this category. If this causes us to question urban Australia's leadership in urban success, then the fact that 50% of Australians will develop cancer – the highest age-standardised incidence of cancer in the world (AIHW, 2012) – provides further pause for thought.

The idea of sustainable futures cannot be introduced without consideration of environmental performance and resource consumption in an era of climate change and growing resource scarcity. Australia can reliably lay claim to some rather disturbing leadership in this area: Australians are the world's largest emitters of CO_2 emissions per capita among major nations at 19 tonnes, followed by the US at 17.3 tonnes and Saudi Arabia at 16.5 (Oliver et al, 2012). Australia is also heavily reliant on scarce fossil resources.

Recent evidence suggests global fossil fuel related emissions have bounced back from the global financial downturn, exacerbating climate change at the high end of predictions. As a result: 'A shift to a 2°C pathway requires immediate significant and sustained global mitigation, with a probable reliance on net negative emissions in the longer term' (Peters et al, 2013: 4). In bulk terms, China's emissions have now surpassed those of many Western nations, such as France, Italy and Spain. However, while China, the United States, the European Union and India together emit the majority of global anthropogenic CO_2 emissions, they do all have policy frameworks in place to tackle them and 'strong and centralized governing bodies capable of co-ordinating such actions' (Peters et al, 2013:6).

This raises serious questions for Australia. Firstly: what is the domestic strategy for reducing emissions and how strong are the 'governing bodies' concerned? A broader question is: given that the 21st century will present new challenges for human development, how well is urban Australia situated to be successful and sustainable in the future? Framed by these questions, our ontological starting point for this chapter is that, internationally, climate change and resource scarcity is set to be the major policy challenge in the post-urbanised world of the 21st century. The key policy challenge is whether political will can be mustered to leave fossil fuels in the ground and position for the post-fossil fuel global economy. In such a context, Australia's reliance on fossil fuels for both running cities and driving the economy via mining exposes the country to significant risks, well beyond the already acknowledged ones of adaptive capacity in the face of more intensive floods, fires and cyclones. In the next section, we outline climate change policy settings and later, progress in urban policy responses, before concluding with reflections on the prospects for a low carbon urban Australia.

Climate change: international perspectives and Australia

Since the 2009 bushfires, climate change related events have accelerated. Australia has followed the prediction of its Commonwealth Scientific and Industrial Research Organisation (CSIRO), and is experiencing severe climate shifts, while elsewhere, 100-year flood events in the UK and Ireland, heatwave-related wildfires in Siberia, a series of hurricanes and tornados of record-breaking strength and damage, and countless other climate-related disasters have unfolded. The 2012–13 Australian summer saw 123 heat and flood-related records broken in 90 days, including the hottest summer and hottest week ever recorded. Eight of the total 21 days in the last 100 years during which Australia exceeded 39°C averaged across the nation took place in 2013. This followed a year when Alice Springs smashed the records for drought and heatwaves, with 157 consecutive days without rain, and even in the following Victorian winter the warmth continued. Indeed, if you are under 25 years old and live in Melbourne, you have only ever experienced above average temperature July days.

Despite these manifestations, climate change mitigation remains a global policy problem. In a neoliberal, post-financial crisis setting, it is unsurprising that policy progress on climate mitigation is pitifully slow. It epitomises market failure by providing competitive advantage to those countries least committed to internalising the external costs of anthropogenic greenhouse gas emissions. Two responses characterise international responses to climate change mitigation in the global North – opposition to neoliberalism (protest), and ecological modernisation policies using tools of market reform and reflexive governance to 'green' the market by internalising carbon (taxes, levies) while promoting 'green' production/consumption systems (rebates, assistance packages, and so on). Here we consider the latter in the international context of Australia.

Global pollution and policy responses can be traced back to Club of Rome and UN reports in the 1970s, and the subsequent publication *Our Common Future* (WCED, 1987). These publications brought to the fore ideas of overconsumption and the need for radical responses to falling intergenerational equity in environmental resources. The Rio Earth Summit in 1992 led to a process culminating in the Kyoto Protocol and the United Nations Framework Convention on Climate Change, setting legally binding obligations for developed countries to reduce their greenhouse gas emissions (UN, 1998). While governments have agreed through Kyoto Protocol processes that the world needs to limit the global temperature increase to no more than 2°C, negotiations are protracted and any new legal obligations will not begin before 2020. Despite diplomatic efforts and those of a myriad of NGOs, the world is drifting further and further from the 2°C track (IEA, 2013), and it is down to countries and regional blocks to provide leadership and action.

As a Kyoto signatory, the Australian Government is bound to national emissions target commitments of 25% below 2000 levels by 2020. This has been prosecuted via various commitments and reversals of commitments around emissions trading schemes, with a controversial scheme finally arriving on the statute books in 2012, but with an uncertain future from the outset. Current policy in Australia is contested and has been shaped in large part by a lack of bipartisan agreement and powerful, nonaligned forces of capitalism vested (a) in the fossil fuel economy and (b) in commitment to the emerging new post-fossil fuel economy.

The most widespread mechanism to reconcile carbon emissions and capitalism is some form of internalisation of the carbon externality, either explicitly or implicitly, by putting a price on carbon. The most long-standing emissions trading and similar schemes, such as the EU Emissions Trading Scheme (ETS), the US based Regional Greenhouse Gas Initiative (RGGI) and the Clean Development Mechanism (CDM) are not without their problems, with fluctuations and value declines affecting the progress of abatement mechanisms, in particular in the EU ETS (EC, 2012). Meanwhile, new emissions trading schemes and related carbon price mechanisms have begun operation in Australia, California, Quebec and Kazakhstan, with plans and pilots including in South Korea and various provinces across China. As IEA (2013) notes, some schemes, including in Australia and the EU ETS, were planned in such a way as to be linked together by 2018.

Alongside fledgling carbon markets there have been significant developments in renewables capacity, and demand-side measures in the form of large-scale retrofit programmes and energy efficiency technology uptake, often associated with new technology, retooling and/or postindustrial restructuring. Some of these might be regarded as successful. For example, there has been significant uptake of domestic solar (photo-voltaic (PV) and hot water) systems in the UK, the US and Australia, and across Europe. Various support schemes have been instituted by national governments to promote the retrofit of these systems to existing dwellings, typically rebates/grants and/or feed in tariff arrangements. By 2013, more than one million rooftop solar PV systems had been installed in Australia, up from 8,000 in 2007 (Climate Commission, 2013).

While there are significant overlaps between the climate policy controversies in Australia and those elsewhere, including in the US and the UK, in Australia there are three particular problematics that arise directly from contemporary political economic conditions.

Firstly, the rush to domestic solar has connected some 2.6 million people (11% of the population) into comanagement arrangements as both producers and consumers in domestic energy arrangements, with apparently unforeseen ramifications for policy. While this is a problem elsewhere, the speed and size of the incumbent industry and shift in Australia is distinctive. There is now genuine concern on the part of the private monopolies and large companies who have significant sunk assets in grid infrastructure predicated upon continuation of a supply–demand divide, where consumers increase demand in a predictable manner, enabling long-term investments to be made in grid development and management. What is not apparent is what might emerge given those millions of customers who may soon have access to storage technology to manage 'their' new resource harvest locally, nor the potential impact of other businesses seeking to take advantage of new opportunities to provide off-grid services.

Secondly, what are the implications of such shifts for an economy that has been resolutely primary industry based, reliant upon cheap exports of fossil fuels? The International Energy Agency provides authoritative scenario analysis and suggests that policy galvanisation around a 450ppm (parts per million) CO_2 concentration is feasible. In this scenario, global demand for coal will fall by 30% over the next two decades, while energy efficiency will provide around half of the emission reduction. This scenario illustrates how exposed Australia will be if it maintains its reliance on 'yesterday's' solutions in the form of a fossil fuel-based domestic energy system and a fossil fuel export-reliant economy.

Thirdly, the uncertainty arising from ongoing politicisation of climate policy in Australia has changed the debate and there are significant associated risks of 'erasing' climate rhetoric from the policy discourse. With the election of coalition state governments since 2010, and federally in 2013, there are notable shifts of policy language away from broader notions of environmental sustainability and/or climate change mitigation, to (a) adaptation/resilience and/or (b) energy efficiency and energy cost/price reduction. For example, the Victorian Government website 'Understanding climate change' (SGV, 2013, available at: www.climatechange.vic.gov.au) has a strong emphasis on adaptation as a topic. Under the greenhouse gas emissions tab, the first paragraph is not explicit about the mitigation challenge: 'Greenhouse gas is a natural part of the atmosphere. It absorbs solar radiation and keeps the earth warm enough to support life. Human activities including burning fossil fuels for energy, land clearing and agriculture have increased the amount of greenhouse gas in the atmosphere'. While such web material and policy rhetoric changes regularly, and can be expected to continue to do so, the point is that the politics of climate change are palpable in Australia in the current era.

This is also reflected in shifts in federal policy and strategy. For example, the selection of Environmentally Sustainable Australia as number one of the four national research priorities established in 2002 was contentious at the time and indicative of a commitment to notions of ecological carrying capacity and intergenerational equity. In 2013, these were replaced by 'the five most important challenges facing Australia', now referred to as 'societal challenges' (Australian Government, nd). These are: living in a changing environment; promoting population health and wellbeing; managing our food and water assets; securing Australia's place in a changing world; and lifting productivity and economic growth. The lack of reference to sustainability and climate change, and focus on management and productivity, are indicative of this broader shift. While there remains a lack of clear consensus on post-Kyoto agreements, this shift is potentially significant in its implications for urban policy and sustainability.

Low carbon urban policy: comparative histories and trajectories

As Burton and Dodson (Chapter 14, this volume) and Orchard (Chapter 12, this volume) point out, the distinctive urban form of

Australian cities is notable in spatial terms by vast suburban tracts of land containing low density, primarily detached housing generally ageing inwards towards the commercial core. These vast suburban landscapes are dominated by fragmented land and property arrangements, home owner dominated tenure arrangements, and an endemic housing affordability crisis.

In this section, we argue that the climate change policy problem in Australia links to an urban policy problem: as a highly urbanised country with growing cities, climate change mitigation and a shifting carbon nexus may render planned growth impossible, relegating Australian cities in the post-carbon era. By 2029, 3.2 million additional homes will be required (SOAC, 2010) and by 2040 the number of urban Australians will double (see Lowe, Chapter 13, this volume). Meanwhile, residential per capita energy use has been rising over recent decades and projections forecast that this will continue, due in large part to increases in space heating, space cooling, lighting and appliances (PMTGEE, 2010; Schultz and Petchey, 2011). Further, the housing stock has poor energy efficiency characteristics and energy efficiency regulations lag behind the US, the UK and Canada (Horne and Hayles, 2008).

In contrast to Australia, the European Union started to develop a more integrated policy set on cities, environment and climate change before Rio in 1992 (European Commission, 1990). To implement these policy guidelines the Council of Ministers set up an Expert Group on the Urban Environment that developed policy advice and research and funded innovations and experiments over a 14-year period. It also published a major policy guideline for European cities (Fudge et al, 1996) and reviewed progress every two years through Europe-wide Sustainable City conferences supported by the European Sustainable Cities and Towns Campaign. This overarching policy framework for the European Union provided member states and cities with comparative understanding and knowledge for their own policy development and ability to transform their norms in relation to planning, environment and city futures. As a consequence, European cities broadly understood the significance of becoming more compact, closing resource loops and preparing for transformation. Australian policy thinking has now recognised that conventional responses to expand existing infrastructure and urban form would be environmentally unsustainable, with rising energy demand and fossil fuel dependency, and increasingly dysfunctional, congested and unaffordable, with declining wellbeing and productivity. In recent decades urban policy has arguably been directed to avoid this outcome and steer a more sustainable, lower carbon course.

Detached dwellings became dominant in the residential form of Australian and US cities in the 19th century (Freestone, 1989; Frost, 1991). Indeed, the history of modern Australia is essentially one of (sub) urbanisation: a settlement pattern reflecting its political economy (Berry, 1984). An export-oriented primary industry-led economy led to growing urbanisation around coastal cities, where export-related and service industries accumulated. This early-20th-century urbanisation was further boosted in the post-war era as the migration programme drove demand for housing. This took on a particular form as post-industrial expectations grew around collective notions of suburban comfort and prosperity. This history is unique, yet it also shares significant parallels. Szelenyi (1981) seeks to explain the distinctions between urban and regional patterns of western settlement between the western US and Australia through the mechanisms of early settlement. In the US, the early settlers were operating outside the state (and sometimes escaping it). Hence, midwest and western settlement significantly predated the arrival of the state, and the new autonomous towns had to work out themselves how to self-govern and self-finance local communal infrastructure. In contrast, in Australia, the state played a major role in planning settlement. It subsidised capital accumulation, including by organising convict labour, providing land grants, and setting prices. It also took on the task of providing communal infrastructure through direct investment and revenues of land sales. By these means, continental settlement was state-controlled.

Szelenyi's account proposes that settlers in the western US became involved from the beginning in the task of building cities, investing their profits, intellectual capital and their other resources in the endeavor, whereas settlers in Australia relied more on state provision and were less concerned with building cities, but were instead concerned only with accumulating capital as quickly and as much as possible. Thus the aristocrats in Australia benefited from the squatter system to move between regions, following opportunities for profit, rather than settling and building towns and cities. Szelenyi cites cases where the state sought to grant more local autonomy and financial responsibility to local governments, but the local governments themselves resisted these.

This history serves to contribute to an explanation of *why* Australia is so urbanised, and of the underdevelopment of public urban and regional infrastructure. In common with cities across the capitalist world, people are drawn to them as centres of postindustrial production, with comparative advantages in terms of the efficiency of their infrastructure, the international connectedness of their city economies, the presence of a workforce with expertise in knowledge-intensive activities and an agglomeration of 'new economy' firms. In Australia, additional forces drew people to the capital cities because of their privileged position, exacerbated by a powerful state exercising control over the regions. This same mechanism, and a relative lack of interest in local financial autonomy, may also explain chronic underinvestment in public infrastructure, at least outside the capital cities.

There have been various attempts in recent decades to more directly shape an increasingly problematic yet still growing footprint of Australian cities. At the national level, Labor Governments – Whitlam (1972–75), Hawke/Keating (1983–96) and Rudd/Gillard (2007–13) – have given some priority to urban growth and its direction, aligned or otherwise with a growing environmental policy agenda, but otherwise urban issues have been off the national policy agenda. At the state government level, the Cain Government in Victoria, for example, went on to lead various reforms, many of which were characterised by liberalisation, but also, and of particular import here, was the focus upon reinventing Melbourne as a global, liveable city. While this was ultimately widely regarded as a successful intervention in urban development, to international acclaim which persists today, the reality of the period was that the urban policy of the various state governments since the late 1970s has been hamstrung by lack of funding and support from the federal government.

For its part, and somewhat paradoxically, the federal experience with urban policy intervention led to a recognition that its direct powers to intervene in cities was extremely limited (Beer, 1995). By the 1980s the federal government had rolled back its urban development programmes as a reaction to what was seen as excessive intervention by the Whitlam Government. This pull-back was temporary, however, and in the late 1980s, during Hawke's last term, Paul Keating, the Treasurer at the time, began promoting the rhetoric of 'rescuing Australian cities' from developers who were left unchecked by state governments. Ironically, such unfettered development was made possible due in no small part to Keating's deregulation of the financial system during his time as Treasurer. As the rhetoric of Better Cities continued, so too did Keating's leadership challenge. Following his first challenge, which failed, in June 1991 Keating was moved to the back bench and the Better Cities proposal was put through Cabinet in time for the budget as a reward to the left faction's support of the Hawke leadership. This programme was to address housing affordability, locational disadvantage, urban transport and energy, the degradation of the urban environment and the financial burden of urban infrastructure (Badcock, 1993).

During the 1990s under Keating, Better Cities became Building Better Cities and took a funding turn to physical infrastructure. Newman and Kenworthy's (1999) analysis showed how the costs of congestion outweighed the short-term benefits of using greenfield land to build low density housing with poor infrastructure on the fringe. This conforms with contemporary ideas emerging from the significant North American originated New Urbanist movement, extolling the social and environmental virtues of more compact urban neighbourhoods. It was estimated that urban sprawl in the early 1990s was costing $4.2 billion per year (Neilson and Spiller, 1992, cited in Badcock, 1993), giving the federal government plenty of impetus to invest in urban development programmes. Ultimately, Badcock (1993) asserts that the federal government's involvement in urban policy was opportunistic and designed to establish itself as an effective crisis manager. Alexander (1994) agrees, describing the plethora of reports that resulted from the federal government's re-entry into urban and regional development as having limited real world impact. Beer (1995) digs deeper into the imperatives driving the federal government's activities in the sphere of urban policy and programmes, and ultimately hails the Building Better Cities programme direction as a success, due to a policy direction being made explicit. There is no doubt that tension between the federal and state governments during the 1980s–'90s was in part due to a significant reduction in commonwealth money given to the states for housing and transport infrastructure.

This was followed by another shift away from commonwealth interest in urban policy, with the Howard Government (1996–2007), coinciding with the planning authorities of all the major states, many with Labor governments, publishing new planning strategies that all broadly focus on containment, consolidation and urban renewal (Forster, 2006). The Rudd Government (2007–10) brought some resurgence of commonwealth interest in urban policy. It set about dismantling the industrial relations reforms that had led to the Howard Government's demise, announced bold aspirations to tackle climate change, modernise the economy through education reform and broadband investment, and mounted a visionary urban agenda through public conversations (such as the 2020 summit), setting up the Major Cities Unit and associated with this, the Infrastructure Australia initiative. The links back to the rhetoric of Better Cities is immediately apparent in the policy goals of these initiatives around productivity, liveability, sustainability and governance. While these bold, if familiar, policy goals were enthusiastically embarked upon in 2007, the reality of the Global Financial Crisis then unfolded, and after June 2010 these ambitions were tempered somewhat by other priorities during the Gillard Government (2010–13).

In summary, urban Australia has unique origins and state–federal relations that explain both the dominance of the 'urban' in the Australian settlement and the policy challenges facing the governing of a low carbon urban Australia. Federalism in Australia is, as Hollander (Chapter 18, this volume) points out, an accidental rather than designed phenomenon, and the on-off nature of attempts to govern urban sustainability leave enduring questions surrounding city obduracy, density, consolidation and environmental efficiency. Unsurprisingly, many academic commentators writing on urban policy are essentially cynical about the politics behind both the state and the federal governments' policy decisions in this field (Badcock, 1993; Alexander, 1994; Bunker et al, 2002; Buxton and Tieman, 2005; Woodcock et al, 2010). Herein lies some explanation as to how chronic infrastructure deficits come about and why congestion is so bad when there is such a lot of room in Australia compared to the rest of the westernised world. As SOAC (2012) indicates, 'the gap between population increase and housing supply in Australian cities is now the largest and most sustained in a century'. Job densities are drivers for prosperity and there is a rising premium for living near the centres of major cities.

Notwithstanding the urban policy context, there are significant shifts taking place in urban Australia that relate to the prospects for low carbon urban futures. Vehicle travel is on the decline, while freight is rising, and there is increasing peak-load stress on infrastructure. Also, as Bill Randolph states: 'Something new has happened to the structure of our cities over the last two decades that can be seen to represent a threshold between earlier phases of urbanisation and what we might, for want of a better term, call 21st century Australian cities' (Randolph, 2004, pp 482–3). These are more polycentric, more distinctively place-based and have reversed inner-city decline through gentrification, with a nascent acceptance of apartment living, especially for the growing number of urban small households who are often renters (Randolph, 2006). Some indicators also suggest improvements in residential energy and water efficiency. For example, in the period 2005–11 there have been step changes in rates of insulation and the aforementioned retrofit of solar domestic systems (ABS, 2011). There is also evidence of increased efficiency in water use associated with retrofitting and social practices (ABS, 2006; Allon and Sofoulis, 2006). These shifts parallel several decades of urban consolidation policies and the question arises as to whether a low carbon urban transition is occurring in Australia.

Conclusion: an urban low carbon transition?

With our precious global commons – the atmosphere – now shifting, it is apparent that Australia is now facing a '*triple* tragedy of the commons' (with apologies to Garret Hardin, 1968). First, there is the global politics of governing and policing the exploitation of the global atmosphere held in common. Second, there is the dominance of consumption as key driver of measurements for wealth and progress, exacerbating the rush to exploit 'free' goods such as the atmosphere. Finally, there is the temptation afforded by holding a stock of fossil fuel resources, meaning the line of least policy resistance is to maximise their exploitation rather than reforming the remainder of the economy.

In an overwhelmingly urban Australia, cities are both living legacies of the past and creative sites of the future. Simultaneously they appear to be obdurate yet dynamic, profit-driven yet social, capitalist and cultural, corporate yet distinctive and place-made. Batty follows Schumpeter (1938) in explaining the creative destruction of cities as a process

> central to a modernity that renews the city so that more and more profit can be extracted through the transformation of development. In this sense these processes are central to all city building. This characterisation of urban dynamics is one in which development is never completed and the city is always 'provisional' in its form and function (Batty, 2007: 3).

Yet within these tensions lie the means to avoid or succumb to the triple tragedy.

To what extent might we regard current urban trends as indicative of a low carbon urban transition? There is a growing 'urban transitions' literature, considering patterns of production and technology, the economy and public policy (Geels, 2004). Often referred to as the 'multi-level perspective', some proponents argue that modern tools of reflexive governance can support sustainable outcomes leading to sociotechnical transitions (Kemp and Loorbach, 2006). While the transitions literature is contested on the grounds that purposive 'steering' and outcomes for consumption are unpredictable (Shove and Walker, 2007), the notion of systemic change requires, in any event, a collective, bipartisan vision and long-term strategy, with clear links between urban and climate policy, and, in the language of ecological modernisation and reflexive governance, a suite of policy settings that are linked to broader social change and where progress is regularly reviewed and adjustments made accordingly.

Controversial and politicised attempts at carbon pricing, together with shifts in rhetoric around carbon mitigation and a history of contested state/federal urban policy initiatives do not bode well for a low carbon urban future in Australia. Policy attempts at building retrofit or urban consolidation are short-lived and at best regarded as only partly successful, while in other silos of government active support is provided to fossil fuel extraction and export. The end of the mining boom may actually be the belated signal that a post-carbon labour market will require significant policy development (see Buchanan and Oliver, Chapter 6, this volume).

As elsewhere, decarbonisation has been confounded by extensive privatisation of energy supply systems, increasing efforts to promote home ownership and consumption, and the prioritisation of the profitability of private enterprise. This 'splintered urbanism' (Graham and Marvin, 2001) complicates attempts to reconfigure cities towards low carbon mobility systems or fundamentally to change static energy-based fossil fuel systems and the buildings they supply, leaving little room for controlling energy grids, with fewer legitimate 'levers' on consumption. Increasingly, the roll of the 'urban' in low carbon governance is recognised as the manifestation of competition and collaboration within and between place-based organisations of governments, markets and civil society. In addition to thinking about technologies and markets, the intensified economic competition between cities in contemporary global capitalism is also understood through the social analysis of intermediaries, carrying new ideas, working across domains, boundaries and scales, and driving change (Guy et al, 2011).

Once we start to examine processes of social change, however, there may be more grounds for optimism. In this context, urban consolidation can be viewed as a response to changing social structures that in turn have led to a higher demand for housing and smaller households. One scenario is that we might end up with greater polarisation, as our inner cities and suburbs fill up with flats, units and townhouses, and the urban fringe with McMansions that will be difficult to retrofit later when smaller households are required – thus limiting housing choice in both models (Randolph, 2004). Another more optimistic scenario is that people will be increasingly drawn to networked and more highly serviced neighbourhoods, while governments and markets will respond through urban service provision, reducing the need for private transport and increasing low carbon retrofit. To cite two examples, urban car share schemes are now emerging, helped by maturing digital sociotechnical infrastructures, and the Greenhouse Alliances in Victoria, covering some 70 of 79 local government areas, are already acting as intermediaries in coordinating retrofit and related community and social change programmes across the state, including in the aforementioned mass movement to domestic solar. While not independent of the state or markets, these are clear examples of the 'interdependencies between production and consumption' that McMeekin and Southerton, (2012: 348) stress must be recognised in the study of sociotechnical change.

While the UK has seen a downward shift in energy consumption, the UK and California have committed to zero-emission housing, and Europe has mandated energy performance disclosure of buildings, Australia lags in the key policy settings most often associated with a low carbon urban transition. However, despite this, and as an apparently unintended consequence of short-lived schemes such as solar rebates, Australia may be witnessing social change that provides opportunities for the emergence of low carbon futures. As Miller states (Chapter 19, this volume, p 334), the issues driving social change in Australia are perhaps 'too serious to be left to politicians' Whether such change is indicative of a low carbon transition, or whether it is reversible, given that the technologies are now available and some are in place, is unknown. However, in prospect, a 'good' policy to guide low carbon transition would factor social practice and change into long-term programmes. Ultimately, this in turn would require a rethink of the neoliberal project and implies re-emergence of the concept of commons – a remaking of 'the making of Australia' project as indicated throughout this book.

References

ABS (Australian Bureau of Statistics) (2006) *Water Account Australia*, Canberra, ABS, Cat. No. 4610

ABS (2011) *Environmental Issues: Energy Use and Conservation*, Canberra, ABS, Cat. No. 4602.0.55.00

AIHW (Australian Institute of Health and Welfare) (2012) *Cancer in Australia: An Overview, 2012*, Cancer series no. 74, Cat. No. CAN 70, Canberra: AIHW & Australasian Association of Cancer Registries

Alexander, I. (1994) 'DURD Revisited? Federal Policy Initiatives for Urban and Regional Planning 1991–94', *Urban Policy and Research*, 12(1): 6-25

Allon, F. and Sofoulis, Z. (2006) 'Everyday water: Cultures in transition' *Australian Geographer* 37(1): 45-55

Australian Government (nd) *Strategic Research Priorities*, Australian Government, Canberra

Badcock, B. (1993) 'The Urban Programme as an Instrument of Crisis Management in Australia', *Urban Policy and Research*, 11(2): 72-80

Batty, M. (2007) 'The creative destruction of cities', *Environment and Planning B: Planning and Design*, 34(1): 2–5

Beer, A. (1995) 'Never Mind the Content, Let's Understand the Process: An Alternative Perspective on Recent Federal Urban Initiatives', *Urban Policy and Research*, 13(2): 107-112

Berry, M. (1984) *The Political Economy of Australian Urbanisation*, Pergamon Press, p 83

Bunker, R., Gleeson, B., Holloway, D. and Randolph, B. (2002) 'The Local Impacts of Urban Consolidation in Sydney', *Urban Policy and Research*, 20(2): 143-67

Buxton, M. and Tieman, G. (2005) 'Patterns of Urban Consolidation in Melbourne: Planning Policy and the Growth of Medium Density Housing', *Urban Policy and Research*, 23(2): 137-57

Climate Commission (2013) *The Critical Decade: Australia's future – solar energy*, Climate Commission, Australia

EC (European Commission) (1990) *The Green Book on the Urban Environment*, Brussels

EC (2012) 'The State of the European Carbon Market in 2012', *Report from the Commission to the European Parliament and the Council*, COM (2012) 652 EC, Brussels

Forster, C. (2006) 'The Challenge of Change: Australian Cities and Urban Planning in the New Millennium', *Geographical Research*, 44(2): 173–82

Freestone, R. (1989) *Model Communities: The Garden City Movement in Australia*, Melbourne, Thomas Nelson

Frost, L. (1991) *The New Urban Frontier: Urbanisation and City-building in Australasia and the American West*, Sydney, New South Wales University Press

Fudge, C., Ludlow, D. and Pauli, S. (1996) *European Sustainable Cities*, European Commission, Brussels

Geels, F. (2004) 'From sectoral systems of innovation to socio-technical systems: Insights about dynamics and change from sociology and institutional theory', *Research Policy* 33 (6/7): 897-920

Graham, S. and Marvin, S. (2001) *Splintering Urbanism: Networked Infrastructures, Technological Mobilities and the Urban Condition*, London: Routledge

Guy, S., Marvin, S., Medd, W. and Moss, T. (2011) *Shaping Urban Infrastructures: Intermediaries and the governance of socio-technical networks*, London, Earthscan

Hardin, G. (1968) 'The Tragedy of the Commons', *Science*, 162, 3859: 1243-8

Horne, R.E. and Hayles, C. (2008) 'Towards global benchmarking for sustainable homes: An international comparison of the energy performance of housing', *Journal of Housing and the Built Environment* 23(2): 119-130

IEA (2013) *Redrawing the Energy-Climate Map: World Energy Outlook Special Report*, International Energy Agency, June

Kemp, R. and Loorbach, D. (2006) 'Transition management: A reflexive governance approach', in: J.-P. Voss, D. Bauknecht and R. Kemp (eds) *Reflexive Governance for Sustainable Development*, Cheltenham, Glos, Edward Elgar: 103-30

McMeekin, A. and Southerton, D. (2012) 'Sustainability transitions and final consumption: practices and sociotechnical systems', *Technology Analysis & Strategic Management* 24(4): 345-61

Neilson, L. and Spiller, M (1992) 'Managing the cities for national economic development: The role of the Building Better Cities program', Paper presented to the Biennial Congress of the Royal Australian Planning Institute, Canberra, 26–30 April.

Newman, P. and Kenworthy, J. (1999) *Sustainability and Cities: Overcoming Automobile Dependence*, Island Press, Washington, D.C.

OECD (2010) *Australia: Towards a Seamless National Economy, OECD Reviews of Regulatory Reform*, OECD Publishing, Paris

Oliver, J.G.J., Janssens-Maenhout, G. and Peters, J.A.H.W. (2012) *Trends in global CO_2 emissions; 2012 Report*, The Hague: PBL Netherlands Environmental Assessment Agency; Ispra: Joint Research Centre

Peters, G.P., Andrew, R.M., Boden, T., Canadell, J.G., Ciais, P., Le Quere, C., Marland, G., Raupach, M.R. and Wilson, C. (2013) 'The challenge to keep global warming below 2 degrees Centigrade', *Nature Climate Change*, 3: 4–6

PMTGEE (Prime Minister's Task Group on Energy Efficiency) (2010) *Report of the Prime Minister's Task Group on Energy Efficiency*, PMTGEE, Canberra

Randolph, B. (2004) 'The Changing Australian City: New Patterns, New Policies and New Research Needs', *Urban Policy and Research*, 22(4): 481-93

Randolph, B. (2006) 'Delivering the Compact City in Australia: Current Trends and Future Implications', *Urban Policy and Research*, 24(4): 473-90

Schultz, A. and Petchey, R. (2011) *Energy Update 2011*, Canberra, Australian Bureau of Agricultural and Resource Economics and Sciences

Schumpeter, J.A. (1938) *Capitalism, Socialism and Democracy*, George Allen and Unwin Ltd, London

SGV (State Government of Victoria) (2013) *Understanding climate change*, SGV. Available at: www.climatechange.vic.gov.au

Shove, E. and Walker, G. (2007) 'Caution! Transitions ahead: Politics, practice, and sustainable transition management', *Environment and Planning A* 39: 763-770

SOAC (2010) *State of Australian Cities 2010*, Major Cities Unit, Australian Government, Department of Infrastructure and Transport

SOAC (2012) *State of Australian Cities 2012*, Major Cities Unit, Australian Government, Department of Infrastructure and Transport

Szelenyi, I. (1981) 'The relative autonomy of the state or state mode of production?' in: Dear, M J and Scott, A J. *Urbanization and Urban Planning in Capitalist Society*, Methuen Publishing

UN (1998) *Kyoto Protocol for the United Nations Framework Convention on Climate Change*, United Nations

WCED (World Commission on Environment and Development) (1987) *Our Common Future* (ed. G.H. Brundtland), Oxford; New York, Oxford University Press

WHO (World Health Organization) (2013) *World Health Organization Better Life Index*. Available at: www.oecdbetterlifeindex.org/countries/australia/

Woodcock, I., Dovey, K., Wollan, S. and Beyerle, A. (2010) 'Modelling the compact city: capacities and visions for Melbourne', *Australian Planner*, 47(2): 94-104

Part Five

POLITICS AND GOVERNMENT

SEVENTEEN

Politics and government

James Walter and Zareh Ghazarian

Introduction

Are politics and government in a state of crisis? On most indicators, Australia fares better than many countries, yet trust in politics is low (Martin, 2010). Commentators assert that the era just past was one of heroic achievement (Kelly, 2009) but that now there is a failure of leadership (Megalogenis, 2010), generating a longer-term difficulty in reaching workable policy decisions on major issues. Some argue that there has been an increase in problem complexity, demanding an adaptive leadership to which current systems are not attuned (see Little, 2012). Others suggest there has been a 'rout of knowledge' when problem complexity is allied to political conflict (Garnaut, 2010), leaving us with simplistic adversarial politics.

These claims question the effectiveness of our political institutions in meeting the expectations of a democratic polity. Are modes of public reasoning promoted by politics informative and responsive? Are the policy processes to which they give rise responding to our needs in ways that satisfy reasonable expectations of just outcomes, encourage trust and contain conflict? Is there a reasonable balance between competing interests preventing undue concentrations of resources, power and influence? These questions are examined in this chapter by focusing on contemporary practices, their effects on policy deliberation and the means of communication that inform public reasoning. We begin by considering the role of parties in the Australian political process before analysing the impact of reforms to the institutional framework of governance, especially the public service. The chapter then discusses whether a form of 'court politics' has developed in the Australian case and analyses the Gillard–led Labor Government. We conclude by addressing the apparent paradoxical divide between Australia's objective position and its public culture. All of these factors, however, must be interpreted in the context of the 'historical moment' in which we find ourselves.

Parties and the decline of party democracy

The mass parties of the 20th century played such a decisive role in shaping the public agenda and providing the channels for opinion aggregation that it was deemed the age of party democracy (Dalton, Farrell and McAllister 2011, 13). The ideological rationale of the mass parties – class division and economic interests – was much diminished in the late 20th century as they evolved to catch-all parties (attempting to net a broad constituency by matching policy to public mood) and thence to electoral professional parties (relying on communications professionals and expert advisers rather than party activists). The importance of mass membership and reliance on party activists dramatically declined. Authority migrated to the parliamentary leadership and the party machine. And as the major parties abandoned ideological coherence, leaders became surrogates for party identity and ethos as the indicators of product differentiation, to be 'sold' to the electorate by the communication experts and 'spin doctors' who are now central to professional party machines. In contemporary elections, it is leadership images rather than party symbols that dominate campaigning. In consequence, party allegiances erode: 'leaders have become more important cues to guide the choice of voters' (McAllister, 2003, p. 275). Leader effects on voting intentions are now demonstrable (Bean and Mughan, 1989). An Australian study, extrapolating from the outlook of some of its respondents, observed that 'the leader may be supplanting the party as the key organizer of people's political thinking' (Brett and Moran, 2006, p. 305).

An underlying thesis is that we have seen the 'mediatisation' of politics, with political leadership driven by communication strategies and greater emphases on image over substance and personality over ideology (Turner 2005; Campus, 2010). There has been an unparalleled 'personalisation' of politics (Blondel and Thiébault, 2009), leading some to argue that there has been a move towards 'presidentialisation' of party leaders even in Westminster systems (Poguntke and Webb, 2005). Some argue that 'leader democracy' is the way of the future. According to its advocates, leaders can step in to 'craft' and stabilise political regimes, integrating strategic elites and giving meaning to politics by 'shaping the agendas of debates, defining issues of concern, identifying the main challenges, establishing public trust ... and providing reassurance to anxious citizens' (Pakulski and Körösényi, 2012, pp 10–11). This is simply a recalibration of democracy, since leaders are subject to citizen recall.

There are four problems with the leader democracy thesis. First, leader dominance potentially threatens to diminish a fundamental principle of liberal democracy: the dispersal of power between different domains intended to ensure that no one element can dominate (Kane and Patapan, 2012). Equally significant, there is a growing body of research among organisational analysts, feminists and complexity theorists indicating that flatter structures with dispersed responsibility are more imperative than ever in contemporary decision making. It beggars belief that any one, dominant leader can comprehend the multiple elements of problem complexity presented by current policy challenges: top-down leadership no longer serves. Hence, a leader should be the person who understands organisational networks, can bring together the 'neural-like' connections within an institution and shape the behaviour of diverse agents in contributing to a solution (see Uhl-Bien et al, 2007). Leader democracy is entirely at odds with these findings. Second, the electoral recall argument is unpersuasive: leaders can still be elevated by and destroyed by their parties without reference to the popular will. And there is a wealth of evidence for the unhappy consequences of decisions made by strong leaders and not subject to sufficient review *between* electoral cycles. Third, while people still support democratic values, they are deeply unhappy with how democracy plays out at present (Judt, 2010) and even more unhappy with their leaders (a point underlined by the dismally low regard in which Australian voters held then Prime Minister Gillard and Opposition Leader Abbott in recent years), raising questions about the trust said to be elicited by leader democracy. Fourth, any stability dependent on the leader is precarious, tied as it is to constant polling and with parties less forgiving than ever when a leader fails to satisfy expectations; witness the removal of Kevin Rudd in 2010 and Julia Gillard in 2013.

In fact, leader authority is now entirely subject to performance: those seen not to deliver can be ruthlessly dispatched, especially in the Australian system where (unlike in Britain or Canada) tenure depends solely on the vote of the parliamentary party. In consequence, the ability of the leader to attend to the task at hand is compromised: they must always be watching their back, careful about sharing knowledge too widely (in case it is used against them). This militates against preparing the ground for new initiatives. Past means of testing novel policy ideas by having a subordinate 'fly a kite', leaving the leader free of obloquy should it fail, are denied them. First thoughts are represented as firm intentions; those that founder are marked against the leader (for example, Julia Gillard's sketchily conceived and widely ridiculed suggestion of a community forum on climate change). Even so, the leader may be driven to a compulsive repetition of 'breakthrough' decisions intended to assert personal authority, but with rushed development limited to an inner circle and insufficiently subject to reality testing, leading to failure – witness Gillard's initiation of the 'Malaysia solution' to deter asylum seekers, or Kevin Rudd's first incarnation of a super profits tax on mining, for example.

To explore such arguments fully, however, we need to consider how leaders function in the complex, multilayered systems of contemporary polities. If parties and leadership have been transformed, what about the surrounding institutions within and through which they must operate?

Institutional reform and policy deliberation

The Australian public service (APS), like its Westminster progenitor, was traditionally the font of policy advice and assumed to be an 'apolitical institution' capable of providing such advice no matter what a government's political complexion. In recent decades significant changes to Australia's political and public policy institutions have undercut these assumptions, enhancing the power of the elected executive in Australia, and introduced additional influential players into policy debate.

Bob Hawke's Labor Government, elected in 1983, adopted neoliberal ideas in response to the growing demands for 'small government' and greater 'efficiency' in the public sector (Ryan and Bramston, 2003). It attempted to balance public expectations of service and social amenity with a reduced role for government by containing wage costs, but with the offset of enhanced social provision (articulated in its 'Accord' with the unions), and by identifying areas where market provision could replace government action (Keating, 2004). The state reduced its direct services by contracting out many functions as well as privatising and deregulating state service agencies (Head, 2005). This was coupled with the adoption by governments of 'new public management' (NPM), which sought to increase the responsiveness of the public service. Head reminds us that NPM had two 'faces': outward and inward. The outward face was towards citizens, now regarded as customers, and the intention of NPM was to improve the quality of service delivery. The inward face referred to NPM providing ministers with the power to exercise tighter control over the bureaucracy, as a result enhancing the power of the political executive (Head 2005, p. 45).

The adoption of NPM also created opportunities for external actors, from think-tanks and consultancies, to participate in the policy making process (see Head, 2005, p 50). NPM was a means for promoting 'contestability'. Consultants and specialist advisers, contracted to deal with particular problems, became increasingly significant. The public service lost its monopoly; it was now seen to be competing with other sources to influence policy (MacDermott 2008, pp 26–30). Competition between different policy advocates, it was said, would lead to more robust decisions. It also gave ministers options: no longer would they be at the mercy of 'mandarins'. This led to what some saw as the 'hollowing out' of the state (Rhodes, 1994).

The neoliberal paradigm was vigorously advanced by free market think-tanks such as the Centre for Independent Studies (CIS) and the Institute of Public Affairs (IPA). They were influential advocates of the privatisation agenda, promoting the ideas of Milton Friedman and Friedrich von Hayek (Marsh, 1994; Stone, 2000). Their activism drew on transnational advocacy networks (Stone, 2008). Countervailing ideas were promoted by think-tanks such as the Evatt Foundation and the Australia Institute, but their belated criticisms could only be directed to implementation problems: the CIS, IPA and others had set the agenda. Governments and policy practitioners may have been less entranced by Friedman and Hayek than were the New Right advocates, but privatisation and resort to market solutions served their cost-cutting purposes. The degree to which these reforms effected a delegation of authority to private networks and non-state actors (Stone, 2008) was scarcely considered.

The Hawke Government reforms also extended to internal APS functions. The Prime Minister's statement in December 1983, calling for efficiency, effectiveness, equity and responsiveness to ministers and the Parliament, foreshadowed the *Public Service Reform Act 1984*. Departments were amalgamated (32 reduced to 16) and cabinet was streamlined, with only senior ministers (responsible for the new super departments) comprising the executive, and assistant ministers (responsible for former departments, now subsidiary elements internal to the new departments) called in as needed. The Public Service Board was abolished. The permanent tenure of departmental secretaries was removed: they were appointed for fixed terms, and subject to performance expectations. These changes addressed ministerial concern that, to gain the full cooperation of senior public servants in implementing their programme, they needed the power to choose their department heads (Stewart, 2006, p 124).

The Howard Liberal-National Party Coalition Government (1996–2007) capitalised on the initiatives of its Labor predecessors. It raised the stakes by sacking six departmental heads on assuming office in 1996; appointing an ideological ally from outside the APS to the key role of Secretary of the Department of Prime Minister and Cabinet (Max Moore-Wilton who, despite state public sector experience, then held a senior post at the Australian Stock Exchange); and cutting 11,000 jobs (8% of the APS workforce) within the first year, with a continuing steep decline until 2000 (Verspaandonk et al, 2010, pp 3–5). Further reform, predicated on arguments for more flexibility, streamlining and cultural change, and enacted in the Public Service Act 1999 and the Parliamentary Service Act 1999, entrenched incentives and management practices characteristic of the private sector.

While the APS was plunged into 'a world of markets and contracts, of competition and consultants' with cascading staff losses (Davis, 2007, p. 480) another important cohort was gaining influence in the decision-making process. Uncommon in the Australian system until the 1970s, political advisers have been incorporated into ministerial offices in the post-war period as the tasks of government have become increasingly complex (Walter, 2006, p 22). The Whitlam Labor Government initiated an enhanced role for ministerial advisers in Australian government in 1972 (Walter, 1986, chapter 3). Expecting that the public service had been habituated to the style of coalition governments and was unprepared for vigorous reform, the government argued that political advisers would provide another source of information to ministers, improving their decision making capacities. Successive governments increased the numbers of advisers. Regulating ministerial staff, however, has been unplanned and ad hoc (Holland, 2002). In 1984 the Hawke Government introduced the Members of Parliament (Staff) Act 1984 (MOP(S) Act), with the aim of regularising the conditions of employment for advisers. The government's intention was to provide protection for public servants who worked in ministerial offices. The resulting framework assumed that ministerial staffers would uphold public service ethics (Walter, 2006, pp 23–4).

Despite the expansion and diversification of advisers (Tiernan, 2004), the MOP(S) Act has not been altered to reflect this (Horne, 2009). Furthermore, many staffers appointed to ministerial offices have been partisan activists with political ambitions of their own. In characterising the modern adviser, Weller (2002) argued that they were 'politically dispensable, convenient scapegoats who will take the bullet for their ministers and protect them from political fallout' (p 72). In recent years, controversies such as the children overboard affair and mistakes concerning immigration detention have highlighted how ministers may defend themselves from criticism by maintaining that staffers failed adequately to advise them (Weller, 2002; Keating, 2003, pp 92–3; Tiernan, 2004). Such cases also made clear the capacity of ministerial staff to intervene in departmental processes, mediating between the political and administrative domains to drive, sieve and skew advice; insisting upon what the minister wants as opposed to the public interest. Moreover, advisers cannot be held accountable, leaving public servants to take the blame (Walter, 2006, p. 24).

Participant observers (for example Button, 2012) still attest to high levels of competence in the APS, and it can be argued that the overall outcome of reform has been that the bureaucracy did manage both to cut back its establishment and to find new means to meet public expectations. Yet there remain significant reservations about the effects on policy deliberation, manifest in prolonged debate between those most closely involved (see for example Podger, 2007a, 2007b; Shergold, 2007), and the concerns of some, such as Michael Keating and Terry Moran (both former Secretaries of the Department of Prime Minister and Cabinet), initially closely engaged in the reform process, eloquent proponents of governmental resort to markets to meet public expectations (Keating, 2004) and the neoliberal adaptation of the APS, but later driven to wonder whether 'responsiveness' has mutated into the sort of 'politicisation' that impedes both the transmission of unwelcome advice and the ability of public servants to ensure due process and the integrity of the system (Keating, 2003; Moran, 2012).

The turn to 'court politics'?

The institutional transitions summarised earlier have led to a modern version of court politics. That is, the combination of emerging 'leader democracy', the hollowing out of parties as the agencies for opinion aggregation and transmission, the attenuation of public sector bodies invested in the public good, and the consequent delegation of authority to private networks and non-state actors has reduced politics to a species of baronial competition (Bevir and Rhodes, 2006, pp 278–82). Court politics captures the manner in which the contemporary pattern of leader dominance has reversed the conventions of dispersed power, open scrutiny and bureaucratic neutrality. The personalisation of politics has proceeded in tandem with the erosion of institutional constraints devised to disperse power. With the diminution of institutions, transparency suffers: court politics implies an incremental privileging of closeted decision making by leaders, with the effect of channelling more and more issues into the inner circle (and away from democratic forums). Service to the leader arguably trumps reality testing in policy analysis; disinterested bureaucracy has either been marginalised (by loyalist personal staff) or has itself succumbed to 'exclusivistic' relationships: a concern that the leader be told only what they want (rather than what they need) to hear prevails (Weller, 2002); key players have no independent base and so tie their ambitions to the leader's needs (see Dexter, 1977, p 268); and the whole enterprise is thus open to private interests (primarily those of leaders, career politicians and private staff with ambitions linked to both of those above) at the expense of the public interest (Walter, 2010).

Arguably, court politics shares the dynamics of groupthink (Janis, 1972). The distinction is that it is seen as a persisting (rather than exceptional) aspect of contemporary governance – the routinisation of relatively closed, inner circle decision making – driving persistent policy fiascos such as those that bedevilled the Rudd and the Gillard Governments (2007–13), and aspects of the final years of the Howard Government (Walter, 2008, 2010). Typically, the policy failures of these governments (for example, Howard's mooted takeover of a state administered hospital; Rudd's Emissions Trading Scheme and his super profits tax on mining; Gillard's 'Malaysia solution' for asylum seekers – one could identify numbers of other examples) manifested a style of decision making redolent of the court. Initiatives were developed by an inner circle and driven from the top (to the detriment of appropriate consultation); the urgency of action was used as licence to ignore the 'normal' checks and balances; it was assumed that power aggregated at the centre.

It is not that these contemporary leaders have been unusually driven, or more recklessly ambitious than their predecessors. Even those whose ambition is relatively realistic can be seduced into resorting more and more to their court, *if* institutions or conventions are insufficiently demanding of dispersed leadership and reality testing. Where court politics prevails, sound policy judgment and the dispersed leadership intended within a liberal democratic polity are in question. But consider the countervailing pressures. Given that so much is demanded of the contemporary leader – having almost alone to articulate a mission that was once distributed across the party and reinforced by widely shared ideological conviction – and yet expecting that since retribution for failure can be swift they must always watch their back, there is every incentive to rely solely on the loyalists of the inner circle. Knowledge garnered is a resource; knowledge shared might give rivals something with which to attack. Repeated announcement of 'breakthrough' initiatives might be a means of asserting personal authority; on the other hand, personalisation of governance inevitably means the leader will in time be seen as the source of all disquiet, eroding that authority. And as the paradigms that shaped political discourse for the past 30 years crumble, there is no safety net, no ground for assuming a baseline consensus other than one gained through hard grinding negotiation.

Governance in question

The travails of the ill-starred Labor Government led by Julia Gillard (2010–13) can be read against this backdrop. The talents Gillard demonstrated – as a negotiator, able to work with others to find compromise solutions – while better suited to minority government than those of Opposition Leader Tony Abbott, were unsuited to the expectations of sure leadership an uneasy electorate demanded. Gillard was embattled and unpopular almost from the moment that she negotiated minority government and, in the interests of consensus decisions, compromised such objectives as her initial promise not to introduce carbon pricing. An early stumble when she said she would now speak as 'the real Julia' played into claims that she would say anything and stood for nothing, a perception enhanced by the deal making integral to sustaining minority government. She failed in the role of communicator-in-chief: little she said appeared to cut through. Seeking to appear decisive when it came to apparently intractable issues, she was prone to serial misjudgements (such as the 'Malaysia solution') that were manifestly inattentive to necessary detail.

Yet despite all, Gillard's was a government of achievement against the odds. It avoided parliamentary deadlock. In the face of a rancorous, disruptive Opposition and withering personal and public attacks such as have faced very few leaders, Gillard remained resilient: her refusal to flinch or concede ground was courageous. She did what was needed to keep the Greens and cross-bench supporters on side, but every matter of substance had to be negotiated. Legislation was passed. Gillard was the closer on initiatives that Rudd had floated, but failed to bring to fruition: carbon pricing, a mining tax, a National Broadband Network; as well as backing new initiatives of substance, such as a national disability scheme, health agreements with the states, plain packaging of cigarettes, GP super clinics, pharmaceutical benefits reforms, educational reform and more. Here then was the paradox: a leader whose stocks hovered stubbornly around the lowest recorded for an Australian prime minister, yet who continued successfully to pursue a legislative agenda in the most adverse circumstances that any prime minister has faced.

Another challenge Gillard faced was the fact that her predecessor, Kevin Rudd, remained in parliament, continually courting the attention of the media and public, fuelling speculation that he would one day return to lead the Labor Party. When induced to challenge Gillard in 2012, he was decisively defeated. Yet in June 2013, some three years after losing the leadership to Gillard, Rudd was re-elected as leader of the Australian Labor Party (ALP) and became prime minister again. That transition was precipitated by Gillard's continuously poor opinion poll results that suggested Labor was destined for disastrous defeat. Rudd, in contrast, had regained popularity and Caucus gambled that he could revive the party's electoral fortunes. Nothing more clearly substantiates the power of the leader-centric trend, since there had been plentiful evidence that Rudd had been a chaotic administrator and was neither liked nor trusted by many of his Caucus colleagues: apparent public popularity alone accounted for his renaissance. The gamble failed: initial indicators of support – the sole reason for Rudd's restoration – quickly dissipated; polls deteriorated to levels little better than those predicted for Gillard; there was no salvation for the embattled Labor Government.

On the one hand, Gillard was the victim of a public culture of anxiety, distrust and cynicism. Parliamentary discord and ruthlessly negative campaigning, not only by the Opposition but also by powerful media interests, against all that the government did, encouraged disquiet about politics in general and leaders in particular. Mediatisation defined politics, as Gillard's personality and image were incessantly analysed while governance was ignored. That Gillard was not to be trusted became an article of faith. Reckless tactical manoeuvres (the dubious appointment of a compromised Liberal MP, Peter Slipper, as Speaker) and recurrent scandal (the Craig Thompson affair; the downfall of Peter Slipper) promoted a perception that national affairs were in the hands of wreckers and chancers. Attempts to set the record straight were not heard: the electorate had stopped listening. On the other hand, achievement against the odds, with a minority government in a divided parliament, depended very much on Gillard's skills in parliament and behind the scenes. It was, as with every leader, an exercise of power, but it was not adapted to the public stage.

The leadership repertoire in this leader-centric age demands a performance that projects decision and vision, along with an ability to draw big pictures (like Gough Whitlam, Paul Keating and, sometimes, Kevin Rudd) or project charisma (like Bob Hawke) or communicate a narrative of belief (like John Howard). Gillard had to engineer agreements, which militated against appearing decisive. A pragmatist, she did not deal effectively in big pictures. Once astute, articulate and quick on her feet, her earnest attempt to adopt the leadership repertoire diminished those skills and failed to capture her strengths. The talents that enabled her achievement in an unusual parliament did not register in the public eye. And she, too, succumbed to court politics, a mode that ensures that public reasoning appears neither informative nor responsive.

Discussion

We can now address that paradoxical divide between Australia's objective position (a relatively successful polity with a strong economy) and its public culture (an endemic pessimism about politics and prospects). Significantly, while legislatures elsewhere (for instance, in the USA) came close to deadlock, the Australian Parliament withstood a rancorous and divisive period: minority government continued to function; a legislative agenda was worked through; even in these adverse circumstances governance could be sustained. Yet the mediatisation of politics obscured this story. The drama of conflict, of alternative leaders as either the locus of error or the only hope of salvation, was ceaselessly replayed. That these leaders were seen to be all too human, and their standing precarious, was bound to provoke unease. That relative prosperity and stability were sustained because institutions continued to work effectively escaped public attention.

This, we argue, is at the core of contemporary disquiet, overshadowing such achievements as there have been. Could it have been otherwise? The problems we canvass are not uniquely Australian. Party decline with a capitulation to political professionals (Katz and Mair, 1995) and an attendant leader-centric trend (Pakulski and Körösényi, 2012) is widespread in Western polities. Concern about the personalisation of politics (Blondel and Thiébault, 2009), with undue emphasis on inner circles rather than representative institutions and mediatisation occluding policy debate (Campus, 2010) is near universal. Such trends are accentuated in Australia by the ease with which leaders can be elevated, and destroyed, by a small subset of actors (the parliamentary party room alone) and the political professionals behind them. Though this merry-go-round is driven entirely by polling, the public sees this outcome as out of its hands, building resentment still further.

What can be done? Parties (on all sides) need drastic reform: a slew of inquiries following electoral failure have identified productive measures, but unless the power of party oligarchies is destroyed, it will not happen. One step would be to reform party preselection, giving greater weight to branch level assessment than to the party executive, which might reverse the tendency for party professionals (with no other life experience) to dominate candidate lists. Another should be to rebuild an activist membership base, allowing it a real voice in party forums; promoting a re-articulation of party ideals; and cooperative networking with other stakeholder groups that share such ideals. Indeed, the network party might be the only option for the future if parties are to remain viable. Many people are drawn into action now not by conventional parties, but by engagement in (and service to) particular objectives, often linking up though new media. But parties could create coalitions of activist groups that may have specific objectives, but are informed by common ideals, acting as the 'peak body' for entities with cognate interests. In the network approach, power is decentralised: 'the defining characteristic of a party is co-operative behaviour, not formal positions. Actors "join" the party when they begin communicating with other members of the network, developing common strategies and co-ordinating action to achieve shared goals' (Koger, Masket and Noel, 2009, p 637). This would require an openness and ability to listen to and learn from others that is beyond the ken of 'political professionals'; it might also, however, re-energise a politics of ideas.

The leader as solution/problem must be tackled: on the one hand, internal reform can re-establish a party's own constraints on leadership excess (and if network parties were to emerge, dispersed leadership among stakeholders, with collective responsibility, would be a prerequisite). On the other, diminishing the options of the parliamentary wing alone in toppling leaders – by requiring votes at an all party conference, for instance – can restrain premature deposition by party room hustlers. An element of greater security (the leader not having constantly to watch their back and surround themself with loyalists) could encourage more collective enterprise.

Policy deliberation must be conducted in circumstances that limit 'inner circle' capture, requiring a better balance between executive action, interest engagement and proper scrutiny. Outsourcing, think-tanks, lobbyists and private office advisers are here to stay; vigorous exchange between competing players is no bad thing if the rules of the game are clear. Accountability measures that apply to all who are involved in deliberative processes (including ministerial staff, consultants and lobbyists) must be established. Each of these, however, operates within a narrow ambit: the APS, given its broader purview, must be allowed a greater degree of autonomy. Regular recourse to deliberative democracy on matters of great moment, involving not only politicians, public servants, advisers and experts but also community and interest representatives, might induce the political class to adopt prudential leadership and ethics (Uhr, 2005, pp 65–8), since its operations would be open to direct observation. Open deliberation would also alleviate the mediatisation of politics, reducing the ability of powerful media interests to dominate representations of debate.

Will changes such as these come about? Kevin Rudd, in his desperate effort to restore ALP fortunes prior to the 2013 election, promised party reform and more open, inclusive and consultative government, which could reshape governance. But could Rudd himself change? Liberal Leader, Tony Abbott, prospered in opposition by unremitting aggression, accentuating his 'strong leadership' (Little, 1988). He also belongs to a traditionally leader-oriented party. He is unlikely to promote dispersed responsibility, or more open forms (such as those of a network party). Nonetheless, the old modes are failing, not only here, but everywhere. Political cycles take time; change is slow; but history is unremitting. The mass parties were a product of particular historical circumstances; when these changed, electoral/professional parties (and increasing leader centrality) were born, and now they too have reached an end-date. The paradox and frustration of contemporary politics suggests the end of a cycle, though we are yet to see the way forward. But leaders and parties that do not adapt to the contingent demands of this historical moment will fail, and in their wake new forms will emerge.

References

Bean C. and Mughan, A. (1989) 'Leadership Effects in Parliamentary Elections in Australia and Britain', *American Political Science Review*, vol 83, pp 1165-79

Bevir, M. and Rhodes, R.A.W. (2006) *Governance Stories*, London: Routledge

Blondel, J. and Thiébault, J. (2009) *Political Leadership, Parties and Citizens: The Personalisation of Leadership*, London: Routledge

Brett, J. and Moran, A. (2006) *Ordinary People's Politics: Australians talk about life, politics and the future of their country*, North Melbourne: Pluto Press

Button, J. (2012) *Speechless: A Year in My Father's Business*, Melbourne: Melbourne University Press

Campus, D. (2010) 'Mediatization and Personalization of Politics in Italy and France: the cases of Berlusconi and Sarkozy', *The International Journal of Press/Politics,* vol 15, pp219-235

Dalton, R.J., Farrell, D.M. and McAllister, I. (2011) *Political Parties and Democratic Linkage: How Parties Organize Democracy*, Oxford: Oxford University Press

Davis, G. (2007) 'Public sector reform', in B. Galligan and W. Roberts (eds) *The Oxford Companion to Australian Politics,* Melbourne: Oxford University Press, pp 479-81

Dexter, L.A. (1977) 'Presidential Staff Relations as a Special Case of a General Phenomenon', *Administration & Society,* vol 9, no 3, pp 267-283

Garnaut, R. (2010) *What if Mainstream Science is Right? The Rout of Knowledge and Analysis in Australian Climate Change Policy and a Chance of Recovery,* Canberra: Cunningham Lecture 2010, Academy of the Social Sciences in Australia

Head, B. (2005) 'Governance', in P. Saunders and J. Walter (eds) *Ideas and Influence: Social Science and Public Policy in Australia,* Sydney: UNSW Press, pp 44-63

Holland, I. (2002) *Accountability of Ministerial Staff?*, Research Paper No. 19 2001–02, Department of the Parliamentary Library, Commonwealth of Australia

Horne, N. (2009) *The Members of Parliament (Staff) Act 1984 Framework and Employment Issues*, Research Paper No. 3 2009–10 (Update), Department of the Parliamentary Library, Commonwealth of Australia

Janis, I. (1972) *Victims of Groupthink*, Boston: Houghton Mifflin

Judt, T. (2010) *Ill Fares the Land,* London: Allen Lane

Kane, J. and Patapan, H. (2012) *The Democratic Leader: How Democracy Defines, Empowers and Limits its Leaders*, Oxford: Oxford University Press

Katz, R. and Mair, P. (1995) 'Changing Models of Party Organization and Party Democracy: The Emergence of the Cartel Party', *Party Politics*, vol 1, no 1, pp 5–28

Keating, M. (2003) 'In the Wake of "A Certain Maritime Incident": Ministerial Advisers, Departments and Accountability'. *Australian Journal of Public Administration,* vol 62, no 3, pp 92-7

Keating M. (2004) *Who Rules? How Government Retains Control in a Privatised Economy,* Sydney: Federation Press

Kelly, P. (2009) *The March of the Patriots: The Struggle for Modern Australia,* Melbourne: Melbourne University Press

Koger, G., Masket, S. and Noel, H. (2009) 'Partisan Webs: Information Exchange and Party Networks', *British Journal of Political Science*, vol 39, no 3, pp. 633-653

Little, A. (2012) 'Political Action, Error and Failure: The Epistemological Limits of Complexity', *Political Studies,* vol 60, pp 3–19

Little, G. (1988) *Strong Leadership*, Melbourne: Oxford University Press

MacDermott, K. (2008) *Whatever Happened to Frank and Fearless?: The Impact of the New Public Service Management on the Australian Public Service*, Canberra: ANU E Press

Marsh, I. (1994) 'The Development and Impact of Australia's "Think Tanks"', in *Australian Journal of Management,* vol 19, no 2, pp 177-200

Martin, A. (2010) 'Does Political Trust Matter? Examining Some of the Implications of Low Levels of Political Trust in Australia', *Australian Journal of Political Science,* vol 45, no 4, pp 705-12

McAllister, I. (2003) 'Prime Ministers, Opposition Leaders and Government Popularity in Australia', *Australian Journal of Political Science,* vol 38, pp 259-77

Megalogenis, G. (2010) *Trivial Pursuit: Leadership and the End of the Reform Era,* Melbourne: Quarterly Essay 40, Black Inc.

Moran, T. (2012) 'Terry Moran in conversation with John Alford', *The Conversation,* Available at: https://theconversation.edu.au/terry-moran-in-conversation-full-transcript-10187

Pakulski, J. and Körösényi, A. (2012) *Toward Leader Democracy*, London: Anthem Press

Podger, A. (2007a) 'What Really Happens: Departmental Secretary Appointments, Contracts and Performance Pay in the Australian Public Service', *Australian Journal of Public Administration*, vol 66, no 2, pp 131-47

Podger, A. (2007b) 'Response to Peter Shergold', *Australian Journal of Public Administration*, vol. 66, n. 4, pp. 498-500

Poguntke, T. and Webb, P. (eds) (2005) *The Presidentialization of Politics: A Comparative Study of Modern Democracies*, Oxford: Oxford University Press

Rhodes, R.A.W. (1994) 'The Hollowing Out of the State: The Changing Nature of the Public Service in Britain', *The Political Quarterly*, vol 65, pp 138-51

Ryan, S. and Bramston, T. (2003) *The Hawke Government: A Critical Retrospective,* North Melbourne: Pluto Press

Shergold, P. (2007) 'What Really Happens in the Australian Public Service', *Australian Journal of Public Administration*, vol 66, no 3, pp 367-70

Stewart, J. (2006) 'Managing and Restructuring the Public Sector', in J. Summers, D. Woodward and A. Parkin (eds) *Government, Politics, Power and Policy in Australia* (8th edn), Frenchs Forest: Pearson

Stone, D. (2000) 'Non-Governmental Policy Transfer: The Strategies of Independent Policy Institutes', *Governance: An International Journal of Policy and Administration*, vol 13, no 1, pp 45–62

Stone, D. (2008) 'Global Public Policy, Transnational Policy Communities, and Their Networks', *The Policy Studies Journal*, vol 36, no 1, pp 19-38

Tiernan, A. (2004) *Ministerial Staff Under the Howard Government: Problem, Solution or Black Hole?* PhD Thesis. Department of Politics and Public Policy, Griffith University

Turner, G. (2005) *Ending the Affair: The Decline of Television Current Affairs in Australia*, Sydney: UNSW Press

Uhl-Bien, M., Marion, R. and McKelvey, B. (2007) 'Complexity leadership theory: shifting leadership from the industrial age to the knowledge era', *The Leadership Quarterly*, vol 18, no 4, pp 298-318

Uhr, J. (2005) *Terms of Trust: Arguments over Ethics in Australian Government*, Sydney: UNSW Press

Verspaandonk, R., Holland, I. and Horne, N. (2010) *Chronology of Changes in the Australian Public Service 1975–2010*, Canberra: Parliamentary Library, Department of Parliamentary Services

Walter, J. (1986) *The Ministers' Minders: Personal Advisers in National Government*, Melbourne: Oxford University Press

Walter, J. (2006) 'Ministers, Minders and Public Servants: Changing Parameters of Responsibility', *Australian Journal of Public Administration*, vol 65, no 3, pp x-xx

Walter, J. (2008) 'Is there a Command Culture in Politics? The Canberra Case', in P. 'T. Hart and J. Uhr, (eds) *Public Leadership: Perspectives and Practices*, Canberra: ANU Press, pp 189–202

Walter, J. (2010) 'Elite decision processes: the "court politics" debate', *Australian Political Studies Association Conference*, University of Melbourne, September. Available at: http://apsa2010.com.au/full-papers.php

Weller, P. (2002) *Don't Tell the Prime Minister*, Melbourne: Scribe

EIGHTEEN

Federalism and intergovernmental relations

Robyn Hollander

The Australian federal system is often seen as a barrier to both the achievement of coherent and cohesive public policy, and the larger social democratic project. The formal limits on sovereignty set out in the constitution; the gross unevenness of financial autonomy (the vertical fiscal imbalance); the inequity in the distribution of policy capacity; and the continuous need to negotiate and renegotiate with unwilling partners all serve to frustrate politicians and public servants alike, and act as a brake on clear policy direction and effective delivery. The situation is exacerbated by weaknesses at local and regional level and the traditional local government emphasis on 'services to property', commonly characterised as 'roads rates and rubbish' (Dollery et al, 2006, 556). While this much is universally acknowledged, the opportunities provided by a federal system to moderate the excesses of neoliberalism and social conservatism at either state or federal level are less commonly recognised. At its best, our system of multilevel governance has the capacity to provide spaces for community engagement, a chance to escape a 'one size fits all' policy straightjacket and facilitate the pursuit of a more progressive policy agenda.

Examples of commonwealth interventions, such as its preservation of the Franklin River and its recognition of the Native Title in the face of sometimes strident state opposition, are well known. While often taken as symptomatic of federalism's failure, they can instead be read as evidence of the strength of split-level governance structures, especially when placed alongside examples of state level policy leadership. We need only to recall it was state Labor governments that in 2007 commissioned the Garnaut review of climate change, which provided the blueprint for federal government policy. Such contests over policy direction cannot always be ascribed to partisanship and the simple right–left divide, as demonstrated by the state-based initiatives in the area of same-sex relationships where we have seen Labor resist federally what has been embraced at state level. In the later part of the 1990s, we also saw the re-emergence of space as central to social inclusion and economic recovery and the need to engage local level structures and networks (Smyth et al, 2005).

The potential of our federation to provide such space is, however, being steadily eroded by two trends – the unremitting grip of new public management, with its emphasis on process and auditing under the guise of transparency and accountability, and the almost unrelenting centralisation of legal authority and financial resources. As with public policy more generally, this centralisation has been characterised by pragmatism. Unlike its counterparts in the US or Switzerland, Australian federalism is not the outcome of a well-developed political theory or consciously articulated regional or cultural identities. Instead, it has developed in response to the practical imperatives of the times (Hollander and Patapan, 2007). As noted in the introduction to this volume, this pragmatism has served us well, but perhaps the time has come to step outside the demands of the present and to consider the possibility of rebalancing the federation and slowing the trend towards centralisation. For any change in direction to occur, however, the commonwealth must be prepared to rethink its existing fiscal model and relinquish its control of the purse strings. Such a move must be accompanied by a reconfiguration of the collective decision making process through reform of the Council of Australian Governments (COAG), a renewed commitment to local and regional level governance, and a reconsideration of introducing an Australian Bill of Rights.

This chapter begins by mapping out Australia's federal landscape and its impact on public policy making. It then goes on to discuss how it has both frustrated and facilitated a more progressive policy agenda. The chapter then turns to examine recent developments, focusing in particular on the increasing domination of the commonwealth, before exploring the possibilities for reform.

Australia's federal framework

Federalism is defined by divided sovereignty, an arrangement whereby government authority is divided between different levels of government, with neither having the legal authority to intervene in areas in the other's sphere of competence. This seemingly straightforward definition assumes a clear allocation of roles and responsibilities, allowing each level of government to operate independently of the other. At first glance, Australia appears to conform to this. Section 51 of the constitution (Constitution Act 1900) explicitly sets out the commonwealth's areas of exclusive responsibility, the so-called 'Heads of Power'. The majority of these powers are concerned with either national borders and external relations, and include immigration, quarantine, and defence, or the establishment of a single national market, including currency, communication and interstate trade. Originally, Section 51 contained very little provision for commonwealth engagement in social policy, limiting it to marriage and pensions, and it was amended in 1946 to include unemployment, medical and other benefits (s 51(xxiiiA)). Implicit was that all other matters – education, transport, law and order, and so on – would remain with the states. At first blush, therefore, Australia presents a picture of 'co-ordinate' federalism, where the two levels of government are able to operate independently of each other.

This image is far from the case, however, because significant elements of 'concurrency', or interaction, were built into the original design. Responsibilities overlapped in areas such as industrial relations, taxation, and after 1967, in Aboriginal affairs. Moreover, the constitution (s 109) provided that the commonwealth would prevail where inconsistency existed between state and commonwealth law. In addition, the financial arrangements guaranteed that the commonwealth and state governments were inescapably intertwined from the outset. There were several key provisions, including arrangements for sharing tariff revenue (s 87), the payment of commonwealth surpluses to the states (s 94) and the ability for the commonwealth to take over state debt (s 105) (Matthews, 1977, p 43). Section 96 allowed the commonwealth to provide financial assistance to the states 'on such terms and conditions as [it] thinks fit' and was of particular significance because these tied or specific purpose payments (SPPs) provided the commonwealth with an increasingly significant lever for intervening in areas of state responsibility.

Over the decades, these original provisions were augmented by determinations of the High Court, the body charged with adjudicating on disputes between the commonwealth and the states. Arguably, the most far reaching of the Court's decisions was in the 1942 First Uniform Tax case, giving the commonwealth priority in the collection of income tax. While the states were still free to levy their own income tax, it could only be an additional impost on tax payers and the commonwealth's tax would take priority. In addition, states that continued to levy their own income tax would not receive commonwealth grants. This had the effect of conclusively cementing the commonwealth's fiscal supremacy. The Court also tended to adopt an expansive interpretation of other constitutional provisions. For example, in the 1984 Tasmanian Dam case, the Court found, under its external affairs power (s 51(xxix)), the commonwealth could make law in relation to environmental protection – a state responsibility – in order to meet its responsibilities under the World Heritage Convention that it had signed up to 1981 (Allan and Aroney, 2008, p 245). This effectively cemented the principle that the commonwealth could use its foreign affairs head of power to make policy in areas of state responsibility as diverse as human rights and industrial relations. The Court also read other heads of power, such as the corporations power (s 51(xx)), expansively. In this way, concurrency, the overlap of roles and responsibility, was established.

Australia's constitutional arrangements did not extend to local government, however. This third tier remained a legislative creation of state governments that has effectively limited its scope and financial base, despite its increasing role in delivering 'services to people' (Dollery et al, 2006, 555).

Federalism and public policy

In this section we briefly survey the ways in which Australian governments have responded to the federal system. We begin by looking at the constraints before considering the opportunities.

Federalism's capacity to limit innovation and frustrate policy making is a well-accepted truism in theory and practice. The jurist H.V. Dicey believed federalism could operate to contain dangerous radical ideas and prevent them from infecting the nation as a whole (Patapan, 1997, pp 262–3). Federalism offered a way of 'restraining the leviathan' by dividing the state power and thereby limiting its capacity to intervene in the private lives of citizens (Fenna, 2012, p 587). Critics argue this has meant national governments have been able to achieve less than their unitary counterparts, especially in areas such as environmental protection and welfare. Weibust (2009, p 3), for example, argues that centralising environmental policy making produces higher levels of environmental protection (all other things being equal). Similarly, Obinger, Castles and Leibfried (2005, pp 3–4) canvass arguments that federalism has acted as an impediment to the development of the traditional welfare state demonstrating lower levels of expenditure and delays in the introduction of programmes. The subnational units in a federation do not necessarily pick up this slack because they are perpetually concerned at putting themselves at a competitive disadvantage vis-à-vis their neighbours, the 'race to the bottom'. Under cover of preventing totalitarianism, federalism has allowed economic interests and local tyrannies to consolidate power (Maddox, 1973, p 95).

In Australia, the Australian Labor Party (ALP) long opposed the federal structure (Galligan and Mardiste, 1992, p 73). For Labor, federalism, with its emphasis on pluralism and minority rights, sat uneasily with its core values of collectivism and utilitarianism. Labor's conception of democracy was majoritarian and the Party had little truck with the championing of minority rights that was part and parcel of federalism. It also married economic modernisation with social conservatism, running counter to Labor's social reformism (Heuglin and Fenna, 2006). In Labor's view, federalism allowed the will of the majority to be subverted by a minority. Hence, Labor has generally favoured a unitary system with a unicameral legislature.

The ALP's position on federalism could not but be reinforced by the Federal Party's experience in government. In the years after World War II, Australia's federal structure served to frustrate the Chifley Government's reform agenda, that envisioned a reconstructed Australia managed by a powerful central government with extensive economic and social powers. The electorate, however, convincingly rejected the 14 Powers Referendum of 1944, which sought to increase the commonwealth's power over employment, housing, health and welfare (Waters, 1969, p 43). Further rejections followed in 1946 and 1948.

In the early 1970s, the Whitlam Labor Government also found federalism a barrier to implementing its reform agenda. Whitlam maintained that federalism was inimical to social democracy, which demands, 'that a *national government* has a direct responsibility to intervene in the distribution of wealth and incomes and social benefits, in order to distribute them more equally and justly' (Whitlam, 1976). Whitlam sought to enhance the commonwealth's power through (unsuccessful) referenda (Starr, 1977, pp 14–16); the expansion of SPPs; and engaging directly with regional and local bodies (Gillespie, 1994, pp 77–8). Such actions generated considerable opposition from the states and ultimately helped bring the government down.

While the Hawke Government adopted a less oppositional approach to working with the states, it still had to find ways to work with them to continue the federation project of building a truly national economy in an increasingly challenging global environment, and promoting horizontal equity in social welfare. In the early 1990s, for example, the commonwealth had to deal with the states to introduce the 1995 National Competition Policy, a microeconomic reform package which rewarded the states for repealing anticompetitive regulation and promoting corporatisation and competition in public utilities and other public services.

This central government frustration with federalism has not been restricted to non-Labor governments. According to Robert Menzies (cited in Page, 2007, p 7), the party's founder, federalism 'protects a measure of individual freedom by not giving us one set of rules'. It was consistent with his party's other commitments to contained government, individual freedoms and regional rights. Despite its tradition of in principle support, however, Liberal governments also chaffed against the restrictions federalism imposed. Successive commonwealth governments managed to achieve much of their policy agenda in the 1950s and 1960s through an increasingly expansive use of SPPs in areas such as housing, education, health, rural development and transport (Parker, 1977, p 41); they were also frustrated particularly in relation to economic management and national development (Tiver, 1976, p 161). Federalism was also sensitive politically and mismanagement of commonwealth state relations could be extremely damaging. It was, for example, one of the factors that contributed to the downfall of Prime Minister John Gorton, who refused to pay lip service to federalist principles.

Prime Minister John Howard has also railed against Australia's federal system, declaring at one point, 'If we were starting Australia all over again, I don't think we ought to have states' (Grattan, 1991, p 5). Although derived from his values and beliefs (Hollander, 2008), his experiences dealing with the states would have undoubtedly helped to consolidate this view. In 1996, for example, in the aftermath of a mass shooting in Tasmania, he proposed that the hotchpotch of state laws be replaced by a common framework which standardised arrangements, also imposed tougher controls on ownership, and banned some types of weapons outright. He could only achieve this through tough negotiating and threats of constitutional change (Hollander, 2008, p 91).

Nor were the states always content with their position within the federation. Although empowered to act in many policy areas, they were constrained by their lack of financial autonomy (Starr, 1977, 18) and continued to periodically press for the return of income taxing powers. In 1970, they presented the commonwealth with a petition requesting that they gain direct access to income tax (Matthews and Jay, 1972, p 248). However, when Prime Minister Fraser offered them the opportunity they declined to take it up (Wilkinson, 2003, p 9). Nor has state dissatisfaction with funding models subsided, despite the introduction of a Goods and Services Tax (GST) in 2000.

This familiar depiction of a conflicted and underachieving policy landscape is only part of the story. Somewhat ironically, the very characteristics which confound the critics also provide opportunities for progressive policy development. The smaller scale, which allows capture, can also translate into responsiveness and a greater receptivity to minority voices that might be overwhelmed in a larger polity. Federalism can provide policy makers with an opportunity to craft policy acceptable to particular constituencies, and more directly responsive to local concerns (Kincaid, 1995). This sensitivity is especially helpful in matters concerning morality, where it can be harder to promote an incremental approach because of its black and white nature (Young, 2005). Mooney (2000), for example, argues that it allows communities to promote the more liberal policies on abortion that would be unacceptable to their more conservative neighbours. Of course, this also means that it allows the persistence of *less* liberal laws, as became evident in Queensland in 2010 when a young couple were charged with seeking to procure a home abortion (Hollander, 2011, 2).

Has this positive potential been realised in practice? The Australian evidence is somewhat sparse, partly because of the absence of the kind of systematic research that is required to establish the case. Nevertheless, there is support for the claim that Australia's federal system has supported progressive policies. First, it has provided the space for state governments to pursue their own distinctive reform agendas. In the 1930s, both Victoria and South Australia set up public housing authorities, an initiative later funded by the commonwealth. Between the late 1960s and early 1980s state governments in South Australia, Victoria and New South Wales (NSW) pursued reform in both policy and administrative practices under Premiers Dunstan, Hamer and Wran (Parkin, 2003:106). Various governments have continued to set the pace at various points in diverse areas including environmental protection, relationship equality and justice (See for example Hollander, 2010; Chappell and Costello, 2011; Rundle, 2011). This is not to deny that they have also, at different times, dragged their feet or actively pursued regressive policy stances, embracing both social conservatism and neoliberal principles and practices, nor that any such progressive achievements were a product of a federal system per se.

Similarly, the flip side of federalism's ability to quarantine radicalism is the potential for policy learning. United States Supreme Court Justice, Louis Brandeis, did much to promote the idea of laboratory federalism. He saw his country's federal structure as a mechanism for resolving pressing problems because it provided secure venues for 'political and social invention' and thus could afford both positive and negative examples of policy performance (Steiner, 1983, p 21). These could then be adopted, adapted or rejected by other states. In Australia, scholars such as Chappell (2001) and Painter (1991) have examined the ways that policy ideas originating in one state have been taken up by others.

The advantage of 'quarantining' has also been evident. For example, in the 1980s, a newly elected Victorian Government embraced an ambitious State Economic Strategy. The Strategy involved identifying and actively supporting areas of competitive strength through such things as cheap energy and finance. Proponents recommended that it be adopted by other jurisdictions in Australia and beyond (Richardson, 1984). Ultimately the Strategy was not a success; it contributed to the burgeoning state debt and the forced sale of the state's bank. It was perhaps fortunate the advice was not heeded.

The states have also influenced the national agenda more directly. Keddie and Smith (2009) show Victoria's leadership was instrumental in the development of the 2006 National Reform Agenda (NRA). The NRA built on the earlier National Competition Policy (NCP), but where NCP focused on economic deregulation, the NRA introduced a human capital dimension by focusing on improving health and skill outcome (Carroll et al, 2008).

The concurrency we find in a federal system is not necessarily negative either. Although one level of government can not usually simply override the other, the overlap can provide safeguards and also opportunities for a broader variety of interest groups to influence that policy process because of the existence of 'multiple and competing venues for policy making' (Baumgartner and Jones, 1991, p 1046). Indeed, Kincaid (1995) argues that one of federalism's great strengths is it '… offers citizens multiple points of access to public power [and] opportunities to appeal to other governments on certain matters when one is unresponsive'.

Evidence of this can be found in Australia's environmental protection record. Many of the environmental success stories of the past three decades have been achieved because of the overlapping powers that exist between commonwealth and state governments. While many, such as protection for the Great Barrier Reef, the wet tropics in North Queensland and areas of Tasmanian wilderness, can be attributed to commonwealth intervention, others, including the cessation of logging in Western Australia's old growth Karri forests or protection of remnant woodland in southeast Queensland were state government initiatives undertaken in the face of commonwealth opposition (Hollander, 2004, 2010).

Our federal system has not necessarily been a barrier to progressive policy making and has even facilitated it at times. However, its capacity to continue to do so is being challenged by accelerating centralisation.

Increasing centralisation

Federations are inherently unstable, subject to both centripetal and centrifugal forces. In Australia, the dominant trend has always been towards centralisation but this has become progressively more pronounced. Between 1996 and 2007, the Howard Government embraced a set of strategies that strengthened the hand of the commonwealth vis-à-vis the states. This centralisation had four dimensions. The first dimension, that of 'fiscal federalism', focused on the GST. Although touted as a state tax – the revenue was to flow to the states – it was, in reality, a commonwealth tax and it remained within the remit of the commonwealth to adjust both overall quantum and the share each state received (Parkin and Anderson, 2007, pp 298–300).

The second dimension, 'regulatory federalism', concerns the way the commonwealth has utilised a rule based approach, supplemented by financial incentives, to ensure state government compliance (Parkin and Anderson, 2007, pp 300–4). This was clearly evident in the drafting of tied grants, where the old 'soft' mechanisms of oversight and enforcement were replaced with tough performance and reporting standards (Hollander, 2006, 2012). The new approach adopted the techniques and tools of new public management, with its emphasis on audit and evaluation, and control of activities through explicit rules and standards, invariably overseen by external bodies (Moran, 2002). The National Competition Council, established to oversee implementation of NCP, provided the model, largely replicated by the COAG Reform Council established in 2007 to report on progress in programme implementation.

The third, 'program federalism', points to the way the commonwealth effectively tightened the conditionality of tied grants, justifying such actions with appeals to the 'national interest' (Parkin and Anderson, 2007, pp 304–6). As we have seen, the nature of Australian federalism means the commonwealth has always intervened in areas of state government responsibility. Traditionally, however, Lingard (2000, p 27) argues this intervention focused on filling gaps and remedying failures. It related specifically to *commonwealth* policy objectives and did not fundamentally change the ways in which the states delivered services. However, over the decades, the commonwealth engagement increasingly focused on the implementation of *national* frameworks aimed at creating uniformity. The transformation is evident in education, for example, where commonwealth engagement has shifted from measures such as providing additional resources for disadvantaged schools in the 1970s, to the implementation of meta-policies around schooling for girls and Indigenous education in the 1980s (Lingard, 2000, p 42), to detailed prescriptions of reading targets, spelling strategies and maths testing in the 1990s and beyond (Stewart, 2005, p 482). Finally, 'parallel federalism' focused on the commonwealth's practice of bypassing the states altogether and instead channelling funds directly to local governments, community groups and other organisations (Parkin and Anderson, 2007, pp 306–8).

Centralisation largely continued apace under Prime Ministers Rudd and Gillard despite the former's promise to usher in a new era in intergovernmental cooperation and 'end the blame game' (McQuestin, 2012), and allow the states more autonomy in the implementation of national goals. In a major reform of commonwealth state financial arrangements, the commonwealth reduced the number of tied grants from approximately 90 to just 5, each linked to a National Agreement which set out agreed objectives along with outputs, outcomes and performance indicators. At the same time, however, the commonwealth entered into allied arrangements known as National Partnership Agreements. Unlike the broad National Agreements, which were long term, large scale and broadly based, the Partnership Agreements focused on specific shorter-term deliverables, often with incentive or reward payments attached. Depending on their nature, they could involve one or more states and ranged from single site water recycling or desalination plants to national pre-apprenticeship training programmes. The danger is that these simply replicate the problems of the past (Twomey, 2009, p 21). Nor was the GST, the so-called state tax, sacrosanct. When the states dallied in committing to his health package, Rudd threatened to claw back GST funds (Fenna, 2012, p 8). Is this increasing centralisation and homogeneity inevitable? The next section considers some proposals for reform.

Rebalancing the federation

The Australian federation has never presented a neat three-tiered division of powers and its governments have always been closely intertwined. Therefore, reform must include a strategy for improving the relationship between them. For scholars and practitioners this has meant reforming COAG. COAG has no formal constitutional status. Established in 1992, it emerged out of the New Federalism of the late 1980s, replacing the often fractious and unproductive annual Premiers Conferences. At the time, it represented significant cultural and institutional change (Carroll and Painter, 1995, p 9; Keating and Wanna, 2000, p 152). In contrast with the tight deadlines and unequal participation of traditional financial Premiers' Conferences, COAG meetings involved considerable preparation and negotiation by both commonwealth and state officials (Edwards and Henderson, 1995, pp 23–4; Keating and Wanna, 2000, pp 137–8). Moreover, unlike Premiers' Conferences, the commonwealth could not adopt its usual 'take or leave it' stance, but instead was forced to bargain with the states to achieve agreement. Another innovation was the inclusion of local government through a representative of the peak organisation, the Australian Local Government Association.

The commonwealth's early enthusiasm for COAG was not sustained (Stewart, 2000) and the infrequency of meetings reinforced this impression – only four were held between 1996 and 2001. It looked as though COAG would only operate when the commonwealth wanted to engage in policy areas for which it needed state cooperation. Part of the problem was that prime ministers were responsible for convening meetings and controlled the agenda. In addition, the secretariat was located within their department. In 2002, the then Queensland Premier, Peter Beattie (2002, p 59) stressed, to function effectively as an intergovernmental forum, COAG needed a routinised meeting schedule, a standardised agenda to which all parties would contribute, and a well staffed, representative secretariat. Others have gone further; Kildea and Lynch (2011) argue that COAG needs formal constitutional recognition if it is to escape domination by the Prime Minister and also become more transparent and accountable.

Fiscal reform must also be explored if the trend towards centralisation is to be slowed. Eccleston (2008) suggests that there are four ways in which the states could reduce their direct dependence on the commonwealth. First, they could explore ways to expand their own revenue base by increasing existing taxes and charges, although the political and economic costs of raising taxes on property, payroll or gambling would likely exceed any financial benefit. Second, they could advocate for an increase in the GST, although this also comes at significant cost. Third, the commonwealth could give the states a fixed share of existing commonwealth taxes, a move not without precedent. Finally, the states could relinquish some of their activities.

If the states transferred responsibility for the public hospital system to the commonwealth, they would be financially better off in the long term because of rapidly rising costs.

The states need to make the most of opportunities to contribute to policy making through organisations such as the Council for the Australian Federation (CAF). The states established CAF in 2006, with the aims of promoting constructive engagement with the commonwealth; developing and sharing innovative policy solutions; and providing leadership in areas of common concern (Tiernan, 2009, p 127). CAF's early achievements were considerable. It made major contributions to a range of policy areas, including climate change, regulatory reform, and health. It subsequently struggled to maintain its early momentum in the face of partisan differences between member governments; changing personalities; and new priorities (Menzies, 2012, pp 66–9). Despite this, CAF has demonstrated, with renewed commitment, that the states can play a more significant role.

In addition, we also need to explore ways to engage at the local level, embracing the shift from local *government* to local *governance*. Such a move involves more than formal constitutional recognition of local government, but instead demands we reconceptualise the role of government at all levels to prioritise community engagement and multilevel decision making (Geddes, 2005). It also means stepping away from the functional approach that has characterised the organisation of government for the delivery of services and adopting a spatially based approach that relies on a 'whole of *governments*' effort (Lawson and Gleeson, 2005). Of course, this will necessitate a renegotiation of the precepts of contemporary managerialism, with its emphasis on rigid auditing and upward reporting, and a greater emphasis on outcomes rather than process. Finally, we need to consider ways to ensure that diversity does not allow injustices to persist. In other federations, such as the United States, this dilemma has been addressed through a bill of rights which establishes a framework for constraining diversity within mutually agreed and commonly accepted norms, thereby making it possible to have one's cake (equity) and eat it (diversity).

Conclusion

This chapter has argued that Australia's federal structure need not be a barrier to progressive policy developments. Federalism acts as a constraint, and, as with any set of rules which limit power, is a mixed blessing, hampering progressive governments at both commonwealth and state level because the commonwealth lacks the constitutional authority to engage directly in many areas of policy making, particularly those relating to social policy, while the states are constrained by their financial dependence on the commonwealth. However, these limitations can also constrain governments wishing to prosecute a neoliberal agenda. This essentially conservative dimension may be complemented by the potential federalism offers for policy experimentation and learning, and for the enhanced opportunities for interest group engagement. Such opportunities, however, are undermined by the accelerating trend towards centralisation, whereby the power of the commonwealth is enhanced at the expense of the states. Any scope for autonomy is further eroded by managerialism, with its emphasis on regulation and audit. Can this trend be moderated to provide space of a reinvigorated federalism? The answer, in the short term, may lie in further fiscal reform; formal recognition and restructuring of COAG; and a recommitment by the states to active leadership. More profound solutions may lie in renewed effort in community building and revisiting the debate around an Australian Bill of Rights.

References

Allan, J. and Aroney, N. (2008) 'An uncommon Court: How the High Court of Australia has undermined Australian federalism', *Sydney Law Review*, vol 30, pp 245-94

Baumgartner, F.R. and Jones, B.D. (1991) 'Agenda dynamics and policy subsystems', *The Journal of Politics*, vol 53 no 4, pp 1044-74

Beattie, P. (2002) 'The immediate challenge regarding COAG reform', *Australian Journal of Public Administration,* vol 61, no 4, pp57–59

Carroll, P., Deighton-Smith, R., Silver H. and Walker, C. (2008) 'The national reform agenda: origins and objectives', Silver, H. (ed) *Minding the Gap: Appraising the promise and performance of regulatory reform in Australia*, Canberra: ANU E Press, pp 63-72

Carroll, P. and Painter, M. (1995) 'The federal politics of microeconomic reform', in Carroll, P. and Painter M (eds), *Microeconomic Reform and Federalism*, Canberra: Federalism Research Centre, ANU

Chappell, L. (2001) 'Federalism and social policy: the case of domestic violence', *Australian Journal of Public Administration*, vol 60, no 1, pp 59–69

Chappell, L. and Costello, M. (2011) 'Australian federalism and domestic violence policy-making', *Australian Journal of Political Science*, vol 46, no 4, pp 633-650

Constitution Act 1900 (Cwlth), www.austlii.edu.au/au/legis/cth/consol_act/coaca430/

Dollery, B. Wallis J. and Allan, P. (2006) 'The debate that had to happen but never did: The changing role of Australian local government', *Australian Journal of Political Science*, vol 41, no 4, pp 553-67

Eccleston, R. (2008) 'Righting Australia's vertical fiscal imbalance: transferring public hospital funding as an option for reform,' *Agenda*, vol 15, no 3, pp 39-52

Edwards, M. and Henderson, A. (1995) 'CoAG – A vehicle for reform' in Carroll, P. and Painter, M. (eds), *Microeconomic Reform and Federalism*, Canberra: Federalism Research Centre, ANU

Fenna, A. (2012) 'Centralising dynamics in Australian federalism,' *Australian Journal of Politics and History*, vol 58, no 4, pp 580-90

Gallingan, B. and Mardiste, D. (1992) 'Labor's reconciliation with federalism' *Australian Journal of Political Science*, vol 27, no 1, pp 71-86.

Geddes, M. (2005) 'International perspectives and policy issues,' in Smyth, P., Reddel, T. and Jones, A. (eds), *Community and Local Governance in Australia*, Sydney: UNSW Press

Gillespie, J. (1994) 'New federalisms' in Brett, J. Gillespie, J. and Goot, M. (eds), *Developments in Australian Politics*, South Melbourne: Macmillan

Grattan, M. (1996) 'PM lashes culture of negativity', *The Age*, 6 July, p 5

Heuglin, T. and Fenna, A. (2006) *Comparative Federalism: A Systematic Inquiry*, Quebec: Broadview Press

Hollander, R. (2004) 'Changing Places? Commonwealth and State government performance and Regional Forest Agreements', paper presented at the Australasian Political Science Association Conference, University of Adelaide, 29 September–1 October

Hollander, R. (2006) 'National Competition Policy, regulatory reform and Australian Federalism', *Australian Journal of Public Administration*, vol 65, no 2, pp 33-47

Hollander, R (2008) 'John Howard, economic liberalism, social conservatism, and Australian federalism', *Australian Journal of Politics and History*, vol 53, no 1, pp 85-103

Hollander, R. (2010) 'Rethinking overlap and duplication: Federalism and Environmental Assessment in Australia', *Publius*, vol 40, no 1, pp 136-70

Hollander, R. (2011) 'Federalism and the moral policy dilemma', paper presented to Australian Political Studies Association Conference, Canberra, September 26-28.

Hollander R. (2012) 'Using Regulation to Effect Constitutional Change: the Case of Higher Education,' in Kildea, P., Lynch, A. and Williams, G. (eds), *Tomorrow's Federation*, Annandale: Federation Press

Hollander, R. and Patapan, H. (2007) 'Pragmatic federalism', *Australian Journal of Public Administration,* vol 66, no 3, pp 280-97

Keating, M. and Wanna, J. (2000) 'Remaking federalism?', in Keating, M., Wanna, J. and Weller, P. (eds), *Institutions on the Edge? Capacity for Governance,* St Leonards, NSW: Allen & Unwin, pp 126-55

Keddie, J.N. and Smith, R.F.I. (2009) 'Leading from below: how subnational governments influence policy agendas', *Australian Journal of Public Administration,* vol 68, no1, pp 67–82

Kildea, P. and Lynch, A. (2011) 'Entrenching "Cooperative Federalism": Is it time to formalise COAG's place in the Australian federation?', University of New South Wales Faculty of Law Research Series Paper 26

Kincaid, J. (1995) 'Values and value tradeoffs in federalism', *Publius ,* vol 25, no 2, pp 29-44

Lawson, S. and Gleeson, B. (2005) 'Shifting urban governance in Australia' in Smyth, P., Reddel, T. and Jones, A. (eds), *Community and Local Governance in Australia,* Sydney: UNSW Press

Lingard, B. (2000) 'Federalism in schooling since the Karmel Report (1973), Schools in Australia: from modernist hope to postmodernist performativity' *Australian Educational Researcher,* vol 27, no 2, pp 25-61

Maddox, G. (1973) 'Federalism: or government frustrated,' *The Australian Quarterly,* vol 45, no 3 pp 92-100

Matthews, R. (1977) 'Revenue sharing and Australian federalism' *Politics,* vol 12 no 2, pp 43-54

Mathews, R.L. and Jay, W.R.C. (1972) *Federal Finance: Intergovernment Financial Relations in Australia since Federation,* Sydney: Nelson

McQuestin, M.-A. (2012) 'Federalism under the Rudd and Gillard Governments' in Kildea, P., Lynch, A. and Williams, G. (eds), *Tomorrow's Federation,* Annandale: Federation Press

Menzies, J. (2012) 'The Council for the Australian Federation and the ties that bind' in Kildea, P., Lynch, A. and Williams, G. (eds), *Tomorrow's Federation,* Annandale: Federation Press

Mooney, C.Z. (2000) 'The decline of federalism and the rise of morality-policy conflict in the United States', *Publius,* vol 30, no 1/2, pp 171-88

Moran, M. (2002) 'Review article: Understanding the regulatory state', *British Journal of Political Science,* vol 32, no 2, pp 391-413

Obinger, H., Castles, F.G. and Leibfried, S. (2005) 'Introduction', in Obinger, H., Leibfried, S. and Castles, F.G. (eds) *Federalism and the Welfare State: New World and European Experiences,* Cambridge: Cambridge University Press

Page, B. (2007) 'A federalist paradox: liberalism, conservatism and the Howard government', Paper delivered at 2007 APSA conference, Melbourne: September

Painter, M. (1991) 'Policy diversity and policy learning in a federation: the case of Australian state betting law', *Publius,* vol 21, no 1, pp 143-157

Parker, R.S. (1977) 'Political and administrative trends in Australian federalism', *Publius,* vol. 7, no 1, pp 35-52

Parkin, A. (2003) 'The states, federalism and political science: a fifty-year appraisal', *Australian Journal of Political Science,* vol 62, no 2, pp 101–12

Parkin, A. and Anderson, G. (2007) 'The Howard government, regulatory federalism and the transformation of commonwealth–state relations', *Australian Journal of Political Science,* vol 42, no 2, pp 295-314

Patapan, H. (1997) 'The author of liberty: Dicey, Mill and the shaping of the English constitution', *Public Law Review,* vol 4, no 8, pp 256-267

Richardson, C. (1984) 'A state economic strategy for sustainable growth', Paper prepared for the 13th Conference of Economists, Perth, WA, August

Rundle, O. (2011) 'An examination of relationship Registration Schemes in Australia', *Australian Journal of Family Law,* vol 25, pp 121-52

Smyth, P., Reddel, T. and Jones, A. (eds) (2005) *Community and Local Governance in Australia,* Sydney: UNSW Press

Starr, G. (1977) 'Federalism as a political issue: Australia's two "New Federalisms"', *Publius,* vol 7, no 1, pp 7-26

Steiner, E.E. (1983) 'Progressive Creed: the experimental federalism of Justice Brandeis', *Yale Law and Policy Review,* vol 2, no 1, pp 1-48

Stewart, J. (2000) 'The Howard government and federalism: the end of an era?' in Singleton, G. (ed), *The Howard Government: Australian Commonwealth Administration 1996–1998,* Sydney: UNSW Press

Stewart, J. (2005) 'Educational policy: politics, markets and the decline of 'publicness', *Policy & Politics,* vol 33, no 3, pp 475-87

Tiernan, A. (2009) 'The Council for the Australian Federation: a new structure of Australian federalism', *Australian Journal of Public Administration,* vol 67, no 2, pp 122–134

Tiver, P. (1976) 'The Ideology of the Liberal Party of Australia: A sketch and interpretation', *Australian Journal of Political Science,* vol 11, no 2, pp 156-164

Twomey, A. (2009) 'The Future of Australian Federalism – Following the Money', *Australasian Parliamentary Review,* vol 24, no 2, pp 11–22

Waters, W.J. (1969) 'The opposition and the "powers" referendum, 1944', *Australian Journal of Political* Science, vol 4, no 1, pp 42–56

Weibust, I. (2009) *Green Leviathan: The Case for a Federal Role in Environmental Policy,* Farnham Surrey: Ashgate

Whitlam, G. (1976) 'The Labor government and the constitution', Opening Federal Anniversary Seminar, Faculty of Law, University of Melbourne, 6 August

Wilkinson, J. (2003) 'Horizontal fiscal equalisation', Briefing Paper 21/03, NSW Parliamentary Library Research Service

Young, E.A. (2005) 'The Conservative Case for Federalism,' *George Washington Law Review,* vol 74, pp 874–88

NINETEEN

Citizen engagement in Australian policy making

Chris Miller

*If liberty and equality ... are chiefly to be found in
democracy they will be best attained when all persons
alike share in the government to the utmost*
(Aristotle)

*Life has become a show at which we are the
audience – and have to buy a ticket*
(Beppe Grillo, leader of the
Italian 5 Star Movement (M5S))

Public and social policy are concerned with defining and responding to
public value which is always open to argumentation and contestation.
Australia currently faces numerous policy challenges, raising new
questions about public value. Many of the issues explored in earlier
chapters – climate change, population growth, the future of cities,
social welfare and the continuing 'gap' between Indigenous and non-
Indigenous Australians – highlight amongst other things uncertainties
about what constitutes public value and the complexities of building
robust policy responses to problems across this terrain.

This chapter argues that to address these uncertainties will require
going well beyond representative democracy to engage more directly
with citizens, embracing what Bently (2005) describes as 'everyday
democracy'. More sophisticated citizen deliberation and participation
is essential, not only for better policy outcomes, but also to rebuild
democratic practices in contemporary society (Mouffe, 2005).
Cornwall (2008) identifies three reasons why participatory democracy
should be extended: it produces more democratic government, more
responsive and engaged citizens, and more efficient and effective
programmes and policies.

In many ways, the engagement of the Australian citizen in political
and policy processes is weak in comparison with experience in

other Western democracies, particularly the European ones. This weakness is, in part, a complex product of the nation's colonial past, its emergence from separate states, the structure of its federal political system, the character of its continuing and increasingly diverse inward migration, and the profound schism between European and Indigenous Australians. The failure of existing political arrangements, the increasingly evident need to respect the diversity of Australian society and culture, and the need to respond creatively to more complex public problems requires the rebuilding and strengthening of Australian citizenship and political participation from the bottom up.

Current uncertainties about future directions of policy are too serious to be left to politicians and the increasingly swollen ranks of a professional political elite. Australia once regarded itself as leading the way in extending democracy, yet today appears more than ever governed by a narrow and exclusive network of elites – politicians, public servants, private consultants, think-tanks, lobby groups, academics and media commentators. The citizen is left playing the role of onlooker or bystander. This is not to dismiss the role and use of expert or elite knowledge in political debate and policy making. Indeed, this role could be much improved, as argued recently in the Australian Academy of Sciences publication, *Live Within Earth's Limits* (Gifford et al, 2010). Rather it is to argue that the significant behavioural change needed for sustainable policy solutions in contemporary Australia will become embedded only after a broad-based process of thoughtful, informed and reflexive dialogue and argumentation involving more elaborate processes of citizen participation and engagement. For this to occur, the role and place of the 'public intellectual', critically engaged with the wider population on social, cultural, political, environmental and economic issues, and their associates, the 'informed community' and a 'public conversation', need to be resurrected and better respected, connections perhaps best made in Donald Horne's vision of the public sphere (Davis, 2010). In the process Australians might halt what David McKnight described (2009) as the decline of a sense of the 'common good' and discover a new 'social philosophy' capable of taking them through the 21st century. While there has been much talk about social capital and interest in the concept of the 'Big Society' (Whelan, 2012), as well as longstanding recognition of the challenges of 'wicked' policy issues, there has been much less commitment to expanding the influence of citizens in policy making (although see Smyth et al, 2005). As Wills and Nash (2012) argue, 'meaningfully involving people in political decisions that determine the quality of their lives' (p 9) is the key challenge facing Australian governments in the 21st century.

Dryzek (2008) identifies three essential prerequisites for participatory democracy: an extension of the franchise to ensure citizens are capable of participating effectively, extending the scope of issues on which citizens are engaged, and extending the degree of authenticity within any act of engagement. Since the 1970s there have also been similar calls for greater 'democratic' policy and programme evaluation. These were led initially by American programme evaluators, acting in response to what was perceived as a widening gap between policy and political discourse and the experiences of the citizen. This turn to democratic evaluation, in which policy effectiveness is judged more by the experience of citizens on whom it impacts, produces a proliferation of narratives and more diverse possibilities about how new policies should respond. It contrasts with mainstream evaluation that is more a 'creature of policy' and often closely supervised by those who fund such evaluations. Traditional expert dominated evaluation can leave citizens denied agency over what is public value, 'squeezed out of politics' and replaced by the 'intensification of single political narratives that brook no argument and which suppress dissent' (Kushner, 2013). Any subsequent loss of trust in government only breeds cynicism and withdrawal from public life, further intensifying a 'decide and announce' approach to policy.

Water reform in the Murray-Darling Basin: a story of policy failure

By way of illustration of the kind of policy challenge that exemplifies the dilemmas Australians increasingly confront, the process of water reform in the Murray-Darling Basin, Australia's food basket is considered here. The basin stretches over a million square kilometres, 14% of the total area of Australia, contains Australian's three largest rivers, has a population of over two million people and its jurisdiction involves the Commonwealth, four states and the Australian Capital Territory (ACT). Water utilisation across the basin for an agricultural industry founded on extensive irrigation has been a longstanding problem. Too much water had been extracted for irrigation to the point where the sustainability of the basin itself was on the point of collapse. The challenge, as stated in the 2007 Water Act, was to determine how much water had to be diverted back to the environment to secure a healthy river system, but to do so in such a way as to minimise the impact on the livelihoods of basin communities. All political parties recognised the need for reform, as outlined in the 2004 National Water Initiative and subsequently in the 2007 Commonwealth Water Act and Water for the Future Program. Cross-party support was further underpinned with the earmarking of $11 billion for reform secured by the Howard Liberal Government and further extended by the Rudd and Gillard Labor Governments. Yet water reform has stumbled, and a sustainable environment has not been secured, in part because government failed to take account of the knowledge and expertise within basin communities and crucially failed to engage those communities in planning for a future with less water available for irrigation.

Water reform was construed as a struggle between two entrenched sides that called upon quite different rationalities. On the one hand, depending on one's position, were firstly the wasteful, prejudiced, privileged and ill-informed city dwellers, led by faceless Canberra bureaucrats who previously had never set a foot on farmland and, secondly, misguided and utopian environmentalists, dreaming of a basin in a pristine natural state, led by a combination of scientists and 'greens' willing to destroy whole communities on the basis of highly contestable 'expert' data. Alternatively, based on the best available scientific data, they were concerned about the basin's sustainability and the degradation caused by overirrigation. On the other hand, again depending on one's perspective, were the farmers, those long-serving and resilient custodians of the land, the real experts, whose forebears, with strong government encouragement, had 'settled' what was a harsh land, in what was a nation-building exercise, and who every day since, regardless of drought, flood or fire, delivered the nation's high-quality food basket. Alternatively, it was a self-serving, wealthy, and powerful farming lobby that was inefficient and wasteful in its irrigation practices, too casual in its disregard for the scarce resource it managed, over-subsidised, reluctant to reform and unwilling to face proven scientific evidence of the imminent collapse of the basin, and with it their own economic livelihoods, nor able to recognise that saving the basin meant that some communities with less water for irrigation would need to find an alternative source of livelihood.

Added to this mix were divisions within the farming community between those sympathetic to reform, who often felt silenced, and the majority steadfastly opposed. South Australian (SA) and Victorian farmers blamed excessive water use on their irrigation inefficient New South Wales (NSW) colleagues, while the latter, along with Queenslanders, argued that since the rivers rose in the east they alone should determine how much flowed west and south. There were competing narratives, too, between farmers and others living in the basin whose livelihoods were outside the industry, between new migrants and established families, alongside differences based on gender and age. Another divide existed between Adelaide, facing a shortage of domestic water and a major environmental disaster at the mouth of the Murray, the only point of exit into the ocean for the whole basin, and the relative lack of concern felt by the seemingly water-plenty citizens of Sydney and Melbourne. Finally, there were the muted voices of the 70,000 Indigenous people living in the basin, for whom water was a source of not only livelihood, cultural and recreational benefits, but also spiritual value (Grafton et al, 2010).

Between these opposing camps stood federal and state politicians, neither of whom displayed much political leadership. This was a Labor Federal Government cynical enough to calculate that there would be few additional votes to be gained from basin communities, and no seats were at risk as a result of any decisions taken. While these were ideal circumstances in which to be seen doing the 'right thing', the smarter option was thought to be to do as little as was necessary to move on. It was also a government criticised for earlier failures in policy implementation, leaving public servants no doubt fearful of further risk taking. Expediency was evident too in the reform package by the unwillingness to invest in a process to enable communities to explore how to secure a sustainable future with less water. While individual 'willing sellers' would benefit financially, paying off debts, possibly exiting from farming altogether and relocating elsewhere, basin communities were left to somehow secure an alternative livelihood.

The Murray-Darling Basin Authority (MDBA), a federal agency created by the Water Act 2007, was tasked to produce an evidence-based sustainable plan for the basin. The Authority undertook the required public consultation on its proposals, a process where its recommendations were derailed by widespread and orchestrated public protest. The Authority's failure to demonstrate basic skills in consultation processes and communication was harshly exposed. Community after community rejected both the proposals and the consultation, making clear their lack of faith in the policy process. This was nothing short of a public embarrassment for both the MDBA and the Federal Government, and led to the resignation of both the Authority's Chair and its CEO. Yet public engagement about the merits and impacts of, and responses to, a scientifically based plan, should be a political task and not one for a bureaucracy, especially one already discredited by previous consultation failures. The subsequent launch of a six-month, all-party Parliamentary Inquiry into the Socio-

Economic Impacts of Water Reform, with members drawn from those with basin constituencies and chaired by the former Independent MP Tony Windsor, with a mandate to listen to the concerns of basin residents, was a lesson learnt too late. Following the anger vented by basin communities, the result was only ever going to be one of retreating from the scientific evidence and offering bland and ultimately worthless reassurances to basin communities.

Throughout the process of producing the first draft basin plan prior to the consultation, little attention was given to the practice-based knowledge, expertise and experience of those living and working in the basin. No opportunities were provided to basin communities to discuss possible options for a sustainable future with less water, although informally there was much talk about the prospect and impact of change, while the complexities of social change went unacknowledged. In addition to expert or elite knowledge, sound public policy formulation needs to recognise non-formal, experiential, innate or practice-driven knowledge, a product of slow maturation over generations passed on largely through an oral tradition. Mature democracies recognise that this still leaves room for considerable uncertainty, on the boundary of knowing and not knowing, 'living on the edge of future time' (Keane, 2010, p 222).

In contrast, the former MDBA Chair was replaced by a NSW former Labor minister, considered better able to 'manage' well organised interest groups, committed to brokering a deal even if that meant a policy outcome that the best scientific evidence says will not produce a healthy river system. 'Evidence' was abandoned, new science was invented and independent peer reviewers denied access to the data, in what became a desperate attempt to remove water reform from the political agenda with the then anticipated forthcoming federal elections. Had water reform been a one-off, not to be repeated 'wicked issue', mishandled by a weak government already prone to gaffs in policy implementation, this could be written off as an example of policy failure to be rectified through the ballot box and its shortcomings addressed by the new more robust incumbents. However, beyond the particular failures of water reform there is a deeper problem. Despite the increasingly global interest in new forms of governance Australians show little appetite for such innovation. Further, the public service has lost the requisite skills, knowledge and capacities to undertake such work, although not long ago it could claim some leadership in community development and social planning (Weeks, Hoatson and Dixon, 2003).

From government to governance and citizen engagement

The global 'deliberative turn' from government to governance is not new and has been well documented (Rhodes, 1997). However, the practices associated with the governance movement are not well advanced in Australia, even if the processes of Australian public policy and public sector reform – more attention to community consultation in strategic planning exercises, public–private partnerships, contracting of government services to the non-profit sector – offer a genuflection in the direction of governance thinking being better associated with smaller government and reducing budgets than improved governance.

Governance is understood as a response to complexity, recognition that neither markets nor governments alone can solve contemporary issues. It is a reaction to a perceived democratic deficit, understood as a loss of citizen faith in political parties and the political system and to a need to relegitimise the state. Regime theorists (Stone, 1989) spoke of the capacity to govern in 'the midst of diversity and complexity', arguing for long-term collaborative coalitions involving government and non-governmental forces in which authority and resources are shared (Stoker, 1995). Such trust-based coalitions, in which participants would 'blend their capacities' (Stone, 1993, p 6), would include the community, the non-profit sectors and trade unions, as well as technical and professional experts (Stoker, 1995). During the last decade such rhetoric became commonplace across a range of policy domains (Forbrig, 2011). New governance 'spaces' have emerged for non-governmental actors to engage, and interest in 'citizen', 'community' and 'third sector' participation has spread globally, albeit with different expressions in different contexts, sometimes at the insistence of global institutions (Deacon, 2007; Cornwall, 2008).

Civil society strengthening has become a central plank of World Bank strategy and civil society participation is a requirement of poverty reduction strategies. United Nations frameworks for human rights, international donor priorities and solidarity networks also support greater democratic inclusion. Such pressures are driving changes in legislation, including constitutional rights that reframe the citizen–state relationship, creating political opportunity structures and new channels of access to public decision making (Tarrow, 1998). Two theoretical standpoints have emerged in response. For governance theorists this shift 'opens up new ways in which citizens can engage in the politics of localities and regions and participate in "project politics" on specific issues' (Newman, 2005, p.4). Cornwall (2004) argues that within government created 'invited spaces', into which non-governmental actors may enter without contention, there are opportunities for 'collaborative activity', and these are as much sites of 'contestation as consensus'. In addition are those 'popular spaces' generated from within civil society and into which governments might be invited. Yet the capacity of non-governmental actors to participate effectively as 'active subjects' (Morrison, 2000) will vary according to context, institutional frameworks and designs, personal capacities and dispositions, linkages with other actors, as well as organisational orientation and capacities (Cornwall, 2008; Howard et al, 2008; Miller et al, 2009). While from this perspective governance represents the 'ultimate in hands-off government' (Rhodes, 1997, p 110), the extent to which participation spaces offer a new vision of the public domain remains contested (Fung et al, 2003; Cornwall and Coelho, 2007).

By contrast, governmentality theory argues that what we are witnessing is a process whereby the state expands its reach and extends its power by governing through non-state institutions, thereby securing the compliance of willing subjects. Thus the non-government (NGO) sector is constructed as a 'governable terrain' (Carmel and Harlock, 2008) and 'community' transformed from a language of resistance into an expert discourse and professional vocation (Rose, 1999). By bringing non-governmental actors and the private sector into governance spaces, government can channel resources (skills, knowledge and networks) and extend further its control. Miller and Rose (2008) argue that 'each of these emergent political rationalities ... seeks a way of governing ... through instrumentalizing the self-governing properties of the subjects of government themselves in a whole variety of locales and localities – enterprises, associations, neighbourhoods, interest groups and, of course, communities' (p 111).

Deacon (2007), however, adopts a position that allows for both possibilities of greater citizen engagement and more extensive government control and concludes that such trends reflect 'the contested terrain of emerging global governance' (p 15), in which he includes both international non-governmental organisations and transnational social movements. Whether or not as intentional as governmentality theory implies, there is a well-documented history of citizen participation as an exercise in tokenism, designed to absorb, exhaust and blunt the criticisms of active citizens.

Similar arguments to those espousing governance, and especially the social and political risks of a disengaged public, are expressed in social capital theory with its emphasis on strong trust-based ties and relationships. They are also present within policy initiatives such as social inclusion, community capacity building, social entrepreneurialism or expanding the role of the non-profit sector (Mair and Ganly, 2010). All focus on the relationship between state and citizen, and the need to strengthen civil society and ensure deliberation and argumentation if democracy is to flourish while confronting complexity. A battery of well-tried methods are available to better engage citizens, including citizen juries and panels, planning for real exercises, deliberative forums, town meetings, citizen report cards, rapid and participatory appraisal, forum theatre, photovoice, deliberative polling and consensus conferences (Wills and Nash, 2012). Critics have highlighted how such approaches are often merely symbolic in intent, designed to better 'manage' dissent while ensuring that dominant interests continue to benefit at the expense of the majority (Mowbray, 2011). However, stifling or inhibiting argumentation is no guarantee that dissenting voices will not emerge elsewhere through the creation of popular spaces. While many invited spaces may fail to meet Dryzek's authenticity criterion, few are so tightly managed as to destroy agency, eliminate rule contestation and prevent voicing the unspeakable.

The attraction of localism

Closely associated with the need for enhanced democracy is the concept of 'localism'. Localism is the process by which governments devolve responsibilities, resources and autonomy for policy making and implementation to a local level. The adoption of a 'steering not rowing' approach still requires government to define the unit of localism, the limits of local autonomy, the degree of independence and oversight from central government and the nature and membership of local governance structures. Governments continue to provide the vision and strategic frameworks and to ensure that local structures meet the tests of good governance being accessible and inclusive. Paradoxically, localism requires a 'whole of government' approach, with greater coordination and collaboration between government departments as well as between the centre and the local. It also requires major cultural and practice changes. Equally, it does not absolve the centre from engaging with its publics in a deliberative dialogue to determine policy objectives. Localism requires a long-term commitment and acceptance of slow, incremental and uneven change, as well as a willingness to work with the tensions on the boundaries of jurisdictional authority (Young Foundation, 2006).

While localism has the potential to maximise citizen involvement, ownership and expertise, it is not a panacea. Few problems or their solutions are exclusively local. Contant and Leone de Nie (2009) point to the tendencies within localism for place-based competition, with little regard for the consequences of actions on neighbours, a failure to appreciate the 'big picture', and the introduction of regional inefficiencies through the pursuit of localised interests. Research in Canada, the UK and Australia has cautioned that there are both intrinsic and contextual limits and, within those limits, dilemmas and challenges to successful implementation, including the proliferation of overlapping local structures (Bradshaw, 2003; Markey et al, 2009; Mowbray, 2011).

Local knowledge and 'know how', while valuable, should not be privileged any more than other forms of knowledge. Not all solutions generated at a local level are likely to be feasible or to take sufficient account of the best available social and physical sciences. Localism does not, however, imply 'isolated' decision-making, but rather a network of local bodies working together, informing and being informed by each other. Localism does not mean leaving communities to fend for themselves, find solutions to what have been intractable dilemmas, make the tough decisions or manage any change process on their own. Localism does not mean governments shedding responsibilities. Rather it means working in partnership to share responsibility for better outcomes, built upon a deeper understanding of the possibilities and constraints in any situation. It offers a new dynamic, greater connectivity and evolving relationship between the local and the centre.

Localism is not unknown in Australia, including the ill-fated attempt by the Whitlam Government in relation to Social Assistance planning (Chapman, 1975). There is also a strong history of localism within natural resource management, including the various catchment management bodies, sometime excessively so, as in the 127 NSW resource management and catchment groups, reported in 1992, and currently evident in the national Regional Development Agencies. Indeed, a flurry of 'place-based' disadvantage programmes in Queensland and Victoria during the 1990s led Smyth et al (2005) to herald somewhat prematurely the arrival of a new model of 'associational governance'. Yet this was short-lived, and Australia continues to have a poor track record in comparison with some European countries, where localism is enshrined in law under the principle of subsidiarity, by which decisions are taken whenever possible at the lowest level of government, as close to the citizen as possible, and conversely those taken at higher levels have to be justified as absolutely necessary. In Brazil, municipalities have extended this principle to the local determination of spending priorities through community participatory budgeting.

Two of the most extensive recent Australian examples are found in Victoria and Queensland. In Victoria, the former Labor Government led by Steve Bracks, having experimented with a localist approach in the 1980s, spoke in its 1999 election platform about building stronger communities and on gaining office introduced its 'Community Capacity Building Initiative', underpinned by a ten-year vision statement, 'Growing Victoria Together' (Mowbray, 2011). Local governments across Victoria began to introduce more systematic 'community planning', while the 2003 Victoria Local Government Act stressed the need to 'take account of the diverse needs of the local community in decision-making'. In their evaluation of eleven community engagement initiatives West and Raysmith (2007) found widespread acceptance of the need for citizen engagement and greater commitment amongst local authorities to undertake community planning, along with better indicator tools to track developments, but also a need for better integration between state and local government.

The most comprehensive state-wide community engagement strategy is that found in the Queensland 'Community Engagement Improvement Strategy', launched in 2003–04 by the then Labor premier Peter Beattie, and continued by his successor Anna Bligh. This sought to embed community engagement across the public sector by ensuring all public servants could deliver the objectives via a range of methods and approaches. The government sought to 'tap into diverse perspectives and potential solutions to improve the quality of its decisions', involve citizens so as to strengthen 'the legitimacy and responsiveness of government, the quality of public policies and programs and the effectiveness of services' and create 'the basis for productive dialogue and ultimately better democracy' (Queensland Government, 2003). Its strategy involved taking government to the community via such mechanisms as regional parliaments, community cabinets, ministerial forums, e-petitions, a web-based single point of access to services and a 'Get Involved' website to encourage citizens. It also funded the on-line 'Community Door' resource clearing-house site for the community sector, managed by Queensland Council of Social Services (QCOSS), provided state officials with an extensive research-based set of data and advice to be used in community engagement practice, adopted the Organisation for Economic Cooperation and Development (OECD) 'engagement model' to distinguish between three levels of engagement – information giving, consultation and active participation – and required all departments to report on and be accountable for actions in community engagement. This was an ambitious strategy in opening up government by changing the public service culture and equipping the workforce with the rationale, knowledge, skills and evaluative tools to create 'invited spaces' for engagement. It has nevertheless been criticised for its one-sided approach, having no strategy for social inclusion and failing to give due recognition to the role of the community sector in enabling citizen engagement (QCOSS, 2009). A radical reform of the public service must be matched by support for civil society organisations to ensure citizens have the capacity to participate effectively.

Other examples of 'invited spaces' at state and local government levels have variously focused on whole of government responses, specific policy proposals or service provision consultations and evaluations (Wills and Nash, 2012). These include the Tasmanian government–civil society partnership, 'Tasmania Together', introduced in 1999, which is underpinned by legislation, funded by government, operates through community forums and surveys and includes an annual youth challenge. Other examples include: Western Australia's 'Dialogue with the city' (2003), a deliberative citizen–based process designed to engage citizens on how to make Perth the 'world's most livable city' by 2030, as well as its 'Consulting Citizens' agenda, established under the premiership of Geoff Gallop; the Far North Queensland Citizen's Jury (2000), focused on environmental impacts of future development of the Bloomfield Track; and Victoria's 'Advancing Country Towns Project' (2011), focused on nine remote and rural towns. There are also programmes such as the NSW 'Community Builder's Program', launched in 1998 and offering funding for community capacity building work. While valuable, such efforts lack national coherence, can be inconsistent within state boundaries and are over-dependent upon the party in office, the orientation of individual ministers and lead public servants. They are often created, as in Queensland and Tasmania, in response to public hostility or disillusionment as a mechanism to manage dissent rather than in acknowledgement that argumentation is fundamental to a vibrant democracy.

In addition there are examples of 'popular spaces' created from within civil society, including those supported by state governments, such as the Australian Women Against Violence Alliance or the Victorian Rural Women's Network. Initiatives such as the 'Citizen's Policy Juries' in Sydney and Tamworth (NSW) on electricity generation have been funded by private bodies such as the New Democracy Foundation. Practitioners and academics have facilitated other spaces, such as the community visioning exercises in various Victorian communities

(Kane, 2007; Mulligan, 2007). Another example is the broad-based campaigning 'Sydney Alliance', comprising civil society groups, faith-based organisations and trade unions, that emerged in 2009–10 and mirrors similar coalitions in North America and the UK (Tattersall, 2010). Across the country there is also a plethora of local community-based popular spaces that make for a rich and diverse civil society but often remain narrow in focus. Virtual spaces exist too with *Crikey*, the daily on-line newspaper running blogs on contemporary issues, while 'Get Up', a national on-line campaigning body, takes up a range of policy concerns through regular e-petitions. 'Get Up' is the sister organisation of 'MoveOn' (USA) and '38 Degrees' (UK), as well as being linked to the global group 'Avaaz'. These organisations follow a particular format in providing opportunities to respond to immediate concerns, but adopt the traditional methods of petitioning and lobbying MPs. While useful for defensive politics, little attention is given to deliberation and they are less effective at making policy. These are valuable additions to political life, often engaging young people for the first time and successful in their own terms, but not a substitute for deliberation.

Towards a policy programme

What might a deepening democracy programme look like? There are strong grounds for Australia following the lead of others and underpinning a policy of citizen engagement with mandatory legislation at all levels of government. To do so would require formal constitutional recognition and the strengthening of local government as a 'third and autonomous sphere of government' (Hearfield and Dollery, 2009; Mowbray, 2011) and the imposition of restrictions and transparency of corporate funding of political parties (Sawer, MacDermott and Kelly, 2010). State governments could be required to enhance community wellbeing and establish citizen forums to deliberate on questions of public value. Non-government and private agencies holding a government contract should be assessed and held accountable for policies and practices for service user engagement. Governments could have a duty placed upon them to provide civil society organisations with core funding, capped at an annually adjusted level, to support the infrastructure of popular spaces. Such actions would need to be underpinned by a thoroughgoing public service cultural shift, revised skills sets and new forms of leadership to undertake citizen engagement work (Wills and Nash, 2012). Such work would also require the recruitment of specialist practitioners located in strategic departments to support the development of public forums and encourage civil society organisations to build their own popular spaces.

If we return to Deacon's notion that this is a contested terrain, Australian civil society at present offers few signs of a revitalised democracy. Traditional bodies such as social movements, the brief exception of the 'Occupy Movement' notwithstanding, appear to have lost an organising capacity. Trade unions are weak, internally divided and discredited, while the Labor Party seems unwilling to democratise itself, although this may develop in the coming period. Without the revitalisation of extraparliamentary politics any formal government-led engagement will always tend towards the incorporation of the citizen. Presently, and despite the emergence of some new popular spaces, there is little sense that Australians are about to reclaim a place in the business of making policy, outside of elections. The deepening of democracy is not a priority for either the national or any of the state councils of social service. Non-government organisations are over-preoccupied with service delivery, maintaining their government contracts, strengthening the sector and securing recognition as professional bodies entitled to influence the policy making process. Few have robust structures to engage their own service users, or the wider community, in deliberations about policies and practice. Few invest in strategies for disadvantaged people to speak for themselves. Civil society may be rich in the number and diversity of organisations and in the level of participation in civil society, but this is largely an instrumental and competitive form of civil society that may make it less susceptible to governmentality tendencies but equally reluctant to recognise commonalities as each pursues its own interests (Miller et al, 2009). A vibrant civil society may give the appearance of the espoused 'Big Society' but it says little about the relationships between civil society, politics and power. Indeed it may obscure a relationship of being politically mugged while participating. Yet this forthcoming period might also be an opportunity for public intellectuals to take a more prominent role, not only through the media, including the rural and regional as well as national media, but also by creating opportunities or spaces for direct public engagement, informing, injecting ideas, encouraging dialogue, and facilitating policy making from the bottom up by building on such conversations. Politicians and elites seeking to protect privileged access to the policy process are often deeply uncomfortable when faced with an engaged citizenry, but ultimately a vibrant local democracy makes for better politics. Yet in a still dominant neoliberal, market-driven, individualistic, self-interested, celebrity and consumerist world, the challenge of how to re-invigorate values of solidarity, equity, social justice, interdependence and sustainability is guaranteed to be a slow process.

References

Bently, T. (2005) *Everyday Democracy: Why we get the Politicians we Deserve*, London: Demos

Bradshaw, B. (2003) 'Questioning the credibility and capacity of community-based resource management', *The Canadian Geographer* vol 47, no 2, pp 137-50

Carmel, E. and Harlock, J. (2008) 'Instituting the 'third sector' as a governable terrain: partnership, procurement and performance in the UK', *Policy & Politics*, vol 36, no 2, pp 155–71

Chapman, R.J.K. (1975) 'Australia's Assistance Plan: A study of ineffective planning', *Australian Journal of Social Issues*, vol 10 no 4 pp 283-298

Contant, C. and Leone de Nie, K. (2009) 'Scale matters: rethinking planning approaches across jurisdictional and sectoral boundaries', in Ross, C. (ed) *Megaregions: Planning for Global Competitiveness*, Washington: Island Press

Cornwall, A. (2008) *Democratizing Engagement: What the UK can Learn from International Experience*, London: Demos

Cornwall, A. (2004) 'New democratic spaces? The politics and dynamics of institutionalised participation', *IDS Bulletin*, vol 35, no 2, pp 1-10

Cornwall, A. and Coelho V.S. (2007) 'Spaces for change? The politics of participation in new democratic arenas', in Cornwall, A. and Coelho, V.S. (2007) (eds) *Spaces for Change? The Politics of Participation in New Democratic Arenas*, London: Zed Books, pp 1-32

Davis, G. (2010) 'The endless seminar: Making of a public man', *Griffith Review 28: Still the Lucky Country?*, Canberra: Griffith University, Autumn, pp 130-161

Deacon, B. (2007) *Global Social Policy and Governance*, London: Sage

Dryzek, J. (2008) *Deliberative Democracy and Beyond: Liberals, Critics, Contestation*, Oxford: Oxford University Press

Forbrig, J. (ed) (2011) *Learning for local democracy: A study of local citizen participation in Europe*, Central and East European Citizen's Network, CEECN

Fung, A. and Wright, E.O. (2003) *Deepening Democracy: Institutional Innovations in Empowered Participatory Governance*, London: Verso

Gifford, R.M., Steffen, W., Finnigan, J.J. and fellow members of the National Committee for Earth System Science (2010) *To Live Within Earth's Limits: An Australian Plan to Develop a Science of the Whole Earth System*, Canberra: Australian Academy of Science

Grafton, Q., Miller, C., Duvnjak, A., Jared, D., Jiang, Q., Nikolakis, W., Ryan, P., Verity, F., Ward, M. and Zutshi, M. (2010) *Potential Water Quality and Quantity Impacts in the Murray-Darling Basin from Communities and Industry responding to Climate Change*, Canberra: Murray-Darling Basin Authority

Hearfield, C. and Dollery, B. (2009) 'Representative democracy in Australian local government', in *Commonwealth Journal of Local Governance*, January, pp 61-75

Howard, J., Lever, J., Mateeva, A., Miller C., Petrov, R., Taylor, M., and Sera, L. (2008) *Participation in New Governance Spaces: The Importance of Habitus*, Paper presented at the Voluntary Sector Studies Network conference, University of the West of England, 14 May

Kane, J. (2007) 'The inspiring story of Coleraine's community bank', *Local-Global: Identity, Security, Community*, vol 4 pp 62-6

Keane, J. (2010) 'Out of the ordinary', *Griffith Review 28: Still the Lucky Country?* Brisbane, Griffith University, Autumn, pp 208-25

Kushner, S. (2013) 'The politics of austerity', Seminar paper presented at School for Policy Studies, Bristol University, July

Mair, J. and Ganly, K. (2010) 'Social Entrepreneurs: Innovating Toward Sustainability', in World Watch Institute (ed) *State of the World 2010: Transforming Cultures from Consumerism to Sustainability*, London: Earthscan, pp 103-9

Markey, S., Halseth, G. and Manson, D. (2009) 'Contradiction in hinterland development: Challenging the local development ideal in Northern British Columbia', *Community Development Journal*, vol 44 no 2, April, pp 209-29

McKnight, D. (2009) 'Thinking about a new progressive vision', CPD 'New Politics Seminar', Sydney, Centre for Policy Development, 29 November

Miller, C., with Howard, J., Mateeva, A., Petrov, R., Serra, L. and Taylor, M. (2009) 'Toward a typology of civil society: Understanding non-government action', in Enjolras, B. and Sivesind, K.H. (eds) 'Civil Society in Comparative Perspective', *Comparative Social Research, Vol 26*, Bingley: Emerald Group, pp 71-103

Miller, P. and Rose, N. (2008) *Governing the Present: Administering Economic, Social and Personal Life*, Cambridge: Polity

Morrison, J. (2000) 'The government-voluntary sector compacts: Governance, governmentality and civil society', *Journal of Law and Society*, vol 27, no 1, pp 98-132

Mouffe, C. (2005) *On the Political*, Oxford: Routledge

Mowbray, M. (2011) 'What became of the local state? Neoliberalism, community development and local government', *Community Development Journal*, vol 46, no S1, January, pp i132-i153

Mulligan, M. (2007) 'Creating community in a changing world', *Local-Global: Identity, Security, Community*, vol 4 pp 82-8

Newman, J. (2005) 'Introduction' in Newman, J. (ed) *Remaking Governance: People, Politics and the Public Sphere*, Bristol: Policy Press, pp 1-15

Queensland Council of Social Services (QCOSS) (2009) *QCOSS Policy Position: Poverty and Social Exclusion*, Brisbane, QCOSS, November

Queensland Government (2003) *Engaging Queenslanders: Get involved. Improving community engagement across the Queensland public sector*, Brisbane, Department of Communities

Rhodes, R.A.W. (1997) *Understanding Governance*, Buckingham, Open University Press

Rose, N. (1999) *Powers of Freedom: Reframing Political Thought*, Cambridge, Cambridge University Press, p 175

Sawer, M., MacDermott, K. and Kelly, N. (2010) 'Strengthening democracy', in Davis, M. and Lyons, M. (eds) *About more than Luck: Ideas Australia Needs Now*, Sydney: Centre for Policy Development Ltd

Smyth, P., Reddell, T. and Jones, A. (2005) (eds) *Community and local governance in Australia*, Sydney, NSW University Press

Stoker, G. (1995) 'Regime theory and urban politics', in Judge, D., Stoker, G. and Wolman, H. (eds) *Theories of Urban Politics*, London: Sage

Stone, C. (1989) *Regime Politics: Governing Atlanta 1946–1988*, Lawrence, KA: University Press of Kansas

Stone, C. (1993) 'Urban regimes and the capacity to govern: A political economy approach', *Journal of Urban Affairs*, vol 15, no 1, pp 1-28

Tarrow, S. (1998) *Power in Movement*, Cambridge, Cambridge University Press

Tattersall, A. (2010) *Power in Coalition: Strategies for Strong Unions and Social Change*, Crows Nest NSW: Allen & Unwin

Weeks, W., Hoatson, L. and Dixon, J. (eds) (2003) *Community Practices in Australia*, Sydney: Pearson

West, S. and Raysmith, H. (2007) *Planning Together: Lessons from Local Government Community Planning in Victoria*, Melbourne, Local Government Victoria, Department of Planning and Community Development

Whelan, J. (2012) *Big Society and Australia: How the UK Government is Dismantling the State and What it Means for Australia*, Sydney: Centre for Policy Development

Wills, J., with Nash, K. (2012) *Redesigning Local Democracy*, City of Swan WA: Local Government Community Development and Services Association

Young Foundation (2006) *Local Democracy and Neighbourhood Governance*, London: Young Foundation

TWENTY

On escaping neoliberalism: concluding reflections

Chris Miller and Lionel Orchard

At first glance neoliberalism has swept all before it across much of the contemporary world. Even those Nordic countries, such as Sweden and Norway, perhaps most committed to social democracy, have been forced to adopt and adjust to the neoliberal pull. The persuasiveness of neoliberalism is such that, despite its obvious shortcomings and sometimes outrageous failures, it remains difficult to imagine any viable alternative approach, or believe that not so very long ago seemingly sensible governments and publics were able to construct modern social democratic states and to conceive of these as the most effective way of pursuing economic growth, while regulating the worst effects of a free market and ensuring basic freedoms and social and political harmony. The neoliberal zeitgeist has succeeded in establishing deep roots in our minds and our practices, no more so than in the field of public policy. Even where neoliberal governments are forced to intervene to regulate markets, build infrastructure, provide or re-introduce systems of social and economic support or extol the virtues of public services, public spaces and social relationships, they do so without, it seems, undermining the rhetoric of neoliberalism, let alone suggesting that it is failing in more fundamental ways.

In part this is because we live in a liberal-democratic, post-socialist age. Liberal and democratic values now shape politics and public policy making across the contemporary world, at least in principle. Nevertheless, questions linger. Just what constitutes a robust reconciliation of liberal and democratic values, and how do we live up to them in our political and policy practices? How do liberal values of individual freedom and choice relate to social democratic values of equality, cohesion and sustainability? Have liberal-democratic practices become too susceptible to neoliberal incursions distorting and undermining the underlying public and social purposes of democratic government and public policy?

Conflict over values and principles, as well as outcomes, and the scope for their better integration, is at the heart of discussion and debate about public policy. The contributions to this book reflect this complexity and ambition. Authors grapple with a wide range of questions about how to reconcile competing ideas, priorities and viewpoints alongside the interests influencing and shaping public policy making as well as the consequences for social groups and society overall of pursuing competing perspectives. Contributors have addressed familiar and more recent concerns including: universalism versus targeting and the balancing of entitlement and responsibility in welfare policy; the defence of social cohesion and collective commitment alongside respect for choice, diversity and individualism in policy making; the relation between centralism, localism, order and participation in the design and practice of public institutions; the balance between material, non-material and post-material orientations in policy development; and the tensions between shorter-term pragmatism and longer-term principles in political and policy debate.

Amid this complexity there are common themes that we want to highlight. We ask how far the arguments presented here address the key starting point for the book, of the place and status of neoliberalism in explaining and shaping recent policy development and change in Australia, and what the priorities for an alternative policy agenda might be.

On economics, welfare and work, the main concerns are with the impacts of the theories and ideas guiding practice and the outcomes produced rather than specific trends and issues in economic policy – taxation, trade, investment and industry. John Quiggin argues that mainstream economic theory stumbles 'zombie-like' along neoliberal paths that are very narrowly based and have proved to be very ineffective in guiding and shaping policy to manage a robust mixed economy. Ben Spies-Butcher points to how economic and employment changes, pursued largely with bipartisan political support, have produced greater levels of structural inequality and social division; aspects contained somewhat by welfare reform involving reconfigured but still strong redistribution through the state. Economic change has also been accompanied by major change in the pattern of work and the labour market, producing much greater levels of vulnerability and impermanence with less protection and public regulation than in the past. John Buchanan and Damian Oliver argue that while neoliberal principles of individual choice are very unsuited to the proper management of these issues, they nevertheless continue to dominate policy practice. Meanwhile, Barbara Pocock and her co-authors emphasise the urgent need for fresh thought about work–life balance, and paid and unpaid work, given wider economic and social change. Indeed, the hallmarks of these various contributions are the need for new recognition of the essential connection of economics to underlying social – welfare and labour – foundations and the corrosive influence of neoliberal policy directions on those foundations. Crucially, the contributions go well beyond conventional neoliberal views to address key dimensions for how the mixed economy can be guided and managed in more equal and inclusive directions.

In other areas of public policy – Indigenous, education, health, housing, and childcare – the main themes centre on the problems of policy inertia and the associated difficulties of developing new policies in responding to the limits of current approaches. Inevitably, the challenges in each area vary considerably, given the level and scale of the problems. In Indigenous policy, Jon Altman argues that current directions are completely out of step with the nature of the problems. Rather, what is required is to move away from conventional responses of both the neoliberal and social democratic kinds, and instead construct models based on a much more active role for Indigenous people in reshaping policy from the bottom up, recognising that while a distinctive approach may be required for those living in remote areas, the great majority of Indigenous people are urban dwellers, and for whom it is far harder to target policy. In education, health, housing and childcare, the key questions centre on rebalancing private and public influences and priorities in public directions, with closer attention paid to the equity impacts of policy change. How this can be achieved varies, given the nature of existing arrangements and the specific issues faced in each area, but all face major problems and in some cases basic failures, unless much more attention is paid to the social democratic case for public involvement and investment.

Policy issues on the environment and culture, particularly in relation to population growth, immigration and diversity, city and urban development and ongoing problems surrounding resource exploitation, are a third major focus of the book. Australia's gradual shift from the 'white Australia' policy to a more multicultural society is generally regarded as having been a success, as George Crowder suggests, although multiculturalism is usually spoken about quite separately from what is perceived as a different relationship between Indigenous and other Australians. Anxieties about the further continuation of this process of multiculturalism, sometimes fuelled by perceptions of events unfolding in more challenging circumstance in Europe and elsewhere, underpin much of the popular discourse on both population growth and refugee and asylum seeker policies. Both neoliberal policy priorities and uneasy relations between arguments for limited and expansive growth have meant that the contests between economic growth, resource conservation and social commitments in immigration, both economic and humanitarian, and population, have not been well handled in recent times.

As our contributors indicate, public policies in these domains have developed in fairly ad hoc ways, with dramatic consequences for the unplanned growth of larger cities, unsustainable environmental exploitation and degradation, for example within the Murray-Darling Basin, and lack of ongoing attention to the carbon economy and future climate change. The development of robust policy in these areas has to, by necessity, go well beyond neoliberal commitments to free markets and unfettered individual choices, a necessity which is yet to be convincingly faced. Rather, neoliberal adherence to an ideological rhetoric that markets simply cannot fail tends to prevent an acceptance that a problem exists at all, and that therefore there is nothing to solve.

The health of Australia's political and public institutions provides a final focus of the book. In many ways, their current state does not provide a strong basis for the development of public policy taking heed of the arguments and issues traversed above. Reflecting trends elsewhere, levels of trust in politics, the turbulence unleashed by social change, the communications revolution, and the resulting decline in confidence of political leaders, seem to be perpetuating erosion in the scope and capacity of public institutions to do the work expected of them. The 'hollowing out the public sphere' analysed by Mark Davis is reflected in James Walter and Zareh Ghazarian's examination of the limits of the 'court politics' currently dominant at the national level in Australia. Despite centralising trends, the strengthening of Australia's federal system of government offers a vehicle to counter the gloom through policy experimentation and democratic engagement at lower levels of government, as Robyn Hollander suggests. On the other hand, as Chris Miller argues, Australia's political culture is not well developed to facilitate this kind of localism and participation. The future of progressive public policy in Australia depends on much greater effort in these areas.

Where does all of this leave neoliberalism in explaining the current impasse in Australian politics and public policy? Perhaps a comment made by Julia Gillard in her concession speech on losing her Prime Ministership in 2013 on the role of gender in the pressures she faced during her leadership is helpful: 'It doesn't explain everything, it doesn't explain nothing – it explains some things. And it is for the nation to think in a sophisticated way about those shades of grey' (Gillard, 2013, p 238).

Indeed it is rare that simple explanations of cause can be discerned in social and political life. Political and policy change in Australia has been profoundly shaped by neoliberal precepts about free markets, negative liberty and the rest. Nevertheless, other ideas and views about freedom, liberty, community and equality continue to figure in political and policy debates. Residues of past ways of thinking and doing things also resonate in political and policy practice. The legacy and positive attitudes to government and social democracy in Australia still lay in the cultural undergrowth awaiting fresh germination.

While Australia is not unique in the way neoliberal ideas have influenced public policy, the specifics of the Australian embrace of those ideas perhaps are. Neoliberal ideas were taken up most strongly and convincingly by reforming Labor Governments – the Hawke/Keating Governments – in the 1980s and 1990s, and applied to many areas of national life. Thus, bank and utility privatisation, the removal of exchange rate control, financial deregulation, national competition policy, the emphasis on productivity in labour relations and managerial reform of the public sector were all pursued vigorously. The political justification for these changes at that time was certainly neoliberal in emphasis – that in order to compete globally, the Australian economy needed to be opened dramatically, and that Australian society needed to squarely face the winds of international competitive pressure. Yet, the Hawke/Keating Governments also pursued policies renovating the welfare state – 'active' welfare pursued with a strong commitment to equity – and did not entirely abandon progressive taxation policy or the case for government action and investment where required. Subsequent Australian governments, both Liberal–Conservative led by John Howard and now Tony Abbott, and Labor and minority Labor Governments led by Kevin Rudd and Julia Gillard, have all operated under the Hawke/Keating shadow. Despite various attempts to tack to the Right or the Left, none has been particularly successful in unsettling the neoliberal/third way consensus struck in the Hawke/Keating era. This is not so surprising, as the consensus was itself an attempt to combine social democratic and liberal ideas.

It is against this background that Julia Gillard's 'shades of grey' idea helps. The contest between liberal and social democratic values and priorities is likely to continue and should do so. Modern social democracy emerged from the ravages of a world war coming hot on the heels of the Depression, itself global in scale. Modern liberalism in its many forms – including British social liberalism, Rawlsian political 'welfarist' liberalism, Berlinian pluralist liberalism, Hayekian free market neoliberalism and Sen and Nussbaum's 'capability' liberalism – both supports and challenges social democracy, depending on the form adopted. In general, liberalism strongly supports individual freedom and private markets, but there is considerable variability in the liberal tradition about the role of government and the welfare state.

Similarly, within social democracy there are many interpretations of how far the state should intervene in the market, private life and the public arena, for example through nationalisation of essential infrastructure, regulation of market conduct and wage levels, redistributive taxation, and the provision of welfare and social insurance. In these ways, social democratic policies ensure that basic needs are met through public provision while access to cultural, leisure and other resources felt to be essential to human development, and equal opportunities maximising individual capacities are supported and maintained.

Such differences in both traditions, while sometimes relating to matters of principle, are also subject to judgments about what response is appropriate in a particular set of circumstances, as well as what is possible politically. In recent times, the Hayekian free market neoliberal view has tended to hold sway in the programmes and policies of Liberal–Conservative governments in the Western democracies from Thatcher and Reagan on. The essential ambition has been to restrict and question, if not halt, the advance of social democracy, even if there are strong arguments in the modern liberal tradition supporting social democratic ambitions.

Neoliberals have held the upper hand intellectually because of the political strength of their argument that governments were ultimately limited in what they could achieve, and that ultimately individual effort and potential, working within a market system, offered the best that could be expected. Social democrats appeared to overreach, suggesting that governments could achieve much more in solving economic, social and environmental problems. The continuation of problems in these areas and the shortcomings of social democracy itself, particularly the limits of its paternalistic and bureaucratic predilections, left its advocates overwhelmed by the resurgence of liberalism of the neoliberal variant. Social democratic and other progressive forces, including liberal ones, need to rediscover their voice, and in doing so must grapple with the neoliberal world as they argue again for social democratic values and goals, spelling out arguments if not for socialism then for a more just and equitable world based on recognition and respect, aware of the limits of finite resources, our obligations as guardians of the environment and our human interdependencies alongside our shared desire for individual creativity. In the Australian setting, as reflected in the various contributions to this volume, policies marrying these progressive social democratic commitments to other varieties of liberalism and communitarian ideas may offer the best hope for rethinking policy priorities and directions.

Reference

Gillard, J. (2013) 'The Concession Speech' in Trenoweth, S. (ed), *Bewitched & Bedevilled: Women Write the Gillard Years*, Hardie Grant Books: Melbourne.

Index

Page references for notes are followed by n

www.ingramcontent.com/pod-product-compliance
Lightning Source LLC
Chambersburg PA
CBHW060021030426
42334CB00019B/2129